Psychoanalytic Explorations of the Masculine and the Maternal

In this book, Yael Pilowsky Bankirer reads into Freud's writings with the unique prism of circumcision as a marker for both the formation of masculine identity, and for matricide, the disappearance of the mother.

Pilowsky Bankirer uses Freud's idea of circumcision within a text as a *Leitfossil*: a key-fossil through which an unresolved unconscious conflict can be traced. She conducts a close reading of Freud's texts – including *Little Hans*, *The Wolf Man*, *Totem and Taboo* and *Moses and Monotheism* – to illuminate and uncover the textual unconscious, deconstruct the explicit narrative and open alternative psychoanalytic possibilities inherent to the encounter with the maternal realm. Throughout the volume, Pilowsky Bankirer informs her analysis by considering the work of Freud in tandem with that of Lacan, Kristeva, Irigaray, Derrida, Benjamin, Butler and more.

Psychoanalytic Explorations of the Masculine and the Maternal: Uncovering the Image of Circumcision in Freud's Works will be of interest to scholars of psychoanalysis and practising analysts alike, particularly those interested in the intersection of gender studies and psychoanalysis.

Yael Pilowsky Bankirer is a psychoanalyst and a poet based in Cambridge, UK. She is a medical doctor and has a PhD in Gender Studies and Psychoanalysis. She is a member of the Site for Contemporary Psychoanalysis and an editor for *Sitegeist – A Journal of Psychoanalysis and Philosophy*.

Psychoanalytic Explorations of the Masculine and the Maternal

Uncovering the Image of Circumcision in Freud's Works

Yael Pilowsky Bankirer

Routledge
Taylor & Francis Group

LONDON AND NEW YORK

Designed cover image: © Getty

First published 2025
by Routledge
4 Park Square, Milton Park, Abingdon, Oxon, OX14 4RN

and by Routledge
605 Third Avenue, New York, NY 10158

Routledge is an imprint of the Taylor & Francis Group, an informa business

© 2025 Yael Pilowsky Bankirer

The right of Yael Pilowsky Bankirer to be identified as author of this work has been asserted in accordance with sections 77 and 78 of the Copyright, Designs and Patents Act 1988.

All rights reserved. No part of this book may be reprinted or reproduced or utilised in any form or by any electronic, mechanical, or other means, now known or hereafter invented, including photocopying and recording, or in any information storage or retrieval system, without permission in writing from the publishers.

Trademark notice: Product or corporate names may be trademarks or registered trademarks, and are used only for identification and explanation without intent to infringe.

British Library Cataloguing-in-Publication Data
A catalogue record for this book is available from the British Library

ISBN: 9781032495439 (hbk)
ISBN: 9781032495392 (pbk)
ISBN: 9781003394334 (ebk)

DOI: 10.4324/9781003394334

Typeset in Times New Roman
by codeMantra

Contents

Preface

This book is an outcome of a long and extensive translation journey. In the first and very literal sense, it is a translation into English of its Hebrew version: *Milim ve-Milot – a feminist journey following the leitfossil of circumcision in Freud's text* that will be published in 2025 in the psychoanalytic series, Narcissus of Resling Publishing. It is also the culmination of a long process of translating an academic work – my PhD thesis – with its particular scholarly language into a more rounded psychoanalytic language. True to the quest to articulate the unspeakable inherent to every written work, this book is a product of a 20-year journey that gradually gave words to my thoughts, a vast translation process which has emerged through conversations, support and generosity of many people.

I would like to thank the people who have shared their wisdom and insights with me, to those who read my work and responded to it, and to those who encouraged and supported me. I am indebted to mothers who shared their thoughts and feelings in relation to circumcision, whose voices and insights continue to echo. I am thankful to Friends, colleagues and other professionals who have read and commented on my writing: to Tali Artman Partock for her unique wisdom and insightful comments and to Tamar Feldberg, Tal Breier Ben-Moha, Keren Limor, Jessa Leff and Dana Lubinsky for their generous listening and readings. During my PhD, I was lucky to be supported by the Gender Studies Program at Bar-Ilan University and particularly by Miri Rozmarin and Ronit Irshai. A special place is reserved in my heart for Henriette Dahan Kalev, who was my PhD supervisor and then became a dear friend and colleague, teaching me through many stimulating conversations. I am grateful to her for her insightful readings of my manuscript.

Many years after finishing my PhD, Dana Amir encouraged me to take the leap and embark on the journey of publishing this book, and I am indebted to her for insightful advice and guidance along the process. I am very grateful to Tim Fox for his wise reading and encouragement throughout many conversations. Aner Govrin gave me priceless comments and remarks about the Hebrew version of the book for which I am grateful. I am exceptionally thankful to Joan Raphael-Leff for her kind words and wisdom, as well as for her valuable reading of my book.

I would like to express my gratitude to all the people who have worked hard on the production of this book: to Sarahjayne Smith, the Production Editor at

Taylor & Francis/Routledge; to the codeMantra team for their outstanding attention to detail and collaborative work in copy-editing, proofreading, and typesetting; to Matthew Willis for the cover design, to Priya Sharma (Editorial Assistant) and, of course, to the Editor, Zoe Meyer, for the outstanding professional handling of my manuscript.

A heartfelt gratitude to my older children, Oren and Yoav Pilowsky Bankirer, for their lessons in English and help in translation, and to my partner, Oded Pilowsky Bankirer, for his endless patience and for our numerous conversations.

My family is indeed an inspiration for me – in a never-ending process of translation.

Introduction

Tracing the Image of Circumcision: A Deep Textual Archaeology

Serving fresh words for all
smiling to guests, waiters, the band, the cooks
you were blessed with bright fortune
that day
but with pain
that night.

A tear of skin abruptly vanished.
Wine pours laughter into cry
muddling blood in red tape.
Torn body disappeared in a cut
of nerve tails.

In the other room
swallowing broken chains of words
a wrench reached your throat
you desired to speak of birth
but could only mutter brit.

(Birth and Brit, Between Our Tongues)[1]

The male Foreskin: that excess of skin covering the tip of the penis is not an organ in my body. I've never had one and I have never been circumcised. As a woman, the foreskin was never a part of my conceptual landscape and for most of my life, I didn't give it a second thought. But as a Jewish woman, during the last few months of pregnancy with my son, I became aware of its presence inside me, a fact that was accompanied with a surge of questions about my relation to an ancient patriarchal tradition – circumcision. My place in the face of this long-standing ceremony that has been practised for thousands of years, transmitted from father to son for generations, violated my rest.

---

1 Yael Pilowsky Bankirer. *Between Our Tongues* (in Hebrew) (Tel-Aviv: Catharsis Publishing, 2023).

DOI: 10.4324/9781003394334-1

Alongside questions I began to explore – and literally embody – in relation to my son's forthcoming birth, I became aware of the movements opposing circumcision, and discovered that there is a widespread and active discourse that goes beyond the Jewish context. Anti-circumcision activism, often referred to as *intactivism*[2] – i.e., activism for bodily integrity – is common in both the United States and Europe. Legal battles accompanied by demonstrations, and social initiatives are constantly emerging in an attempt to recognise male circumcision as an act of male genital mutilation, MGM, with similar political implications as FGM (Female Genital Mutilation). In various countries, attempts have been made to change the laws governing the ceremony, to regard circumcision as incurring harm to the helpless and the vulnerable leading to traumatic emotional effects, and to ban non-medical procedures. Numerous films created, books and papers that were published on the matter, reveal the emotional turmoil attached to circumcision, intensities that also came up in personal conversations with people around me. I was surprised to find that even among the secular, complete atheists and people with little relation to traditional Judaism, circumcision raises the tone in conversations and harsh words ignite discourse like arrows of fire, as if a wound had been exposed.

Why does circumcision carry such high intensity? It is "the oldest enigma in the history of surgery", David Gollaher writes, and it is difficult to imagine

> what inspired the ancients to cut their genitals or the genitals of their young … Yet, long before medicine and religion branched into separate streams of wisdom – indeed, long before history itself – cutting of the foreskin of the penis was invented as a symbolic wound; thus, circumcision became a ritual of extraordinary power.[3]

It is much older and broader than Judaism – about one-sixth of the world's population circumcise their sons and the custom is practised in different parts of the world, for different reasons, in different forms.[4] The earliest evidence of its existence dates back long before the biblical mention of the covenant made between God and Abraham threading back to ancient Egypt.

2 The idea of the intact body echoes Hellenistic philosophy in which life should be lived according to the wholeness of nature. From a psychoanalytic perspective, as Jordan Osserman emphasises in his book, the term "intactivist" invites criticism, since it "refers to "intactness" that psychoanalysis tends to consider a major defensive fantasy against the subject's foundational fracture—the wish to "restore" a prelapsarian unity and wholeness that never, in fact, existed". Jordan Osserman. *Circumcision on the Couch: The Cultural, Psychological, and Gendered Dimensions of the World's Oldest Surgery* (London: Bloomsbury Publishing, 2022), p. 2.

3 David Gollaher. *Circumcision: A History of the World's Most Controversial Surgery* (New York: Basic Books, 2000). Preface, p. xi.

4 For example, as traditional rites of passage in East African tribes; among many Muslims around the world; tribes in the Pacific Islands and the ancestral population of Australia; For Jews around the world, the ceremony is held at the age of eight days; And in the United States, it is practised as a medical and surgical procedure performed after birth (less common today).

Although throughout the history of circumcision this symbolic wound carried different meanings in various cultures, it seems that its association with 'otherness' has consistently been surfacing, and Freud explains that circumcision is "the deepest unconscious root of anti-semitism; for even in the nursery little boys hear that a Jew has something cut off his penis—a piece of his penis, they think—and this gives them a right to despise Jews".[5] Indeed, historically, circumcision has been a practice that sustained phantasies of otherness – whether Jewish or another – and has been a sign of those who represent difference, yet, curiously at the end of the 19th century it has also been adopted by the mainstream of English-speaking countries as a surgical practice. At the beginning of the 20th century, medical circumcision swept the United States and, to a lesser extent, Britain, turning its skin from being a symbol of otherness to becoming a sign of good hygiene and high status. Large amounts of resources and funds were invested in research on the healing abilities of surgical circumcision, in order to prove not simply its better hygiene and aesthetics but also its effectiveness as a prophylactic surgery to prevent diseases such as epilepsy, joint diseases, urinary tract disorders, as well as to cure various mental illnesses originating from sexual overstimulation and masturbation. Although most of these 'treatments' did not survive the test of time, one can observe through them the powerful aura surrounding circumcision.

As a physician who is preoccupied with the human psyche, I was fascinated by the medicalisation of this ritual and the way in which ancient boundaries are blurred, revealing the connection – that Freud speaks of – between science and religion, surgery and ritual. The surgeries' therapeutic virtues, healing and protective abilities that were apparent throughout the history of circumcision were interlinked with its internal question of otherness and indeed Freud recognises the powerful effect of circumcision, providing the people with a sense of otherness that also carries "an unexampled capacity", the ability to defy "misfortunes and ill-treatment" that have also "earned the hearty dislike of every other people".[6]

How are circumcisions' healing attributes related to the question of otherness embodied in the ritual tradition? How are symbolic meanings of growth and protection connected to what Eliza Slavet calls "Racial Fever"[7]: an uncontrollable desire to define the identity of the subject and the group, to find the heritage, to cast and discover (and sometimes invent) the history that marks the subject and group as separate from the other? Tracing the *Leitfossil* (key-fossil) of circumcision in ancient Jewish texts Freud recognises the labyrinthine nature of this practice in relation to

5 Sigmund Freud. "Analysis of a Phobia in a Five-Year-Old Boy". In: James Strachey (ed. & trans.) *The Standard Edition of the Complete Psychological Works of Sigmund Freud* 10 (1909) (London: The Hogarth Press and the Institute of Psycho-Analysis, 1955), pp. 1–150, 36.
6 Sigmund Freud. "*Moses and Monotheism*, Three Essays." In: James Strachey (ed. & trans.) *The Standard Edition of the Complete Psychological Works of Sigmund Freud* 23 (1939) (London: The Hogarth Press and the Institute of Psycho-Analysis, 1964), pp. 1–138, 105.
7 Eliza Slavet. *Racial Fever: Freud and the Jewish Question* (New York: Fordham University Press, 2009).

others, asking why, in their journey to separate from others, in order to differentiate themselves, Jewish people chose a sign so wildly used by others? He writes:

> As a mark that is to distinguish one person from others and prefer him to them, one would choose something that is not to be found in other people; one would not choose something that can be exhibited in the same way by millions of other people.[8]

Freud's question opens a window into the circularity of otherness inherent to the image of circumcision, in which the memory of the other always echoes within. In pointing to the uncanniness of this blurred boundary, he identifies the conflictual core in relation to otherness not as a result of their radical difference but rather in their similarity. For Freud, it is precisely the proximity and familiarity of the other; the blurred boundaries between self and other that provoke the conflict. Thus, this constituent sign of identity bears the mark of alienation, as it is a constant reminder of its paradoxical nature in relation to the other; of the subject's inability to separate and become identical only to itself.

Thus, circumcision, as Freud portrays it, is a conflictual sign simultaneously marking the separation and similarity from/to the other. Exploring identity and otherness in my own encounter with the question of circumcision, this understanding led my attention to the gender axis, and I began to wonder in what way is Jewish circumcision, which takes place on the eighth day after birth, related to the nine months of blurred boundaries, and lack of identity that occur during pregnancy. Or to put it more clearly: is this otherness that Freud speaks about in relation to circumcision the racial other or the gendered one? As my son was growing inside me, I became aware of this interlaced question hidden beneath the question of race: we were one that is two and two that are one, a mix of male and female, a body inside a body. The fact that the *Brit*, Jewish circumcision, the cutting of male genitalia, is so temporally, symbolically – and also linguistically – close to *birth*, implies a psychic complexity around gender and invites questions about the relationship between motherhood and circumcision.

Eric Kline Silverman's writing touches on this complexity, portraying circumcision as a sort of matricide[9] stemming from repressed feelings of both envy towards and identification with the mother. According to him, the act of ceremonial circumcision mediates between nature and culture by providing a masculine response to the maternal in which separating the male infant from the mother is repeating the process of birth.[10] The cut of the foreskin repeats the cut of the umbilical cord. If the seven days of menstruation (which Jewish texts refer to as *niddah;* Hebrew: נִדָּה)

---

8 Sigmund Freud. "*Moses and Monotheism*, Three Essays." *The Standard Edition of the Complete Psychological Works of Sigmund Freud* 23 (1939), p. 45.

9 Murder of the mother.

10 Eric Kline Silverman. "Circumcision and Masculinity: Motherly Men or Brutal Patriarchs?" In: Harry Brod and Shawn Israel Zevit (eds.) *Brother Keepers: New Perspectives on Jewish Masculinity* (Harriman, TN: Men's Studies Press, 2010), pp. 34–56.

represent female fertility, on the eighth day a new cycle of fertility begins – masculine rather than feminine, symbolic rather than physical, cultural instead of natural. According to Silverman's analysis, circumcision reflects the intricacies of the unresolved Oedipal conflict in relation to the maternal. It "mirrors the development of the male self vis-a-vis motherhood" revealing "male envy of female parturition and inverts menstruation and birth". It erases motherhood and enables separation by symbolically replacing her presence with a male rite. Circumcision, according to Silverman's interpretation, "differentiates men *from* women by transforming men *into* women".[11]

In a similar way, reading Leviticus, Julia Kristeva analyses the Jewish masculine identity as one that is formed in circumcision by separating from the mother and through abjecting the feminine.[12] "What the male is separated from", she explains, "the other that circumcision carves out on his very sex, is the other sex, impure, defiled". As she explains, Judaism repeats the "natural scar of the umbilical cord at the location of sex", in order to proliferate laws of impurity, to duplicate and displace "the preeminent separation which is that from the mother".[13] For men to identify with the image of the one God, Judaism is flooded with laws of abjection – abominations, impurity and prohibitions that multiply and diverge into many other laws – all rooted in the attempt to separate from the phantasmatic power and horror of the mother.

While the baby, enclosed within the circle of his male relatives, receives his masculine Jewish identity inscribed onto his male genitalia, symbolising the relationship within the male lineage of the son-Father-God, the mother is usually in another room, behind a closed door, away from the singing voices. Are there any words arising from this other room that can be listened to? Women's exclusion from the main event, and more significantly from language is reflected in Hebrew, in which circumcision means not just a circular incision, a ring-shaped cut but also a word (*Mila*). *Brit Mila*, circumcision, also means the covenant of words, reflecting the way a subject enters the realm of culture and of language, a rite of passage that bounds the masculine and particularly the male organ with the ability to speak. If, circumcision is "that singular and immemorial archive" as Derrida refers to it, inscribed on the skin as a wounded testimony for Jewish conflict of otherness, what does it mean for women who remain beyond the covenant of the ceremony (*Tekes*) and outside the text? what will be the faith of those who are exiled even from the exile itself?

11 Silverman, Eric Kline. "The Cut of Wholeness: Psychoanalytic Interpretations of Biblical Circumcision." In: Elizabeth Wyner Mark (ed.) *The Covenant of Circumcision: New Perspectives on an Ancient Jewish Rite* (London: Brandies University Press, 2003), pp. 43–57, 56. Indent in the original.

12 Julia Kristeva. *Powers of Horror: An Essay on Abjection* (New York: Columbia University Press, 1982).

13 Julia Kristeva. *Powers of Horror: An Essay on Abjection* (New York: Columbia University Press, 1982), p. 100.

At a *Bris* event I attended that is engraved in my memory to this day, the mother was absent. Weak and exhausted, eight days after giving birth, still in a whirlwind of merging day and night, in which pain and anxiety are inseparable from sweet moments of happiness, she handed over her baby, small and helpless to a stranger who would injure his genitals and with a cut of a knife bring him into the covenant of masculine tradition. She said nothing about her experience and feelings, kept silent and left the room. I, on the other hand, as a young and curious medical doctor, took my place in the front row among a crowd of men. From where I was standing, I heard the baby crying. But his cries were drowned out by the circle of men around him, between the sounds of prayer, the commotion of joy and the cheers of the dining guests. I watched as the baby's grandfather held him and the *mohel* (circumciser) secured his hands and feet to a wooden board while passing the wine cup among the guests. I thought about his mother who was absent, closing herself in the other room and wondered about the way this ritual of circumcision is carving gender gaps into the baby's body.

What are the "broken words" of the other room? This question became louder for me, and at the beginning of my research – which ended as a psychoanalytic reading, and is here before you – I interviewed mothers, trying to listen to the voices that disappeared from the main narrative about circumcision. I held interviews with mothers – some after their son's circumcision and some who chose not to circumcise their sons – in an attempt to uncover the words hidden in that other room, to listen to the language of those who remain beyond the ceremony and outside the text.

Women spoke about leaving the room, and about closing themselves in a different room, behind a closed door, outside the event. They talked about a sense of split. Some described how the baby's crying changed after circumcision and how until then, his crying felt different to them. They talked about physical sensations such as pain in the chest and in their breasts, a need to breastfeed, and uterine cramps. Many of the women talked about the need to protect the baby in the face of social and cultural demands, a sense of betrayal, alongside excitement and great anxiety. Crying was a central motif in their stories – listening to the baby's cries, a muddle of milk and tears dripping at the event.[14]

I sought to be a witness for these unspoken words; to gather the voices that are dropped from the familiar narrative. It seemed to me that alongside the main ceremony, women were going through a sort of ritual of their own, an initiation into motherhood under a patriarchal culture. Perhaps this wound does not only introduce the male child into his masculine Jewish lineage in the covenant of men but also construct the maternal as a position without words. In the process of botanical assembly, a branch is cut off and the base remains as a hollow vessel, which cannot grow its own fruit, but only support the new branch that is assembled and through

---

14 The mothers that were interviewed gave me permission to share their words in publications without names or identifying details, of course.

which the new fruit is fed. In a similar way, perhaps mothers remain committed to the baby's pain, with a growing need to hold, preserve, and protect but without words of their own. In the process of exclusion from the main room, where the body is bound and language released, the cry of maternal silence takes shape.

The interviews I conducted never grew into proper research and were never published. In parallel to the course of my life in the direction of psychoanalysis, I turned to Freud's texts to perform a close reading analysis, exploring questions of Gender through the image of circumcision. The relationship between the ritual (in Hebrew:*tekes*) and text revealed itself as a reciprocal movement that, reproduces a similar matricidal movement at the basis of psychoanalytic theory. While Freud identifies circumcision as that ambivalent motif that simultaneously connects and separates the subject from their "other", I use this understanding to identify the conflictual gendered dimension repressed in his own texts – repeatedly revealing the hidden face of the mother.

Freud's Key-fossil

Imagine that an explorer arrives in a little-known region where his interest is aroused by an expanse of ruins, with remains of walls, fragments of columns, and tablets with half-effaced and unreadable inscriptions. He may content himself with inspecting what lies exposed to view, with questioning the inhabitants— perhaps semi-barbaric people—who live in the vicinity, about what tradition tells them of the history and meaning of these archaeological remains, and with noting down what they tell him—and he may then proceed on his journey. But he may act differently. He may have brought picks, shovels and spades with him, and he may set the inhabitants to work with these implements. Together with them he may start upon the ruins, clear away the rubbish, and, beginning from the visible remains, uncover what is buried. If his work is crowned with success, the discoveries are self-explanatory: the ruined walls are part of the ramparts of a palace or a treasure-house; the fragments of columns can be filled out into a temple; the numerous inscriptions, which, by good luck, may be bilin- gual, reveal an alphabet and a language, and, when they have been deciphered and translated, yield undreamed-of information about the events of the remote past, to commemorate which the monuments were built. Saxa loquuntur![15]

In his 1896 lecture 'The Aetiology of Hysteria', Freud lays the foundation for con- ceptualising psychoanalytic work as archaeological reconstruction. In this meta- phor, he marks the psychoanalytic process as one that is drawn beyond what is laid on the surface: the obvious conclusion, the visible evidence, the simple narrative

---

15 Sigmund Freud. "The Aetiology of Hysteria." In: James Strachey (ed. & trans.) *The Standard Edi- tion of the Complete Psychological Works of Sigmund Freud* 3 (1896), pp. 187–221, 192. London: The Hogarth Press and the Institute of Psycho-Analysis, 1953.

that is told, and unceasingly strives using symbolic pickaxes and shovels, to dig deep in order to uncover the remains of the palace, the inscriptions and the temples hidden beneath the ground. Stones that at first seem to be meaningless objects, Freud argues, can speak and open for the psychoanalyst a passage to uncover the hidden and concealed, a window to the reconstruction of the *historical truth*.[16]

Freud teaches us that stones can speak. Clods of earth and rocks that may appear insignificant can become, according to this metaphor, a living structure encapsulating a cardinal testimony in his quest for the truth, evidence of a forgotten layer buried beneath the surface. In his last book, *Moses and Monotheism*, Freud's language shifts from an archaeological rhetoric to a paleontological one, marking the covenant of circumcision as a "key-fossil" (*Leitfossil*) in his investigation. It becomes a sign of conflict, evidence of a living dimension that had been congealed and remained forgotten and buried in stone. As Freud explains in his analysis of Jewish texts, a textual fossil is formed due to two opposite movements that simultaneously seek to reveal and conceal the "truth": one endeavours to show the origin of the Jewish people and the other seeks to hide it, and such ambivalence leaves behind a trail of evidence in the text. Circumcision is the distinctive mark of Jewish identity, Freud explains, differentiating Jewish men from other men, but at the same time, it is precisely the sign that can connect the Jewish people to the otherness of their origin in Egypt from which they seek to escape. Thus, circumcision remains a valuable sign of conflict in the text: a struggle between two opposing textual movements to both reveal and conceal the 'origin'. Like bodily symptoms of trauma, circumcision becomes a *mausoleum*, a marker for the emerging compromise of repression in these texts.

While *castration* is an anxiety-provoking phantasy encapsulating the ambivalence towards the father – which Freud describes as a necessary stage in the subject's psychosexual development – *circumcision* reveals another layer. This textual image does not point solely towards the father but reveals the conflict in the relationship with the mother as well, exposing an otherness that must be "cut off" for the subject to formulate a coherent sense of identity. As evidence of ancient trauma that has been repressed, circumcision is the stone – or rather the fossil – that must be turned to reveal the traumatic origin buried beneath the surface. It is a textual symptom uncovering an archaic split between nature and culture, between self and other, between man and woman; a boundary line that has served me in identifying the Archimedean point through which Freud's various texts were read.

Freud metaphorically borrows tools of excavation from the archaeological domain to depict the analytic process as a quest for truth beneath the stones. In this description, psychoanalytic interpretation emerges from what Paul Ricoeur later referred to as "hermeneutics of suspicion",[17] characterized by disbelief toward

---

16 For more on Freud's distinction between *material truth* and *historical truth*, see Chapter 3.
17 Paul Ricoeur. *Freud and Philosophy: An Essay on Interpretation* (New Haven: Yale University Press, 1970).

what appears given and self-evident, aiming to uncover hidden meanings and bring to light the untold, the unspeakable. Like an archaeologist, Freud doesn't readily accept the manifest narrative, directing his efforts into deeper layers of the unconscious. Digging deeper to find fragments of stones, remnants of ancient artefacts that have been forgotten, he strives to reconstruct from them the structure that once stood there; to recreate from ruins and remnants left behind a concealed ancient truth.

Reading the texts as a multilayered psyche with contradictions, incoherences, emissions and slips makes it possible for the investigating analyst and the attentive reader, just like the archaeologist, to identify the locations where digging should uncover what lies hidden beneath, the deeper layer of psychical and cultural reality. Thus, psychoanalytic theory – and Freud's texts specifically – constitutes in my reading both the analytic tool and the field of investigation. The textual fossil, circumcision, not only sends its long arms into a deep conflict in the human psyche, and not only serves as a marker for Freud to identify the way to reconstructing Jewish history but can also be directed towards Freud's psychoanalytic texts, enabling the revelation of the underlying ambivalence beneath the coherent theory that emanates from his various writings. In my reading, circumcision is not merely a marker used by Freud in his investigations but emerges as a powerful symbol in the Freudian text itself, through which one can open a window into the repressed dimension in the text, into what eludes and escapes it, to the spectral otherness that moves beneath the stones.

The Freudian Texts

Numerous anthropological studies of various circumcision rituals across the world demonstrate the fact that it is not only a ritual that binds men to their masculine lineage but also a powerful motif in separating male children from their mothers. This motif of separating from the mother runs through different rituals – from Muslim circumcision, through rites of passage in African cultures to Jewish circumcision. Scholars have shown that circumcision plays both a part in separating boys from their mothers, and, in different societies, a central role in gender relations, in the exclusion and the marginalisation of women.[18] The decision to explore questions

18 For further information see David Gollaher. *Circumcision: A History of the World's Most Controversial Surgery* (New York: Basic Books, 2000); Arnold Van Gennep. *Rites of Passage*. Translated by M.B. Vizedom and G.L. Caffe (Chicago: University Chicago Press, 1960); Terence Turner. "Social Body and Embodied Subject: Bodiliness, Subjectivity, and Sociality Among the Kayapo." *Cult. Anthropol.* 10 (1995): 143–170; Jhon Layard. *Stone Men of Malekula* (London: Chatto & Windus, 1942); Maurice Bloch. *From Blessing to Violence: History and Ideology in the Circumcision Ritual of the Merina of Madagascar* (Cambridge: Cambridge University Press, 1986); Maurice Bloch. *Prey Into Hunter: The Politics of Religious Experience* (Cambridge: Cambridge University Press, 1992); K.E. Paige and J.M. Paige. *The Politics of Reproductive Ritual* (Berkeley: University California Press, 1981); Michio Kitahara. "A Cross-Cultural Test of the Freudian Theory of Circumcision." *Int. J. Psychoanal. Psychother.* 5 (1976): 535–546; Lester Richard Hiatt. "Indulgent

of gender through the image of circumcision echoes the symbolism of the ritual as a matricidal moment, leading to this one specific theoretical thread that was pulled out of the web of entangled otherness. It is a feminist reading, a journey that focuses on conflicts in relation to the maternal. Whereas Freud recognises the emotional ambivalence that produces fossils, I identify moments of ossification in his own work and the conflictual layer solidified within it – revealing a textual ambivalence that repeatedly covers, represses and repudiates the maternal.

The process of writing the book begins precisely where Freud identified the key-fossil: circumcision, namely, in his texts in which the image of circumcision arises: *Analysis of a Phobia in a Five-Year-Old Boy* (1909); *Leonardo da Vinci and a Memory of His Childhood* (1910); *Totem and Taboo* (1912–1913); *From the History of an Infantile Neurosis* (1918); *Moses and Monotheism* (1939). In these texts, Freud touches on circumcision – sometimes in great detail, as in *Moses and Monotheism*, and sometimes only in a footnote, as in *Leonardo da Vinci and a Memory of His Childhood* and *Totem and Taboo*. Across his various writings, he describes circumcision in different ways: as a symbol of castration; as a motif that evokes the Oedipal anxiety of the Father; as a mark that provokes antisemitism and misogyny; as a paradigmatic sign of trauma; as a vital element in the child's psychosexual development; And as a fossil, a key metaphor harbouring an unsolvable ambivalent aspect. However, in all of them, circumcision also serves as a dominant image that operates within the texts themselves and aided me to identify its symptomatic structure, as a 'key-fossil' leading to an ambivalent textual movement through which the maternal dimension can be revealed.[19]

Fathers and Collective Male Violence." In: Ariane Deluz and Suzette Heald (eds.) *Anthropology and Psychoanalysis: An Encounter Through Cultures* (London: Routledge, 1994), pp. 171–183; Theodor Reik. *Ritual: Four Psychoanalytic Studies* (New York: Grove Press, 1946); Bruno Bettelheim. *SymbolicWounds: Puberty Rites and the Envious Male* (Glencoe, IL: Free Press, 1954); Vincent Crapanzano. "Rite of Return." *Psychoanal. Stud. Soc.* 9 (1981): 15–36; Geza R'oheim. *The Eternal Ones of the Dream: A Psychoanalytic Interpretation of Australian Myth and Ritual* (New York: International Universities Press, 1945); Geza R'oheim. "The Symbolism of Subincision." *Am. Imago* 6 (1949): 321–328; Geza R'oheim. "Transition Rites." *Psychoanal. Q.* 11 (1942): 336–374. Roger V. Burton and John W.M. Whiting. "The Absent Father and Cross-Sex Identity." *Merrill-Palmer Q. Behav. Develop.* 7 (1961): 85–95; John W.M. Whiting and Anthony R. Kluckhohn. "The Function of Male Initiation Ceremonies at Puberty." In: T.M. Newcomb, E.L. Hartley and E.E. Maccoby (eds.) *Readings in Social Psychology* (New York: Henry Holt & Co., 1958), pp. 359–370; Gilbert H. Herdt. "Fetish and Fantasy in Sambia Initiation." In: Gilbert H. Herdt (ed.) *Rituals of Manhood: Male Initiation in Papua New Guinea* (Berkeley: University of California Press, 1982), pp. 44–98; Gilbert H. Herdt. *Guardians of the Flutes: Idioms of Masculinity* (New York: McGraw Hill, 1981).

19 Freud also touches on circumcision in his writings "Introductory Lectures to Psychoanalysis" (1916–1917) - Lecture No. 10, "New Introductory Lectures to Psychoanalysis" (1933) - Lecture No. 32 and "The Taboo of Virginity" (1918), but in these texts he refers to circumcision as part of a collection of examples that he cites for initiation ceremonies, rituals involving blood, symbolism in a dream, and castration anxiety - topics that he develops and discusses at length in the other texts concerning circumcision that are analysed in the book.

Freud's writings that pertain to circumcision, which were closely analysed in my reading, can be divided into three theoretical layers, encompassing the individual, cultural, and historical aspects of Freud's theory. These are represented in the three chapters of the book: The first chapter, *In her Shadow: Three Case Studies*, represents his individual-focused theory, the layer of the subject. It is based on three clinical case studies analysed by Freud, which also serve as significant building blocks in his theory of childhood psychosexual development. These case studies, which unfold memories and events from early childhood, allow readers to delve into the emotional complexity embedded in the mother-child relationship and enabled me to explore the way the metaphor of circumcision marks the textual moment in which, the maternal is both revealed and concealed. Using this metaphor, Freud provides a "solution" that shifts the focus from the mother to the Oedipal narrative and to the father. It delineates a boundary between the male subject and the maternal object, leaving circumcision as an ambivalent key-fossil that indicates the otherness that has been "cut off".

In the second chapter, *Totem and Taboo: Phantasies of Origin*, I analyse the text *Totem and Taboo*, extracting Freud's theory on the development of culture and the beginning of social life. In this book, Freud weaves the myth of the origin of religion and the formation of societal structures, connecting the subject's psychic development to the formation of culture. Through the image of circumcision, both individual and cultural development are theoretically linked to the Oedipal narrative of the murder of the father. The sacrificial ritual described in the text, with the image of circumcision emerging from it, creates a set of dichotomous splits pivoting around the gender axis. Through these sets of binary oppositions, pointing towards the separation from the maternal, a renewed fertility cycle emerges – masculine rather than feminine, transcendent rather than bodily, cultural rather than natural. Keeping in mind the maternal pole enables an exploration of thoughts and theories that Freud brings up but then neglects to follow; Theories that open the door to questions of maternal subjectivity, to linking parenting with maternal sexuality, and to exploring maternal body, phantasy and symbolism in their significance to the origins of culture.

While the second chapter demonstrates the collapse of textual narratives in the encounter with maternal subjectivity, the third chapter, *The Jewish Key-fossil*, illustrates further a haunted text. In this chapter, representing the historical layer and addressing the question of Judaism, Freud's narratives about the origin of monotheism, the formation of the Jewish people, and the life of Moses, are all revealed to be embedded in the return of the repressed (m)other. Unlike the texts analysed in previous chapters, in which circumcision serves as a turning point in the text, an image that shifts the gaze away from the maternal, cementing the Oedipal narrative as an origin, in *Moses and Monotheism*, Freud himself marks circumcision as a key-fossil, a motif whose petrification indicates the conflict simmering beneath. Yet, as the text progresses and as Freud strives for the truth buried under the stones, he too is drawn into a cycle of erasures that omits the maternal. Gradually, Freud's epistemic position changes, moving from deconstruction to reconstruction, from a question to a conclusion. In the course of this movement, the image of circumcision also changes its character, transforming from an ambivalent fossil into a trans-historical Oedipal sign of cutting and separating from an other.

Throughout the book, it becomes apparent that these three dimensions – the individual, the cultural, and the historical – are not standalone entities but intricately connected to each other. Freud weaves threads between the various texts and layers of his theory, intertwining the subject's psychic development with historical and cultural movements – all around an Oedipal core. In each of the texts, circumcision constitutes a central motif that is interwoven in various ways throughout the textual journey. In each of them, a different movement of eliminating the maternal and a different shade of the conflict towards the mother becomes apparent. Through this metaphor, Freud "circumcises" the text, bringing to the fore castration anxiety but at the same time it also unveils something about this masculine wound and its connection to the unspoken relationship with the mother.

Through a close and in-depth reading, I highlight the moments when the image of circumcision arises and identify the circumcising movements within the text which, while striving to construct an Oedipal narrative, also conceals and erases the maternal. Throughout the analysis, I drew from psychoanalytic and philosophical theories to enable a renewed reading of Freud's writings. The insights of thinkers such as Jacques Lacan, Gilles Deleuze, Félix Guattari, Luce Irigaray, Julia Kristeva, Jessica Benjamin, Carl Gustav Jung, Erich Neumann, Maurice Merleau-Ponty, Jacques Derrida, Judith Butler, and others allowed me to explore the repressed maternal dimension and open Freud's texts to new interpretations and meanings. Using the theoretical thinking of these scholars, I performed an analysis of various layers of the Freudian theory, bringing to the fore the conflicted relationship with the m/other, and opening new avenues of thought.

The image of circumcision leaves a trail of evidence in the various texts, deletions and gaps, which lead to maternal otherness, or rather to (m)otherness. Analysing these textual conflictual moments and allowing this wounded realm to surface, opened Freud's writing to the various possibilities inherent within it. The encounter with the maternal dimension evokes in the text the paradoxes that underline the subject's coherent identity and brings to the foreground a range of alternative ways of thinking not only in psychoanalytic theory but also within language and culture itself.

Chapter 1

In Her Shadow
Three Case Studies

The three clinical case studies explored in this chapter are childhood stories thoroughly analysed by Freud. *The Wolf Man*[1] is a description of the childhood neurosis of a patient, Sergei Pankejeff, who came to Freud for analysis at the age of twenty-three. Analysing his famous dream of wolves, Freud delves into the repressed memories of Pankejeff's childhood, unveiling new interpretations and meanings emerging from his patient's unconscious. The case study of *Little Hans*[2] is a fascinating clinical description of a five-year-old boy who gradually developed equinophobia (horse phobia). The analysis in this clinical description was carried out by Hans's father, under the supervision and guidance of Freud, and it lays out for the readers captivating conversations and occurrences that took place between the five-year-old boy and his parents. While *The Wolf Man* case study is a retrospective analysis of the patient's childhood, and the case of *Little Hans* is a remote-real-time analysis conducted by Freud through correspondence with Hans' father, the third case description in this chapter, *Leonardo's childhood memory*,[3] is an analysis that Freud performs through a time capsule, without ever meeting the patient. Four centuries after the death of the artist and researcher Leonardo da Vinci, Freud analyses this iconic figure's childhood through da Vinci's artworks and one single childhood memory discovered in his writings.

The three clinical descriptions serve as a significant volume of evidence through which Freud moulds his theory on childhood psychosexual development. All three case studies touch upon fragments of memory and events that occurred during early childhood, and therefore, provide a gateway to delve into the depth of the

---

1 Sigmund Freud. "From the History of an Infantile Neurosis." In: James Strachey (ed. & trans.) *The Standard Edition of the Complete Psychological Works of Sigmund Freud* 17 (1918), pp. 1–124. Edited and translated by James Strachey. London: The Hogarth Press and the Institute of Psycho-Analysis, 1955.

2 Sigmund Freud. "Analysis of a Phobia in a Five-Year-Old Boy." In: James Strachey (ed. & trans.) *The Standard Edition of the Complete Psychological Works of Sigmund Freud* 10 (1909), pp. 1–150. London: The Hogarth Press and the Institute of Psycho-Analysis, 1955.

3 Sigmund Freud. "Leonardo Da Vinci and a Memory of his Childhood." In: James Strachey (ed. & trans.) *The Standard Edition of the Complete Psychological Works of Sigmund Freud* 11 (1910), pp. 57–138. London: The Hogarth Press and the Institute of Psycho-Analysis, 1957.

DOI: 10.4324/9781003394334-2

mother-child relationship, opening a door to the emotional complexity embedded within this relational framework. In all three texts, circumcision, although not lengthily elaborated on, appears as a central image, revolving around the gender axis, through which the focus is redirected from the mother to the Oedipal narrative, to castration anxiety and to the relationship with the father. Yet, at the same time, it also remains as a key-fossil, an ambivalent marker for the textual anxiety, both covering and uncovering the complexity of the relationship with the mother. It is a window to a textual conflict in which the discussion of the maternal is limited and the complexity of the mother-child relationship is reduced to a preoccupation with maternal lack, anxiously drawing a boundary line between the subject and the (m)other.

Each of the case studies evokes a different angle of the relationship with the mother and opens a doorway to discussing a concept or an aspect of the Freudian theory of childhood psychosexual development: The case study of *The Wolf Man*, following his famous dream of wolves, invites an exploration of the concept of the 'primal scene' and the different meanings of this powerful image. The description of *Little Hans* provides an insightful opening into the depth of the Oedipal conflict within the child's inner world, and *Leonardo's childhood memory* reveals numerous implications hidden within the concept of the 'Phallic Mother', opening a discussion of the complexity and paradoxes inherent to maternal power. In the three case studies, while with one hand Freud opens the door to the various theoretical dimensions inherent to the relationship with the mother, he also covers it with his other hand, leaving circumcision as an ambivalent image that at the same time reveals and conceals a wounded maternal realm.

I

THE WOLF MAN: THE POSTERITY OF THE PRIMAL SCENE

The Wolf Man is a case study that Freud dealt with intensively, between the years 1910–1914. Sergei Pankejeff was a young man of Russian origin, who came to Freud for analysis for his obsessional neurosis. The text published by Freud in 1918 is an analysis of Pankejeff's childhood neurosis, which was conducted by Freud 15 years after its onset, when the patient was 23 years old. In the case description, Freud explores the events of Pankejeff's childhood, weaving together pieces of memory, fantasies and anxieties, with childhood imaginative associations, dreams and fairy tales. Through these detailed association chains, some narratives collapse while others are revived. The reconstruction that appears before the eyes of the readers is based on the analysis of Pankejeff's famous dream of wolves, which was dreamt just before he was four years old, granting the case study with its name:

> I dreamt that it was night and that I was lying in my bed. (My bed stood with its foot towards the window; in front of the window, there was a row of old walnut trees. I know it was winter when I had the dream and night-time.) Suddenly the window opened of its own accord, and I was terrified to see that some white wolves were sitting on the big walnut tree in front of the window. There were six or seven of them. The wolves were quite white, and looked more like foxes or sheep-dogs, for they had big tails like foxes and they had their ears pricked like dogs when they pay attention to something. In great terror, evidently, of being eaten up by the wolves, I screamed and woke up.[4]

The horror and meaning of the white wolves appearing in the dream are the windows through which Freud enters the unconscious world of the four-year-old patient. That ominous dread signifies the existence of an event or an experience waiting to be deciphered in the child's unconscious. The description of the case that is woven around the dream leads Freud to conceptualise *The Primal Scene*, signifying the child's exposure to the sexuality of the parents and the erotic relationship between them. Whereas for Freud the 'primal scene' is a psychic phantasy introducing the child to the parent's sexuality, and specifically to the power relations and hierarchy between the sexes, another thread within the text reveals an alternative possibility inherent in this concept, opening the door to an encounter with maternal sexuality.

Premature Birth

One association with the dream of wolves brought forward a memory of a severe epidemic that affected the livestock near the patient's childhood home: "shortly before

---

4 Sigmund Freud. "From the History of an Infantile Neurosis." *The Standard Edition of the Complete Psychological Works of Sigmund Freud* 17 (1918), p. 29.

the time of the dream—an epidemic broke out among the sheep", Freud writes. "His father sent for a follower of Pasteur's, who inoculated the animals, but after the inoculation, even more of them died than before".[5] The high status of Pankejeff's family produced hope for the animals to be cured by the hands of science. But the hope soon faded, and the situation worsened. A promise of healing and subsequent failure, which appears as an association to the dream, can be heard as a blueprint for a terrifying recurring motif in the patient's life; one that also shapes his attitude towards analysis and plays a significant role in his neurosis. Not only that the proximity to power and money fail to help, but a traumatic conglomerate involving hierarchical power relations appears to be entangled in the patient's psyche.

Sergei Konstantinovich Pankejeff was born into a wealthy Russian family of nobles and landowners. As described by Mikkel Borch-Jacobsen, his father used to organise wolf-hunting expeditions on their estate, followed by grand celebrations that were held around the pile of hunted wolves. "The Library of Congress" as Borch-Jacobsen describes, "holds several photos of the young Sergius standing with his mother and sister in front of a heap of slaughtered animals".[6] Alongside the abundant wealth, festivities and public life, Sergei's father suffered from alcoholism and was diagnosed with bipolar disorder (manic depression illness) and psychosis, which were discreetly treated by another 'wolf', a psychiatrist and psychoanalyst named Moshe Wulff. Other family members also suffered severe mental crises: Sergei's paternal grandfather died of alcoholism. His wife, who was Sergei's paternal grandmother, fell into depression after the death of her only daughter and likely committed suicide by taking an overdose of medication. One of Pankejeff's paternal uncles developed paranoia and was hospitalised. Two of his maternal cousins suffered from schizophrenia and were also treated by Moshe Wulff. Anna, Sergei's older sister, also committed suicide at the age of eighteen, a fact that deeply affected Sergei's mental state. Following Anna's suicide, his mother experienced prolonged mourning and depression, and in 1908, two years after the suicide, his father also took his own life by consuming an overdose of medication.

It seems that the wolves in the dream lead to a thread of associations that weaves between the slaughtered wolves and the family members who fell ill and needed the help of the psychiatrist Moshe Wulff.[7] These associations and meanings, which were not referred to in Freud's dream analysis, nonetheless reveal a sediment trail of evidence in the text, marking the violence embodied in the patient's life. Despite the abundance of wealth and the families' hope for the best treatment by psychiatry

---

5 Sigmund Freud. "From the History of an Infantile Neurosis." *The Standard Edition of the Complete Psychological Works of Sigmund Freud* 17 (1918), p. 30.

6 Borch-Jacobsen, Mikkel. *Freud's Patients: A Book of Lives* (London: Reaktion Books, 2022), p. 162.

7 It is important to note that Moshe Wulff treated the family in the years after the famous dream of wolves, and therefore it was not an aetiology for the dream in its direct sense. However, it might have arisen as an association or as an aetiology for the dream from the patient's adult life, in which, Pankejeff knew Wulff as a psychiatrist and psychoanalyst who treated his family. The dream, which was brought to analysis when the patient was 23 years old, even if was dreamt during childhood, is always re-created, as Freud explains, through the experiences, thoughts and phantasies of the adult.

and psychoanalysis, the mental crises in Pankejeff's family spread like a plague in a flock of sheep. Even before Sergei's birth, the family legacy oscillated between the promise for good fortune and a life filled with trauma, loss and pain and Freud indeed points out these traumatic cycles in the patient's life. Yet, this oscillation between upper and lower, which involves power dynamics and hierarchies also extends to the analytic process itself and, subsequently, to the textual structure which climbs, at times, to great heights, while at other times, plunges into depths. Recognising this movement in the patient's psyche, Freud writes that

> [a]t a decisive point, therefore, a transposition has taken place; and moreover, this is indicated by another transposition in the manifest content of the dream. For the fact that the wolves were sitting on the tree was also a transposition, since in his grandfather's story they were underneath, and were unable to climb on to the tree.[8]

Between these extreme polarities of upper and lower, the story of Sergei Pankejeff unfolds.

This motif of great promise and subsequent failure becomes increasingly evident in Freud's case description, with an image of premature birth. Pankejeff states that he lived his life with a kind of veil from the world, a sense of alienation that detached him from his surroundings and prevented him from feeling truly alive. "His principal subject of complaint was that for him the world was hidden in a veil, or that he was cut off from the world by a veil",[9] Freud writes explaining that

> The complaint that he made was in reality a fulfilled wishful phantasy: it exhibited him as back once more in the womb, and was, in fact, a wishful phantasy of flight from the world. It can be translated as follows: 'Life makes me so unhappy! I must get back into the womb!'[10]

Thus, according to Freud, Pankejeff's symptom of a masking veil – "which hid him from the world and hid the world from him"[11] – was a result of the patient's narcissistic structure expressed in the wish to return to the womb and to envelop himself in a protective cocoon.

Another aspect of this structure, revealed in the course of the analysis, is that Pankejeff "was born with a caul. He had for that reason always looked on himself

---

8 Sigmund Freud. "From the History of an Infantile Neurosis." *The Standard Edition of the Complete Psychological Works of Sigmund Freud* 17 (1918), p. 34.

9 Sigmund Freud. "From the History of an Infantile Neurosis." *The Standard Edition of the Complete Psychological Works of Sigmund Freud* 17 (1918), p. 75.

10 Sigmund Freud. "From the History of an Infantile Neurosis." *The Standard Edition of the Complete Psychological Works of Sigmund Freud* 17 (1918), p. 100.

11 Sigmund Freud. "From the History of an Infantile Neurosis." *The Standard Edition of the Complete Psychological Works of Sigmund Freud* 17 (1918), p. 100.

as a special child of fortune whom no ill could befall".[12] The amniotic sac is usually ruptured before or during birth, but in rare cases, the baby is born with it, wrapped in its fluids, and this is considered a sign of luck for life for the newborn. The fact that Pankejeff was born wrapped in his amniotic sac, might have also created a moment of connection in the analysis, since Freud himself, according to rumours, was born with a *lucky dome*. From the very beginning of the analysis, and even before this fact is revealed, Freud felt a connection that brings with it a great promise for both the therapist and the patient. As he puts it in his letter to Ferenczi: "I have taken on a new patient from Odessa, a very rich Russian with compulsive feelings, but I am more capable of accomplishment than ever".[13]

For Pankejeff, the wealth and family status into which he was born were both a protective shell and his traumatic repetition. A metaphor of a screen, or rather the lifting of a screen, is used by Anat Tzur Mahalel to describe this drama that took place in both the life of the Wolf Man and in the analytical process. The repetitive screen-lifting is characterised by panic at the moment of unveiling: opening the window (as in the dream), opening the eyes, and revelations in analysis that sent him fleeing back into the womb. As Tzur Mahalel elaborates,

> the dialectic between the internal and the external turned, in Pankejeff's case, into a neurotic symptom of feeling caught behind a veil, as a repetition of the conflict evolving around the experience of being prematurely torn from the quiet serenity of the womb.[14]

This traumatic cycle of revelation and concealment was entangled with anxiety, bringing with it therapeutic stagnation, and hindering his process of development and change in analysis. The many gaps in the patient's life – the great promises to which he was born and the traumatic falls from heights of fortune – generated a repetitive structure of traumatic falling: falling from the tree, falling from wealth into poverty, falling sick, a fall from analysis, a fall from the womb in a premature birth, a miscarriage.

The structure of the patient's anxiety and this powerful image of premature birth emerging from the text raise questions about the patient's relationship with his mother and the history of his separation from her. Birth encapsulates a separation from the mother, which is, in a way, always premature. Mothers do not only give birth to their children but also, as psychoanalysis shows, introduce them to an inherent experience of separation – a necessary and ongoing creation of gaps, of fractures, and of separations, which are part of early life within the relationship with

---

12 Sigmund Freud. "From the History of an Infantile Neurosis." *The Standard Edition of the Complete Psychological Works of Sigmund Freud* 17 (1918), p.99.
13 The Correspondence of Sigmund Freud and Sándor Ferenczi 1 (1993): 1908–1914, 25: 1–571, pp. 133–134.
14 Anat Tzur Mahalel. "The Wolf Man's Glückshaube: Rereading Sergei Pankejeff's Memoir." *J. Am. Psychoanal. Ass.* 67, no. 5 (2019): 789–814, 794.

the mother. This repetitive 'cutting of the umbilical cord', provokes in the infant feelings of interruption, of abandonment and even sometimes deadening anxieties. Thus, the patient's desire to return to the womb may testify to this early unprocessed and anxiety-provoking conflict towards the maternal.

Freud indeed points out the difficulty Pankejeff experienced as a child in the absence of his mother, who rarely spent time with her children, partly due to the gastrointestinal illnesses she suffered from. "[H]e was aware of his mother's weak health even in his early childhood", Freud writes, and "as a consequence of it she had relatively little to do with the children".[15] As was customary in the provinces of the rich and upper class during this period – and it is interesting to think that Freud grew up in a similar way – Pankejeff was cared for by a nanny, "an uneducated old woman of peasant birth, with an untiring affection for him. He served her as a substitute for a son of her own who had died young".[16] The absence of the mother is also evident in the initial childhood onset of Sergei's neurotic illness, as the anxiety was triggered by the experience of separation from the parents. The parents left the siblings for the summer under the care of an English governess who "turned out to be an eccentric and quarrelsome person, and, moreover, to be addicted to drink".[17] The neurosis began, as Freud describes it, "when his parents came back from their summer holiday, they found him transformed. He had become discontented, irritable and violent, took offence on every possible occasion, and then flew into a rage and screamed like a savage".[18] Tantrums continued into his adulthood and similar incidents repeated throughout his life, in which even "[h]e himself was puzzled by his behavior". Pankejeff would "lose control", accusing his mother that "she did not love him, that she was trying to economize at his expense, and that she would probably rather see him dead so as to have sole control over the money".[19]

Pankejeff's memories throughout the text reveal the young child's identification with his mother. It emphasises the mother's tendency to express somatic depression and raises questions about Pankejeff's identification with her through his own somatic symptoms. Like his mother, he was preoccupied with his intestinal movements, had difficulty with spontaneous bowel movements and, identifying with her menstruation, he claimed that his stool had blood in it. He repeated his mother's words saying that "he could not go on living like that",[20] and, like his

15 Sigmund Freud. "From the History of an Infantile Neurosis." *The Standard Edition of the Complete Psychological Works of Sigmund Freud* 17 (1918), p. 13.

16 Sigmund Freud. "From the History of an Infantile Neurosis." *The Standard Edition of the Complete Psychological Works of Sigmund Freud* 17 (1918), p. 14.

17 Sigmund Freud. "From the History of an Infantile Neurosis." *The Standard Edition of the Complete Psychological Works of Sigmund Freud* 17 (1918), p. 15.

18 Sigmund Freud. "From the History of an Infantile Neurosis." *The Standard Edition of the Complete Psychological Works of Sigmund Freud* 17 (1918), p. 15.

19 Sigmund Freud. "From the History of an Infantile Neurosis." *The Standard Edition of the Complete Psychological Works of Sigmund Freud* 17 (1918), p. 73.

20 Sigmund Freud. "From the History of an Infantile Neurosis." *The Standard Edition of the Complete Psychological Works of Sigmund Freud* 17 (1918), p. 76.

mother, expressed his emotions through physical symptoms. Many textual moments provide insight into the way in which the wolves-dream, and the patient's anxiety about wolves are connected to his complex ambivalent feelings towards his mother. These symptoms not only reflect an identification with the mother and a need to "return to the womb", but also suggest rage at separating from her. Alongside Freud's Oedipal interpretations of the wolves anxiety, pointing to the fear of the father, another thread emerges from the text, indicating an earlier source of anxiety rooted in the intricate relationship with the mother.

These clinical observations are picked up by Freud, but he does not elaborate on their connection to the patient's anxiety and of course, does not develop them into theoretical understandings in relation to the maternal. Recognising the structure of premature birth as well as the anxiety in the transference of the analytic process, Freud describes the way in which, in response to loss, Pankejeff clings to the therapist in a dependent and frightened manner, resisting any possibility for change. He highlights the stillness and lack of movement in the wolves-dream, as well as the absence of bowel movements in the patient's symptoms of constipation, reflecting the patient's difficulty in digesting his encounters with the world. Freud writes: "The patient with whom I am here concerned remained for a long time unassailably entrenched behind an attitude of obliging apathy. He listened, understood, and remained unapproachable". Due to the slow therapeutic progress and the patient's resistance, Freud decided to take a drastic step and set an end date for the analysis. "Under the inexorable pressure of this fixed limit", he explains, "his resistance and his fixation to the illness gave way, and now in a disproportionately short time the analysis produced all the material which made it possible to clear up his inhibitions".[21]

In response to Freud's "Wolf Man" case study, Otto Rank writes that in any analysis, "the patient attempts to repeat in a quite obtrusive way the process of birth", and that the challenge faced by the analyst is to allow the patient a gentle separation, in a way that does not repeat the traumatic structure of their birth.[22] Although the therapeutic process that Pankejeff underwent with Freud was undoubtedly profound, intensive and long, it nevertheless repeated the trauma of his premature birth. Despite Freud's understanding of this structure dominating the patient's psyche, and despite his attempts to create a different movement, a traumatic separation is reproduced in the analysis.

Freud's abrupt amniocentesis – continuing the metaphor of premature birth – did not lead to a healthy separation that would allow the patient to stand on his own two feet but left him swallowed even more in the psychoanalytic world, and in fact throughout his life Pankejeff remained dependent on various analyses, continuing

21 Sigmund Freud. "From the History of an Infantile Neurosis." *The Standard Edition of the Complete Psychological Works of Sigmund Freud* 17 (1918), p. 11.
22 Otto Rank. "The Trauma of Birth in Its Importance for Psychoanalytic Therapy." *Psychoanal. Rev.* 100 2013 (1924): 669–674, esp. p. 670.

to engage in numerous encounters and interviews that placed him at the centre of psychoanalytic writing – a subject, or in fact, an object for many analysts and re-searchers.[23] The fact that Pankejeff remained trapped in the memory of his analysis with Freud is also evident in the way the patient continued to refer to himself as a clinical case, identifying by the name "The Wolf Man" throughout his life. Thus, while Freud described the regressive phantasy of returning to the mother's womb that characterised the Wolf Man, the analysis he conducted with him also repeated the same traumatic structure.

Pankejeff's absorption within the analytic world may indicate the difficulty of treating trauma-saturated cases and the way in which analysis might collaborate with a patient's internal traumatic structure. Despite the intention to facilitate thera-peutic progress, Pankejeff was immersed in the reenactment of trauma, and as I will show, an anxious entanglement was shared by both therapist and patient. As I will argue, Pankejeff's analysis with Freud did not allow for a gradual process of separation, partly due to a shared anxiety about the maternal. By constantly turning the analytic gaze towards the Oedipal model and the relationship with the father, the complexity of the relationship with the mother, the need for identification with her and the anger toward her could not be explored or worked through, leading to a repetition of the same traumatic birth in the analysis itself. Using the image of cir-cumcision, I will identify the textual moments in which the traumatic structure ap-pears, revealing the way both therapist and patient are intertwined in the fear of the maternal dimension. The inherent dependency in the relationship with the mother repeatedly evokes textual attempts – and one might say hysterical attempts – to cling to the phallus, to grasp masculinity and identify it with the upper side of the hierarchical relationship; a structure that at the same time leaves circumcision as a conflictual marker of a wounded dimension simultaneously covering and revealing its vulnerability.

The Circumcision Wound

A tailor was sitting at work in his room, when the window opened, and a wolf leapt in. The tailor hit after him with his yard—no (he corrected himself), caught him by his tail and pulled it off, so that the wolf ran away in terror. Some time later the tailor went into the forest, and suddenly saw a pack of wolves coming towards him; so he climbed up a tree to escape from them. At first the wolves were in perplexity; but the maimed one, which was among them and wanted to revenge himself on the tailor, proposed that they should climb one upon another till the last one could reach him. He himself—he was a vigorous old fellow—would be the base of the pyramid. The wolves did as he suggested, but the tailor had recognized the visitor whom he had punished, and suddenly called out as he

23 Myself included.

had before: "Catch the grey one by his tail!" The tailless wolf, terrified by the recollection, ran away, and all the others tumbled down.[24]

The conflict identified by Freud relates to Pankejeff's narcissistic response to his own identification with the mother. "It seems, therefore, as though he [the patient] had identified himself with his castrated mother during the dream", Freud writes,

> and was now fighting against that fact. 'If you want to be sexually satisfied by Father', we may perhaps represent him as saying to himself, 'you must allow yourself to be castrated like Mother; but I won't have that.' In short, a clear protest on the part of his masculinity![25]

This protest of masculinity, Freud explains, creates in the patient the structure of anxiety that, while identifying with the mother, he is also terrified of the possibility of being "castrated like Mother". As portrayed in the story of the tailor and the wolf, in which the wolf flees in response to any small reminder of its severed tail, thereby toppling the ladder of wolves, so it is in the patient's masculine structure. Any hint of his vulnerability is understood as a possibility of falling into the inferior side of the hierarchy, experienced as a "blow to his narcissism",[26] causing him to flee in panic from any feminine identification.

In portraying Pankejeff's narcissistic fragility, Freud identifies a structure of masculinity in which the subject is terrified of his own vulnerability. One can read the emerging subjectivity of the child who has experienced extreme difficulties and trauma but is prohibited from expressing pain. He is expected to grow up, to man up, learning that pain and vulnerability must be projected onto women. Pankejeff heard these expectations from the very beginning of his life: in the disappointed statements about the position he took compared to his sister who "was very much his superior, [and] used to tease him"[27]; In the raising of eyebrows in the face of his gentle behaviour, which often got the response "that he ought to have been the girl and his elder sister the boy"[28]; In the descriptions of his behaviour after being left by his parents for the summer as "unbearable". Although Freud recognises the rigid gender construct in the patient's psyche and the anxieties it produces, he too continues to affirm rigid fixation of gender representations, interpreting the patient's vulnerability as "hysterical", criticising his identification with his mother and understanding it under hierarchical structure defined by the male sexual organ.

24 Sigmund Freud. "From the History of an Infantile Neurosis." *The Standard Edition of the Complete Psychological Works of Sigmund Freud* 17 (1918), pp. 30–31.

25 Sigmund Freud. "From the History of an Infantile Neurosis." *The Standard Edition of the Complete Psychological Works of Sigmund Freud* 17 (1918), p. 47.

26 Sigmund Freud. "From the History of an Infantile Neurosis." *The Standard Edition of the Complete Psychological Works of Sigmund Freud* 17 (1918), p. 99.

27 Sigmund Freud. "From the History of an Infantile Neurosis." *The Standard Edition of the Complete Psychological Works of Sigmund Freud* 17 (1918), p. 29.

28 Sigmund Freud. "From the History of an Infantile Neurosis." *The Standard Edition of the Complete Psychological Works of Sigmund Freud* 17 (1918), p. 15.

The image of circumcision comes up in one of Pankejeff's memories, as a moment of encountering vulnerability:

> When I was five years old, I was playing in the garden near my nurse, and was carving with my pocket-knife in the bark of one of the walnut-trees that come into my dream as well. Suddenly, to my unspeakable terror, I noticed that I had cut through the little finger of my (right or left?) hand, so that it was only hanging on by its skin. I felt no pain, but great fear. I did not venture to say anything to my nurse, who was only a few paces distant, but I sank down on the nearest seat and sat there incapable of casting another glance at my finger. At last I calmed down, took a look at the finger, and saw that it was entirely uninjured.[29]

The moment of panic, like the panic induced by the dream, is a moment of encounter with a wound – not that of the mother but, rather, that of a human male child who can bleed. Despite being born wrapped in ample protections – amniotic membrane, extreme wealth, high status and masculinity, injury and pain are still a possibility. This emerging possibility of the finger being cut causes panic precisely because vulnerability is not an option. The young child, who experienced traumas and losses, encounters through this dream-hallucination both his masculine vulnerability and its inherent prohibition.

The tip of the finger hanging by a thin piece of skin evokes immense fear in the child in its echo of the Jewish ritual in which the baby's foreskin is cut and Freud indeed explains that this hallucination occurred around the time when the patient became familiar with "the ritual circumcision of Christ and of the Jews in general".[30] The imagery of circumcision, which appears several times in the text, opens a door to that injury and allows an exploration of the patient's wound, and the structure of masculine subjectivity. Following this image, one can observe both the panic evoked by this "wound" and the solution that transpires in an anxious collaboration between the therapist and the patient. In this collaborated solution, a binary hierarchical division between the sexes is established, and the wounds are projected onto the mother (and women in general).

Despite being familiar with this Jewish wound as a Jew, Freud repeats the panic of that structure in the text. Following the young patient's mental preoccupation with circumcision, Freud explains, the child developed an awareness of castration, giving rise to fear of the father, and an identification with the masculine position was solidified:

> we shall perhaps be justified in reaching the interpretation that the tree meant a woman to my little patient as well. Here, then, he was playing the part of his

29 Sigmund Freud. "From the History of an Infantile Neurosis." *The Standard Edition of the Complete Psychological Works of Sigmund Freud* 17 (1918), p. 85.
30 Sigmund Freud. "From the History of an Infantile Neurosis." *The Standard Edition of the Complete Psychological Works of Sigmund Freud* 17 (1918), p. 86.

father, and was connecting his mother's familiar haemorrhages with the castration of women, which he now recognized,—with the 'wound'.[31]

The possibility that the wound may exist in men and not just in women symbolically topples in a panic the tower of wolves – challenging the structure of the patient's masculine subjectivity in response to which, gender variabilities are repressed and the binary and hierarchies of sexual relation must be reinstated through interpretation: The tree represents the wounded and bleeding woman; the young child takes on the role of the father, carves into the tree with his awl, and understands the significance of the feminine "wound", the "lack" of the mother and women's sexual role in relation to men.

Although Freud's exploration of the patient's desire to perform a cut with his knife until blood flows is directed towards the mother, questions about the child's ambivalent feelings towards her are denied by the analyst. Alongside "playing the part of his father",[32] the aggression and desire to cause bleeding could reflect Pankejeff's response to the mother's 'absence', but in a different sense: not her absent male sexual organ but her absence for him. Perhaps it is not, as Freud suggests, a case of the child taking on the father's position (the normal masculine position) in relation to the mother, but an expression of his anger towards the mother in response to her absence, to the separation from her in times of vulnerability and trauma; it is perhaps an unspoken conflict directed towards an inherent maternal ability to separate from her children – to cut the umbilical cord and the breast, a maternal "cutting" which is always premature. In other words, perhaps the aggression towards the mother-tree is not a "healthy" response to her absence-of-male-organ, but a vindictive response to a different absence – her painful absence for him. And perhaps even more, the aggression towards her is a manifestation of jealousy of her freedom to express vulnerability as a woman – possibilities that the textual narrative does not dwell on.

In the face of these possible interpretations, which cry out from the text, Freud portrays an image of masculine sexual aggression as "healthy" – normal male aggression that wounds women and causes them to bleed. In response to the imagery of circumcision and to other masculine wounds appearing in the text, the hierarchical binarism of sexual difference is highlighted, as an evasion of that wound. Freud states that "women are castrated, … instead of a male organ they have a wound which serves for sexual intercourse" and explains that "castration is the necessary condition of femininity".[33] Introducing the 'primal scene', Freud describes the parents' sexuality – according to him in the eyes of the child – as a "violent act" in which the father injures the mother and causes her to bleed.

31 Sigmund Freud. "From the History of an Infantile Neurosis." *The Standard Edition of the Complete Psychological Works of Sigmund Freud* 17 (1918), p. 86.

32 Sigmund Freud. "From the History of an Infantile Neurosis." *The Standard Edition of the Complete Psychological Works of Sigmund Freud* 17 (1918), p. 86.

33 Sigmund Freud. "From the History of an Infantile Neurosis." *The Standard Edition of the Complete Psychological Works of Sigmund Freud* 17 (1918), p. 78.

These descriptions of Freud, highlighting a violent hierarchy of sexuality organised according to the gender axis, are created as a textual response to the image of the masculine "wound". In all of them, the woman is wounded by the man – negating any possibility of exploring the other side of the relationship – the depth of the masculine wound in relation to the maternal.

Throughout the text, Freud lays out various events in which the threat of castration is raised by different women in the patient's life. For example, when Pankejeff, as a child, "began to play with his penis in his Nanya's presence, and [...] [h]is Nanya disillusioned him; she made a serious face, and explained that that wasn't good; children who did that, she added, got a 'wound' in the place".[34] On another occasion, "when the children were given some coloured sugar-sticks, the governess, who was inclined to disordered fancies, announced that they were pieces of chopped-up snakes",[35] and Freud, of course, referred to this as an association aimed at castration. In a third incident, Freud recounts from fragments of memory an earlier scene in the young patient's life, in which he was threatened with castration by a previous governess: "When he saw the girl scrubbing the floor he had micturated in the room and she had rejoined, no doubt jokingly, with a threat of castration".[36] The threats of castration coming from female characters in the patient's life might have led to an exploration of the ambivalence towards the mother and even to an interpretation of the *'primal scene'* as an *event in which the child encounters the mother's ability to cut*. Alongside other interpretations, the child's 'primal scene' phantasy can be understood as an encounter with maternal sexuality and the mother's ability to place a cut into a dyadic continuum. Separating the baby from the breast and shifting her attention to a relationship with 'a third', the mother introduces the infant to the cut of the 'primal scene'. All these constitute fertile grounds for the development of a complex emotional relationship towards the maternal, which contains conflicting feelings of love, anger, jealousy and anxiety.

Ambivalent feelings towards the patient's mother, as well as other feminine figures in his life, might have served as a gateway to a deeper exploration. Although Freud indeed lays out the events that could have led to an in-depth discussion, the image of circumcision is never explored as a masculine wound in its relationship to the maternal, and Freud retroactively provides an Oedipal solution to all the open questions when he explains:

Although the threats or hints of castration which had come his way had emanated from women, this could not hold up the final result for long. In spite of everything it was his father from whom in the end he came to fear castration.

---

34 Sigmund Freud. "From the History of an Infantile Neurosis." *The Standard Edition of the Complete Psychological Works of Sigmund Freud* 17 (1918), p. 24.

35 Sigmund Freud. "From the History of an Infantile Neurosis." *The Standard Edition of the Complete Psychological Works of Sigmund Freud* 17 (1918), p. 25.

36 Sigmund Freud. "From the History of an Infantile Neurosis." *The Standard Edition of the Complete Psychological Works of Sigmund Freud* 17 (1918), p. 92.

In this respect heredity triumphed over accidental experience; in man's prehistory it was unquestionably the father who practised castration as a punishment and who later softened it down into circumcision.[37]

Freud's explanation regarding the role of circumcision in the early history of humankind is central to his psychoanalytic theory, as it connects individual development with the broader human history in which the Oedipal myth becomes a precursor to a universal cultural experience. While, in the early days of life, the "threats of castration", cuts and separations are imminent to the relationship with the maternal, Freud explains, following the image of circumcision, that in the early days of human history, castration was instituted by the father. Following this image, both clinically and theoretically, castration is positioned as a cardinal phantasy in childhood development focused solely on the relationship with the father. Connecting individual development to human social development, Freud weaves in this textual movement his patient's life with the historical and the cultural, ontogenesis with phylogenesis. He anchors an origin, tightening a rope around the Oedipal narrative as the single human myth preceding any individual experience – one exclusive psychological phantasy that shapes all experiences from personal to the universal and explains at the same time the lives of patients, historical and cultural development. Without diminishing the significance of the Oedipal metaphor in the child's development, I would like to point to the textual moment in which it becomes the sole narrative. Through this textual movement that begins with the masculine wound of circumcision, the possibility of unlocking the complexity in the patient's life story collapses into a single solution, and different voices in the understanding of childhood psychosexual development are sealed. At this moment, individual reality is cast into a phylogenetic pattern with only one meaning, as Freud explains:

> These scenes of observing parental intercourse, of being seduced in childhood, and of being threatened with castration are unquestionably an inherited endowment, a phylogenetic heritage, but they may just as easily be acquired by personal experience. With my patient, his seduction by his elder sister was an indisputable reality; why should not the same have been true of his observation of his parents' intercourse? All that we find in the prehistory of neuroses is that a child catches hold of this phylogenetic experience where his own experience fails him. He fills in the gaps in individual truth with prehistoric truth; he replaces occurrences in his own life by occurrences in the life of his ancestors.[38]

Does the phylogenetic pattern dictate a single interpretive meaning? This question, which touches on all primary phantasies including 'castration', and 'the primal

---

37 Sigmund Freud. "From the History of an Infantile Neurosis." *The Standard Edition of the Complete Psychological Works of Sigmund Freud* 17 (1918), p. 86.

38 Sigmund Freud. "From the History of an Infantile Neurosis." *The Standard Edition of the Complete Psychological Works of Sigmund Freud* 17 (1918), p. 97.

scene', will require an in-depth discussion (which I will go into later in the chapter). Following the encounter with the maternal, a specific textual movement appears, through which an interpretive playfulness for these primordial phantasies becomes impossible. In these textual moments, circumcision remains an ambivalent marker, in which the wound is concealed and revealed at the same time. Freud marks the preoccupation with circumcision as a turning point in the child's life through which Pankejeff's childhood neurosis is resolved by introducing him to castration anxiety and paternal law. He explains that through engagement with the image of circumcision, the relationship between the sexes was internalised according to the Oedipal structure. According to this interpretation, becoming familiar with the ritual of circumcision, the child was subjected to an image that provoked the primal phantasy of castration anxiety, and subsequently internalised the dichotomous structure and hierarchy of the relation between the sexes: the mother's lack; the father's strength and their erotic division into binary poles – active and passive, dominant and submissive, penetrator and penetrated.

In this way, Freud merges the image of '*circumcision*', '*castration*' and the '*primal scene*', assigning them all with a single interpretation. As in the dream of the patient, in which a window opens and closes in a panic, so it is in Freud's text: the preoccupation with the Jewish ritual constitutes the textual moment that both opens and closes the door to a wound. Through this image, an ongoing interpretative process inherent to the 'primal scene' ceases. The 'primal scene' might have been an opening into an initial triadic space in which the subject can playfully identify with both the mother and the father, to move between the positions of an object and a subject, and perhaps particularly – to engage with maternal sexuality and subjectivity – draw to a close. Once castration is established as a representation of the relationship with the father alone, the relationship with the maternal is repressed and the "masculine" identity of the child is sealed. Circumcision then remains an ambivalent marker in the text which, while solidifying the emotional complexity into an Oedipal dichotomy, also provides a glimpse into the child's wound, in their relationship with the maternal, and the need to identify with her.

Throughout the case description, in response to the encounter with the many wounds in the patient's life, Freud repeatedly sets gender boundaries presenting to the patient a hierarchical understanding of 'masculinity' and 'femininity' in which the wound is projected onto the mother. Despite recognising the patient's "narcissistic masculinity", describing his anxiety and his 'masculine protest' in response to vulnerability,[39] Freud too, like the patient in response to the wound, closes all the open windows that mix between inside and outside, self and other, masculine and feminine. The potential for creative interpretations inherent in the 'primal scene' phantasy is erased under an interpretation that views the dream in terms of a gender hierarchy centred around the phallus. Despite asking: "[w]as the wolf a female

---

39 Sigmund Freud. "From the History of an Infantile Neurosis." *The Standard Edition of the Complete Psychological Works of Sigmund Freud* 17 (1918), p. 110.

creature[?]",[40] thereby acknowledging the conflict with the mother – the patient's need to identify with her as well as the fear of her and the rage towards her – Freud quickly explains that the wolf cannot represent any content other than the father. As he elaborates, "[h]is fear of his father was the strongest motive for his falling ill, and his ambivalent attitude towards every father-surrogate was the dominating feature of his life as well as of his behaviour during the treatment".[41]

The Primal Scene

Throughout the text and in his various writings, Freud raises the question of whether the 'primal scene' is an actual event or, alternatively, a childhood phantasy reconstructed retroactively:

> I should myself be glad to know whether the primal scene in my present patient's case was a phantasy or a real experience; but, taking other similar cases into account, I must admit that the answer to this question is not in fact a matter of very great importance. These scenes of observing parental intercourse, of being seduced in childhood, and of being threatened with castration are unquestionably an inherited endowment, a phylogenetic heritage.[42]

Thus, Freud portrays the primal scene as a universal phantasy assigned to the category of those

> primal phantasies, as I should like to call them, and no doubt a few others as well, are a phylogenetic endowment. In them the individual reaches beyond his own experience into primaeval experience at points where his own experience has been too rudimentary.[43]

By granting the 'primal scene' the status of phylogenetic inheritance, Freud situates it as an archaic event, a memory without an object of memory, a pre-event that awakens the body and to which there are no words. It can be understood – similarly to other archaic events – as a transitional event, located between phantasy and reality. Freud's interpretation of the 'primal scene' identifies the event as an enigma, one that continuously creates an excess that evades translation. Inscribed in the

---

40 Sigmund Freud. "From the History of an Infantile Neurosis." *The Standard Edition of the Complete Psychological Works of Sigmund Freud* 17 (1918), p. 25.

41 Sigmund Freud. "From the History of an Infantile Neurosis." *The Standard Edition of the Complete Psychological Works of Sigmund Freud* 17 (1918), p. 32.

42 Sigmund Freud. "From the History of an Infantile Neurosis." *The Standard Edition of the Complete Psychological Works of Sigmund Freud* 17 (1918), p. 97.

43 Sigmund Freud. "Introductory Lectures on Psycho-Analysis." In: James Strachey (ed. & trans.) *The Standard Edition of the Complete Psychological Works of Sigmund Freud* 16 (1917), pp. 241–463, London: The Hogarth Press and the Institute of Psycho-Analysis, 1963. p. 371.

child's psyche as a necessary riddle in childhood psychosexual development, the 'primal scene' becomes an open question continuously seeking interpretation.[44]

As argued by Lacan, Freud's exploration of the Wolf Man's case study delineates a psychoanalytic picture that goes beyond content and touches upon the fundamental structure of the psyche and the significance of analytical work, where, while interpretation points to the real, it also demonstrates the impossibility of reaching it. For Lacan, the very construction of the 'primal scene' in the case description also introduces a radical interpretation of the term 'truth', placing it outside the patient's subjective memory, the significance of which lies in illustrating the way phantasy operates in relation to the inaccessible real.[45] The Wolf Man case study serves as a quintessential model for the existence of 'truth' outside the dyad between patient and analyst, opening the door to a radical conceptualisation of 'reality' as a third – neither belonging to the analyst nor existing in the analysand's memories. It demonstrates the paradoxical nature of the psychoanalytic endeavour which involves a movement towards the real, while recognising its primordial elusiveness and inaccessibility.

Richard Boothby, who expands on Lacan's interpretation, explains that Freud, while insisting on the importance of truth-seeking and reaching the origin of the neurosis, in his conceptualisation of the 'primal scene', also introduces a schism between historical reality and human reconstruction. This radical interpretation marks an uncertainty between what Freud calls 'material truth' and 'historical truth' – between the search for truth in the archives of memory and the possibility of reaching it. The conceptualisation of the 'primal scene' is an inter-textual interpretation that denies the event its ontological foundations and locates a necessity of free interpretive play in the gap between the significance of the origin and its inherent absence.[46]

The case of the Wolf Man proves that the nature of this interplay between phantasy and the real can never be fully grasped. Historical truth, as Freud defines it, is essential for healing, but only because it is irreproducible within the inaccessibility that characterises the Real. The 'primal scene' operates as an elusive interpretive enigma that simultaneously holds both the burden of truth and its impossibility. When memory fails and the question of origin remains unanswered, the role of analysis is to bring the patient to the edge of an uncrossable abyss beyond which one cannot see; to that terrifying moment that perpetuates prehistoric forgetfulness, which covers and obscures the origin that lies beneath.

---

44 Laplanche characterises this as an intergenerational communication between mother and baby containing enigmatic messages that stimulate the infant to the study of sexuality. For further reading see: Jean Laplanche, "The Theory of Seduction and the Problem of the Other." *Int. J. Psychoanal.* 78 (1997): 653–666.

45 Jacques Lacan, "The Function and Field of Speech and Language in Psychoanalysis." Écrits: A Selection (Trans. Alan Sheridan. London: Tavistock, 1977), pp. 30–113.

46 Richard Boothby. *Freud as Philosopher: Metapsychology after Lacan* (New York: Routledge, 2001).

The sense of panic awakened by the Wolf Man's dream and the anxiety that gripped him throughout his childhood neurosis revealed to both analyst and patient the presence of an actual and powerful experience that preceded the dream. The question that arises – what is the traumatic event that took place in the past which is revealed by the dream? – must remain open to initiate a textual search for that 'truth'. Yet, while the concept of 'primal scene' points to an inaccessible origin, Freud's solution comes quickly, translating every detail into "the one event" that took place when the patient's age,

> was n + 1½ years. He had been sleeping in his cot, then, in his parents' bedroom, and woke up, perhaps because of his rising fever, in the afternoon, possibly at five o'clock, the hour which was later marked out by depression. It harmonizes with our assumption that it was a hot summer's day, if we suppose that his parents had retired, half undressed, for an afternoon siesta. When he woke up, he witnessed a coitus *a tergo* [from behind], three times repeated; he was able to see his mother's genitals as well as his father's organ; and he understood the process as well as its significance.[47]

Freud goes on to explain that there is "no other possibility [...]either the analysis based on the neurosis in his childhood is all a piece of nonsense from start to finish, or everything took place just as I have described it above".[48] This particular interpretation of the dream not only traces a precise historical event but also provides an undisputable translation of the patient's psychic process developed by witnessing this 'primal scene'. He concludes that following the dream,

> [The patient] discovered the vagina and the biological significance of masculine and feminine. He understood now that active was the same as masculine, while passive was the same as feminine [...]he had identified himself with his castrated mother during the dream, and was now fighting against that fact. 'If you want to be sexually satisfied by Father', we may perhaps represent him as saying to himself, 'you must allow yourself to be castrated like Mother; but I won't have that.' In short, a clear protest on the part of his masculinity![49]

As Lacan argues, due to Freud's need to appropriate the case study to his conceptualisations of childhood psychosexual development, he was not patient enough to allow the patient an independent playful interpretation and, subsequently, his own reconstruction of its meaning. Struggling to hold on to the interpretative tension

---

47 Sigmund Freud. "From the History of an Infantile Neurosis." *The Standard Edition of the Complete Psychological Works of Sigmund Freud* 17 (1918), p. 37.

48 Sigmund Freud. "From the History of an Infantile Neurosis." *The Standard Edition of the Complete Psychological Works of Sigmund Freud* 17 (1918), p. 56.

49 Sigmund Freud. "From the History of an Infantile Neurosis." *The Standard Edition of the Complete Psychological Works of Sigmund Freud* 17 (1918), p. 47.

in analysis, he hastily solved the dream, fixing the 'truth' he discovered, thereby driving a wedge of alienation between the patient and the narrative of truth that was constructed for him from the outside. Pankejeff could never recall the event Freud had narrated for him, and despite the therapist's attempts, until the end of the analysis and in fact until the end of his life, he did not come to terms with its 'truth'. Consequently, a gap, an abyss remained that continuously drew him back, almost obsessively, throughout his life. In fact, it entangled together throughout their lives both the patient – who developed symptoms of paranoia, and the analyst, who returned to the case in his various writings.

If the 'primal scene' is structured as a phantasy that allows the continuous unfolding of different meanings in relation to an inaccessible origin, Freud's interpretation seals a necessary gap between reality and the real, placing a single truth as the sole origin. The way each detail of the dream is translated as a component of that event indicates that the dream indeed holds another meaning beneath the surface, however by quickly providing a rigid solution Freud also closes the door to the possibilities inherent in this interpretive movement. The text reveals the collapse of tension necessary to continue introducing new possible interpretations, and the disappearance of curiosity originating in the desire to uncover an inaccessible truth. The narrative is constructed as pieces of historical truth in which the relationships between the sexes are reduced to hierarchical binary power relations.

The gap between the 'primal scene' as a fertile ground for relational possibilities and Freud's interpretation of the child's understanding of the "true facts"[50] of sexual relationships, raises questions about what might be negated in a psychoanalytic language that collapses into this binary structure. Although Lacan recognises this binary structure, he too offers a psychoanalytic theory that is based on the construct of oppositions.[51] For Lacan, masculinity and femininity are not psychological patterns formed through the constellation of biological sexuality but rather categories shaped within an arbitrary system of linguistic differences that take on hierarchical meaning within culture. In the transition to the symbolic order, the phallus does not represent male genitalia, but rather points to the unreachable in the binary linguistic process of becoming a subject, and only later, through cultural practices, does it grow into a representation of power and desire identified with the male organ. Lacan then can recognise, on one hand, the linguistic structure that underlies the polar division between the sexes and identifies it in various cultural contexts, but on the other hand, like Freud, he creates a circular array in which only one sex exists.

50 Sigmund Freud. "From the History of an Infantile Neurosis." *The Standard Edition of the Complete Psychological Works of Sigmund Freud* 17 (1918), p. 25.

51 Jacques Lacan. *Feminine Sexuality: Jacques Lacan and the ecole freudienne* (Edited by J. Mitchell & J. Rose. New York: Norton, 1982); Jacques Lacan. *The Seminar XX, Encore: On Feminine Sexuality, the Limits of Love and Knowledge* (Edited by Jacques-Alain Miller. Translated by Bruce Fink. New York: W.W. Norton & Co., 1998); Jacques Lacan. "The Mirror Stage as Formative of the I Function I as Revealed in Psychoanalytic Experience." *Écrits* (Translated by Bruce Fink, New York and London: W. W. Norton, 2006 (1949)), pp. 75–81.

Under the structure of symbolic language to which the entrance gate is the phallus itself, the only subject position is one in which both desire and the ability to speak are masculine.[52]

Whether gender binarism is a structure of language or a biological and cultural fact, psychoanalysis cannot escape repeating a similar interpretation in which the feminine is structured as negation of the male subject. A solution is a liquid comprised of different elements, as Boothby points out.[53] What is sealed in this textual transition that solidifies the solution of the 'primal scene' is a vast web of phantasies, feelings and experiences in response to the closed door of the parent's bedroom, particularly erasing the interpretations regarding the mother's other. The text solidifies and closes the door on possible interpretations not only in relation to the patient's life but also for psychoanalytic theory, which remains within the realm of a binary language. Forming a rigid structure of subjectivities based on this binarism, it repudiates any interpretation that touches on the relationship with maternal subjectivity and sexuality.

The (Hierarchical) Ladder of Wolves

One association to the wolves dream, as described before, was the *tale* of the *tailor*, and the *tail* that was cut, collapsing the ladder of wolves. This story, which Pankejeff heard from his grandfather, invites a closer look into the hierarchical ladder that characterises the patient's neurotic anxiety. As Freud elaborates, a perverse eroticisation of power relation characterised the patient's relationships throughout his life: "all the girls with whom he subsequently fell in love—often with the clearest indications of compulsion—were also servants, whose education and intelligence were necessarily far inferior to his own".[54] Similar perverse attributes were also reflected in the structure of Pankejeff's animal phobia, which oscillated between the anxiety arising from external threats and aggressive acts he committed. As a child, he would often express anxiety about animals and aversion to reptiles but, on the other hand, occasionally engage in acts of cruelty in which he used to dissect

52 Following Ferdinand de Saussure's linguistic theory, and Claude Lévi-Strauss' structural theory, Lacan sees language as a system of differences – between basic units of consonants (signifiers) and meanings (signified) – underlying the binary opposition between the sexes. Perhaps at first glance, Lacan seems to be proposing a solution for feminist psychoanalysis by transferring Freudian theory from biologic essentialism to the structural realm, but a second look reveals that the challenges his theory poses for feminist thinking does not make it easier to introduce the missing symbolic language to conceptualise both femininity and motherhood. Lacan restructures the Freudian 'historical truth' as a linguistic truth, but in this way, he also positions the phallus as the privileged signifier only through which one can enter the symbolic. While recognising the lack from which language is created, he also theorises the symbolic as a closed system which excludes women.

53 Boothby refers to the dream solution in a different context, regarding Irma's dream, and interprets the *solution* as the seminal fluid. I took from his words the idea of a solution as a fluid interpretation, and the symbolic contrast between liquid and solid interpretations in the analytical position.

54 Sigmund Freud. "From the History of an Infantile Neurosis." *The Standard Edition of the Complete Psychological Works of Sigmund Freud* 17 (1918), p. 22.

beetles and caterpillars. This neurotic structure, which Freud elaborates on, echoes, as I have mentioned, in the legacy of his family's story who were trapped in oscillation between higher and lower, and was manifested in the image of the wolf: between the hunting expeditions of wolves and relying on the help of the psychiatrist Moshe Wulff. These power dynamics resurface repeatedly throughout the text in cycles of projection and introjection of aggression that characterise the patient's relationships and also cast its shadow on the analytic process itself.

While identifying the opposing binaries and power dynamics that characterise the patient's relationships, the hierarchical ladder is preserved in Freud's analytic interpretations in relation to the gender axis. Although Freud recognises the rigidity of oppositions that govern the patient's inner world, his interpretations repeat a similar hierarchical structure in his conceptualisations of gender and sexual relations. In a sort of collaboration with the patient's inner structure, the analysis of the wolves-dream theorise sexual relation as a split between "the man [who occupy the] upright [position], and the woman [who] bent down like an animal".[55]

The panic of the wolf recalling his wounded tail characterises not only the patient's inner world but also the textual structure in which a splitting movement, constantly separating the masculine from the feminine, is generated in the face of a masculine wound. In every encounter with the memory of that wound, and particularly when "gender norms" are challenged, as happens around the patient's delicate behaviour and his desire to identify with the mother, a hierarchical binary structure around the gender axis is re-instated. The patient's need to identify with the mother is explained as an exceptional case that can "be regarded as a characteristic of his congenital sexual constitution", namely, as an abnormal variant of the male structure. As a result of this different structure, the patient assumed, according to Freud, "a passive attitude, and showed more inclination towards a subsequent identification with women than with men".[56] Freud concludes that Pankejeff's nature of being a "very good-natured, tractable, and even quiet child",[57] testify to an innate tendency that relegated him to a "passive and masochistic feminine sexual role".[58]

Both the identification with the mother and the conflict towards her are never explored in the text as significant theoretical and clinical aspects. Identification with the mother, with all its possible meanings, is explained through a binary structure

55 Sigmund Freud. "From the History of an Infantile Neurosis." *The Standard Edition of the Complete Psychological Works of Sigmund Freud* 17 (1918), p. 39.
56 Sigmund Freud. "From the History of an Infantile Neurosis." *The Standard Edition of the Complete Psychological Works of Sigmund Freud* 17 (1918), p. 81.
57 Sigmund Freud. "From the History of an Infantile Neurosis." *The Standard Edition of the Complete Psychological Works of Sigmund Freud* 17 (1918), p. 14.
58 Elsewhere in the text, Pankejeff's 'feminine' identification is explained differently – not as a constitutional tendency but as the product of a traumatic sexual experience, in which the patient underwent seduction by his sister "in the first inheritance when he was still very young" (ibid., p. 36). Whether the cause is a congenital factor or acquired trauma, the feminine-passive-lower coupling remains, and the need to identify with the mother, with its various meanings, is explained hierarchically through her attitude to the male genitalia.

pivoting around the phallus. Freud's phallocentric language reduces an array of symbolic meanings into a fixed pattern organised according to the relationship to the male sex organ: to be a mother (bringing life into the world, giving birth, containing, nurturing, creating – to name a few) is to be sexually passive, penetrated by the penis. The child's desire to identify with the mother (the phantasy to become pregnant and to give birth, or, alternatively, an identification with the mother's somatic depression) takes on the sole meaning of the desire to be satisfied by the penis. Being a woman and a mother, according to Freud's interpretation, places one picture in the mind of the child: being castrated, losing the phallus and craving it. The wolves phobia – despite the many clues to an aetiology rooted in the relationship with the mother – is interpreted as castration anxiety, a terrifying fear of losing the male organ. The phallocentric pattern is organised as a system of binary and hierarchical opposites in which no space for questions is left for the emotional complexity vis-à-vis the maternal.

This pattern is consistent throughout Freud's interpretation of the wolves-dream from which he goes on to develop the concept of the 'primal scene' as the discovery of a hierarchical structure of sexual relations between the parents. Following the dream, Freud writes, the boy discovered "the biological meaning of masculinity and femininity". As he elaborates,

> The activation of the primal scene in the dream now brought him back to the genital organization. He discovered the vagina and the biological significance of masculine and feminine. He understood now that active was the same as masculine, while passive was the same as feminine.[59]

The 'primal scene' represents, according to Freud, the moment when the child understands the sexual relationship as hierarchical power dynamics with an inherent dichotomous structure. He even goes on further to portray the sexual relationship between the parents (and heterosexual relations in general), as perceived by the child, as one in which the father is beating the mother. For him, the enigmatic event at the same time arouses the child sexually and evokes aggressive and sadistic phantasies: the child concluded that "in front of him a scene of violent movement" and that "[u]nder the influence of the primal scene he came to the conclusion that his mother had been made ill by what his father had done to her" – "A conclusion which was probably not far from the truth" – Freud adds in a footnote.[60]

In his essay on "*Negation*", Freud explains that the idea of negation is key to an unconscious structure of uniting contradicting opposites that constantly seek

59 Sigmund Freud. "From the History of an Infantile Neurosis." *The Standard Edition of the Complete Psychological Works of Sigmund Freud* 17 (1918), p. 47.
60 Sigmund Freud. "From the History of an Infantile Neurosis." *The Standard Edition of the Complete Psychological Works of Sigmund Freud* 17 (1918), p. 78.

to merge and create a third element.[61] "Negation is a way of taking cognizance of what is repressed",[62] he writes, explaining that it facilitates an encounter with repressed emotions and thoughts that we might otherwise find difficult to connect with. It is an unconscious attempt to first recognise and then integrate an otherness, which has been split and repressed. Freud indeed identifies the structure of splitting with "the sharp distinction",[63] between the masculine and the feminine in the patient's life, as well as the symptoms generated by their rigidity. Despite recognising the symptomatic inability of these opposites to integrate into a third, Freud continues to insist on similar binary oppositions throughout his interpretation: up and down, lower and higher, motionless – agitated movement, I observe – I am being seen, subject and object – a hierarchical system that corresponds to the prototype man-woman. While the role of a tailor – to use an image from the associations to the dream – similar to that of an analyst, is to stitch together a rift, merging both sides of the wound, this integration of opposites, does not occur in Freud's text.

A Beaten Organ, Hysteria

An interpretation of the 'primal scene' in terms of hierarchy and sexual violence seems to be reflected in recurring anxiety characterising both Pankejeff's inner world and the textual movement: the splits in the text; the panic movement that rushes to seal questions concerning sexuality; the recurring substitution of sexuality with power hierarchies; and the way in which the 'primal scene' is depicted through a binary language as an intersexual power dynamic and violence – all these raise questions about the way in which traumatic realities permeate the analytical process.

Traumatic memories, as argued by Judith Lewis Herman, are not accessible to the analyst as a clear, structured narrative from beginning to end. They appear as confusing fragments of memories calling to be deciphered.[64] Although writing about "screen memories"[65] and recognising the rigid and violent structure of the patient's sexuality, Freud, not only reconstructs the 'primal scene' as a power

61 Sigmund Freud. "Negation." In: James Strachey (ed. & trans.) *The Standard Edition of the Complete Psychological Works of Sigmund Freud* 19 (1925), pp. 233–240. London: The Hogarth Press and the Institute of Psycho-Analysis, 1961.

62 Sigmund Freud. "From the History of an Infantile Neurosis." *The Standard Edition of the Complete Psychological Works of Sigmund Freud* 17 (1918), p. 154.

63 Sigmund Freud. "From the History of an Infantile Neurosis." *The Standard Edition of the Complete Psychological Works of Sigmund Freud* 17 (1918), p. 111.

64 Judith Lewis Herman. *Trauma and Recovery: The Aftermath of Violence – from Domestic Abuse to Political Terror* (New York: Basic Books, 1992).

65 Reconstructed memories which are "are often distorted from the truth, and interspersed with imaginary elements" in later life, and these "scenes, like this one in my present patient's case, which date from such an early period and exhibit a similar content, and which further lay claim to such an extraordinary significance for the history of the case, are as a rule not reproduced as recollections, but have to be divined—constructed—gradually and laboriously from an aggregate of indications". Sigmund Freud. "From the History of an Infantile Neurosis." *The Standard Edition of the Complete Psychological Works of Sigmund Freud* 17 (1918), p. 51.

struggle between the sexes but also presents it as the sole universal solution to this "primal polygenetic phantasy". As in the dream, the textual movement is saturated with anxiety at the opening of the window – a moment in which the inside and the outside, masculine and feminine, subject and object blend. In order to prevent the possibility of mixing, of intertwining, of tailoring and integrating the edges, both the therapist and the patient oscillate between the binary poles, projecting the split onto a gender axis.

Abraham and Torok's study, tracing linguistic chains, identifies a spectral uncanniness or rather a linguistic crypt, created in the Wolf Man's speech.[66] They identify the Wolf Man's poetic language as a symptom that refuses to resolve the question of its origin in either phantasy or reality. Thus, with this continual struggle to escape an "event" or "trauma", the Wolf Man created himself as an unresolvable enigma. Those cryptic messages that have folded into themselves in the gap between signifiers and signified are the spiralling trail of an inaccessible occurrence that has been commended silence, with no prospect of accessing the linguistic domain. The manner in which the patient's sexuality is associated with violence and humiliation, the extremely early sexuality of his sister, and his own early seduction scenes, suggest the occurrence of an early trauma (which does not exclude but, rather, goes hand in hand with early seductive phantasies). Following the linguistic path, Abraham and Torok arrive at the brink of childhood sexual trauma that occurred within the family that was accompanied by a command not to speak and was therefore psychically sealed as a knot of silence, a linguistic crypt. If previous interpretations that I have referred to, position the 'primal scene' as an inaccessible origin that cannot reach the layer of language, this interpretation highlights the traumatic event at the heart of the Wolf Man's dream as a symptom that creates a hole in the linguistic system. It is the injunction of silence and concealment that accompany the trauma that generates recurring anxiety both for the patient and in the analytic process.

According to this conceptualisation of trauma, the difficulty in encountering archaic events does not originate in sexuality itself, nor in the inability to translate the event that occurred into linguistic expression. Instead, it is rooted in the command of silence that accompanies these events. It is the obligation not to say that generates the panic every time the window opens for words to enter. As in the Wolf Man's dream, the analytic gaze (which contains a command: speak!) evokes the archaic terror of violating the imperative (do not speak!) consequently shutting the window in terror, leaving a mark in the text, as an ambivalent symptom torn between the edges. The inaccessible memory, longing for translation, also contains within it the necessity not to speak, leaving the patient anxiously captive in its impossibility – a structure that is repeated in the analytic process. Immersed in an endless conflict, Pankejeff creates linguistic crypts, a broken language through which he can continue talking without making a decision.

---

66 Nicolas Abraham and Maria Torok. *The Wolf Man's Magic Word: A Cryptonymy*. Translated by Nicholas Rand (Minneapolis: University of Minnesota, 1986).

In analysing the patient's reaction to the 'primal scene', Freud dwells on Pankejeff's anal sexuality and interprets it as an identification with the mother's sexuality, which is, as he describes it, feminine, masochistic and even hysterical. Pointing out that "his mother had been made ill by what his father had done to her", he explains that the patient's feminine identification is expressed through the intestines: "The disorders in the function of this zone [the intestines] had acquired the significance of feminine impulses".[67] Freud's interpretations throughout the text exchange female genitalia – the uterus and vagina – with the bowels, interlacing between the process of digestion and pregnancy, between defecation and birth, and linking the patient's anal position – both constipation and pleasure – to female sexuality.

The language Freud uses to describe the patient's bowel reaction, "hysterically affected organ",[68] may reveal something of the panic movement accompanying the text and open up further thoughts about the layers of trauma beneath. In these words – hysterically affected organ – he describes the bowel's participation in the analytic conversation, however connecting Pankejeff's symptoms with hysteria points again in the direction of trauma and the symptoms generated in women (as well as men), who are expected to digest the impossible and the unspeakable, and thus, remain silent and, therefore, hysterical. Freud indeed emphasises the masochistic structure of such behaviour, but further reading into this interpretation raises a question about the traumatic impossibility of the material the patient is required to digest. The patient's "hysterical bowels", as well as the oscillation between binary opposites in the text, may reflect a similar ambivalent position, a hysterical position, in the face of an unbearable, unspeakable wound.

As Jessica Benjamin explains, the blind spot of psychoanalysis, which was born out of the psychonalytic work with hysteria patients, lies in the disavowal of the connection between violence and hysteria, often manifesting as a refusal to examine the dimensions of pain and trauma, as a result of which silence is imposed – both for the patient and for psychoanalysis itself.[69] The mother, Freud writes, seemed to have undergone "an act of violence", but the expression on her face "did not fit in with this", and was an "expression of enjoyment" [70]. Following these words, one can interpret Pankejeff's identification with his mother as relating to a hysterical dimension that is required to remain silent, conceal the trauma and at the same time continue smiling. Being commanded silence can be recognised in both the patient's symptoms and in the analytic relationship, in which, just like his mother, Pankejeff too, continues to smile, ostensibly cooperating with Freud's psychoanalytic guidance, but at the same time, beneath the surface, carrying a "full stomach" of words

67 Sigmund Freud. "From the History of an Infantile Neurosis." *The Standard Edition of the Complete Psychological Works of Sigmund Freud* 17 (1918), p. 78.

68 Sigmund Freud. "From the History of an Infantile Neurosis." *The Standard Edition of the Complete Psychological Works of Sigmund Freud* 17 (1918), pp. 113–176.

69 Jessica Benjamin. *Shadow of the Other* (New York & London: Routledge, 1998).

70 Sigmund Freud. "From the History of an Infantile Neurosis." *The Standard Edition of the Complete Psychological Works of Sigmund Freud* 17 (1918), p. 45.

that can neither be digested nor expressed. Freud, who acknowledges the existence of a "wound", and, to a large extent, even that of a trauma, repeatedly attaches it to the mother, as part of her body, avoiding the possibility of touching the wounds of the patient, which are crying out in their silence.

What are the traumatic realms that impose silence on psychoanalysis? The phrase "hysterically affected organ" is meant to describe the way the patient's bowels join the analytic conversation. However, in the translation of Freud's text into Hebrew, the word "beaten", or "stricken" is used to translate affected, linking hysteria to another wounded organ, the circumcised male organ. Thus, the Hebrew translation reveals the textual movement that collaborates with this hysterical anxiety arising in the encounter with the wounded organ. Every encounter with the possibility of a masculine wound leads to textual hysteria that is preoccupied with concealing the traces of the trauma. Encountering the masculine wounded organ, in the image of circumcision, awakens an anxiety that consequently projects the bleeding wound onto the biology of women, with their lack of male organs and monthly bleeding, while at the same time normalising violence, trauma and power relations as healthy "violent muscular activity, directed upon the object".[71]

The patient's story raises questions about the reality that these children lived through and the traumatic world into which they were born. Pankejeff's story repeatedly indicates trauma, manifested in the way violence and humiliation are incorporated into the patient's psychic life, and revealed by the descriptions of his sister's very early sexuality which apparently led to early seduction scenes between her and Pankejeff.[72] In collaboration with this hysterical psychic structure the textual movement is characterised by an inability to hold a space of questions in relation to trauma in which, encountering wounded realms leads to a panicked grip onto a phallic binary structure. The interplay between languages reveals something of this textual response to the masculine wound, which nonetheless leaves a trail of evidence in the text.[73] The image of circumcision becomes a recurrent key-fossil that simultaneously signifies vulnerability, and initiates the pathway to an anxious textual response, projecting the wound onto the mother, and grasping onto a binary structure of gender relations.

The Collapse of the 'primal scene'

In contrast to Freud's portrayal of the 'primal scene' as an event that introduces the child to the one true "biological meaning of masculinity and femininity", later

---

71 Sigmund Freud. "From the History of an Infantile Neurosis." *The Standard Edition of the Complete Psychological Works of Sigmund Freud* 17 (1918), p. 108.

72 Efi Ziv marks Freud's abondanment of seduction theory as rooted in the imperative of silence imposed on psychoanalysis: Efi Ziv, "Incest." *Mafte'akh A lexical Journal of Political Thought (in Hebrew)* (2020): 15, 13–34..

73 In the German origin, the expression is more similar to that found in the English translation: "hysterisch affiziertes organ" (hysteria affected organ).

discussions of the 'primal scene' shift the focus from discovering traumatic sexual hierarchies towards being a part of a vital and playful axis in the developmental array of the child's object relations. Analysts such as Ogden, Meltzer and Aron emphasise the contribution of the 'primal scene' to creativity and development. The 'primal scene' represents for them the stage in which a triangular space opens up and the subject's inner world and in which they can identify themselves within a field of external forces operating around them.[74] The internalised 'primal scene' is a playful space in which the child can "get it all": identify as multi-gendered, shift between identification with each of the changing parental figures, alternate between different sexual roles, and develop a dynamic sense of self that creatively encompasses various interactions with different representations, which can be both intertwined and contradicting. The 'primal scene' is thus, essentially a transition from a dyadic relationship with the mother (and in fact with each parent separately) to a triangular space in which the child fundamentally participates in a complex field of relationships, including the relationship between the parents.[75] The triangular space allows the observing of a relationship between two others or, alternatively, engaging in a relationship with another while acknowledging the presence of a third observer. The phantasy of the 'primal scene' allows the child to position him/herself as a spectator or participant in relationships and thus, develop the mental possibility of moving between observation and participation – a psychic flexibility that also precipitates the movement from immediacy to symbolisation. They can then navigate between thinking about themselves as an object and existing as a subject. While they are active subjects towards each participant, they are also objects being observed by a third party. The 'primal scene' represents the development of a complex self-awareness that encompasses triadic interaction and movement between being a subject and being an object. Only then does the image of the parents as complete, connected and separated subjects, which can also serve as objects for another, emerge. The phantasy of the 'primal scene' encapsulates a complex relational system in which both parents are bound by a meaningful relationship that excludes the child, but at the same time, they are each connected to the child in a meaningful relationship in a way that excludes the other parent.

One key implication of the 'primal scene' lies in the playful internalisation not only of parental figures but also of the relationship between the parents, and the unveiling of the *'other room'*. Through these new internal representations, the child begins to develop an in-depth dimension of relational configurations, discovering maternal desire for a third beyond him/her. While the primary mother-child dyad is described as a relationship between two, the 'primal scene' represents the challenge encapsulated in the mother's ability to look beyond the child, with an introduction into the

---

74 Lewis Aron. "The Internalized Primal Scene." *Psychoanal. Dial.* 5 (1995): 195–237; Donald Meltzer. *Sexual States of Mind* (Perthshire, Scotland: Clunie, 1973); Thomas H. Ogden. *The Primitive Edge of Experience* (Northvale, NJ: Aronson, 1989).
75 The concept of the 'primal scene' corresponds in many ways with Klein's conceptualisation of the 'combined parental figure', which I will elaborate on later.

triadic space of maternal desire and sexuality. This experience in the child's inner world sparks curiosity, anticipation and arousal alongside a sense of alienation and exclusion. The child discovers – even without being consciously aware of that – that the mother's gaze is carried elsewhere, her libidinal energies are directed beyond the realm of the maternal-child continuum and that she desires an other, a third. At this symbolic moment, the dyad is penetrated by an unfamiliar dimension and the mother establishes a relationship of pleasure from which the child is excluded and thus, evokes feelings of absence and lack, abandonment and separation – a wounded unspeakable rapture within the relationship with the maternal.

It is interesting to notice that while this interpretation of the 'primal scene' echoes feelings of absence and rapture in the child's experience, Freud performs a projective inversion, attributing the lack, the absence to the mother's genitalia. Does Freud identify with the rage that the child experiences towards the mother and is, therefore, unable to explore and conceptualise it? Without delving into the depth of this question, I have pointed out the way in which the complexity of feelings towards the maternal – the sense of longing, dependency and vulnerability is repudiated in Freud's interpretations. Both in Freud's interpretation of Pankejeff's childhood and in the way he theorises the 'primal scene', he turns the gaze towards the "healthy masculine violence" and focuses on the biologically castrated mother.

According to Aron, the 'primal scene' represents an important developmental stage that does not necessarily have to be traumatic. Through this mental phantasy, the child develops the ability to hold powerful contradicting emotions, unfolding for the first time a complex, three-dimensional realm. However, he argues, if these gaps and contradictions cannot be held, if there is no capacity for a dialectical movement between identifications and no space for multi-gender playful creativity, the 'primal scene' does not fulfil its purpose and might become traumatic. If the developmental creative movement is interrupted, the subject develops a rigid gender structure, clinging onto one side, reducing a triangular relational complexity into a binary hierarchical image.[76]

It is important to mark Freud's innovative perspective – writing at the beginning of the 20th century, within a conservative society in which the separation into gender roles was rigid – in his ability to point out the child's need to identify with the mother. However, as I have argued, due to the anxiety in the face of the complexity of the relationship with the mother, the rigidity persists in the interpretive process, and challenging gender binaries emerging in the analysis does not find its way into psychoanalytic theory.

Freud's psychoanalytic interpretations, demonstrate the difficulty of holding the contradictions and paradoxes that are always part of gender complexity: alternating phantasies between female and male identifications are eruptive in the text, reducing each time an inter-gender multiplicity into a narrow binary structure; Freud repeatedly emphasises the need to choose between masculine-active and

---

76 Lewis Aron. "The Internalized Primal Scene." *Psychoanal. Dial.* 5 (1995): 195–237.

feminine-passive and avoids exploring the dialectical movement between subject and object and the way in which they are endlessly intertwined. The desire to return to the womb, which Freud perceives as an anxious retreat from the world, may also be interpreted as the need to return to that playful intermediate space in which oppositions can merge and intertwine, providing an outlet to the binary and hierarchical perception.

The three-dimensional structure that could have been created in the encounter with the 'primal scene' repeatedly collapses into a two-dimensional, binary structure due to the reluctance to allow three-dimensional space for the mother's figure. Each time the text introduces the question of maternal subjectivity i.e., with the question of the mother's existence as a subject of desire that is always both within and beyond the dyadic relationship with the child, Freud shifts the gaze – on the one hand, to the mother's phantasy to be satisfied by the male organ, and on the other hand, to the child's fear of undergoing castration (like the mother) and losing that same organ. At the heart of the inability to contain triadic complexity lies the difficulty of encountering maternal subjectivity. Freud's understanding of the 'primal scene' reduces the complex, ambivalent feelings that arise in this triangular space by conceptualising them through phallocentric language, veiling the relationship with the mother with the male genitalia.

In this way, Freud's psychoanalytic conceptualisation of the 'primal scene' transforms from a phantasy that opens a window into a triadic intermediate space and creative playfulness into a traumatic event in which the child internalises the relations between the sexes as hierarchical binaries. Under this phallocentric perspective, the possibility of encountering maternal subjectivity inherent in the 'primal scene' is transformed into the child's gaze at the mother's biological lack. Paradoxically, the complex representation of triadic relationships that might have been developed through the 'primal scene' image collapses under Freud's interpretation into a structure that contains only one: the phallus and its negation.

Although it is not possible to reach the single origin of the Wolf Man's dream, and despite the fact that it is indeed impossible to draw the actual historical memory that led to it, by marking the textual places in which the 'wound' loses its layers of complexity, the dialectical tension collapses and the desire and curiosity to reach an origin disappears, it is possible to outline Freud's blind spot and perhaps that of psychoanalysis as well.

II

LITTLE HANS: A DOUBLE-LAYERED MATRICIDE[77]

The case study of Little Hans tells the story of a young boy, now known as Herbert Graf, who, at the age of four, began to express symptoms of horse phobia, an anxiety that gradually escalated until it became difficult for him to leave the house. Hans's parents, who knew Freud, turned to him for help, but the analysis itself was not carried out by Freud, but by Hans' father (Max Graff), who documented his conversations with his son, sent them to Freud and received guidance from him.[78] The description of the case, written in 1909, contains fascinating dialogues between the father, the mother and the child, while in between the detailed events Freud presents his thoughts, analysing step by step, the inner world of the young patient.

The child's therapeutic journey, his symptom development and his fascinating conversations with his parents, serve as clinical observations that allow Freud to delve into the deep layers of the human psyche in order to draw conclusions about childhood sexuality. The child, he explains, reveals the sexual origin of neurotic symptoms that in the adult we have to put a lot of effort into exposing: "observing in children at first hand and in all the freshness of life the sexual impulses and wishes which we dig out so laboriously in adults from among their own débris".[79] Thus, the observations made by Hans's father and the detailed records he passed on to Freud serve as fertile ground for conceptualising the origin of neurotic symptoms and childhood psychosexual development.

Freud describes the process of Hans's development, analysing his fascinating conversations with his parents, his dreams, his fantasies and phantasies, as well as his raw anxieties and his infantile curiosity which is revealed to the reader in all its vitality and playfulness. Closely reading the movements in the child's inner world, Freud plunges into the deep layers of his psyche in order to discover the source of his phobia. However, as I will show, Freud does not remain a passive observer of the child's rich inner world, but directs him, through his father, to the Oedipal metaphor, which contains within it a very specific understanding of his fears, desires and dreams. Throughout the therapeutic work, he is actively shaping the way the

---

77 Parts of my analysis in this chapter have been published as an article in the journal *Conversations* (in Hebrew): Yael Pilowsky Bankirer. "'I Really Was the mummy' The Double Act of Matricide." *Conversations* 3, no. 2 (2022): 155–162.

78 Hans's parents were among Freud's first followers. He maintained friendly relations with them. His father, Max Graf, regularly participated in a group that met at Freud's house on Wednesdays. Hans's mother was one of Freud's first patients. Even before the analysis and development of the phobia, the parents, on Freud's recommendation, agreed to educate their child in accordance with the psychoanalytic worldview.

79 Sigmund Freud. "Analysis of a Phobia in a Five-Year-Old Boy." In: James Strachey (ed. & trans.) *The Standard Edition of the Complete Psychological Works of Sigmund Freud 10* (1909): 1—150. London: The Hogarth Press and the Institute of Psycho-Analysis, 1955, p. 6.

child understands himself, in constructing his worldview, his relation to his own body as well as the bodies of others and directing his desire according to the analyst's interpretation.

Using his typical apologetics, Freud explains that "psychoanalysis is not an impartial scientific investigation, but a therapeutic measure. Its essence is not to prove anything, but merely to alter something", and therefore,

> during the analysis Hans had to be told many things that he could not say himself, that he had to be presented with thoughts which he had so far shown no signs of possessing, and that his attention *had to be turned in the direction from which his father was expecting* something to come.[80]

Thus, many times Hans's experiences and words are discarded and he, as well as the readers, are insistently directed towards understanding Hans's phobia through the phallus and the Oedipal narrative.

Alongside Freud's Oedipal understanding, I will present in this chapter an alternative interpretation that opens a window into Hans's preoccupation with motherhood, pregnancy and childbirth. Hans's words, behaviour and dreams reveal both a phantasy to identify with the mother and difficult feelings towards her in response to the birth of his sister. Using the theoretical framework of Deleuze and Guattari, I will point to the way in which Hans's various libidinal desires and diverse identifications are packaged under the Oedipal super-signifier. I will highlight how his complex relationship towards the maternal is replaced by her lack, leaving circumcision as an organising metaphor – a key-fossil that at the same time fortifies the familiar Oedipal metaphor and paradoxically evades it.

The Carrying Horse

The onset of symptoms was preceded by a nightmare from which Hans woke up crying in a panic lest his mother disappear: "When I was asleep I thought you were gone and I had no Mummy to coax with".[81] In the following period, the child regressed, constantly needing his mother's presence. Every stroll outside the house made him panic and he had to ask to go back home so he could be with his mother. Young Hans, who was "kind-hearted and affectionate",[82] suddenly became crippled by anxiety, frightened and dependent.

80 Sigmund Freud. "Analysis of a Phobia in a Five-Year-Old Boy." *The Standard Edition of the Complete Psychological Works of Sigmund Freud* 10 (1909), p. 104. Emphasis added.

81 Sigmund Freud. "Analysis of a Phobia in a Five-Year-Old Boy." *The Standard Edition of the Complete Psychological Works of Sigmund Freud* 10 (1909), p. 23.

82 Sigmund Freud. "Analysis of a Phobia in a Five-Year-Old Boy." *The Standard Edition of the Complete Psychological Works of Sigmund Freud* 10 (1909), p. 112.

In constructing the aetiology of the anxiety, Freud explains that

[i]n his attitude towards his father and mother Hans confirms in the most concrete and uncompromising manner what I have said in my *Interpretation of
Dreams* and in my *Three Essays* with regard to the sexual relations of a child to
his parents. Hans really was a little Oedipus who wanted to have his father 'out
of the way', to get rid of him, so that he might be alone with his beautiful mother
and sleep with her.[83]

For Freud, the simple solution to the riddle of Hans's neurosis is Oedipal: it is
triggered by his erotic desire towards his mother, which provokes difficult feelings
and aggressions towards his father. The fear of the horse biting represents the fear
of the father who may punish him with castration for wishing to take his place in
relation to the mother.

Despite this salient interpretation, it gradually becomes clear that the fear of
horses began following an incident in which Hans observed the fall of a horse
carrying a heavy load, and a different explanation emerges. As Freud explains,
it becomes evident that the nature of the phobia might be more complicated and
that "[b]ehind the fear to which Hans first gave expression, the fear of a horse biting him, we had discovered a more deeply seated fear, the fear of horses falling
down".[84] Hans's phobia was not limited to fear of the horse's bite but was deeply
anchored by the anxiety of the fall of *the horse that was carrying heavy cargo*.
From this moment on, the young boy began to fear horses carrying wagons, carts or
other loads, horses that in his imagination might fall. Freud interprets this fear in a
similar way, as an Oedipal anxiety explaining "that Hans at that moment perceived
a wish that his father might fall down in the same way—and be dead".[85] According
to this analysis, the neurosis erupts as a result of a conflict in which young Hans,
who loves his father, cannot bear the ambivalent feeling towards him and therefore
transfers his feelings from the father to the horse.

However, beneath the Oedipal veil of this repeated interpretation in the text,
emerges a rich world of content related to the maternal: motherhood, pregnancy
and childbirth. As Anat Palgi-Hecker explains in her analysis of the case, while
Freud and the father are preoccupied with castration anxiety and the Oedipal complex, "Hans is preoccupied with entirely different questions: how can he be like his
mother, and what exactly is it that he has to give up?"[86]

---

83 Sigmund Freud. "Analysis of a Phobia in a Five-Year-Old Boy." *The Standard Edition of the Complete Psychological Works of Sigmund Freud* 10 (1909), p. 111.

84 Sigmund Freud. "Analysis of a Phobia in a Five-Year-Old Boy." *The Standard Edition of the Complete Psychological Works of Sigmund Freud* 10 (1909), p. 126.

85 Sigmund Freud. "Analysis of a Phobia in a Five-Year-Old Boy." *The Standard Edition of the Complete Psychological Works of Sigmund Freud* 10 (1909), p. 52.

86 Anat Palgi-Hecker. *From I-mahut to Imahut* (in Hebrew, Tel-Aviv: Am Oved, 2005), p. 61. My
translation from Hebrew.

Alongside the descriptions of anxieties, Freud indeed portrays Hans's reactions to the approaching birth of his sister, the conflicts, anxieties and curiosity that arise in him around her birth. Hans notices his mother's pregnancy, and despite his parents' attempts to tell the young boy the story of the 'stork', he realises that something is growing inside her, a new life:

> The arrival of his sister brought into Hans's life many new elements, which from that time on gave him no rest. In the first place he was obliged to submit to a certain degree of privation: to begin with, a temporary separation from his mother, and later a permanent diminution in the amount of care and attention which he had received from her and which thenceforward he had to grow accustomed to sharing with his sister.[87]

With the birth of his little sister, Hanna, approaching, Hans gradually realises that a baby will soon penetrate the dyadic relationship with his mother; that a 'third' will soon interfere his intimate "coaxing" with her. He understands that his life is about to change and that his mother will be busy. Her energies of love, desire and care will also be directed towards his sister. He gradually learns that the space between him and his mother may be invaded by a third dimension that will alter their relationship and force him to reposition himself in relation to her. The heavy load of the cart carried by the horse echoes *the "heavy load" of the pregnant mother* carrying Hans's sister in her womb and thus, Hans's anxiety about the carrying horse might point to a different interpretation, shifting the analysis in the direction of the maternal.

The mother's pregnancy is indeed a heavy baggage for Hans, and the process of anticipating the birth of his sister leads him to engage with questions of pregnancy and childbirth. He is preoccupied with maternal birthing abilities and maternal care, which can be life-giving, and nurturing, but may also, as in his case, inhabit rejection and separation. This preoccupation is expressed, for example, in Hans's imaginary games with "his children", in which he is doing with them "everything one does with children"[88]; in his attempts to convince his father that he "laid an egg"[89]; and in his insistence on continuing to hold on to the fantasy of being a mother. The father's reaction to Hans's play with his imaginary children often involves judgment about the possibility of identifying with the mother: "are your children still alive?" he asks him, "[y]ou know quite well a boy can't have any children".[90] But Hans wants to tell him more about them, and it seems that the

---

87 Sigmund Freud. "Analysis of a Phobia in a Five-Year-Old Boy." *The Standard Edition of the Complete Psychological Works of Sigmund Freud* 10 (1909), p. 132.

88 Sigmund Freud. "Analysis of a Phobia in a Five-Year-Old Boy." *The Standard Edition of the Complete Psychological Works of Sigmund Freud* 10 (1909), p. 97.

89 Sigmund Freud. "Analysis of a Phobia in a Five-Year-Old Boy." *The Standard Edition of the Complete Psychological Works of Sigmund Freud* 10 (1909), p. 85.

90 Sigmund Freud. "Analysis of a Phobia in a Five-Year-Old Boy." *The Standard Edition of the Complete Psychological Works of Sigmund Freud* 10 (1909), p. 96.

father's judgment causes Hans's children to multiply: "I had them to sleep with me, the girls and the boys" and

> [w]hen I couldn't get all the children into the bed, I put some of the children on the sofa, and some in the pram, and if there were still some left over I took them up to the attic and put them in the box, and if there were any more I put them in the other box.[91]

Describing his playful preoccupation with the maternal role, Hans tries to convince his father that although his mother is carrying a baggage that takes a lot of her attention, there is still room in him for other children, and takes him into the realm of identification with the mother: "really I was their Mummy", he explains.[92]

The Double Layer of Matricide

Pregnancy and childbirth introduce Hans to the emotional complexity of the relationship with the maternal. Following the birth of his sister, a rift is formed within their relationship, and he understands that his mother now has an other. In the face of this separation and loss, not only identification but also anger is expressed. Hans's anger is revealed in his fantasies of hitting a horse, of breaking a window on a train and in a dream that he shares, in which

> there was a big giraffe in the room and a crumpled one; and the big one called out because I took the crumpled one away from it. Then it stopped calling out; and then I sat down on top of the crumpled one.[93]

Freud concludes that these aspects of aggression arise out of rage and jealousy towards the father, however, they can also be understood as *matricidal* – arising from the phantasy of murdering the mother, a term that Freud never spoke of and of which theoretical and clinical implications are absent from his texts. The concept of *matricide* contains a rich array of meanings other than the difficult (matricidal) emotions towards the mother. It also refers to the different cultural and social aspects in which the maternal is suppressed, negated and excluded. The term may also highlight the gap between the incessant engagement with the mother as an object and the absence of the mother's voice as a subject. Although this concept has been recently gaining recognition in feminist psychoanalytic theory, it is still – perhaps as cyclic testimony to the absence it seeks to describe – one of the least discussed

91 Sigmund Freud. "Analysis of a Phobia in a Five-Year-Old Boy." *The Standard Edition of the Complete Psychological Works of Sigmund Freud* 10 (1909), p. 94.
92 Sigmund Freud. "Analysis of a Phobia in a Five-Year-Old Boy." *The Standard Edition of the Complete Psychological Works of Sigmund Freud* 10 (1909), p. 94.
93 Sigmund Freud. "Analysis of a Phobia in a Five-Year-Old Boy." *The Standard Edition of the Complete Psychological Works of Sigmund Freud* 10 (1909), p. 37.

psychoanalytic concepts. Similar to patricide, matricide encompasses a variety of fantasies and phantasies – both conscious and unconscious – related to the murder of the mother.[94] However, what makes it complex is the fact that the archaic act of matricide is obscured within a culture that is fundamentally matricidal. A culture, as Irigaray specifies, that distances women from the symbolism of the feminine body, limiting them to the corporeal and material, hindering the symbolic value acquisition of unique experiences such as pregnancy, childbirth and motherhood.[95]

Irigaray refers to 'matricide' as reflecting the Oedipal process within Western society, in which, identifying the father of the law at the same time erases the maternal. As the child is faced with the Oedipal challenge of recognising difference, they learn to navigate difference by using what she refers to as 'sameness' – renouncing the mother and identifying with the father. The father is perceived as the edge of existence, while the mother is exiled from the symbolic order, and can only be approached through a relationship of negation, turning her into a 'reverse mirror' of subjectivity, identified as the position of the object, the lack (of a male organ), of the material and the corporeal.

Feminist psychoanalytic explorations have highlighted the radical absence of maternal subjectivity at the root of the Oedipal narrative. Theorists have pointed out the way Oedipus is generated as an organising structure of psychoanalytic theory, which repeatedly imprisons mothers in the position of the ultimate other. Amber Jacobs brings the forgotten myth of Metis, Athena's mother, as an example of the process of the mother's erasure.[96] The goddess Athena, who emerges fully grown and armed from the head of Zeus, her father, is commonly portrayed as a daughter without a mother. However, beneath the multiple layers of defensive armour she wears, another aspect of her story may be revealed, reminding us that, in fact, she had a mother – Metis – who was raped and swallowed by Zeus. Jacobs reminds her readers of this forgotten myth of Metis and points out the centrality of her absence as Athena's mother, who is so famously known in both philosophy and psychoanalysis, as a goddess without a mother. The long-standing tradition of referring to Athena as a motherless goddess is an example of the double-layered matricidal process, in which the mother is not only murdered, but also the myth describing the murder is erased. Forgetting the myth of the mother's murder is what prevents the maternal from returning from the unconscious as an active component of the human psyche.

In the case study of *Little Hans*, his ambivalent feelings towards the mother – jealousy, rage and the phantasy of killing her – are deeply buried under layers of a matricidal culture in which an Oedipal language does not allow for the complexity of the relationship with the mother to be explored. The mother is excluded from the

---

94 Melanie Klein distinguished between conscious *fantasies* and those that are repressed unconscious *phantasies*.

95 Luce Irigaray. *Sexes and Genealogies* (New York: Columbia University Press, (1987) 1993).

96 Amber Jacobs. *On Matricide: Myth, Psychoanalysis, and the Law of the Mother* (New York: Colombia University Press, 2007).

symbolic, and the radical separation from her becomes the 'gold standard' and the only option, even for psychoanalysis itself. Going back to the giraffe dream, it is possible to listen to the erased aspect of the relationship towards the mother, and to the way it is covered by the relationship towards the father. In contrast to Freud's Oedipal interpretation of the dream as a "rebellious phantasy" towards the father, in which the child wishes to snatch the little mother from the bigger father and sit on her, that is, to control her and coax with her, one could propose a different interpretation: perhaps the wrinkled little giraffe represents the newborn baby, and the rage is directed, in fact, at the mother for introducing a third element into the dyad?

Freud's Oedipal interpretation, by covering the difficulty in the relationship with the mother, demonstrates the double act of matricide. The duplicity of the murder of the mother becomes evident in the way Hans is consistently denied the opportunity to think about himself, about his life and about his body through the relationship with his mother.[97] A double-layered matricide is revealed not only in Hans's difficult feelings towards the mother but also in the avoidance of exploring and working through the emotional complexity of the relationship with the maternal – both the rage towards her and the identification with her. An Oedipal language that repeatedly positions the mother solely as an object reduces the emotional complexity of the relationship with her, eliminating the possibility of understanding and developing through it. Under this closed Oedipal interpretation, the mother can only be introduced as an object, as a radical otherness and through the demand for separation. The meaningful encounter with the maternal as a subject, with a variety of desires, needs, phantasies and fantasies, might have opened the door in Hans's inner world to the convoluted relationship with the mother, and the theoretical landscape might have taken on a different path, diverging from the familiar Oedipal structure.

Encountering maternal subjectivity, Hans is presented with an opportunity to acknowledge the otherness of the mother – not only in the sense of being different from him – but her presence as an other, who is able to carry a third dimension beyond him; a third, which is simultaneously beyond their relationship and an essential component within it. Contrary to the mother's position as an object, her subjectivity allows her to choose otherwise, to shift her gaze to another direction beyond him; yet it is precisely this ability, that opens a new kind of intimacy in the space between them. As Alison Stone writes, "this desire is a component of the relation as inherently triadic, a relation between two whose psyches differ and intersect from their position of difference".[98] If maternal subjectivity can be held, the space between mother and child becomes essentially triadic as their relationship inherently contains a third.

Hans indeed encounters his mother's otherness not only in terms of sexual difference – his physiological difference from her and her ability to conceive and

97 Yael Pilowsky Bankirer. "'I Really Was the Mummy' The Double Act of Matricide." *Conversations* 3, no. 2 (2022): 155–162.

98 Alison Stone. "Against Matricide: Rethinking Subjectivity and the Maternal Body." *Hypatia* 27, no. 1 (2012): 118–138, 10.

give birth as a woman – but also her otherness as a subject beyond the relationship with him; a subject that has a 'third' and is able to choose to separate in turning her gaze in a different direction.[99] At the core of maternal subjectivity lies the recognition of the triadic nature of the relationship with her and thus, her ability to choose regarding the nurturing and caring for the child.

As external reality changes, Hans's identification with the mother appears to be increasing, and his behaviour seeks to cultivate within himself maternal qualities, perhaps in order to preserve within, what has been denied for him on the outside. However, this maternal identification seems to provoke a strong reaction from his surrounding male 'therapists' as this encounter with maternal subjectivity is precisely what the culture, within which Hans has grown, struggles to accommodate. The birth of Hans's sister is an opportunity to grapple with a complex set of emotions within the triadic space with the mother. Yet, while he is entangled in a powerful conflict with the mother – which includes, on the one hand, matricidal feelings, and on the other, his desire not only to unite with the mother, but also to identify with her – Hans encounters the intensity of cultural pressure, which demands radical separation, encouraging him to understand the maternal solely as an object, and difference, only through the male organ.

In the face of the new challenges in Hans's relationship with the maternal, and in response to his preoccupation with motherhood, pregnancy and childbirth, the men in his life – Freud and his father – shift away his gaze, framing the richness of his experiences under a very particular understanding of the Oedipal metaphor. They prevent him, to the best of their ability, from playful identification with maternity, guiding him to think of himself in Oedipal terms. While it is the mother who turns her gaze from Hans to the new baby, they explain to him that the fear of the falling horse is an expression of castration anxiety directed towards the father. While it is the mother who creates the gap between her and Hans, within the Oedipal conceptualisations it is the father who tears the child away from their maternal dependency. Freud teaches the young child to understand his anger and aggression as feelings directed solely towards his father, and Hans learns that the emotional conflicts that arise in him are products of a competing relationship with the father over the mother. He is distanced from the challenges before him, from the opportunity of encountering maternal subjectivity, and is led to a phallocentric view of the maternal, in which the mother serves only as an object of desire.

When Freud and the father encounter the child's desire to identify with his mother, they try to "correct", aggressively at times, guiding him to take on the role expected of him according to the Oedipal drama. Freud instructs the father to "take away this aim [to identify with the mother] from Hans by informing him that his mother and all other female beings (as he could see from Hanna) had no *widdler*

---

99 Simply put: if an object is an existence without the ability to choose, maternal subjectivity requires a space in which there is a choice, a triadic space.

at all".[100] While Hans is preoccupied with the birth of his sister, with the way she arrived into the world, and the mother's care for the baby, that is to say, with maternal presence, Freud shifts his gaze to her lack and to her 'absence' of male organ, directing Hans towards understanding the privileged status of male genitalia.

Hans finds himself at the centre of a conflict, caught in a struggle between conflicting internal and external forces. He is trained to understand himself, his desires and his various experiences through a very particular image of the Oedipal triangle – the desire for the mother and the fear of the father. Freud leads him to the Oedipal metaphor, ignoring many things that are said, alternative directions of thought and different modes of desire. While Hans is drawn to the spontaneous engagement with motherhood, Freud and his father continuously convey a demand to separate from the mother, to give up the identification with her and to abandon fantasies of pregnancy and childbirth. They steer him to think of himself in Oedipal terms, repeatedly explaining that feelings of anxiety are an expression of castration anxiety and fear of the father. They incessantly direct him to recognise his difference from his mother and sister, emphasising the privileged position of the male sex organ, and positioning him as a subject in relation to women – having a penis and, therefore, having the ability to desire.

The case study of Little Hans brings to the fore the necessity to discuss the difference between biological identity, social identity and identification. These three triangular vertices are different from each other and the relationship between them, which was rigid in Freud's time, allows for a more fluid movement today, when a space can be carried between them. Engaging with the discourse of masculinity, Ken Corbett points out the vitality of allowing different types of gender fantasies, phantasies and identifications. In other words, to allow – as a society and as subjects – a gap between identity (biological or social) and identification.[101] As humans, we don't have wings and can never fly, but our identification with birds (our becoming birds to use the language of Deleuze and Guattari) is not only possible but also essential for establishing a flexible sense of self. Identifications in these areas border fantasy, fuelled by phantasy and are vital not only for the development of a depressive position, recognising our limits (and the existence of castration that Freud elaborates on), but also in order to form a complex sense of self, in which fantasies, desires and identifications become a playful realm. Even if Hans will not be able to carry a baby in his womb, his identification with his mother is essential to develop different psychic representations of care, empathy, containment and symbolically for being able to carry heavy loads.

The emotional intensity that surges in the child encountering the carrying/caring horse could have provided a window into the relationship with the mother. But the opportunity is missed, and Freud concludes that "both kinds of horses,

---

100 Sigmund Freud. "Analysis of a Phobia in a Five-Year-Old Boy." *The Standard Edition of the Complete Psychological Works of Sigmund Freud* 10 (1909), p. 28.
101 Corbett, Ken. *Boyhoods: Rethinking Masculinities* (New Haven, CT: Yale University Press, 2009).

the biting horse and the falling horse, had been shown to represent his father, who was going to punish him for the evil wishes he was nourishing against him", and as he recognises, "[m]eanwhile the analysis had moved away from the subject of his mother".[102] Hans gradually experiences the possibility of identifying with his mother being taken away from him and feels the withdrawal of a significant aspect of his inner world. Psychic aspects such as containment, nourishing and perhaps the ability to carry heavy emotional luggage, are gradually eradicated by the men around him. His need to play "being the mother" in response to his baby sister's birth – a playful realm of identification, creatively internalising the carrying and caring maternal aspects, which are being removed from without – is navigated to an Oedipal perception that rejects the identification with motherhood in all its various shades.

Thus, an alternative interpretation of the carrying horse relates to the loss of the maternal aspect in Hans's inner world. Just as the child is not allowed to carry the symbolic image of pregnancy, so can the horse drop its heavy load and fall, with the cargo no longer contained in its wagon. Not only that Freud's Oedipal interpretation, seducing him into a phallocentric position, does not relieve Hans' symptoms, but, as I will point out, it increases the anxiety of this imminent fall. Under this cultural demand to let go of the identification with the maternal, Hans' anxiety worsens, as a containing dimension of his inner world is about to die.

Oedipalisation of Rhizomatic Movements

The case description does not only deal with the story of Little Hans but serves Freud to demonstrate and establish his theory of childhood psychosexual development. Using this case study he marks the Oedipal complex and castration anxiety as a cardinal universal stage in the development of children and as an aetiological origin for neuroses in adults. The textual structure of binding multiple symbolic possibilities into their predetermined Oedipal conclusion can be explored through the theoretical concepts of Deleuze and Guattari. Their critique of Freud's work describes the way various possibilities are sealed under a narrow Oedipal solution and is specifically used here to analyse the negation of maternal relationship under the Oedipal metaphor.

In their book *Anti-Oedipus*, Deleuze and Guattari criticise the way psychoanalysis interrupts the productive becoming of the unconscious. The interpretation of desire as a predetermined Oedipal construct, and the representation of the body as a dimension separated from its surroundings, is reducing multiplicity, as they argue, under the one signifier of Oedipal sexuality, obstructing what they refer to as the *rhizomatic movement of the unconscious*.[103] The rhizome is a kind of weed with a non-hierarchical labyrinth of interacting sprouts, spreading through a wide array of

---

102 Freud. "Analysis of a Phobia in a Five-Year-Old Boy." p. 126.
103 Gilles Deleuze and Félix Guattari. *Anti-Oedipus: Capitalism and Schizophrenia* (Minneapolis: University of Minnesota, 1983).

intersections without a beginning or an end, and growing simultaneously in multiple directions. It is a chaotic anarchical network that cannot be organised according to a systematic structure – represented as a single summation, replaced by a concise description, or confined by one super-signifier. The concept of the rhizome does not describe an essence but rather an ongoing event, an evolving occurrence in an unstable movement through space-time in various directions, deviating from any regularity, intentionality and order. Spreading along unexpected paths, the rhizome intersects momentarily with different ways of thinking, and continues expanding without observing its transformative power. Like a machine, the rhizome contains an incessant becoming, a fluid movement that continually transforms itself.[104]

As explained by Ariella Azoulay and Adi Ophir, the rhizome can be understood by contrasting it with the metaphor of the *tree* – a stable hierarchical system with directional growth. The tree metaphor contains an organised structure of predetermined connections; a family tree in which various parts are arranged through a clear one-dimensional genealogy construct. In contrast, the rhizome does not preserve any one connection between two points in its spreading complexity. It moves in all directions without a defined order and thus contains transformations within it, generates creative movements and incessant becoming.

Within a culture of anxiety about chaos, rhizomatic expansions are subjected to what Deleuze and Guattari call *territorialisation*, by systems and organisations of power, law and control, seeking to provide territory, order and direction and attempting to explain chaos through organised signifiers. As they explain, the Oedipal pattern is a clear example of such a territorialisation structure in which the connections between its various elements are pre-organised and are ordered in a structure that regulates the movements of desire. Rhizomatic flux is subjected to constant territorialisation of desire as a response to its inherent counter-movement of *deterritorialisation*, seeking to evade it. Freudian theory began with a representation of desire as multiple and scattered across the body. However, despite conceptualising the unconscious as a constant rhizomatic movement, Freud solidifies adult sexuality within the Oedipal structure, the organisation of which is pre-determined. Freud's radical move, detaching sexuality from the genital and reproductive organs and showing how desire permeates the human body, is itself a deterritorialisation of sexuality. Yet, this movement is accompanied by a parallel territorialisation in his theory and thus, while psychoanalysis began by liberating the constant becoming of the unconscious and dismantling traditional views of desire and sexuality, it also engages in a parallel counter-movement of territorialisation expressed in the convergence of psychoanalytic thinking into the Oedipal model, which, once again organises the libido around the male genitalia, under a pre-determined systemic structure.

The story of the little Hans serves as one of the cornerstones in theorising childhood psychosexual development and constitutes a key point in Freudian

---

104 Ariella Azoulay and Adi Ophir. "We Don't Ask 'What Does It Mean' but 'How Does It Work': An Introduction to a Thousand Plateaus." *Theory and Criticism* (in Hebrew), 17 (2000): 123–131.

conceptualisation of the Oedipal metaphor and as a central system that organises desire. For Deleuze and Guattari, the case study is precisely an example of the Oedipalisation of desire illustrating the way psychoanalysis shapes the subject within a culturally familiar structure organised around the phallus. Hans learns to suppress his range of desires, his multi-gendered libidinal movements and gradually moves to think about himself by clinging to the privileged male genitalia, which becomes an organising image. *It is no longer simply a functional organ among many others, but rather a super-signifier of the projected privileged position of being a man.* The child undergoes socialisation and Oedipalisation, and his rhizomatic movement is buried under the organising structure of a phallocentric psychosocial system.

In children's psychoanalytic case studies, Deleuze and Guattari write, it is possible to clearly see how creative expressions, the multiplicity of libidinal desires, and the making of the unconscious are all reduced to a predetermined Oedipal pattern. In *Two Regimes of Madness*, Deleuze presents a gap – a table with the words of Little Hans (and other children who underwent psychoanalysis) on one side, and on the other side the psychoanalytic interpretation given to them; the words that psychoanalysis was able to hear under the super-signifier of the phallus and the Oedipal narrative.[105] For example, when Hans tells his father that he is afraid of the horse, his father explains to him, "you were most likely frightened when you saw the horse's big widdler".[106] When he returns from the zoo frightened by the animals in the cage, his father explains to him: "Do you know why you're afraid of big animals? Big animals have big widdlers, and you're really afraid of big widdlers."[107] Under Freud's guidance, the father repeatedly explains to him about his Oedipal feelings for his mother. He asks him, "What would you like to do if you were Daddy?" to which Hans replies: "And you were Hans? I'd like to take you to Lainz every Sunday—no, every week-day too. If I were Daddy I'd be ever so nice and good". Hans's desires are focused elsewhere in areas that do not fit the Oedipal narrative, but the father continues: "But what would you like to do with Mummy?" to which Hans replies: "Take her to Lainz, too".[108] Then the father goes on to explain to him, that he'd "like to be Daddy and married to Mummy".[109] The child is trained to understand himself, his various desires and experiences through the Oedipal triangle: the desire for the mother and the fear of the father. Freud leads him to the Oedipal metaphor, ignoring many things that are said, different thoughts,

105 Gilles Deleuze. *Two Regimes of Madness* (New York: Semiotext, 2006).
106 Sigmund Freud. "Analysis of a Phobia in a Five-Year-Old Boy." *The Standard Edition of the Complete Psychological Works of Sigmund Freud* 10 (1909), p. 34.
107 Sigmund Freud. "Analysis of a Phobia in a Five-Year-Old Boy." *The Standard Edition of the Complete Psychological Works of Sigmund Freud* 10 (1909), p. 33.
108 Sigmund Freud. "Analysis of a Phobia in a Five-Year-Old Boy." *The Standard Edition of the Complete Psychological Works of Sigmund Freud* 10 (1909), p. 89. Lainz is a suburb of Vienna where Hans's grandparents lived.
109 Sigmund Freud. "Analysis of a Phobia in a Five-Year-Old Boy." *The Standard Edition of the Complete Psychological Works of Sigmund Freud* 10 (1909), p. 92.

phantasies and desires, and circling him in an immuring structure in which other possible psychoanalytic interpretations fade away.

Hans presents a rhizomatic system of desires that evade representation and territorialisation. He goes outside his house to make contact with other children and crosses the street to explore the garden and fields. He creates different *assemblages* and moves from one to the other: when he is tired of playing alone at his parent's house, he looks for encounters with other children and is drawn to creating new assemblages. The relationship with his surroundings is not a reflection or product of the relationship with his parents and cannot be conceptualised through the Oedipal triangle alone. Each libidinal interaction has its own unique relational assembly that cannot be characterised by one super-structure. Hans's relationship with his parents, his relationship with the building, with the neighbours, with the different animals in the zoo, with the horses all represent a specific activity of the child's fluid libido. Gradually, however, Hans's creativity and libidinal multiplicity are limited through the Oedipal metaphor imposed on him, his outward movement of inquiry is inhibited, and he is guided to think of himself through a single organising metaphor.

Through the social discourse introduced by the men around him, Hans is gradually led into an Oedipal understanding of his body, which provides a very specific meaning to his desires. Not only Freud and Hans's father are preoccupied with this phallic discourse, but the social preoccupation with the male genitalia is also evident in the culture into which Hans was born – a discourse which is reflected in the child's daily life and in Hans's conversations with his parents. He notices, for example, that "his mother was powdering round his penis and taking care not to touch it".[110] Hans's father and the Professor are continuously eliciting information about his preoccupation with this organ. They repeatedly ask him to observe and internalise the binary reality in which "his mother and all other female beings (as he could see from Hanna) had no widdler at all".[111] His parents cover and hide their own sexual organs repeatedly emphasising the prohibition "not to put his hand to his widdler". They warn him before bedtime and then, after he wakes up, they inquire about it and he admits "he had put it there for a short while all the same".[112] Being tuned to their repeated rhythm, Hans understands that 'this organ' is different from all other organs of the body. He learns to perceive it not as a functional organ (the organ through which he urinates), but as an organ that marks the differences between the sexes and dictates how he should understand his desires and approach the world.

110 Sigmund Freud. "Analysis of a Phobia in a Five-Year-Old Boy." *The Standard Edition of the Complete Psychological Works of Sigmund Freud* 10 (1909), p. 19.

111 Sigmund Freud. "Analysis of a Phobia in a Five-Year-Old Boy." *The Standard Edition of the Complete Psychological Works of Sigmund Freud* 10 (1909), p. 28.

112 Sigmund Freud. "Analysis of a Phobia in a Five-Year-Old Boy." *The Standard Edition of the Complete Psychological Works of Sigmund Freud* 10 (1909), p. 24.

The process of Oedipalisation can also be seen in Hans's fascinating account of sexual curiosity and, specifically, his investigation into what he calls *'widdlers'*.[113] As Freud explains,

> the first reports of Hans date from a period when he was not quite three years old. At that time, by means of various remarks and questions, he was showing a quite peculiarly lively interest in that portion of his body which he used to describe as his 'widdler'.[114]

Hans identifies 'this organ' in the various animals in the zoo, investigates the objects around him, and asks his mother if she has one as well. After a while, he explains to his father that "A dog and a horse have widdlers; a table and a chair haven't", and Freud, enthusiastic about Hans's conclusion, confidently asserts that the toddler succeeded in identifying "an essential characteristic for differentiating between animate and inanimate objects".[115]

Although the German original of the word widdler is *wiwimacher*, literally meaning the organ that produces urine, existing in both males and females, Freud referred to it as the male organ insisting that "little girls and women, ... have no widdlers",[116] while at the same time praising Hans's discovery that the presence of a widdler is the sign differentiating an inanimate object from a live subject. Freud is disappointed that the little researcher could not yet discover that it does not exist in women. "One might well feel horrified at such signs of the premature decay of a child's intellect", he writes about other boys reporting similar observations, "[w]hy was it that these young enquirers did not report what they really saw—namely, that there was no widdler there?"[117]

Is the male genitalia the hallmark that distinguishes living beings from inanimate objects? While Hans's words express a profound sensitivity in reflecting the culture into which he was born and raised, Freud leads him as well as the readers one step further, providing this phallic dominance an ontological stamp, validating the male

---

113 The German origin "wiwi-macher" may have represented the urinary organ in both sexes as described by Jarome C. Wakefield following Jonathan Lear – Hans exploration focuses on the functional character of this organ. Jarome C. Wakefield. "Concept Representation in the Child: What did Little Hans mean by 'Widdler'?" *Psychoanal. Psychol.* 34, no. 3 (2017): 352–360. Using the word 'widdler' refers only to the male organ, and thus expresses something of Freud's conviction that "little girls and women, ... have no widdlers." In this way the English translation demonstrates something of the way Hans learns to understand his organ.

114 Sigmund Freud. "Analysis of a Phobia in a Five-Year-Old Boy." *The Standard Edition of the Complete Psychological Works of Sigmund Freud* 10 (1909), p. 7.

115 Sigmund Freud. "Analysis of a Phobia in a Five-Year-Old Boy." *The Standard Edition of the Complete Psychological Works of Sigmund Freud* 10 (1909), p. 9.

116 Sigmund Freud. "Analysis of a Phobia in a Five-Year-Old Boy." *The Standard Edition of the Complete Psychological Works of Sigmund Freud* 10 (1909), p. 31.

117 Sigmund Freud. "Analysis of a Phobia in a Five-Year-Old Boy." *The Standard Edition of the Complete Psychological Works of Sigmund Freud* 10 (1909), p. 11, footnote.

organ not only as a symbol of sexual difference but also as the signifier for the distinction between subject and object. Throughout the text, he is encouraging Hans to hold on to both conclusions and align them into one: the male sexual organ is the mark separating between male-subject and female-object.

Indeed, Hans, a wise and sensitive child reflected the centrality of the "widdler" in culture and discourse. However, prior to his symptom development, he could peacefully coexist with this phallic power, as the dominance of the male organ did not negate other forces, he experienced within him and did not necessitate separation from his feminine and maternal abilities. For example, when Hans arrives at the cowshed and sees a cow being milked: "'Oh, look!' he said, 'there's milk coming out of its widdler!'"[118] Freud explains to the readers that the child behaves according to the fact that "the ego is always the standard by which one measures the external world; one learns to understand it by means of a constant comparison with oneself",[119] and therefore, Hans identifies his organ in the cow's udders as well. But perhaps a different interpretation can be applied here. Maybe the opposite is true, and Hans does not learn about reality through his own body, but learns to understand his body through the discursive reality? Perhaps, during this period before the onset of symptoms, Hans was able to identify with the maternal and think of himself as having the ability to nourish. Before the Oedipal amputation, this widdler – which later becomes the signifier of sexual difference – is an abundant organ, which has the power to nourish and fill the void and absence with milk.

This subtle textual reversal of causality is used in order to establish an argument that the phallocentric perspective constitutes the child's natural perspective, and Freud continues to explain that, in fact, this natural curiosity

> aroused in him the spirit of enquiry, and he thus discovered that the presence or absence of a widdler made it possible to differentiate between animate and inanimate objects. He assumed that all animate objects were like himself and possessed this important bodily organ.[120]

Thus, through this investigation, he learns facts about the world, distinguishes between the living and the inanimate; examining the different animals; researching his own body and his parents'. According to Freud, he presents "the need for making a comparison", assuming that the child interprets the world through his own body (and the male organ). However, as Deleuze and Guattari point out, it is, in fact, the territorialisation movement of an Oedipal discourse through which the body is shaped; an Oedipalising movement that creates itself as a reference point that

---

118 Sigmund Freud. "Analysis of a Phobia in a Five-Year-Old Boy." *The Standard Edition of the Complete Psychological Works of Sigmund Freud* 10 (1909), p. 7.
119 Sigmund Freud. "Analysis of a Phobia in a Five-Year-Old Boy." *The Standard Edition of the Complete Psychological Works of Sigmund Freud* 10 (1909), p. 107.
120 Sigmund Freud. "Analysis of a Phobia in a Five-Year-Old Boy." *The Standard Edition of the Complete Psychological Works of Sigmund Freud* 10 (1909), p. 106.

frames everything around the male sexual organ. Although, in his early life, Hans presents a structure of desire which is fluid, polymorphic and produced within specific contexts, in every corner he is infected with the Oedipal virus, pushed into a phallocentric worldview, learning to understand his desire according to a very specific template of the Oedipal triangle. His emerging sexual identity is a product of discourse, an effect of policing the body into two distinct opposing identities which are structured around the male sexual organ.

Is it the horse phobia that led to Freud's Oedipal cure, or is it cultural and Freudian Oedipal fixation itself that triggers the child's anxiety? The anxiety intensifies after Hans's father explains to him, following Freud's guidance, that "little girls and women, ... have no widdlers: Mummy has none, Anna has none, and so on".[121] After this explanation, when he goes to the zoo with his father, he presents with exacerbated anxiety showing "signs of fear at animals which on other occasions he had looked at without any alarm".[122] His father explains to him again that the return of "his nonsense" has to do with the size of widdlers he encountered at the zoo. But is it possible that the anxiety stems from the Oedipal cage that is closing in on him? Perhaps just as Hans found it difficult to see the domestication of the large wild horse, so was the surge in his anxiety a response to the sight of large animals confined in cages? He felt the grip of the Oedipal narrative closing in and understood his father's explanation as an all-encompassing demand to access the world through his male organ – a structure that obliges him to tear away from the maternal, cementing in him an understanding of himself through the binary divisions organised around the phallus.

Applying a Deleuzian interpretation, it is possible to understand the fear of the horse as a de-territorialisation attempt under the molar Oedipal regime. Watching the collapse of the horse under the heavy burden, the child identifies with its struggle, with the reins placed onto his eyes and mouth. That big, powerful animal, a symbol of wildness and freedom is domesticated and tied by human hands. The fascination with the horse and the anxiety of it is Hans's way to express his conflict under the all-embracing Oedipal system. Through this animal-becoming, he expresses identification with the horse's domestication process and with the burden imposed on the falling horse. Through this identification, he reflects both the strength of the wild animal fighting to bite and break free and the burden of its Oedipal chains. Like the horse, he too is vehemently bound to a specific understanding of himself, of his life and of his desires. He too, like the horse, feels the need to escape from his shackles, by biting or kicking to break free of the bridle and reins, almost falling under the cargo placed onto him.

121 Sigmund Freud. "Analysis of a Phobia in a Five-Year-Old Boy." *The Standard Edition of the Complete Psychological Works of Sigmund Freud* 10 (1909), p. 31.

122 Sigmund Freud. "Analysis of a Phobia in a Five-Year-Old Boy." *The Standard Edition of the Complete Psychological Works of Sigmund Freud* 10 (1909), p. 33.

Footnotes and Otherness

Following Deleuze and Guattari's conceptualisation, it is possible to explore Hans's neurosis as originating in the Oedipal prohibitions imposed on him, and in the nature of its relation to a whole system of cultural representations. This Oedipalisation is a clenching movement that organises desire, navigating his polymorphic curiosity through various discursive representations towards a very specific understanding of himself and causing his neurosis. Hans's possibilities for de-territorialisation are diminishing, he gradually understands the sacrifices he must make, relinquishing the multiplicity of assemblages and submitting to a dichotomous system characterised by the phallus. Under this territorialising system, he succumbs to the forces exerted upon him, suppressing the productive nature of his desire and learning to think in binary Oedipal terms and to understand himself through the categories prescribed to him.

Focusing on Oedipal sexuality, Freud performs a negation of the maternal and establishes the locus of phallic power in the triangular structure solely with the father. When the male sexual organ is marked as the unit of power, the gaze shifts from the relations with the mother and from the power inherent in motherhood that preoccupies the child. Throughout the text, Freud and Hans's father strive to teach him that women have "no widdler at all",[123] and that the privileged organ, the symbol of cultural power, is not found in mothers. In the face of Hans's preoccupation with pregnancy and birthgiving, with maternal strength in relation to children, they continuously redirect his preoccupation through the Oedipal narrative to the father. Freud and Hans's father try to teach Hans not only that boys cannot give birth but also that they should not identify with this position, that they should not fantasise or imagine pregnancy and birthing as a symbolic possibility. They convince him to look at his mother's and women's organ as a lack, repeatedly asking for his observations of his mother and sister's "missing" penis. They demand that he abandons his position of identification with the mother, while, at the same time, emphasising to him the privileged position of the male organ, if he would only agree to accept it.

Young Hans wishes to continue to identify with his mother, he wants to "be a mother" and to internalise what he perceives as her strength. The anxiety and resistance that arise when he is forced to separate from his mother or to separate from his identification with his mother on various occasions aggravate his conflict – reflecting both the Oedipal territorialisation movement and the resistance to it. In the face of the demand to abandon the maternal and to hold onto the male organ as the sole symbol through which the world can be grasped, his anxiety intensifies.

The Oedipal triangulation exerts a continuous pressure on Hans, driving him to give up the fantasy of being a mother, the close relationship with his mother and the perception with maternal power in his life. Continually shifting the attention from the maternal conflicted realm to the relationship with the father, this textual

---

123 Sigmund Freud. "Analysis of a Phobia in a Five-Year-Old Boy." *The Standard Edition of the Complete Psychological Works of Sigmund Freud* 10 (1909), p. 28.

movement persists even when the act of separating him (and threats of castration) comes from the mother. As revealed in the analysis of other case studies, the question of castration is entangled with the separation from the mother, but Freud makes an effort to fill the gaps in the text, shifting the gaze from the mother's castration threats to the Oedipal narrative, and the conflicted feelings shift to the relationship with the father. He overlooks the significance of the mother's ability to cut, redirecting the readers as well as Hans from the emotional complexity towards her to the Oedipal ambivalence towards the father.

In 1923, Freud added a footnote in which he described his resistance to a similar theorising of castration complex in relation to the maternal, which was developed by his successors – Lou Andreas-Salomé [1916], A. Stärcke [1921], F. Alexander [1922], and others. They introduced the hypothesis that every separation, and specifically weaning from the mother's breast, might be viewed as a prototype of a castration complex:

> every time his mother's breast is withdrawn from a baby he is bound to feel it as castration (that is to say, as the loss of what he regards as an important part of his own body); that, further, he cannot fail to be similarly affected by the regular loss of his faeces; and, finally, that the act of birth itself (consisting as it does in the separation of the child from his mother, with whom he has hitherto been united) is the prototype of all castration.[124]

Any detachment of the mother's breast from the baby's mouth, they argue, triggers in the baby an experience of anxiety about losing an essential part of his/her body. Every interruption to the dyadic continuum with the mother, every time the baby experiences a gap in maternal immediacy, castration anxiety is awakened and the encounter with absence is evoked with growing feelings of ambivalence towards the mother. Freud strongly opposes this view insisting that "the term 'castration complex' ought to be confined to those excitations and consequences which are bound up with the loss of the penis".[125] In doing so, he ignores the various meanings inherent in maternal power as anxiety-inducing, dismissing it as irrelevant through a phallocentric gaze. In Hans's case, it is the mother who threatens with castration: she is the one who evidently separated him from the nurturing breast, and she is the one who carried and gave birth to Hans's sister.[126] The emotional

---

124 Sigmund Freud. "Analysis of a Phobia in a Five-Year-Old Boy." *The Standard Edition of the Complete Psychological Works of Sigmund Freud* 10 (1909), p. 8, footnote.

125 Sigmund Freud. "Analysis of a Phobia in a Five-Year-Old Boy." *The Standard Edition of the Complete Psychological Works of Sigmund Freud* 10 (1909), p. 8, footnote.

126 Regarding the specific question of whether Little Hans was breastfed, the information available from Freud's case study does not provide explicit details about the infant's breastfeeding history. This is an interesting question to overlook considering Hans's anxiety started in separating from his mother. Information about Little Hans's early feeding experiences is missing from the available literature on the case.

complexity towards the mother remains unresolved, and Freud insists on the exclusivity of the Oedipal phantasy, in relation to castration complex.

The emotional intensity that arises in Hans in relation to his mother upon the birth of his baby sister is reshaped through the Oedipal structure, and his ambivalent feelings are redirected from the mother to the father. Faced with the opportunity to encounter the mother as a subject, embodying the ability to "cut", Hans comes to perceive his mother merely as an object of desire. This movement nullifies maternal power, overlooking the opportunity to explore the challenge in their relationship – both aggression and identification. Within the Oedipal triangulation, maternal ability to cut, to look beyond the child, is repudiated and thus the power inherent in maternal ability to nourish is also erased. The maternal remains matter, a two-dimensional object, a repressed and inaccessible pre-human existence. In the textual movement of reducing the maternal to an objectified (m)otherness, the image of circumcision emerges, testifying for an unspeakable 'wound'.

The footnote about circumcision appears in the text when Freud analyses the worsening of Hans's anxiety after his father explained to him that "little girls and women... have no widdlers: Mummy has none, Anna has none, and so on".[127] After the explanation, given to him under Freud's guidance, Hans developed an aggravated fear of animals, refusing to leave the house.[128] As Freud explains, Hans's regression stems from his resistance to the explanation given to him about women. He revolted against his father's words and therefore it "had a shattering effect upon his self-confidence" and "no therapeutic results".[129] Had he been willing to accept the explanation and to hold onto to the privilege of the male organ, the anxiety would have died down.

Refusing Oedipalisation and wishing to hold onto his identification with his mother, Hans does not accept the father's explanations about the dichotomy between the sexes organised around the male organ. The conflict intensifies, and Hans's anxiety is getting worse as he refuses to accept the social demand, represented by the father and Freud, to give up maternal strength. Hans responds, as I have interpreted, in an exacerbated anxiety in seeing large, caged animals in the zoo, due to the intensified conflict towards his own Oedipalising cage. At this point in the text, marked by Hans's growing conflict towards his process of Oedipalisation Freud adds a long footnote concerning circumcision:

> I cannot interrupt the discussion so far as to demonstrate the typical character of the unconscious train of thought which I think there is here reason for attributing to little Hans. The castration complex is the deepest unconscious root of

127 Sigmund Freud. "Analysis of a Phobia in a Five-Year-Old Boy." *The Standard Edition of the Complete Psychological Works of Sigmund Freud* 10 (1909), p. 31.

128 Sigmund Freud. "Analysis of a Phobia in a Five-Year-Old Boy." *The Standard Edition of the Complete Psychological Works of Sigmund Freud* 10 (1909), p. 50.

129 Sigmund Freud. "Analysis of a Phobia in a Five-Year-Old Boy." *The Standard Edition of the Complete Psychological Works of Sigmund Freud* 10 (1909), p. 36.

anti-semitism; for even in the nursery little boys hear that a Jew has something cut off his penis—a piece of his penis, they think—and this gives them a right to despise Jews. And *there is no stronger unconscious root for the sense of superiority over women.* Weininger (the young philosopher who, highly gifted but sexually deranged, committed suicide after producing his remarkable book, Geschlecht und Charakter [1903]), in a chapter that attracted much attention, treated Jews and women with equal hostility and overwhelmed them with the same insults. Being a neurotic, Weininger was completely under the sway of his infantile complexes; and from that standpoint what is common to Jews and women is their relation to the castration complex.[130]

This footnote not only encapsulates the textual response to Hans's neurotic conflict but also marks Freud's personal involvement in this case. Much has recently been written, analysing this footnote beyond being a psychoanalytic statement about circumcision and castration.[131] This note is an echo to the various conflicting identities of Freud himself – encapsulating questions of religion, ethnic origin, sexuality and gender – and thus, demonstrates the way in which psychoanalytic theory is intertwined with Freud's attempts to reconcile his own relation to otherness.

In analysing this footnote, Jay Geller points out that throughout the case study, Freud makes no mention of the fact that it was he who encouraged Hans's father to circumcise his son. As he explains, in the growing antisemitic atmosphere in Europe, Hans's father considered raising his son as a Christian. However, in correspondence with Freud, he was persuaded that if he did not allow his son to grow up as a Jew, he would deprive him of "energy forces" that cannot be replaced, "and in this way Freud effectively served as godfather in the circumcision of Hans, handing the baby to the mohel".[132] As Geller argues, when anchoring circumcision as part of a universal 'castration complex' in this footnote, Freud seeks to shed the responsibility for Hans' upbringing as a Jew, with all its accompanying meanings and implications. Analysing Hans's identifications with the mother – and perhaps with the circumcised Jew – as a temporary stage that follows the course of universal developmental process, minimises the question of his Jewishness, and Freud's guilt in relation to that. In juxtaposing circumcision with castration complex, he is able

130 Sigmund Freud. "Analysis of a Phobia in a Five-Year-Old Boy." *The Standard Edition of the Complete Psychological Works of Sigmund Freud* 10 (1909), p. 36, footnote.
131 For further reading see: Jay Geller. "The Godfather of Psychoanalysis: Circumcision, Antisemitism, Homosexuality, and Freud's 'Fighting Jew'." *J. Am. Acad. Relig.* 67, no. 2 (June 1999): 355–385; Sander Gilman. *The Case of Sigmund Freud: Medicine and Identity at the Fin de Sidcle* (Baltimore: Johns Hopkins University Press, 1993); Sander Gilman. *Freud, Race, and Gender* (Princeton: Princeton University Press, 1993); Daniel Boyarin. *Unheroic Conduct: The Rise of Heterosexuality and the Invention of the Jewish Man* (Berkeley/Los Angeles: University of California Press, 1997).
132 Max Graf. "Reminiscences of Professor Sigmund Freud." *Psycho-Anal. Quart.* 11 (1942): 465–476.

to depict the way Hans's anxiety is following a normal route that will eventually bestow him with the 'right' form of masculine power as promised.

Freud's text, Geller explains, is a symptom of the complexity of being a Jew in Europe of that time, in which the image of the Jew was associated with femininity and weakness.[133] The footnote is revealed as a textual anomaly, a *'synecdoche'* that marks in the lower (and unconscious) text the missing core of the upper (and conscious) text: the question of Jewish identity and the way it is intertwined with Freud's conceptualisation of otherness as feminine at that historical time. The footnote opens a window to thinking about otherness but at the same time also solves it, gathering various meanings under the universal castration complex. The absence of this central question from the conscious text signifies, according to Geller, the footnote as a 'synecdoche' or perhaps, as I would like to show, as a key-fossil.

In contrast to Freud's understanding of circumcision as an initiation that places the child in the covenant of masculinity, focusing on the relationship between father and son, Daniel Boyarin points to the question of the relation to the other inherent in it. He describes circumcision as a ritual that positions the Jew as an eternal other and thus opens up a space for encounters with that otherness. The act of removing the foreskin, according to Boyarin, undermines the dichotomous divisions that underlie Western culture – body and spirit, feminine and masculine, nature and culture and connects the Jew to the memory of an inherent otherness. The sign of the covenant is itself a recognition of relation, of dependency and therefore challenges binary categories: individual and collective identity, autonomous subjectivity and dependency, masculine identity and feminine identity – in a way that continuously opens the door to an otherness.

The footnote concerning circumcision contains its opposite within and therefore becomes a key-fossil marking the conflictual truth bubbling beneath the surface. Analysing through the lens of Deleuze and Guattari's theory allows an analysis of Freud's response to Hans's resistance (exacerbated anxiety) as a counter-movement of textual territorialisation relating to the question of otherness. Freud responds to Hans's resistance by a territorialisation movement that unites various otherness under the Oedipal supra-signifier and castration anxiety: emphasising similarities between the attitude towards Jews and women, he bundles together in one basket misogyny and antisemitism. Being an other, according to Deleuze and Guattari, is a constant rhizomatic becoming, which is characterised by the fact that it has no model or signifier. The textual movements seeking to conceptualise and frame these various otherness are built on the same dialectic structure to which de-territorialisation constitutes an incessant force of resistance.

---

133 At the end of the 19th century, the beginning of the 20th century, a discourse emerged in Europe that linked the image of the Jewish man, (passive, pale and weak), to the image of an effeminate man with homosexual orientations. As Daniel Boyarin explains, within this cultural reality, Freud invented psychoanalysis focusing on heterosexual Oedipal masculinity. Daniel Boyarin, "Freud's Baby, Fliess's Maybe: Homophobia, Antisemitism, and the Invention of Oedipus," *GLQ: A Journal of Gay and Lesbian Studies*, 2, no. 2 (1995): 115–147.

When resistance prevails and anxiety intensifies, Freud turns to unite castration and circumcision under one phallic metaphor, thus, carrying out a process of renewed territorialisation in the encounter with difference. In doing so, he also theorises the attitude towards Jews and women, pointing out the similarities between misogyny and antisemitism and uniting them under one (Oedipal) signifier. Faced with the question of otherness and the 'wound', Freud consolidates a diversity of relationships under the binary of presence or absence of the male organ, explaining the relationship between man and woman, in a similar phallic way as that between the circumcised Jew and the uncircumcised European. In this united narrative, the fear of losing the male organ is the reason for both antisemitism and misogyny, erasing layers of complexity with the reduction of various relational fields to the binary of castration complex. Although this footnote could raise questions about multiple otherness, and the role of a range of different identifications in the process of childhood development, it is positioned in the text as a repetition of the same castrating act that has always already happened in the transition to culture. Whereas Hans is preoccupied with dependency, anger and the need to identify with maternal strength, Freud overturns the tables concluding that "there is no stronger unconscious root for the sense of superiority over women" than the existence of a penis. Under this point of view, the encounter with the other is only enabled through the phallus and both the relationship with women and the relationship with being Jewish are reduced according to the attitude towards the male genitalia: hatred towards women stems from her lack, just as the "despise" of Jews is a result of the fact that "a Jew has something cut off his penis".[134] Through this footnote, the attitude towards different otherness is channelled into the binary and hierarchical division presence/absence of the male organ, in a way that interrupts the movement of rhezomatic flux and fixes all otherness under this phallocentric worldview.

Another encounter with otherness hidden in this paragraph relates to homosexuality, an unspoken dimension in the text that is explored by both Geller and Boyarin.[135] Freud addresses this issue in his summary in which he concludes that

> it was not to homosexuality that our young libertine proceeded, but to an energetic masculinity with traits of polygamy; he knew how to vary his behaviour, too, with his *varying feminine objects*—audaciously aggressive in one case, languishing and bashful in another.

Ignoring various libidinal objects that Hans exhibits as part of his rhizomatic desire, Freud defines homosexuality in a similar way to the Oedipal structure. Hans is homosexual, he argues, "as all children may very well be... quite consistently with

---

134 Sigmund Freud. "Analysis of a Phobia in a Five-Year-Old Boy." *The Standard Edition of the Complete Psychological Works of Sigmund Freud* 10 (1909), p. 36.

135 Geller. "The Godfather of Psychoanalysis." 1999; Boyarin. *Unheroic Conduct: The Rise of Heterosexuality*, 1997.

the fact, which must always be kept in mind, that he was acquainted with only one kind of genital organ—a genital organ like his own".[136] Homosexuality is a result of the psychic structure of children in which only the male organ exists, adding a footnote in 1923 does not allow an escape from the binarism: "I have subsequently (1923e) drawn attention to the fact that the period of sexual development which our little patient was passing through is universally characterized by acquaintance with only one sort of genital organ, namely, the male one".[137]

Freud's footnote appears as a response of the policing-teritorialising Oedipal system in its encounter with resistance and therefore marks the conflicted position in the face of otherness – not only for Hans but also, I would like to propose, for Freud and for psychoanalysis. Although stating he is reluctant to "interrupt the discussion",[138] Freud stops, adding a footnote that touches on the question of the other – the Jew, the feminine and the homosexual. Different modes of desire, alternative ways of relating to the body, other ways of self-understanding, and various interactions with the world – all gathered together and reduced under the known Oedipal structure. Coupling circumcision and castration, every attempt at de-territorialisation, every pain, every challenge in encountering the other is organised according to the male sexual organ.

The Navel of the Dream

The key-fossil of 'circumcision' marks a textual moment that simultaneously contains the question of otherness and its fixation under the Oedipal super-signifier. The intricacies of the conflict are revealed in the condensation movement that unites various otherness (ethnic-religious-gender-sexual) under a phallic signifier, grasping onto the male genitalia, but at the same time leaving an open textual wound, as the mark of the unconscious.

The point of view of the child in relation to this process is revealed in a sequence of dreams-fantasies in which Hans portrays a sort of enforced surgery he is going through. He describes a mechanical procedure in which the bath and some of his organs are first dismantled and then replaced. At the end of this surgery, a large metallic prosthesis, is attached to his belly, forcefully screwed into his abdomen. "I was in the bath", he tells his father, "and then the plumber came and unscrewed it. Then he took a big borer and stuck it into my stomach".[139] A few days later, he continues: "The plumber came; and first he took away my behind with a pair of pincers, and then gave

---

136 Sigmund Freud. "Analysis of a Phobia in a Five-Year-Old Boy." *The Standard Edition of the Complete Psychological Works of Sigmund Freud* 10 (1909), p. 110. Emphasis added.

137 Sigmund Freud. "Analysis of a Phobia in a Five-Year-Old Boy." *The Standard Edition of the Complete Psychological Works of Sigmund Freud* 10 (1909), p. 110. Footnote, emphasis added.

138 Sigmund Freud. "Analysis of a Phobia in a Five-Year-Old Boy." *The Standard Edition of the Complete Psychological Works of Sigmund Freud* 10 (1909), p. 36.

139 Sigmund Freud. "Analysis of a Phobia in a Five-Year-Old Boy." *The Standard Edition of the Complete Psychological Works of Sigmund Freud* 10 (1909), p. 65.

me another, and then the same with my widdler".[140] This surgical procedure, which echoes the ritual of circumcision, is a wonderful metaphor for the therapeutic process that Hans undergoes under Freud's hands, reflecting, in fact, the psychological process of children under the Oedipal super-signifier that closes in on them. Freud explains that going through castration complex and identification with the father, the male child completes his developmental process: recognising sexual difference, separating from his mother and realising that he can no longer have everything. Indeed, the Oedipal challenge could have opened the door to a movement that recognises loss, and partiality as part of every encounter with otherness. However, as Jessica Benjamin writes, at the heart of the Oedipal solution lies a paradox, a central paradox in psychoanalysis that has been repressed.[141] The Oedipal solution, in which the only option is to renounce the mother and identify with the father, contains within it the collapse of the three-dimensional structure into a construction of a binary language that does not recognise difference beyond negation. As Benjamin writes, "the idea of phallic monism is clearly at odds with the acceptance of difference that the Oedipus Complex is supposed to embody. It denies the difference between the sexes or rather it reduces difference to absence, to lack".[142] This textual movement of teritorialisation prevents an understanding of otherness as a living presence, through which the subject continues to evolve – a process in which the other is indeed recognised as a signifier of the partiality of the self; that is, as a representation of absence, that is not outside (the mother's lack) but inside.

Is identification only with the father the only possible solution? What would happen if, alongside identification with the father, identification with the mother could also occur? What if Hans could continue to hold onto his image of pregnancy and childbirth and his milk-producing abilities? Does this require falling beyond the boundaries of language – into psychosis? Does the ability to continue holding the maternal necessarily mean narcissistic regression? An omnipotent stance unwilling to acknowledge loss? And what would change in the structure of the male – as well as female – subject if identification with the maternal was not hindered by the Oedipal process?

Freud proudly concludes by explaining that in

Hans's last phantasy the anxiety which arose from his castration complex was also overcome, and his painful expectations were given a happier turn. Yes, the Doctor (the plumber) did come, he did take away his penis, but only to give him a bigger one in exchange for it.[143]

140 Sigmund Freud. "Analysis of a Phobia in a Five-Year-Old Boy." *The Standard Edition of the Complete Psychological Works of Sigmund Freud* 10 (1909), p. 98.

141 Jessica Benjamin. *The Bonds of Love: Psychoanalysis, Feminism, and the Problem of Domination* (New York: Pantheon Books, 1988).

142 Jessica Benjamin. *The Bonds of Love: Psychoanalysis, Feminism, and the Problem of Domination* (New York: Pantheon Books, 1988), p. 166.

143 Sigmund Freud. "Analysis of a Phobia in a Five-Year-Old Boy." *The Standard Edition of the Complete Psychological Works of Sigmund Freud* 10 (1909), p. 100.

In these words, Freud describes the surgical process of Oedipalisation. Under the hands of psychoanalysis, Hans's penis was removed and replaced by a larger, metallic prosthesis: the phallus. In this process, Hans learned to understand his body differently, to perceive his penis not simply as a functional organ but as an organising image of the entire culture, as a metallic vessel with huge dimensions and boundless power. From this moment on, he will only be able to look at the world from within that organ. The operation is complete and from now on every encounter with others, every interface with his environment and every desire will be translated through the metal tool jutting out of his belly.

A framework is established that would serve as an organising structure for the variety of Hans's libidinal encounters: the child is taught to perceive the world through his masculine organ and to understand any encounter with otherness through this dichotomous and hierarchical structure. Freud's Oedipal guidance is in collaboration with a phallic cultural perception that lures the child to understand his multiple encounters – with animals, with his friends, with his mother, with his sister, with his Jewish identity, with his multiple-object rhizomatic desire– under the binary of its relation to the male organ. The image of circumcision is coupled with that of castration and thus multiple possibilities converge under the Oedipal metaphor, in which, the rhizomatic movement of desire is continually reorganised and any possibility of encountering others beyond the self is blocked by the dichotomous and hierarchical phallic axis of have/have nots.

The first step in this surgical process, as the dream shows, is the dismantling of the bath. Perhaps a symbol of pregnancy and containment, the image of the bath incorporates the possibility of fluid, non-linear movement – rhizomatically spreading and extending shoots in all directions. This womb of fluids is dismantled in Hans's inner world, as a precondition for receiving the prosthetic phallic organ. The doctor, the mohel (circumciser), the surgeon, the plumber – first removes the enveloping, maternal dimension, dismantling the range of maternal identifications in his inner world, uprooting the phantasies for conceiving and the desire for birthing. In its place, the child is connected like an external life support machine to the Oedipal narrative.

This initiation ceremony described by Hans himself is an extraordinary metaphor for the therapeutic process, for the exchange that took place in his mental world, and for the closure that took place in the entire text. The bath is dismantled, Hans's organs are replaced, and he receives from the plumber a metal phallic device which will be attached to his stomach. Echoing the ritual of circumcision, in which a piece of soft skin is cut off from the penis in the process of assuming masculine identity, this process of Oedipalisation begins with erasing the maternal. Merging circumcision with castration through this unifying image, the wide range of desire-structures disappears, and the developmental challenge of encountering otherness gives way to one phallic signifier. This ceremony is the Oedipal initiation of the child, in which the penis is replaced by the symbolic phallus, in the surgical – and psychoanalytic – procedure that violently attaches a metal prosthetic organ, which will henceforth serve as an organising axis for his life: his phallic masculinity.

III

LEONARDO: A CHILDHOOD MEMORY OF MATERNAL PHALLUS

In *The Wolf Man* case study, analysed in the first sub-chapter, Freud presents an analysis that he himself performed. In the case study of *Little Hans* the analysis was conducted by the father under Freud's guidance. The third case study in this chapter, *Leonardo da Vinci's childhood memory* delves into Freud's attempt to analyses the childhood years of a man he had never met. Centuries after his death, Freud traces the childhood years of the 15th-century artist and scientist Leonardo da Vinci, exploring his memories, his relationships, and the psychoanalytic meaning embedded in his works. Specifically, Freud focuses on the analysis of some of Leonardo's famous paintings, including the 'Mona Lisa' and 'The Virgin and Child with Saint Anne', as well as a detailed analysis of a short childhood memory, on which Freud elaborates:

> so far as I know, only one place in his scientific notebooks where Leonardo inserts a piece of information about his childhood. In a passage about the flight of vultures he suddenly interrupts himself to pursue a memory from very early years which had sprung to his mind: 'It seems that I was always destined to be so deeply concerned with vultures; for I recall as one of my very earliest memories that while I was in my cradle a vulture came down to me, and opened my mouth with its tail, and struck me many times with its tail against my lips.'[144]

Leonardo's childhood memory in which the tail of a bird of prey was shoved into his mouth while he was in the cradle leads Freud to the mythological realms of ancient Egypt, to the goddess Mut and to the concept of the *'phallic mother'*. Due to Leonardo's circumstances, who grew up in his early years with only his mother, this case contains Freud's response and theoretical explorations of the dyadic relationship between a child and his mother, enabling a closer look at his analysis of maternal power in the child's life. The concept of the 'phallic mother', holding together both the maternal and the phallus, introduces Freud's question about "the puzzling psychological fact that the human imagination does not boggle at endowing a figure which is intended to embody the essence of the mother with the mark of male potency which is the opposite of everything maternal".[145] How is it possible,

---

144 Sigmund Freud. "Leonardo Da Vinci and a Memory of his Childhood." In: James Strachey (ed. & trans.) *The Standard Edition of the Complete Psychological Works of Sigmund Freud* 11 (1910): 57—138. London: The Hogarth Press and the Institute of Psycho-Analysis, 1957. p. 82. There was an error in the German translation and the original Italian text refers to a *kite* rather than a vulture. The analysis here deals with the Freudian theory and therefore this error is irrelevant to Freud's associations and the theory derived from it.

145 Sigmund Freud. "Leonardo Da Vinci and a Memory of his Childhood." *The Standard Edition of the Complete Psychological Works of Sigmund Freud* 11 (1910), p. 94.

he asks, that human imagination can combine the maternal image with the masculine power that is its opposite? The uncoupling of the phallus and the male genitalia opens a window into maternal subjectivity and enables the theoretical exploration of the child's relationship with both maternal power and maternal sexuality. However, as I will show, while Freud opens the door to this discussion, he also shifts his gaze from the potential it encapsulates, repeatedly warning of the danger in preserving maternal power to both the child's 'masculinity' and his sexual orientation. Leading readers from maternal phallus to the discussion of her lack (of a male organ), the textual trajectory strives to pair the phallus with the actual penis leaving the image of circumcision as a key-fossil, that both reveals and conceals a wound.

Maternal Split

Little is known about Leonardo's early life, Freud explains. He was an illegitimate child of "Ser Piero da Vinci, a notary and descended from a family of notaries and farmers who took their name from the locality of Vinci". His mother, "was *a certain Caterina*", most likely a peasant girl.[146] The father refused to marry Leonardo's mother, and thus, in the first years of his life the young boy grew up with only his mother. Leonardo's father married a wealthy woman from Florence, but "the marriage of Ser Piero with a certain Donna Albiera remained childless, and it was, therefore, possible for the young Leonardo to be brought up in his father's house".[147] When he was about five years old, the boy moved in with his father and into his new family.[148] At this point in his life, he separated from his mother and there is no mention of him ever meeting her again.[149] As Freud explains, "the fact which the vulture phantasy confirms, namely that Leonardo spent the first years of

---

146 Sigmund Freud. "Leonardo Da Vinci and a Memory of his Childhood." *The Standard Edition of the Complete Psychological Works of Sigmund Freud* 11 (1910), p. 81. Emphasis added: it is important to notice the way Freud's writing introduces the name of Leonardo's father compared with the name of his mother.

147 Sigmund Freud. "Leonardo Da Vinci and a Memory of his Childhood." *The Standard Edition of the Complete Psychological Works of Sigmund Freud* 11 (1910), p. 81.

148 Freud concludes that this was at the age of three or five. He writes: "In the same year that Leonardo was born, the sources tell us, his father, Ser Piero da Vinci, married Donna Albiera, a lady of good birth; it was to the childlessness of this marriage that the boy owed his reception into his father's (or rather his grandfather's) house—an event which had taken place by the time he was five years old, as the document attests. Now it is not usual at the start of a marriage to put an illegitimate offspring into the care of the young bride who still expects to be blessed with children of her own. Years of disappointment must surely first have elapsed before it was decided to adopt the illegitimate child—who had probably grown up an attractive young boy—as a compensation for the absence of the legitimate children that had been hoped for. It fits in best with the interpretation of the vulture phantasy if at least three years of Leonardo's life, and perhaps five, had elapsed before he could exchange the solitary person of his mother for a parental couple. ...". Sigmund Freud. "Leonardo Da Vinci and a Memory of his Childhood." *The Standard Edition of the Complete Psychological Works of Sigmund Freud* 11 (1910), p. 91.

149 Although there are other opinions, which Freud refers to, suggesting that Leonardo met his mother at least once more before her death when he was 41 years old.

his life alone with his mother, will have been of decisive influence in the formation of his inner life".[150]

Although recognising the cardinality of this early relationship, Freud interprets the influence of the dyad between Leonardo and his mother in the early years of his life as evidence of the danger inherent in maternal love. The mother's devotion testifies, according to him, to the deprivation of the unmarried woman who is longing for the presence of a man. "Like all unsatisfied mothers", Freud writes, "she took her little son in place of her husband" and while nourishing the child with love, warmth and tenderness, she also "robbed him of a part of his masculinity".[151]

Analysing the mother's substitution of her deprivation (of a man and a phallus) with the love of the male baby, Freud focuses the text on the reverse substitution in which maternal love creates a deprivation of masculinity in the child. According to him, through her care, nourishing and love, Leonardo was imprisoned "under the dominance of an inhibition which forbade him ever again to desire such caresses from the lips of women".[152] With love, she takes away his masculinity, chaining him with tenderness in maternal shackles that would seal his fate and rob him of his future.

Evidence of Leonardo's sex life is scarce, and Freud concludes that he abstained from sexual contact with women and raises the suspicion – which was also raised by others – that Leonardo had homosexual relations with his students. Using this case study, Freud draws a theoretical link between homosexual orientation to a developmental process with a "very intense erotic attachment to a female person, as a rule their mother",[153] in which due to the abundant warmth, tenderness and love "lavished" upon them by their mothers, and due to the absence of the father, these children refuse to let go of the phallic power attached to the maternal role. "We should have to translate it thus", Freud writes, "It was through this erotic relation with my mother that I became a homosexual".[154] The mother, he argues, following Sadger's work, is characterised in these cases by vigorous masculine traits, which often exclude the father from his role, leaving the child bound to maternal influence. Thus, a boy becomes homosexual when he does not give up the image of the phallic mother, and therefore continues to narcissistically seek his own image of love, just as his mother loved him.

Through this analysis, Freud links the memory of the beak opening the mouth of the infant Leonardo to an interpretation describing the relationship with the mother

150 Sigmund Freud. "Leonardo Da Vinci and a Memory of his Childhood." *The Standard Edition of the Complete Psychological Works of Sigmund Freud* 11 (1910), p. 92.
151 Sigmund Freud. "Leonardo Da Vinci and a Memory of his Childhood." *The Standard Edition of the Complete Psychological Works of Sigmund Freud* 11 (1910), p. 117.
152 Sigmund Freud. "Leonardo Da Vinci and a Memory of his Childhood." *The Standard Edition of the Complete Psychological Works of Sigmund Freud* 11 (1910), p. 117.
153 Sigmund Freud. "Leonardo Da Vinci and a Memory of his Childhood." *The Standard Edition of the Complete Psychological Works of Sigmund Freud* 11 (1910), p. 99.
154 Sigmund Freud. "Leonardo Da Vinci and a Memory of his Childhood." *The Standard Edition of the Complete Psychological Works of Sigmund Freud* 11 (1910), p. 106.

as the source of homosexuality. The passivity of the baby's lips is interpreted as a homosexual oral phantasy and the mother is portrayed as robbing the baby of his masculine power. As he suckles breast milk, she draws his masculine strength and phallic power from him. Emphasising Leonardo's gentle character, Freud highlights his "homosexual passivity" as well as his artistic tendency and innovative research as a result of this dominant primary dyad. According to Freud, from an early age, he learned to sublimate, redirecting his desire towards his intellectual pursuits: "He had merely converted his passion into a thirst for knowledge; he then applied himself to investigation with the persistence, constancy and penetration which is derived from passion",[155] investing in art and research with the same passion with which a person seeks sexual contact. Skipping between notions of gender identification and sexual orientation, Freud connects his thoughts about Leonardo's sexuality with evidence of his relaxed and pleasant nature:

> He was gentle and kindly to everyone; he declined, it is said, to eat meat, since he did not think it justifiable to deprive animals of their lives; and he took particular pleasure in buying birds in the market and setting them free.[156]

A split in maternal image is portrayed in these discussions, in which the mother is depicted, on one hand as a good, compassionate and nourishing figure, but on the one hand, as deceitful and treacherous.[157] Leonardo received from the relationship with his mother, "one of the forms of attainable human happiness",[158] but within it a different maternal aspect is revealed, a treacherous mother who will rob him of his masculinity. This image of a split mother is used by Freud to interpret the meaning inherent in his artwork, specifically the smile of the Mona Lisa. The smile, he explains, contains a dual experience, taken from Leonardo's life circumstances, a double meaning encapsulating

> the charm of deceit, the kindness that conceals a cruel purpose, — all this appeared and disappeared by turns behind the laughing veil and buried itself in the poem of her smile ... Good and wicked, cruel and compassionate, graceful and feline, she laughed.[159]

---

155 Sigmund Freud. "Leonardo Da Vinci and a Memory of his Childhood." *The Standard Edition of the Complete Psychological Works of Sigmund Freud* 11 (1910), p. 74.

156 Sigmund Freud. "Leonardo Da Vinci and a Memory of his Childhood." *The Standard Edition of the Complete Psychological Works of Sigmund Freud* 11 (1910), p. 69.

157 Plagi-Hecker describes a repeated pattern in Freud's writings in which the tender mother is revealed as cruel.

158 Sigmund Freud. "Leonardo Da Vinci and a Memory of his Childhood." *The Standard Edition of the Complete Psychological Works of Sigmund Freud* 11 (1910), p. 117.

159 Sigmund Freud. "Leonardo Da Vinci and a Memory of his Childhood." *The Standard Edition of the Complete Psychological Works of Sigmund Freud* 11 (1910), p. 109, containing the quotation of The Italian writer Angelo Conti.

Leonardo's separation from his mother at a very young age – according to Freud between the ages of three and five – is enough to indicate the absence of the mother that accompanied the artist's life. However, intriguingly, Freud's discussion focuses on maternal "excess", on the absence of the father and on the damage caused by the mother raising the child alone. He does not dwell on Leonardo's separation from his mother and does not ponder how it affected him. He does not raise questions about the child's traumatic loss in his early parting from his mother nor does he touch on his feelings of loneliness, abandonment and alienation in his new home. Certainly, he does not dwell on Leonardo's psyche being affected by his mother's subjectivity – her experience and struggles in life – the conditions and process of him being taken away from her, her response to it, and the power relations between the parents. Instead, he focuses on the poverty that prevailed early in his life with his mother, emphasising that he was an illegitimate child and uses rhetoric describing the absence of the father:

> It is here that the interpretation of the vulture phantasy comes in: Leonardo, it seems to tell us, spent the critical first years of his life not by the side of his father and stepmother, but with his poor, forsaken, real mother, so that he had time to feel the absence of his father.[160]

It is unclear what had happened in Leonardo's early life: did the mother leave, or was the child forcefully taken away from her to live with his father? What were her feelings towards the father for his abandonment? What were Leonardo's feelings? Did she fight to keep him, or did she give up quickly in the absence of financial resources? In contrast to the father – who was wealthy in both money and social status – the mother was undoubtedly lacking the means to support herself and the child. In the face of this early and most probably traumatic loss of the mother at an early age, Freud is preoccupied with the absence of the father. How is it that Freud specifically chooses a weak and resourceless woman to depict the overbearing deeds of maternal power? How is it that Freud chooses what he himself describes as a poor and impoverished woman, in order to open the theoretical discussion about the *phallic mother*?

Freud does not take the time to ask these questions, and the painful loss of the mother is repressed and only echoing from the textual unconscious. Despite the evident absence of the mother, Freud shifts the readers' gaze highlighting maternal surplus and the absence of the father. Once again, the complex feelings in the relationship with the mother are repudiated and reversed in Freud's text, which focuses on the father's absence in the mother's world and in the child's upbringing. His descriptions of the early years of Leonardo's life depict a threatening danger in mother-son relationship, in which maternal tenderness, love and nourishing become an overflow that disrupts the psychosexual development of the child.

---

160 Sigmund Freud. "Leonardo Da Vinci and a Memory of his Childhood." *The Standard Edition of the Complete Psychological Works of Sigmund Freud* 11 (1910), p. 91.

The Phallic Mother

I recall as one of my very earliest memories.[161]

According to Freud, consciousness, like a historian, produces memories from fragments of information from dreams and phantasies within which a kernel of truth resides. He analyses at length Leonardo's childhood memory in which he was lying in a cradle and a vulture descended, opened his mouth and "struck me many times with its tail".[162] Childhood memories, such as Leonardo's, he explains, are a distorted reflection of reality, since historical records often express "present beliefs and wishes rather than a true picture of the past". History, as he elaborates, was not written as a result of "objective curiosity" or love of truth, but because its writers sought to "influence their contemporaries, to encourage and inspire them, or to hold a mirror up before them".[163] Many things in history have been forgotten, others have been distorted, while some have been misinterpreted in order to conform with existing conceptions. Leonardo's memory, according to Freud is similarly a reconstruction that was made in his adulthood and, thus, includes many elements repainting the truth in different colours.

Freud's words resonate in his own text, as he reconstructs Leonardo's childhood memory, according to his developing theory. He too rebuilds history according to the desires of the present and seeks to tell a story that will correspond to his emerging understandings of childhood psychosexual development. Alongside searching for the truth about Leonardo's life, and beyond the attempts to support the emerging Oedipal theoretical framework, Freud's reconstruction is demonstrating his own unprocessed relationship with the maternal. As Palgi-Hecker explains in her analysis, "The attempt to decipher a secret such as the Mona Lisa's smile is linked to other questions Freud is preoccupied with, in the context of femininity and motherhood". She identifies "a pattern that appears in many of Freud's case studies in which the mother (or nanny) seduces and then cheats and humiliates".[164] Recognising a similar inverse reaction in which the tender and nourishing mother becomes aggressive and deceitful in many of Freud's texts, Plagi-Hecker argues that this pattern is testifying to his own complicated relationship with the maternal.

This inability to encounter the maternal is folded within the Oedipal structure itself from its very beginning and can be demonstrated within the case study of Leonardo. The gap between Leonardo's painful early separation from his mother and Freud's analysis, which emphasises her overbearing dangerous presence in

---

161 Sigmund Freud. "Leonardo Da Vinci and a Memory of his Childhood." *The Standard Edition of the Complete Psychological Works of Sigmund Freud* 11 (1910), p. 82.

162 Sigmund Freud. "Leonardo Da Vinci and a Memory of his Childhood." *The Standard Edition of the Complete Psychological Works of Sigmund Freud* 11 (1910), p. 82.

163 Sigmund Freud. "Leonardo Da Vinci and a Memory of his Childhood." *The Standard Edition of the Complete Psychological Works of Sigmund Freud* 11 (1910), pp. 82–83.

164 Anat Palgi-Hecker. *From i-mahut to Imahut* (in Hebrew. Tel-Aviv: Am Oved, 2005), p. 75, my translation.

the child's life, raises questions about Freud's emotional response in encountering the relationship with the mother, leading to a matricidal textual movement that in turn permeates the realm of psychoanalytic theory. In his reconstruction of Leonardo's phantasmatic memory, Freud fills in the gaps using the Oedipal model and asks – but at the same time frightened of the answer – what happens in the psychosexual development when the father is not present during the child's early years? This question introduces Freud, as well as psychoanalytic theory, to the possibility of looking beyond the Oedipal narrative and the relationship with the father. It allows a view into the pre-Oedipal period, into the relationship with the mother, focusing the questions in the direction of the maternal. The concept of the 'phallic mother', arising from the theoretical discussion, has the potential to think of the phallus of the maternal, beyond its automatic affiliation to the male genitalia and allows an exploration of the way in which the mother's phallus is connected to the power inherent to maternal nourishing, breastfeeding and sexuality.

Indeed, Freud interprets the tailed vulture in Leonardo's memory as a symbol of the power inherent in the act of maternal breastfeeding. As he explains,

> it only repeats in a different form a situation in which we all once felt comfortable—when we were still in our suckling days ('*essendo io in culla*')[2] and took our mother's (or wet-nurse's) nipple into our mouth and sucked at it.[165]

In the act of maternal breastfeeding, according to this interpretation, lie the roots of oral sexuality and the first buds of pleasure in a person's life. Leonardo's memory of these tender moments with his mother leads Freud to the conclusion that the vulture next to the baby in the crib represents the mother and the tail that opens its mouth is the male genitalia, the penis attached to the mother. Readers follow an association chain leading to the hieroglyphs of ancient Egypt, in which the maternal was represented as a vulture in the image of the goddess *Mut*. Ancient Egyptians worshipped this vulture-headed goddess called Mut, who presented with a vulture head, woman's breasts and a male penis in a constant state of erection.[166] They also believed that the vulture was a female-only specie that naturally reproduced without a male, impregnated by the wind penetrating their vaginas. The image of the goddess Mut represents a parthenogenetic phantasy as an ancient symbol resonating, as Freud points out, in both the Christian belief in the Virgin Mother and in the life of Leonardo who grew up, at least during his early years, without a father.

The historical period in which the image of the maternal goddess with a male penis prevailed represents, according to Freud, the phylogenetic equivalent to the childhood stage in which the mother "is given a combination of male and female

---

165 Sigmund Freud. "Leonardo Da Vinci and a Memory of his Childhood." *The Standard Edition of the Complete Psychological Works of Sigmund Freud* 11 (1910), p. 87.

166 It is important to emphasise again that in the Italian original it was not a vulture and therefore the chain of associations is, of course, Freud's and not Leonardo's.

sex characters".[167] The ancient Egyptian's belief in the phallic power of the goddess corresponds to a stage of development in which the child equips the mother with both strength and with a male organ – the period of the *'phallic mother'*. The concept of the 'phallic mother' can be thought of in Kleinian terms through what she describes as *'Combined Parental Figure'*, an image containing both the maternal breast and the paternal penis at the same time. The combined parental image initially exists for the baby within the mother figure, holding both the maternal and the paternal images in an androgynous state: a universal representation of primary creativity in which the feminine and masculine components are intertwined.[168]

As a sexual-hybrid symbol, this image is also an early phantasy for maternal sexuality. An existence that contains both sex organs, (in the phantasy of both boys and girls), also comprises of an internal ability for sexual pleasure outside the dyad with the baby and thus, contains the buds of the 'primal scene' image discussed in the previous subchapter. It is an image of an entity that can satisfy itself in the mixture of libidinal and aggressive urges comprised in it. Like the parthenogenetic Egyptian belief that the female vulture is capable of self-impregnation, so is the 'combined parental figure' and the 'phallic mother' for the child phantasies of maternal self-satisfaction, or perhaps a budding phantasy of *the other of the mother*. As such, it opens the door both to maternal sexuality and to the experience of the child's exclusion from the parental dyad of the 'primal scene'.

The image of the 'phallic mother' contains the roots of the developmental challenge inherent in the relationship with maternal subjectivity, awakening in the child an ambivalent array of emotions: curiosity, anticipation and arousal, as well as a sense of exclusion and anger. Through the phantasy of the 'phallic mother', a window opens in his/her inner world to maternal sexuality and a realisation begins to emerge that the mother's gaze may be directed towards another that can satisfy her. Through this androgynous maternal image of 'combined parental figure', the relationship between the child and the mother will unfold in a later stage into the 'primal scene' – the emerging of a phantasy in which there is space and movement between three relational figures.

In addition to this image as the roots of triadic relationship, the mother's phallus is also a recognition of her power, not because she has a third (and thus her subjectivity lies beyond the relationship with the child) but because of her power within the relationship: in her cardinal presence for her children, in their dependency, and in the mother's desire within the dyadic relationship itself. The image of the mother with the phallus represents the child's experience in the face of that maternal strength, his/her recognition of her active ability to nourish and mother, a realisation (albeit unconscious) of her desires, as well as the experience of dependency in relation to her. The power ingrained in the mother's ability to breastfeed is

167 Sigmund Freud. "Leonardo Da Vinci and a Memory of his Childhood." *The Standard Edition of the Complete Psychological Works of Sigmund Freud* 11 (1910), p. 94.
168 Melanie Klein. "The Oedipus Complex in the Light of Early Anxieties." *Int. J. Psychoanal.* 26 (1945): 11–33.

always already intertwined with her ability to detach the baby from the breast, and therefore the concept of 'phallic mother' entails the ability to 'cut' inherent to maternal subjectivity, the encounter with which, provokes strong conflicting feelings in the infant.

However, the image of the 'phallic mother', as described by Freud, refers to the temporary representation of her power, and thus, this image of the phallus also incorporates its vanishing quality: the essence of its disappearing charade in the movement from *projection* of omnipotent-power to the *projection* of castration. The phallus, in Lacanian terms, represents the privileged signifier, the empty signifier of desire itself, through which the subject gains access into the symbolic. It incorporates within it, not only the imagery projection of omnipotence (in the form of male organ) onto the mother, but also the movement between this projection of power to that of castration – which is, again, first and foremost that of the mother. Maternal power inherent in the concept of the 'phallic mother', as coined by Freud, signifies the vanishing power inherent in the maternal role itself – the disappearing power of the maternal position of nourishment and that of her desire for the baby.

The case study of Leonardo, in its polarity in relation to the mother, portrays this movement in the split image of the maternal – the gap between her poverty and weakness and her powerful ominous image as described by Freud; the disparity between the image of the 'phallic mother' and her diminished social position; the descriptions of her excess presence in Laonardo's life given the fact that he was separated from her at the age of three or five; and, of course, the schism in maternal images throughout the text – all testify to this particular attribute of the phallus as a simulacrum of power only indicating a void, the emptiness of the symbolic itself. Although demonstrating this movement in the text, the vanishing power of the maternal as a theoretical realm is neglected, and Freud rushes to attach the phallus to the male organ clinging at the same time to "the reality" of her castration, portraying the *projection* of castration onto the maternal as a moment of truth. As he explains, once the boy realises the mother's lack, he views,

> the female genitals in a new light; henceforth he will tremble for his masculinity, but at the same time he will despise the unhappy creatures on whom the cruel punishment has, as he supposes, already fallen.[169]

The gap in which the phallus is oscilating between totality and absence, the whole and the hole, can only be portrayed through castration anxiety about the actual penis, and thus both the child and the textual movement skip the opportunity to explore this theoretical realm within the relationship with the mother.

Analysing the concept of the 'phallic mother', which does not give the mother a male sex organ but emerges from the understanding of the separation between the

---

169 Sigmund Freud. "Leonardo Da Vinci and a Memory of his Childhood." *The Standard Edition of the Complete Psychological Works of Sigmund Freud* 11 (1910), p. 95.

concrete penis and the symbolic phallus, may give rise to new theoretical meanings. Indeed, the word *phallus*, originating in Greek, literally means to inflate, to swell, an attribute of its charade being projected with larger dimensions than it actually is, but also representing the evasive abilities of maternal body to inflate and change dimensions – the womb during pregnancy and the breast during its cycles of breast-feeding. This etymological reminder of the word phallus itself echoes Klein's revised conception of the phallus as relating to the breast. Castration concept, as she envisioned it – long before the process of Oedipalisation is rooted in the most primary separation from the maternal breast. The breast as a primary signifier, resonating in Leonardo's memory and his preoccupation with birds throughout his life, testify to this unexplored relationship with his mother and her potency.[170]

Describing the emotions that arise in the infant in relation to the mother, Klein presents a different understanding of the accompanying mechanism of splitting. She describes the childhood experience as oscillating between the 'good breast' and the 'bad breast', between satisfaction and love on one hand, and jealousy and persecution on the other, without the ability to contain both simultaneously. She shows that these conflicting emotions present a developmental challenge for integration of the fragmented early self, that may lead to reconciliation between contradictory and ambivalent feelings. This schizoid-paranoid position splits between positive and negative feelings, and the child alternates between projecting and introjecting aggression. The object (the mother) is sometimes perceived as persecuting and threatening, while at other times as pure and entirely good but at risk of being destroyed by the child's threatening "badness".[171]

A similar movement is unfolded in Freud texts, in which, according to Palgi-Hecker,

> Freud fails to maintain these conflicting feelings of aggression and love in relation to the mother. he demonises the mother, who, according to him, steals her son's masculinity and pushes him to homosexuality. Alternatively, he paints her as ideal in her maternal love. In so doing, he deprives the mother of the possibility of being a complex figure.[172]

The splitting accompanying the text in the figure of the mother indicates the difficulty of the author in dealing with the emotional forces arising in the face of the image of the 'phallic mother'. Like the child struggling to hold together a complex picture of maternal subjectivity, the textual splitting shifts between projection and introjection of aggression, and the mother figure oscillates between being "Good and wicked, cruel and compassionate, graceful and feline".[173]

---

170 Melanie Klein. "Notes on Some Schizoid Mechanisms." *Int. J. Psychoanal.* 27 (1946): 99–110.
171 Melanie Klein. "Mourning and Its Relation to Manic-Depressive States." *Int. J. Psychoanal.* 21 (1940): 125–153.
172 Anat Palgi-Hecker. *From i-mahut to Imahut* (Tel-Aviv: Am Oved, 2005), p. 76, my translation.
173 Sigmund Freud. "Leonardo Da Vinci and a Memory of his Childhood." *The Standard Edition of the Complete Psychological Works of Sigmund Freud* 11 (1910), p. 109.

Freud is aware of the complex feelings that arise in him in relation to the maternal. In his analysis of da Vinci's Mona Lisa and her smile, he describes his ambivalent attitude toward the painting. He identifies in it

> the most perfect representation of the contrasts which dominate the erotic life of women; the contrast between reserve and seduction, and between the most devoted tenderness and a sensuality that is ruthlessly demanding—consuming men as if they were alien beings.[174]

Although he is aware, Freud's response to this emotional complexity does not allow for an in-depth theoretical discussion and the conflicting emotions that arise lead to a reaction that juxtapose the phallus with the male genitalia denying the possibility of exploring maternal power, and the relationship with it. Although Freud recognises that the breast is "the first source of pleasure in our life", and thus a first source of power to which the term 'maternal phallus' refers, this memory of Leonardo with the bird in his crib, quickly shifts from the early experience of breast-feeding to the totality of the penis.

The image of the phallic mother is, according to Freud, a temporary developmental phase that must be passed or corrected, a stage in the child's life in which "he still holds women at full value",[175] as he still believes that she is similar to him, attributing to her the male genital organ and imagining "that all human beings, women as well as men, possess a penis like his own".[176] The desire in the child's relationship to the mother, Freud emphasises, is "a longing for her genital organ, which he takes to be a penis".[177]

Does the child bestow the mother with phallic power as a result of a misbelief that she has a male genital organ? or is the child aware of the maternal abundance, and his/her dependency – acknowledging maternal power in relation to his physical and emotional needs? Freud argues that the child is "confused" and temporarily attributes the male genitalia to the mother, but it seems that it is Freud who confuses the phallus – which is a symbol of power and social recognition – with the concrete organ. The image of breastfeeding, for which the lips are opening in Leonardo's childhood memory, is soon replaced by the male penis, and the power attached to the breasts is explained as confusion that is part of the child's developmental process, in which the child temporarily pairs the male penis with the mother. In an attempt to rectify the confusion, Freud asserts—while rallying the entire psychoanalytic

---

174 Sigmund Freud. "Leonardo Da Vinci and a Memory of his Childhood." *The Standard Edition of the Complete Psychological Works of Sigmund Freud* 11 (1910), p. 108.

175 Sigmund Freud. "Leonardo Da Vinci and a Memory of his Childhood." *The Standard Edition of the Complete Psychological Works of Sigmund Freud* 11 (1910), p. 96.

176 Sigmund Freud. "Leonardo Da Vinci and a Memory of his Childhood." *The Standard Edition of the Complete Psychological Works of Sigmund Freud* 11 (1910), p. 95.

177 Sigmund Freud. "Leonardo Da Vinci and a Memory of his Childhood." *The Standard Edition of the Complete Psychological Works of Sigmund Freud* 11 (1910), pp. 95–96.

community behind him—that "we have asserted that…the vulture's 'coda' cannot possibly signify anything other than a male genital, a penis".[178]

Perhaps the one crucial difference between the images of phallus-breasts and that of the phallus-penis, negated under the economy of the 'one organ', is that *the breast is always more than one*, freeing the baby from the grip of the one phallic breast, and allowing a triadic relationship.

Leonardo's Debt

In her reading of psychoanalytic texts and specifically Freud's writings, Palgi-Hecker points out the profound psychological difficulty of relating to the maternal; A difficulty that is also inherently connected to a philosophical lacuna, in which the concept of 'the mother' consistently and persistently evades theorisa- tion as a subject. The mother appears as a theoretical essence that can only be approached through biological and physical language. Palgi-Hecker draws atten- tion to what she describes as the "maternal erasure mechanism" from the realm of subjectivity leading to the mother's repeated perception in psychoanalytic theories as an object – a need-fulfilling function for the child-subject. As she explains, the challenges in conceptualising maternal subjectivity are masked by a split over- reaction in which the mother is either glorified or blamed, while a more complex image remains inaccessible.

One unexplored array of feelings sitting at the roots of this erasure, she argues, is the inability to emotionally and culturally recognise what she calls the *'the debt'* to the mother. Following Winnicott, she highlights the fact that not only the child is completely dependent on the mother but there is also an extreme diffi- culty of recognising that dependency, leading to fear of women.[179] The basic human condition – being structurally born dependant on a mother, who's devotion, care and nourishing are essential to sustain the child's life and psychic development – creates an unpayable debt. This archaic debt, which isn't processed, leads to a psychic mechanism of fragmentation, repression and denial and ultimately to the "erasure of the mother". In her analysis of Freud's texts, Palgi-Hecker identifies this inabil- ity to recognise the debt to the mother, leading to a recurring pattern of attraction and repulsion – a pull-push movement towards and from the maternal that is then projected onto the mother figure, who is portrayed as "initially seductive, then hu- miliating and ultimately erased".[180]

178 Sigmund Freud. "Leonardo Da Vinci and a Memory of his Childhood." *The Standard Edition of the Complete Psychological Works of Sigmund Freud* 11 (1910), p. 93.

179 Donald W. Winnicott. *The Child and the Family* (London: Tavistock Publications; New York: Basic Books, 1957), p. 141.

180 Anat Palgi-Hecker. *From i-mahut to Imahut* (Tel-Aviv: Am Oved, 2005), p. 16, my translation.

In one of Leonardo's elaborated accounts, he writes in orderly fashion a list of "expenses after Caterina's death for her funeral".[181] Although it is said that Leonardo never met his mother after leaving to be raised by his father, Freud suggests, following Merezhkovsky, that he met her one last time before her death and paid for her funeral expenses. This meticulously detailed account, in which Leonardo calculates his expenses after her death indicates, according to Freud, his neurotic way of engaging with his overwhelming feelings of love and desire for her, which are "distorted out of all recognition".[182] Recognising his "obsessional neurotic" way of expressing mourning, Freud does not pause to explore the question of debt, Leonardo's ancient account in relation to his mother, that was never settled and which can never be resolved. Instead, he concludes that this obsessional trait – "Leonardo's libidinal impulses finding expression in a compulsive manner and in a distorted form" – asserts his assumption that "Leonardo's erotic life did really belong to the type of homosexuality".[183]

Leonardo's case study tells us the story of an impoverished woman getting impregnated by a powerful man, who abandoned her and then forced her in some way or another to give up her child. Whether that was done with a struggle or under financial and social pressure, it occurred within a power-system in which she was an inferior in relation to the father. How did Leonardo feel in relation to his mother's struggles as a woman? Who did he identify with in the power struggle between his parents? How did he grow up as a man carrying not only the unpayable debt to the mother described by Winnicott but also the ripples of her being so wronged?

Listening to the details of Leonardo's identification with the feminine – his pleasant character, his being "gentle and kindly to everyone", as described by Freud, it is possible to imagine his identification with his mother. While Freud analyses the effect of maternal power on the child's masculinity, pointing out the peril in providing her with such a phallic image – I'd like to suggest that Leonardo's character, behaviour, inventiveness and art point to an identification with his mother's position in relation to patriarchal power. Thinking about his core beliefs of condemning "war and bloodshed", his "avoidance of all antagonism and controversy" and his refusing to eat meat "since he did not think it justifiable to deprive animals of their lives", one might speculate on his sense of guilt as a man towards his mother. Thinking about the experience of his parents' separation in the context of their power relation, it is easy to recognise his sense of the injustice done to her in his conviction that man is "not so much the king of the animal world but rather the worst of the wild beasts". His "particular pleasure in buying birds in the market and

181 Sigmund Freud. "Leonardo Da Vinci and a Memory of his Childhood." *The Standard Edition of the Complete Psychological Works of Sigmund Freud* 11 (1910), p. 104.
182 Sigmund Freud. "Leonardo Da Vinci and a Memory of his Childhood." *The Standard Edition of the Complete Psychological Works of Sigmund Freud* 11 (1910), p. 105.
183 Sigmund Freud. "Leonardo Da Vinci and a Memory of his Childhood." *The Standard Edition of the Complete Psychological Works of Sigmund Freud* 11 (1910), p. 106.

setting them free",[184] can testify to layers of shame and guilt in relation to women's caged position and his privileged position as a man.

Freud analyses Leonardo's fascination with birds and flight throughout his life as a manifestation of his restrained sexuality that he did not allow himself to experience fully. "[W]hy do so many people dream of being able to fly?" Freud asks,

> The answer that psycho-analysis gives is that to fly or to be a bird is only a disguise for another wish, and that more than one bridge, involving words or things, leads us to recognize what it is. When we consider that inquisitive children are told that babies are brought by a large bird, such as the stork; when we find that the ancients represented the phallus as having wings; that the commonest expression in German for male sexual activity is 'vögeln' ['to bird': 'Vogel' is the German for 'bird']; that the male organ is actually called 'l'uccello' ['the bird'] in Italian—all of these are only small fragments from a whole mass of connected ideas, from which we learn that in dreams the wish to be able to fly is to be understood as nothing else than a longing to be capable of sexual performance.[185]

While Freud portrays Leonardo's relation to birds as a sign of repressed masculine desire, I'd like to offer an interpretation in which Leonardo, through this identification with caged birds, identified in fact with the mother in the power relation with his father – who seduced her and then abandoned her with a child. Whereas Freud is focused in his analysis on the ominous maternal effect on the child, I'd like to offer that perhaps his memories and paintings can tell something about his mother's life and her struggles. Leonardo's gaze at the sky, this fascination of flying birds, indicates perhaps a desire to release the iron grip with which the human imprisons the body, and men oppress women, like a bird in a cage. Gazing upon the world from above the boundaries marked by men, Leonardo wishes to redraw his landscape as if on a blank canvas that has not yet been painted.

Freud's subtle textual movement, in which phallic power collapses into the male penis alone, skips the theoretical discussion about the phallic mother beyond its "danger" to masculinity – or a "mistake" that must be solved by repudiation – as an opening into the challenges of the relationship with maternal subjectivity and maternal sexuality. Although with his one hand, Freud opens the discussion about the phallic mother, with the other, he closes the possibility of pouring different meanings into this concept, in a way that will express a complex dialogue in relation to both maternal power and its removal. When describing the experience of dependency that characterises infancy, he 'skips' the mother and explains that "small human child's long-drawn-out helplessness and need of help; and when at a later date

---

184 Sigmund Freud. "Leonardo Da Vinci and a Memory of his Childhood." *The Standard Edition of the Complete Psychological Works of Sigmund Freud* 11 (1910), p. 69.

185 Sigmund Freud. "Leonardo Da Vinci and a Memory of his Childhood." *The Standard Edition of the Complete Psychological Works of Sigmund Freud* 11 (1910), pp. 125–126.

he perceives how truly forlorn and weak he is when confronted with the great forces of life".[186] When the childhood experience of helplessness and dependency arises, Freud negates the debt to the mother. He does not recognise the way it expresses itself in the relationship with the mother, rooted in an archaic dependency; a dependency that does not simply come about in the encounter "with the great forces of life", but with those of the maternal. The discussion diverts the gaze from the mother and quickly resorts to the solution in the relationship with the father.

Just as in the description of Leonardo's life, so it is in the theoretical discussions in the paper – Freud does not directly refer to the relationship with the mother, and instead, he quickly speaks of the protective father figure saving the child from a difficult and distressing childhood experiences. Although the phallic mother concept is coined, maternal power as a relational term is erased, as a result of which maternal split images are sharpened – the mother is either good and powerless or a powerful swallowing monster. Within these textual contradictions in the maternal image oscillating between the uncanny edges of desire and horror, another ambivalent textual image emerges, that of circumcision.

The Missing Wound of Circumcision

At this textual moment stimulated by the discussion of the 'phallic mother' and the symbol of the goddess Mut, Freud addresses "the puzzling psychological fact",[187] the riddle of binding together motherhood with the symbol of masculine power. How is it possible, he asks, for humans to link together these two opposites: motherhood and phallic power? Perplexed by the question, he performs a textual manoeuvre, in which, while introducing the possibility of discussing the power of the maternal, he also closes it off with an apotropaic grip of the male organ, juxtaposing the penis with the phallus.

In this discussion, Freud replaces maternal phallus with maternal lack, explaining that the possibility of absence of a male genital organ in women arouses in the child a strong fear rooted in the dread of castration. In the narrative he outlines, the dramatic observation of female genitalia leads the boy to the realisation that the penis may be "missing in other people" and castration anxiety rises in him as he imagines that "little girls too had a penis, but it was cut off and in its place was left a wound".[188] Looking at the girl's or the mother's genitalia, the child fears this 'nothing', this 'wound' as the sign of maternal castration that emerges as the first sign of sexual difference: "henceforth he will tremble for his masculinity, but at the same time he will despise the unhappy creatures on whom the cruel punishment

186 Sigmund Freud. "Leonardo Da Vinci and a Memory of his Childhood." *The Standard Edition of the Complete Psychological Works of Sigmund Freud* 11 (1910), p. 123.

187 Sigmund Freud. "Leonardo Da Vinci and a Memory of his Childhood." *The Standard Edition of the Complete Psychological Works of Sigmund Freud* 11 (1910), p. 93.

188 Sigmund Freud. "Leonardo Da Vinci and a Memory of his Childhood." *The Standard Edition of the Complete Psychological Works of Sigmund Freud* 11 (1910), p. 95.

has, as he supposes, already fallen".[189] The fear of the genital absence provokes an unbearable anxiety, which is resolved by the antidote of a protective seizing of the phallus – a terrified masculine structure continuously seeking to couple the phallus and the penis. The boy, Freud confirms, will from now on engage with an "intense desire" in "sexual research[es] with particular thoroughness" to ensure the existence of (the power of) his organ.

Yet, as Dorothée Bonnigal-Katz point out "Despite Freud's insistence of evacuating the mother from the situation…the castration the boy really fears is not his own: ultimately, it is the maternal phallus that he naturally fears for – and rightfully so".[190] Using Lacanian terms, she examines the concept of castration as deeply rooted in Freud's description of the vanishing phallic mother, depicting, in fact, the way maternal authority disappears in order to establish paternal law and patriarchal power. "What is the repressed material embedded in the obvious and senseless fact of locating maternal authority in the backstage of patriarchal power?", she asks. Recognising the gap in relation to maternal power, which is both obvious truth and uncannily nonsensical, she highlights its reappropriation by the "glorified paternal" as a fundamental structure of the perceived transition from omnipotence to castration. This movement creates the maternal, as a result, as a 'monster', that cannot be approached or looked at.

The strong opposition that arises from Leonardo's case study between the power of maternal phallus and her weakness as a woman, testify to this neglected theoretical realm – which cannot be approached or explored as the focus of Freud's text, and later on psychoanalysis, is shifted to a structural position that can only see maternal ominous effect on the child's masculinity, and to the necessary reality of her lack. This shift in the simulacrum of power from the mother to the father can be observed not only in the analysis of the child's psychic life but also in the textual movement itself. In response to the coupling of the "mark of male potency" with the maternal, Freud continues with his own textual coupling and adds a footnote concerning circumcision:

> The conclusion strikes me as inescapable that here we may also trace one of the roots of the anti-semitism which appears with such elemental force and finds such irrational expression among the nations of the West. Circumcision is unconsciously equated with castration. If we venture to carry our conjectures back to the primaeval days of the human race we can surmise that originally circumcision must have been a milder substitute, designed to take the place of castration.[191]

---

189 Sigmund Freud. "Leonardo Da Vinci and a Memory of his Childhood." *The Standard Edition of the Complete Psychological Works of Sigmund Freud* 11 (1910), p. 95.

190 Dorothée Bonnigal-Katz. "From Medusa to Kronos: The Fragile Illusion of the Maternal Phallus." *Psychoanal. Cult. Soc.* 25 (2020): 114–121.

191 Sigmund Freud. "Leonardo Da Vinci and a Memory of his Childhood." *The Standard Edition of the Complete Psychological Works of Sigmund Freud* 11 (1910), p. 95.

The rising and pervasive antisemitic feelings, Freud explains, are rooted in human history, at the beginning of which circumcision was a *real* substitute for castration. Thus, these emotions contain a transhistorical, phylogenetic component surfacing in the child's (the boy's) developmental process, in which the universal fear of the castrating father is embedded, leading the (male) child to carefully preserve his genital organ, protect it, hold firmly to his masculinity and develop feelings of hatred towards others whose genital organ is "lacking".

It seems that the same panic that Freud describes in the child's psyche is also reproduced in the text itself, rushing to pair the phallus with the penis and to mark the separation between the masculine and the feminine, between the haves and the have-nots. Alongside this movement that both theorises and displays a fragile masculinity structure of defending the phallus-penis attachment, the footnote is initiating a denial of maternal phallus as a paternal origin is anchored. Since "the primaeval days of the human race", Freud explains, the fear originated in paternal *real* castration – a narrative that disconnects any power from the maternal, leaving her merely as an object.

If the image of the phallic mother is a projection of omnipotence onto her – why is the image of her castration cannot similarly be seen as a projection as well? If the phallus is the symbol of the vanishing power, why is the coupling of the phallus with the male genital organ, not another projection of omnipotence rooted in the negation of dependency on the mother? Although both maternal omnipotence and maternal castration are projections originating in the child's variety of feelings and phantasies in relation to maternal power, Freud anchors one side (omnipotence) in the wrong and the other (castration) in the right; one side becomes a "confused phantasy" of the child and the other is understood as the mature realisation of reality.

In this textual moment, through the use of circumcision, the patriarchal phallocentric perspective becomes the only possible one – it is both transhistorical and all-encompassing. In the early days of humanity, Freud explains, circumcision was a substitute for castration. Circumcision – also translated from Hebrew as the covenant of the word – is the symbolic representation of the actual castration and a reminder of an unconscious primal anxiety at the base of human (masculine) existence. It is the gateway into the symbolic and language itself, a super-signifier that represents castration anxiety as an 'ancient' element, through which the primacy of patriarchal phallocentric gaze is established. Both castration and circumcision could have been different representations of partiality in the encounter with the other, however, through their coupling with the masculine sexual organ, the rope is tightened around the Oedipal dominance, or rather, around the neck of the mother. Circumcision emerges as a universal moment of panic in the encounter with the other, initiating a phallic gaze that will search to defend its masculinity. This point in the text signifies Freud's inversion and solidifies the existence of castration of the male organ as primal causality for all relational forms.

The comment concerning circumcision did not appear in the original text itself but was added in the margin of the page, in a footnote, ten years later in 1919. As Jonte-Pace explains, a footnote marks a 'hole' in the text, and the later addition of the footnote indicates that a dimension remained open and turbulent in the textual unconscious.[192] Ten years after writing the text, Freud returns to this 'hole' in order to place circumcision – the (masculine) covenant of the word – at the moment of encountering maternal phallus. In this footnote, he provides an answer to maternal phallus and her ability to 'cut' in the form of the castrating father. In the place of (the boy's) wounded partiality in the encounter with another (the mother), he projects the wound onto the genital of the other (the feminine or the Jew), a movement through which symbolic meanings of both castration and circumcision are reduced to the actual wounded genitals, placing in particular, maternal lack instead of her power. By adding this footnote, Freud positions circumcision, like a tombstone on a grave, as a mark indicating that something is buried underneath. Yet at the same time, it remains guarding, preventing the mother from reaching out from beneath the surface, prohibiting the return of the repressed.

In the process of childhood development described by Freud, circumcision is a signifier of the eternal existence of castration anxiety and therefore becomes a super-signifier of paternal power. At this moment, the encounter with the other takes place not only in relation to the phallus (and thus to the question of where power is located) but also through providing an answer (and only one answer) to this question by attaching the symbolic phallus to the male genital organ. While the phallus represents the symbolic and thus the vanishing power as an always deferred position, the masculine (and textual) panic movement collapses the gap that characterises the symbolic by clinging onto the male genitalia. Through the preoccupation with circumcision (both textual and psychic), the encounter with the other becomes an event of protection of the male organ as a phallus, anxiously projecting the phallus again, this time onto the penis itself.

According to Freud, in an encounter with women or with Jews, feelings of contempt are awakened towards the unfortunate creature –women as well as Jews – whose "cruel punishment has... already fallen",[193] and fate has already robbed him/her of that organ. Being an event that arouses an eternal anxiety of the castrating father, any encounter with an other will become one that takes place under a phallocentric gaze, projecting castration onto the other and holding on to the masculine organ. This is no longer one interpretation among many, but the moment in which the curtain is drawn on the possibility of an open, curious and developing encounter with others beyond oneself. Whereas the discussion of the 'phallic mother' opens the door to an encounter with others through which the self can recognise his or her own partiality and symbolic castration, the image of circumcision in its coupling to castration establishes the phallic power as one that is attached only to the male genitalia positioning castration anxiety as a transhistorical dimension only through which the subject encounters the other.

192 Diane Jonte-Pace. *Speaking the Unspeakable: Religion, Misogyny, and the Uncanny Mother in Freud's Cultural Texts* (Berkeley: University of California Press, 2001).

193 Sigmund Freud. "Leonardo Da Vinci and a Memory of his Childhood." *The Standard Edition of the Complete Psychological Works of Sigmund Freud* 11 (1910), p. 95.

While the concept of the 'phallic mother' grants the maternal with phallic image that can both separate and penetrate, recognising that this maternal other can detach herself from the child, the shifting of the gaze towards paternal castration connotes the maternal to the immediacy of the real. By solidifying castration as a mythical dimension that occurred by the paternal ancestor in the early days of humanity, Freud links the primacy of the father's power to his writings in *Totem and Taboo* and later in *Moses and Monotheism*, engendering circumcision as the symbol that signifies paternal primacy and the fear of the father. "[W]e can surmise that originally", Freud writes, in "the primaeval days of the human race…circumcision must have been a milder substitute, designed to take the place of castration". Thus, connecting individual developmental process (as in the story of Leonardo) to the history of the Jewish people (*Moses and monotheism*) and the development of human culture as a whole (*Totem and Taboo*), through the image of circumcision, Freud grants paternal castration a primeval status that encompasses all, transferring the difficult and ambivalent feelings from the (phallic) mother to the image of father threatening with castration.

In this way, Freud explains not only antisemitic sentiments but also misogyny, repudiation of the maternal and contempt towards women. He points out the way in which the encounter with the other – the Jew as well as the woman – takes place from a worldview that pivots around the male genital organ, as a sort of 'negative hallucination': a psychic process that denies the existence of an object or an other. This psychic phenomenon of 'negative hallucination' was linked by Freud to hysterical massive repression that occurs when an unbearable reality cannot be perceived.[194] This process creates a hole, a gap in the place of the erased object that is then 'glued' onto that other, i.e., – the missing organ of the mother. The partiality of the self that is revealed in an encounter with an other will be projected onto that other and marked as his or her 'absence'.

Freud indeed portrays this process in detail, yet he too repeats a similar textual movement, attaching psychoanalytic blind spot through a phallocentric gaze to the 'genitals of the other'. From this textual moment on, the discussion of the maternal relates to her 'lack' and the emotional experience in the face of that object, or rather that subject – an existence beyond the self, is translated into a 'wound', a cut that has already occurred in (m)other's genitals. Clinging to the penis as a defence, might be read as a description of the 'negative hallucination' and the hysterical response of the (male) child in the face of the maternal other but in portraying it as the only route for development, leading psychoanalysis to the Oedipal metaphor as a sole theoretical possibility in the encounter with the other/maternal, Freud denies, this time on the level of theory, psychoanalytic discussion of this relationship.

---

194 Sigmund Freud. "Delusions and Dreams in Jensen's 'Gradiva'." In: James Strachey (ed. & trans.) *The Standard Edition of the Complete Psychological Works of Sigmund Freud* 9 (1907): 7–95. London: The Hogarth Press and the Institute of Psycho-Analysis, 1959.

Failing to step beyond the binary oppositions, the blind spot of psychoanalysis is produced at the location of refusing that challenge in the encounter with a new worldview, a different morphology. In the analysis of Leonardo, Freud negates Leonardos' conflicted emotional debt as a man towards his mother, skipping the opportunity to explore his matricidal conflict. In the context of the obvious power relation between the parents, the absence of clinically exploring and theoretically recognising the psychic intricacies of his privileged position in relation to her is quite jarring. Instead, he collaborates with masculine hysterical coupling of the phallus and the penis, depicting the mother as a monster that will rob of his masculinity due to 'her lack'.

In response to a question about the phallic mother, the text condense circumcision and castration, thus repeats the binarism that splits – using the male genitalia – between the masculine and the feminine, turning the gaze away from the possibility of exploring the 'phallic mother' with all its possible symbolic meanings. At the same time, this textual movement exposes a masculine 'wound' as a key-fossil that momentarily blurs the familiar dichotomy between the sexes. The 'phallic mother', the Egyptian goddess Mut and the androgynous image reveal an encounter with maternal power which exposes at the same time, the wound of the male subject – a forbidden vulnerability un/covered in the text through the relic of circumcision.

From the encounter with maternal power, the textual gaze is shifted towards her lack, outlining a normal developmental process as an Oedipalisation in which the child internalises the privilege of the male organ, affiliating any source of power to the actual penis. Irigaray's conceptualisation of the *'logic of sameness'* enables an in-depth exploration of this process of negation, in which the maternal 'is' is replaced by her 'absence' of male sexual organ. Attaching the male sexual organ to the phallus, any encounter with an other can be denied, or reduced through a comparison with the penis-self to a hole, a lack that confirms the phallic-penile-masculinity as a sole possible existence.

Irigaray and the Gaze at (the Organ of) the Mother

Irigaray's project of reading Freud's and Lacan's psychoanalytic texts is one of the central enterprises of feminist psychoanalysis. In her analysis, she examines the historical determinants of the psychoanalytic discourse, revealing the way, despite presenting as scientific and universal, it is embedded in phallocentric conceptions.[195] Language, according to Irigaray, is shaped in the image to the male body, particularly that of the male genital organ – One, Rigid, Visible. Through this image, women are excluded and silenced, or framed by feminine stereotypes of having nothing; produced as the negation of that masculine ideal. Thus, Masculine

---

195 Luce Irigaray. *Speculum of the Other Woman* (Translated by Gillian C. Gill, Ithaca: Cornell University Press, 1985a); Luce Irigaray. *Marine Lover of Friedrich Nietzsche* (Translated by Gillian C. Gil. New York: Colombia University Press, 1991); Luce Irigaray. *I Love to You: Sketch of a Possible Felicity in History* (Trans. Alison Martin. New York: Routledge, 1996).

subjectivity develops through woman's imprisonment in the instinctual and emotional chaos of the body and through their positioning as a negative to the representation of the masculine ideal. For Irigaray, the phallomorphism of discourse is not an intrinsic attribute of language itself but rather a symptom of a culture that denies difference, in which the feminine is erased in an obsessive preoccupation with the image of the male organ, excluding multiplicity and difference. Under this *'one'* image, aspects that are characteristic of female sexuality – the polymorphic body, multiple sexuality, maternal transformations and openness – are all prevented from crossing the threshold into language and therefore the possibility of creating symbolic alternatives is denied.[196]

In her writing, Irigaray criticises Western culture that constitutes itself by excluding the feminine from the symbolic-social order. She exposes the structure of subjectivity as formed through a masculine monologic structure that divides the world into categories, which are either identity or negation with the 'one' logic and does not recognise difference beyond negation.[197] Under this perception, the subject is constructed through what she calls the *'logic of sameness'* – an all-embracing process of perception and conceptualisation in which otherness can only be understood by being measured against the self. This 'logic of sameness' is symbolically and intrinsically linked to an imagery of the ideal of the masculine, and therefore creates the feminine as its negation. Western culture, Irigaray argues, from Plato to Freud, speaks a language that only recognises one subject, the masculine, and thus, does not acknowledge a non-oppositional sexual difference. Men are perceived as the only subject with consciousness and meaning, while women are the other, the object, a supportive and invisible entity. Every encounter with otherness is reduced to a familiar pattern under which the spectrum of subjectivities is solidified into a pre-set concept created through comparison with the familiar 'one'.[198]

In the analysis of Leonardo, Freud explains that when a male child turns his curiosity to the riddle of sexuality, he is led by his interest in his own penis:

He finds that part of his body too valuable and too important for him to be able to believe that it could be missing in other people whom he feels he resembles so much. As he cannot guess that there exists another type of genital structure of equal worth, he is forced to make the assumption that all human beings, women as well as men, possess a penis like his own.[199]

196 Luce Irigaray. *This Sex Which Is Not One* (Ithaca, NY: Cornell University Press, 1985b).
197 Luce Irigaray. *An Ethics of Sexual Difference* (Trans. Gillian Gill and Carolyn Burke. Ithaca: Cornell University Press, 1993).
198 Luce Irigaray. *Speculum of the Other Woman* (Translated by Gillian C. Gill, Ithaca: Cornell University Press, 1985a); Luce Irigaray. *This Sex Which Is Not One* (Ithaca, NY: Cornell University Press, 1985b).
199 Sigmund Freud. "Leonardo Da Vinci and a Memory of his Childhood." *The Standard Edition of the Complete Psychological Works of Sigmund Freud* 11 (1910), p. 95.

At the beginning of his life, Freud argues, the child (the male child) encounters the world through the familiarity of his own body, and since he sees himself as the measuring standard for the external world, he cannot conceive the existence of difference, attributing all people, including women, a similar sexual organ as his. For Irigaray, this phallocentric assumption establishes a circular movement between the gaze (childhood curiosity, searching to understand the world) and the male genitalia. While investigating otherness, it also anchors the phallocentric view of the world as primary and thus erasing this otherness under the logic of sameness. For the male child and, in turn, for psychoanalysis, the starting point for (understanding) childhood sexuality, as conceptualised by Freud, stems from the male sexual organ through which the child recognises the world. This, in turn, becomes the starting point for psychoanalysis, that anchors its investigations of sexuality in the male sexual organ.

Irigaray uses the imagery of *the speculum* to illustrate how Western philosophical discourse, and Freud specifically, relies on the logic of sameness. The speculum is a gynaecological instrument used to examine female genitalia. For Irigaray, it represents a mirror that reflects in reverse everything standing before it: an instrument with a phallic morphology designed to penetrate the mysteries of womanhood but approaches the encounter with the female (genitalia) through its inherent masculine morphology. It is a means of exploring the feminine, but the image of the male organ is inherently guiding the gaze and the ability to look at women. In this way, under the guise of a scientific neutral investigation, Irigaray explains, Freud looks at women as a man looks in a mirror or as Narcissus is gazing at his reflection, seeing only himself. As a result, he is unable to give expression to any meaningful or symbolic aspects in the feminine, but only as a contrast to the masculine, her 'nothingness' reflects his phallic possession, and her 'absence' reveals his presence.

Irigaray begins her book with Freud's formulation of the riddle of femininity (in Freud's *"femininity"*) and critically examines his arguments using the concept of speculum. She points out that his interpretation of femininity and sexual difference rests on a premise of sameness in which phallic morphology is a starting point for both the masculine and the feminine. The male child, according to Freud's interpretation, looks at his mother through his genitals, and encounters the other through an approximation to a familiar morphology. For Irigaray, this text is revealing the economy of representations underlying the Oedipal house of cards: a desire and search for the familiar structure, the repetition of a similar masculine identity, homo-auto-eroticism, the gaze from the logic of sameness that repeatedly prevents a genuine and curious encounter with an other beyond oneself.

The Freudian interpretation analyses the relationship with the mother from a phallocentric perspective in which the child identifies the world through a male gaze. When he looks at the mother or her genitals, he can only see himself, terrified that the sign of masculinity will be taken from him, and therefore giving her the penis he loves so much. The possibility of difference arouses in the child the panic, which, according to Freud, is due to the fact that the "mother's wound" reminds the child of the existence of castration. Whereas for Freud, castration relates to the possibility that the male organ will be taken away from Irigaray's perspective, an alternative apprehension arises for that fear of 'absence'. This appearance, which has 'nothing' in it, may, she argues, represent a different morphology, an existence that does not align with sameness in any way. As such, this encounter with difference challenges the singularity of the Oedipal metaphor and the totality of the phallic image, portraying it as a monologic representation lacking a regulating system. Opening into an alternative existence, it may serve as a signifier for a different libidinal economic system, an otherness not yet recognised in the discourse of desire. When a man looks at a woman through the phallus, she claims, he indeed sees nothing, she has nothing resembling a penis, or that may be a substitute for the male genitalia. The phallocentric gaze cannot recognise difference, or rather – its anxiety response is an attempt to negate difference, as a result of which it must consolidate otherness as nothing. Thus, the feminine becomes a representation of nothingness, and remains as an inverted mirror to the only essence possible – that of the male organ.

Freud defines the 'phallic mother' phantasy as a temporary stage that children must overcome in their psychosexual development. He frames the discussion of maternal power as a danger to Leonardo's sexuality, focusing on the absent father in his early years. Instead of exploring the effect of the mother's absence from his life, he quickly moves to discuss her physical lack ('absence'). According to him, the young child in his early years does not yet recognise 'reality' – that women have 'nothing', outlining the process by which the child understands the 'absence' (of male genitalia) of the mother as an essential stage in psychosexual development. The solution to this 'impossible' encounter with maternal power and otherness lies in an Oedipal process of grasping the phallus and attaching it to the actual male sexual organ. Through this Oedipalisation process masculinity remains an unstable identity that must keep on chasing its own tail for validation, continually denying any encounter with otherness.[200]

While Freud marks the child's view of the world as emerging from the male sexual organ, Irigaray shifts the focus to the conflict that arises at the encounter with the other. She explores the fear, the panic, the uncanny feelings that arise in encountering the feminine or maternal lack: What is so threatening and paralyzing in an encounter with something that does not exist? – she asks. The existence of a different structure of desire outside the phallocentric system of representations collapses, she argues, the exclusivity of the phallus and takes masculine desire out of its two-dimensional structure, adding a third point and creating a space for movement. The panic arises due to the possibility of an encounter with an other that does not echo the familiar logic of sameness, an encounter between two which might lead to a recognition of the partiality of the self. An understanding that the male genital organ is not the only essence, introduces the masculine to an existence

---

200 Luce Irigaray. *Speculum of the Other Woman* (Translated by Gillian C. Gill, Ithaca: Cornell University Press, 1985a).

beyond the self, presenting an existence of a power that is not coupled to the penis. The castration complex, Irigaray continues, is operating to escape otherness and relationship between the sexes, reducing emotional complexity to a binary pattern of one organ and its negation. The definition of female sexual organs as 'lack' is a censorship on the encounters with otherness, with a non-phallic morphology, representing a different structure of desire.

If the essence of masculinity is clinging to the male genitalia as the only source of power, then Freud is right in his analysis that continuing to believe the phantasy of the phallic mother will rob the child of what he describes as normal masculine sexual development, since recognising another power that is not coupled to the actual penis collapses the Oedipal house of cards. Holding on to the possibility of maternal phallus separates the phallus as a signifier from the actual male penis and therefore dismantles the exclusivity of phallic power as existing only in men. Although the morphology of that authority might be similar, as in the image of Mut, the possibility of detaching it from the concrete penis opens the door to other images of power enabling the phallus to develop and move away from the image of only one organ.

Just before the image of the goddess Mut emerges in the text, following Leonardo's memory, Freud pauses to recognise that the bird's beak, although carrying phallic morphology represents breastfeeding. The phallic power of nursing arises in the text prior to Freud's chain of association leading the readers into the realm of maternal phallus beyond the male organ. This textual opening does not lead to further exploration of this encounter with maternal power, and Freud seals his conclusions with the Oedipal narrative and castration complex.

From Irigaray's perspective, the castration complex is an unsuccessful solution of encountering the other, and Oedipal masculinity is seen as a psychic construct rooted in defensive refusal to recognise otherness beyond the self: facing the challenge inherent in the encounter with femininity, female sexuality is marked as castrated; faced with a different morphology, Freud defines it as absent. Instead of an encounter with otherness outside the phallocentric system of representations, Freudian analysis portrays a hole, a missing organ, nothingness. A circular contract is written, Irigaray explains, between visual dominance and the 'One' genital organ, identifying the feminine with its inversion: "The contract, the collusion between one sex/organ and the victory won by visual dominance therefore leaves woman with her sexual void, with an 'actual castration' carried out in actual fact".[201] The impossibility of seeing, as she explains, is transformed into a conclusion that women *have nothing*. A man looking at a woman through the male organ cannot see beyond himself, thus declaring: the problem is not in the gaze, but in the actual lack of the female organ, projecting his blind spot onto women.

The panic of the phallocentric gaze in encountering (the absent male sexual organ of) the mother arises from the fact that the encounter with otherness requires

---

201 Luce Irigaray. *Speculum of the Other Woman* (Translated by Gillian C. Gill, Ithaca: Cornell University Press, 1985a), p. 48.

recognition of self-partiality, breaking the dominance of male monologic representation. As Irigaray explains, the fear of the feminine stems from the fear of recognising the partiality of the male subject – a recognition inherent to every encounter with difference outside the logic of sameness. Acknowledging the existence of a different worldview and an essence beyond the self, shatters the centrality and exclusivity of male phalomorphism. It opens the door to exploring femininity beyond the immediate response of framing difference under the logic of sameness: negating it by either reducing the other to the complete opposite of the 'one' or, alternatively, by 'swallowing' the other, incorporating her into the realm of the subject. Thinking about sexual difference enables Irigaray to conceptualise difference beyond negation and, in her later writings, to revive the imagery of the female body in language.

This perspective of Irigaray and her description of the phallocentric encounter with otherness essentially turns Freud's theoretic bowl upside down: Whereas Freud claims that the child explores the world according to his familiar body and sexual organ, Irigaray's conceptualisation reveals that clinging onto the penis-phallus is not primary but produced as a defensive response to the encounter with otherness and to the possibility of self-partiality. For her, it is a resistance to an open dialogue with otherness, stemming from the fear of the challenges inherent in an encounter between two who are not one. Grasping onto the male sexual organ is a response to the developmental challenge of maternal power, which requires to work through both dependency and vulnerability in relation to the mother, who has the power to both nourish and cut. While Freud interprets castration fear, as the primary fear of losing the penis that shapes the attitude toward the other, Irigaray's perspective reveals the possibility that it is precisely the attitude toward the other, or the difficulty in this encounter with the (m)other, that leads to the development of the Oedipal narrative and castration complex.

A similar interpretation can be applied to the textual movement in the case study of Leonardo in which the encounter with the 'phallic mother' directly leads the readers from maternal power to her lack, from the vulnerability and dependency in the relationship with the mother to the relationship with her 'absence' – a movement that can be interpreted as defence in the encounter with maternal subjectivity. In this textual process, the image of circumcision is a key-signifier that both reveals and conceals the 'wound'. From this perspective, the 'absence' of the mother or her lack is revealed as negative hallucination, a reversal of the partiality of the subject, projected onto the mother. The 'lack' of the female sexual organ is an expression of a discourse that marks the body, of which an (m)otherness has been stolen – the nothingness projected onto the mother's body is a symptom expressing what is erased in the psychoanalytic discourse itself.

Textual Fossilisations

Irigaray's conceptualisations reveal the way in which the inability to bear the partiality of the self in the face of an (m)other, the difficulty of recognising difference beyond negation, leads to the projection of 'absence' onto women's body.

This view allows for an in-depth exploration of the textual anxiety in the theoretical encounter with the 'phallic mother' and can be dwelled on a little more through what Freud himself writes about the uncanny effect, in his 1919 essay.[202] The anxiety arising in the text, (following the key-fossil – the image of circumcision), involves a similar kind of terror, a petrifying feeling that can only be described by the word *unheimlich*.

As Freud explains, the psychic meanings of the uncanny can be derived, from the etymology of the German word unheimlich, which contains both the home and its opposite, introducing the subject to the experience of alienation in the known and familiar, and to the moment of strangeness in what is supposed to be close and intimate, in the homely. These two contradictory opposites are intertwined in the German word *unheimlich* in which the homely (*Heimlich*) slowly absorbs the meanings inherent in its opposite, unheimlich until "it finally coincides with its opposite".[203] As Ernst Jentsch argues, "It is an old experience that the traditional, the usual and the hereditary is dear and familiar to most people, and that they incorporate the new and the unusual with mistrust, unease and even hostility".[204] While the familiar and the known evoke a sense of comfort, and the new and unknown evoke an experience of discomfort, uncanny feeling of anxiety emerges from intertwined situations in which uncertainty and novelty creep into the old and familiar.[205]

Both *circumcision* and the image of the *phallic mother* evoke the uncanny due to blurring of familiar boundaries between the masculine and the feminine, allowing both vulnerability in the masculine and phallic power in the feminine, and thus, challenging the rigidity of gender binary of the Oedipal schism between sexes. Irigaray's perspective and her writing on the "logic of sameness" further develop this understanding of the uncanny anxiety in the face of the maternal: the uncanny experience arises when the mother is revealed as a subject which is not completely swallowed into the world of the self. She is no longer a transparent familiar existence but a subject beyond the self, with power and otherness, introducing the child-subject to the challenge of difference and thus marking their partiality. Releasing the grip of the male penis (and the insistence on castration anxiety as the sole reason for the awakening of uncanny feelings), an alternative meaning

202 Sigmund Freud. "The Uncanny." In: James Strachey (ed. & trans.) *The Standard Edition of the Complete Psychological Works of Sigmund Freud 17* (1919): 217–256. London: The Hogarth Press and the Institute of Psycho-Analysis, 1955.

203 Sigmund Freud. "The Uncanny." *The Standard Edition of the Complete Psychological Works of Sigmund Freud* 17 (1919), p. 226.

204 Ernst Jentsch. "On the Psychology of the Uncanny". 1906. Translated by Roy Sellars, *Angelaki: Journal of the Theoretical Humanities* 2, no. 1 (1995): 7–16. p. 4.

205 This thesis of the uncanny experience arising in intermediate states of uncertainty and ambiguity is introduced in Freud's paper following Ernst Jentsch's essay. Freud discusses this thesis but ultimately (once again) rules in favour of castration anxiety as the origin of the uncanny. Although he concludes that the uncanny experience originates in the fear of the father, his essay also leads to other less explored realms of the maternal dimension.

emerges from the text – a moment of encounter with an other, which brings with it a terrifying opening into the subject's partiality.

"No-one in the world is surprised under usual circumstances when he sees the sun rise in the morning", Jentsch writes.[206] One cannot expect any surprise from the sun that will certainly reappear tomorrow and the following day, and therefore there is no reason to wonder about it, to question its existence, to be curious about it. Under phallocentric economy, in which the entire world of 'being' is created through placing the boundary line (un), only two ways of existence are possible in relation to the other: to absorb the other into one's own world as familiar, completely swallowed – with no need for further curiosity – or to place it beyond oneself as an absolute other, a radical otherness which can only be represented as negation or 'nothingness'. Both movements are but one as they both stem from the logic of sameness leaving the worldview unchanged, without realising the challenge and potential in the encounter with an other. While under phallocentric view, the alien-familiar contrast constitutes a dichotomy – two lingual meanings, each in opposition to the other through the prefix of negation un (un/Heimlich) – the uncanny sensation is provoked in moments of blurred boundaries in which radical difference is undermined, revealing that otherness is neither totally othered nor completely swallowed by the subject.

In contrast to the binary view, in which otherness can only be radically different, encountered through negation, Irigaray presents an alternative philosophical perspective into difference, in particular, sexual difference.[207] Challenging the meaning of difference as dichotomous, she opens a space for difference as two dynamic beings, which are essentially infinite, open to each other and to the world. She portrays a relationship between two in which subjectivity is a process of continuous becoming through difference and otherness. Driven by the sense of their own partiality, these two beings are continuously curious about each other and do not approach the other through sameness and comparison to oneself, as Freud describes in the text, but precisely through the understanding that there is another worldview outside the familiar that cannot be narrowed under a system of pre-known concepts.

Freud analyses the uncanny petrification through the mythological story of '*Medusa*' explaining that primordial fear as a product of castration anxiety overwhelms the subject when gazing at the mother's genitalia.[208] Looking at the Medusa, with her snake-like hair and petrifying gaze, a man turns, out of terror, into a stone – hardening like the erected penis and clinging onto his phallic organ.

206 Ernst Jentsch. *On the Psychology of the Uncanny* (Translated by Roy Sellars, 1906), p. 4.

207 Luce Irigaray. *An Ethics of Sexual Difference* (Trans. Gillian Gill and Carolyn Burke. Ithaca: Cornell University Press, 1993); Luce Irigaray. *I Love to You: Sketch of a Possible Felicity in History* (Trans. Alison Martin. New York: Routledge, 1996).

208 Sigmund Freud. "Medusa's Head." *The Standard Edition of the Complete Psychological Works of Sigmund Freud* 1718 (1922), pp. 273–274.

The petrification and display of the erected male penis is an apotropaic movement, an act of preserving and protecting what has not yet been lost.

It is interesting to think about what Irigaray defines as the circular 'contract' between visual dominance and the 'one' genital organ, in relation to the image of Medusa, whose sight generates anxiety and petrification, and whose hair symbolise, according to Freud, castration complex and the 'lack' of female genitalia. Why is it in her sight of all things – the encounter with her eyes – that turns men into stone? And how does Medusa's impossible gaze relate to her representation of masculine fear of the female genitalia?

"You only have to look at the Medusa straight on to see her. And she's not deadly". Cixous writes, "She's beautiful and she's laughing".[209] Cixous's writing, like Irigaray's theory, does not recoil with fear at the face of the phallus' disappearing act, but rather she is able to step beyond the 'nothingness' of women and explore the panicked projection that occurs at the moment of encounter, through the complexity of the mythological story. Perseus 'overpowered' the Medusa by not gazing into her eyes, blocking the encounter with a shield or a mirror, or perhaps – to borrow Irigaray's metaphor – with a speculum. The mirror held in front of her can only allow Medusa to see masculine projections. She does not see her own face, but rather a reflection of the terrifying image projected onto the feminine in relation to the phallus.

What is so frightening about Medusa, Cixous asks, that men cannot face her face? In her early life, Medusa was a beautiful young woman who was raped in one of Athena's temples by Poseidon. Athena punished Medusa by exiling her and transforming her beautiful hair into horrible snakes. The blame for the terrible act was projected by the sovereign on Medusa, transforming her into a monster the eyes of whom no man can encounter. From this moment on, looking at her face, her eyes, her piercing glare would turn any man into stone expressing the petrifying encounter with the layers of guilt and shame. The petrifying shame of the abuser evoked by the traumatic memory of those who harmed – and not only harmed, both raped and then blackened, erased her existence – turned her memory into a monster.

While the prevailing view focuses on Medusa as a representation of the castrated woman – a symbol of the female sex organ and the primal fear it arouses in men who gaze upon it – Cixous presents the possibility that she is beautiful and laughing. In doing so, she raises questions about the masculine fear as an aspect projected onto women. Laughing in the face of her monstrous representation, she rejects and returns the projections imposed onto her, liberating the playful and creative aspect of the feminine.

Thus, beneath the terror of the mother's 'nothingness' emerges an uncanny feeling that stems from the difficulty of turning the probing-nosal inwards, looking inside to encounter the subject's own partiality, and working through layers

---

209   Hélène Cixous. "The Laugh of the Medusa." *Signs* 1, no. 4 (1976): 875–893, 885.

of shame and guilt. In Leonardo's case, Freud's preoccupation with the 'phallic mother' might be an intuitive response to the unspoken question of the relationship between the parents in the text. Freud indeed recognises the weak social position of the mother, who was seduced – to put it gently – by the father who was a man of status, money and power. With no social premise to refuse, she was then abandoned and rejected, left to raise the child in poverty on her own, before having the child taken from her. Resonating the story of Medusa, the textual movement interestingly portrays the mother in the inner world of the child as a monster that is a peril to his masculinity. While Freud is focused on the mother-monster's overbearing effect on Leonardo's psychic development, I listened to the story his personality and psychic position can reveal about his mother and her emotional struggles within the power relations of her life. Leonardo's personality and character reveal the conflicted stance of a man who is aware of the danger in his own privileged position, who is imbued with guilt in relation to his power, and who can recognise his debt to his mother.

Similarly to Cixous, Bracha Lichtenberg Ettinger delves into the uncanny effect projected onto women. She broadens the discourse on the maternal creating a new language rich in imagery originating from maternal body. Her theoretical framework rethinks subjectivity through what she describes as "matrixial border space" – a border space of differentiation-in-co-emergence, separation-in-jointness and distance-in-proximity.[210] This imagery of an in-between space of co-emergence is a powerful image of encounter with an other in which there is neither absorption nor alienation of the other. It is a space where castration has not yet occurred, allowing for psychic possibilities of coexistence at the border between symbiosis and separation. This perspective opens the door to thinking about the maternal beyond familiar terms of absolute symbiosis, through the uncanny transformative space where ambiguous boundaries and blurred lines enable a field of relationships, where the self and the other are intertwined but also, at the same time, distinct.[211]

Ettinger refers to the gap between the post-Oedipal perception of the mother and that which is made possible through the matrixial space. She apprehends, in its wake, the uncanny anxiety that arises after the Oedipal castration has already occurred, leaving behind the maternal space again – as a monster: as an incestuous dimension associated with death that continues to lure into symbiotic fusion, signifying the loss of subjectivity. Once subjects learn to identify themselves through categories of separation (and the male sex organ), symbolic castration surges as a

---

210 Bracha Lichtenberg Ettinger. "Matrixial Trans-Subjectivity." *Theor. Cul. Soc.* 23 (2006): 2–3; Bracha Lichtenberg Ettinger. "The Sublime and Beauty beyond Uncanny Anxiety." In: F. Dombois, U.M. Bauer, C. Marais, and M. Schwab (eds.) *Intellectual Birdhouse. Artistic Practice as Research* (London: Koening Books, 2012).

211 Bracha Lichtenberg Ettinger. "The Feminine/Prenatal Weaving in the Matrixial Subjectivity-as-Encounter." *Psychoanal. Dial.* VII, no. 3 (1997): 363–405; Bracha Lichtenberg Ettinger, "Matrix and Metamorphosis Metramorphosis." In: *Trouble in the Archives*, Special issue of *Differences*, 4, no. 3: 176–208, Bloomington: Indiana University Press, 1992.

defence against the possibility of a threatening and impossible encounter with the maternal, with its imagery connection between the womb and the tomb.

Like the encounter with Medusa's eyes, a process of petrification can be identified in the textual clinging onto the phallus arising from the conflict vis-à-vis the mother's face. Freud's text illustrates the difficulty of looking beyond 'nothingness' at the face of the mother, encountering an unbearable debt in the relationship with maternal subjectivity. As in Medusa's story, every time her gaze appears, Freud holds on to an Oedipal narrative, with a petrified refusal to look beyond the masculine self-existence. With every reminder of the partiality of the self, of the experience of shame, vulnerability or internal lack – the maternal is blackened, maternal subjectivity erased and the gaze is diverted to the male phallus-penis in order to hold onto it. The maternal is quickly covered with phallic part objects and with a stroke of the pen, the Oedipal answer erects as the only possible explanation.

It is not for nothing that Freud calls circumcision *a fossil* in his investigations. It marks the mausoleum created by encountering a wound; a living dimension so petrified that it turns into stone echoing the effect provoked in response to the gaze of the Medusa. With a growing urge to both look and not look at the 'missing organ', Freud chooses a third path – grasping onto a male organ as a fetish, which enables the subject to look without seeing. Fossilised by uncanny anxiety, the subject holds onto the phallic object and denies the conflicted experience underneath. The terrifying encounter with the maternal dimension – a dimension in which boundaries are blurred and through which otherness steps beyond complete negation, leads psychoanalysis to the Oedipal defence concealing the conflict in relation to maternal subjectivity by grabbing the phallic-part object in repetition. Although Freud describes this process in relation to Medusa's gaze and her snake-like hair, in which "the multiplication of phallic symbols" (the Medusa's hair),[212] is both a defence and a reminder of castration (and self-partiality), a similar movement occurs in his Leonardo text. As he both describes and repeats in the textual movement, a repetition of the Oedipal coupling of the phallus-penis functions as a grave-stone to what is buried underneath. Thus, through aligning circumcision with the Oedipal castration complex, vulnerability is projected onto the maternal and the conflict is negated by repeatedly shifting the gaze towards the relationship with the father. Maternal dimension becomes the forbidden aspect against which the terror of castration and the Oedipal narrative emerge as the only answer. Maternal 'nothingness' and 'lack' allow the subject to continue believing the phallus has not yet been lost. Circumcision thus, remains as a textual reminder to the compromise inherent in this fetish movement – a tombstone, a key-fossil, a *Leitfossil* that simultaneously opens and closes a window into the maternal.

Through the coupling between the image of circumcision and castration, a monolithic worldview emerges in the Freudian theory, pivoting around the phallus-penis,

---

212 Sigmund Freud. *Medusa's Head* (1922). In: Neil Hertz (ed.) *Writings on Art and Literature* Stanford, CA: Stanford University Press, 1997, 1922.), p. 273.

narrowing the relation to the other through a 'logic of sameness'. The curiosity that accompanies the interface with (m)otherness becomes an attempt and aspiration to reduce the (m)other to the familiar world of the one. When the ego boundaries are experienced as the edges of the universe, the limitations of the self cannot be recognised. Uncanny experience emerges out of any reminder, however partial, of an otherness that cannot be defined by the male genitalia that might open a window to the uncoupling of the phallus and the penis. Uncanny experience is provoked by the very fact that it dismantles the phallocentric position, raising the possibility of self-partiality, and leading to the castrated self – the recognition of the existence of a (m)otherness beyond the self.

Portraying the phallus as a super-signifier that can only be attached to the male genitalia repudiates an exploration of maternal power. Conflicted feelings towards the mother's phallus, the debt towards the maternal, identification, desire and aggression – are all transferred to the paternal vertex, in a way that preserves the image of the mother as a split figure. This attachment to the phallus-penis allows Freud to depict the mother as a soft, good figure incapable of harm but at the same time illustrate the danger in attributing power to the maternal: the possibility of maternal power becomes a peril to subjectivity as masculine. Repeated Oedipalisation envelopes both child and psychoanalytic theory within a phallic wall through which only one can be recognised.

Like the severed head of the Medusa, the theoretical encounter with the eyes of the maternal, evokes an unmediated, encounter with what has always already been castrated – an inherent self-partiality in relation to an (m)other. The overwhelming terror does not stem from the fear of encountering the 'nothingness' of the (m)other, but from an uncanny experience that emerges in the face of the unknown (m)other, a representation of an essence beyond oneself.

Chapter 2

Totem and Taboo
Phantasies of Origin

This chapter explores another layer in Freud's writing. While the first chapter, *In her Shadow: Three Case Studies*, remains focused on the realm of the subject, the following chapter unfolds the image of circumcision within Freud's writings in *Totem and Taboo* on the roots of culture. In this book, Freud traces the foundations of totemism in order to put forward a theory about the beginnings of religion, society and culture.[1] Following a variety of anthropological, sociological and psychological interpretations of totemic cultures, Freud presents a story centred on the primacy of the murder of the father, the ancestor – the patricide from which the law of the father emerged both as an intrapsychic element and as a cornerstone of culture. The myth he outlines is at the same time a story about the beginnings of religion and a theory of the structure of psychic representation.

Linking anthropological and sociological theories to psychoanalytic insights, *Totem and Taboo* weaves cultural structures with the subject's psychical edifice tying together the history of religion to the emergence of neurosis. Being among Freud's favourite works, it explores a range of literary and mythological sources, and a variety of clinical cases, unfolding before the readers multiple examples from different cultures. The textual movement between social reality and mental reality, the connections it weaves between phylogenesis and ontogenesis and the diversity of illustrations, position this book as a cardinal text that anchors the question of society and culture to the entire Freudian theory.

Anthropology and Psychoanalysis – a Brief Background

"[A] large number of customs and usages current in various societies ancient and modern, ... [are] to be explained as remnants of a totemic age",[2] Freud writes. Totemism, according to him, is a sort of origin, an archaic historical phase in the formation of human culture, relics of which can be found in various societies, both

---

1 Sigmund Freud. *Totem and Taboo: Some Points of Agreement Between the Mental Lives of Savages and Neurotics* (Translated by James Strachey. Routledge, [1912–1913] 2003).
2 Sigmund Freud. *Totem and Taboo: Some Points of Agreement Between the Mental Lives of Savages and Neurotics* (Translated by James Strachey. Routledge, [1912–1913] 2003), p. 117.

DOI: 10.4324/9781003394334-3

ancient and modern. This prehistoric phase contains clues, Freud explains, into later development and current human social behaviour. Quoting Wundt, he portrays totemic culture as revealing a historical 'origin', a social structure from which human culture and religion emerged: "totemic culture everywhere paved the way for a more advanced civilization, and, thus, that it represents a transitional stage between the age of primitive men and the era of heroes and gods".[3] Thus, an in-depth investigation of the foundations of totemism, might open a door to understanding the first stages of the existence of human culture and outline the connection between cultural progress and individual development.

The meaning of the word 'Totem' is derived from an American Indian origin (Ojibwa)[4] – meaning kinship between brothers and sisters who are descended from the same mother and are forbidden to marry. It is the belief that human thought is spiritually connected with some natural entity. The Totem is an animal or a symbol taken from nature, characterising in various ways a specific group of people, a tribe or a clan. At the time of Freud's writing – the end of the 19th century and the beginning of the 20th century – many scholars explored totemic religions and developed a wide range of theological, sociological and anthropological theories around them. The polemic about totemism in the early 20th century included debates over the meanings of the totems, the religious basis of totemic cultures, and the structure of the underlying social systems.

Freud acknowledged that the numerous theories surrounding totemism were "a matter of dispute", explaining that even "the facts themselves are scarcely capable of being expressed in general terms" and there is "scarcely a statement which does not call for exceptions or contradictions". Nonetheless his *Totem and Taboo* is an attempt to gather these various theories, outline the main points, the questions and the controversies in order to "decide whether we should regard [them] … as a true picture of the significant features of the past or as a secondary distortion of them".[5] Throughout the text, Freud unfolds a rich array of findings and debates, placing his theory in conversation with other thinkers such as Frazer,[6] Lang,[7] Spencer,[8] McLennan,[9]

---

3 Sigmund Freud. *Totem and Taboo: Some Points of Agreement Between the Mental Lives of Savages and Neurotics* (Translated by James Strachey. Routledge, [1912–1913] 2003), p. 117, quoting from: Wundt, W. Elemente der Völkerpsychologie, Leipzig. (Trans.: Elements of Folk Psychology, New York and London, 1916, 1912), p. 139.

4 Ojibwa are a large group of Indigenous Americans, of Native American descent.

5 Sigmund Freud. *Totem and Taboo: Some Points of Agreement Between the Mental Lives of Savages and Neurotics* (Translated by James Strachey. Routledge, [1912–1913] 2003), p. 4, footnote.

6 James G. Frazer. *Totemism and Exogamy: A Treatise on Certain Early Forms of Superstition and Society* (London: Macmillan, 1910).

7 Andrew Lang. *Social Origins* (London, New York and Bombay, 1903); Andrew Lang, *The Secret of the Totem* (London, New York, 1905).

8 Herbert Spencer. "The Origin of Animal Worship" *The Fortnightly Review* 7 (1870): 535–550.

9 John Mc'Lennan. "The Worship of Animals and Plants, Part I". *Fortnightly Review*, New Series, 6 (1869): 407–427.

Durkheim,[10] Wundt,[11] William Robertson Smith[12] and many others, with the intention to extract the 'truth' and the 'original', to sort the wheat from the chaff and refine the answer to the question of religion.

For Freud, the epistemological thread that outlines the way to distinguish between the various theories, to choose between the different assumptions laying before him is that of psychoanalysis. Drawing on his clinical cases, theoretical concepts and understanding of the human psyche, he seeks to achieve a theory of the roots of culture and religion, which is based on the assumption that there is a parallel between individual psychology and the development of cultures. Just as the human psyche matures from childhood to adulthood, so do societies hierarchically evolve from initially primitive social structure to a more developed form of religion that manifests itself in an advanced understanding of human reality:

> There are men still living who, as we believe, stand very near to primitive man, far nearer than we do, and whom we therefore regard as his direct heirs and representatives. Such is our view of those whom we describe as savages or half-savages; and their mental life must have a peculiar interest for us if we are right in seeing in it a well-preserved picture of an early stage of our own development. If that supposition is correct, a comparison between the psychology of primitive peoples, as it is taught by social anthropology, and the psychology of neurotics, as it has been revealed, by psycho-analysis, will be bound to show numerous points of agreement and will throw new light upon familiar facts in both sciences.[13]

The premise on which *Totem and Taboo* is based is the fundamental assumption of parallelism between phylogenesis and ontogenesis, between the development of the human species and that of the individual.[14] This hypothesis encapsulates a hierarchical perception of growth from the primitive to the modern, from the child to the adult and from the neurotic to the normal. Arguing for the psychological proximity between childhood experience and neurotic behaviour, both of these are juxtapositioned to the lives of "primitive peoples".

10 Émile Durkheim. *Incest: The Nature and Origin of the Taboo* (New York: Lyle Stuart, Inc., 1963).

11 Wilhelm Wundt.. *Mythus und Religion*. Vol. 2 of *Völkerpsychologie*. Leipzig: Wilhelm Engelmann, 1906.

12 Wiliam Robertson Smith. *Lectures on the Religion of the Semites* (First Series, London: The Fundamental Institutions, 1894).

13 Sigmund Freud. Totem and Taboo: Some Points of Agreement Between the Mental Lives of Savages and Neurotics (Translated by James Strachey. Routledge, [1912–1913] 2003), pp. 1–2.

14 This assumption is also based on a biological and embryological concept that was prevalent in the 19th century and was later abandoned, according to which ontogenesis – the development of the individual, repeats phylogeny – the evolutionary development of the entire species. According to the biogenetic law (also called the law of recapitulation) formulated by the biologist and naturalist Ernest Haeckel, *the organic development of a living organism is a kind of summary of the history of its taxonomic* species and mimics the evolution of that species.

Using a language, which is easily recognised today as inappropriately racist – such as the term "savages" – Freud explains that these ancient cultures express the emotional life of children, or, alternatively, the psychic regression of the neurotic. "[I]t is enough to draw attention to the great care which is devoted by the Australians, as well as by other savage peoples, to the prevention of incest", he writes, "It must be admitted that these savages are even more sensitive on the subject of incest than we are. They are probably liable to a greater temptation to it and for that reason stand in need of fuller protection".[15] Just as children uninhibitedly express desires and impulses, so too these people express according to Freud, an earlier and even ancient psychic reality.

Many have criticised Freud's *Totem and Taboo* for this Eurocentric view, which positions Western culture as advanced and developed compared to other cultures. Lévi-Strauss in his book *Totemism* argued that Western's depiction of ancient totem cultures (as well as those that exist today) as primitive and wild is a colonialist projection aimed at aligning the West with the opposite – rational and enlightened.[16] Human consciousness does not depend on social context, and thus, the use of natural analogies (such as the totem animal) to explain the environment is no less rational than today's definitions of the relationship between nature and culture and therefore is not an indication of a more 'primitive' or inferior mental structure. In fact, the totem, like any other structuralist principle, is intended to delineate the system of social relations through characteristics of similarity and difference. Since Lévi-Strauss's analysis, consensus was established that totem cultures could not be unified and seen as an earlier social concept on a hierarchical scale. Totemism functioned in different forms in different tribes and areas and should not be analysed as a single system. The reason for adopting an object or animal in different tribes as a totem varies greatly reflecting different ways of giving meaning to the relationship between nature and culture that does not stand in hierarchical relation to the meaning given to it in Western culture.[17]

Although, in many ways, this argument pulls the rug from underneath any investigation of 'totemism', as understood in Freud's time, this text can nevertheless be approached as a window into the question of 'origin' and the human myth underlying Freudian theory. Freud's exploration of totemic cultures is an opening into his conceptualisations of representation; into the psychological origins yielding cultural, religious and symbolic meanings. This chapter does not seek to touch on historical reality or describe the different cultures, but rather to analyse the

---

15 Sigmund Freud. *Totem and Taboo: Some Points of Agreement Between the Mental Lives of Savages and Neurotics* (Translated by James Strachey. Routledge, [1912–1913] 2003), p. 11.

16 Claude Lévi-Strauss. *Totemism* (Boston: Beacon, 1963).

17 Lévi-Strauss separates the totem from the prohibition of incest. While the totem functions in different ways in different societies, the prohibition of incest is the foundation on which social life is based. It is a universal taboo that establishes the social structure as a system of substitutions which, according to him, in parallel with linguistic ability, puts ancient societies and modern societies on a similar structural level.

psychoanalytic myth about the dawn of humanity; the primal 'origin', before the formation of law, that constitutes the early conditions for social life. Just as it is a story about the beginnings of social life and the beginning of religion, *Totem and Taboo* is a phantasy about the emergence of paternal law, about the process of subject-formation, about the structure of subject-object relationship and about the psychological substrates from which the ability for symbolisation emerges. Reading Freud's analyses following these cultures with the questions he raises and the narratives he portrays, allows an examination of the totems—and perhaps the key-fossils—of psychoanalysis itself.

The Totems of Psychoanalysis

"What is a totem?" Freud asks, explaining that "It is as a rule an animal (whether edible and harmless or dangerous and feared) and more rarely a plant or a natural phenomenon (such as rain or water), which stands in a peculiar relation to the whole clan".[18] Each tribe or clan is named after its totem and follows several basic rules in order to maintain loyalty to the totem. It is a representation that binds the kinship between the members of the clan, assigning them to the social system and providing a shared meaning. It establishes the lawful foundation and the boundaries of the tribe, regulating their relations with other tribes and formulating the ties within – both between the members of the tribe and between the tribe and the totem itself.

The attitude toward the totem, according to Freud, expresses an emotional conflict in which, on the one hand, "the clansmen are under a sacred obligation (subject to automatic sanctions) not to kill or destroy their totem and to avoid eating its flesh (or deriving benefit from it in other ways)",[19] and on the other hand, once in a while, the members of the tribe turn the killing of the animal into a feast in which the flesh of the totem is eaten. At first glance it seems that the abstention from eating or using the totemic animal is at odds with the solemn sacrificial ceremony in which the totem is slaughtered by all members of the tribe but, as Freud explains,

> one thing would certainly follow from the persistence of the taboo, namely that the original desire to do the prohibited thing must also still persist among the tribes concerned. They must therefore have an ambivalent attitude towards their taboos. In their unconscious there is nothing they would like more than to violate them, but they are afraid to do so; they are afraid precisely because they would like to, and the fear is stronger than the desire.[20]

---

18 Sigmund Freud. *Totem and Taboo: Some Points of Agreement Between the Mental Lives of Savages and Neurotics* (Translated by James Strachey. Routledge, [1912–1913] 2003), p. 3.
19 Sigmund Freud. *Totem and Taboo: Some Points of Agreement Between the Mental Lives of Savages and Neurotics* (Translated by James Strachey. Routledge, [1912–1913] 2003), p. 3.
20 Sigmund Freud. *Totem and Taboo: Some Points of Agreement Between the Mental Lives of Savages and Neurotics* (Translated by James Strachey. Routledge, [1912–1913] 2003), p. 37.

In fact, both murderous desires and prohibition are intertwined in the formation of the law and express the attitude towards the father in which, as Lacan puts it, "repression and the return of the repressed are one and the same thing, the front and back of a single process".[21]

All these threads can be tied together through one coherent narrative, Freud explains, "in substituting the father for the totem animal in the formula for totemism".[22] Using clinical case studies of the development of neurosis in children, he concludes that "the totem animal is in reality a substitute for the father",[23] and the contradictory attitude represents the complexity of the relationship with the father on which the social system is based. The ambivalent attitude expressed in the prohibition against harming the totem and the celebration that takes place while feasting together on its flesh expresses the conflictual feelings towards the father: the desire to kill him as well as the love and admiration for him. The two basic laws that Freud identifies as characteristic of totemism – the prohibition against killing or harming the totem and the prohibition to have sexual relations with members of the totem of the opposite sex – are rooted, as Freud concludes, in the Oedipal relationship:

> If the totem animal is the father, then the two principal ordinances of totemism, the two taboo prohibitions which constitute its core—not to kill the totem and not to have sexual relations with a woman of the same totem—coincide in their content with the two crimes of Oedipus, who killed his father and married his mother, as well as with the two primal wishes of children, the insufficient repression or the re-awakening of which forms the nucleus of perhaps every psychoneurosis.[24]

Psychoanalysis weaves a common thread between these two laws – the murder taboo and exogamy – incorporating them into an Oedipal narrative through which both psychic life and the growth of culture are explained simultaneously. In linking the *taboo on incest* – with which the book begins – with the *taboo on the murder* of the father, Freud posits the Oedipal triangle and the conflict between father and son as the primordial myth; a myth that becomes, not just a primary story for the emergence of culture but also, as Amber Jacobs points out, the only story that can be applied to explain human lives.[25] Although *Totem and Taboo* opens with the question of incest and the relationship with the mother, it soon turns the gaze to the

21 Jacques Lacan. *The Seminar of Jacques Lacan, Book 3: The Psychoses 1955–1956* (trans. by R. Grigg, ed. by Jacques-Alain Miller, W. W. Norton & Company, 1993), p. 60.

22 Sigmund Freud. *Totem and Taboo: Some Points of Agreement Between the Mental Lives of Savages and Neurotics* (Translated by James Strachey. Routledge, [1912–1913] 2003), p. 152.

23 Sigmund Freud. *Totem and Taboo: Some Points of Agreement Between the Mental Lives of Savages and Neurotics* (Translated by James Strachey. Routledge, [1912–1913] 2003), p. 163.

24 Sigmund Freud. *Totem and Taboo: Some Points of Agreement Between the Mental Lives of Savages and Neurotics* (Translated by James Strachey. Routledge, [1912–1913] 2003), p. 153.

25 Amber Jacobs. *On Matricide: Myth, Psychoanalysis, and the Law of the Mother* (New York: Colombia University Press, 2007).

father, marking the Oedipal structure as the sole archetype from which language, law and culture originate.

Oedipus fled from Corinth, the city where he grew up, to escape the oracle of Delphi's prophecy that he would murder his father and marry his mother. However, as some have pointed out, the myth begins before Oedipus, when the prophecy is given to his father, King Laius, for abducting and raping Chrysippus. After the birth of Oedipus, Laius revealed the secret of the prophecy to Jocasta and ordered the child, Oedipus, to be killed. Fearing that the predicted events will come true, Laius had his son's ankles pierced and tethered together so that he could not crawl, and Jocasta gave the boy to a servant to be abandoned to death on Mount Cithaeron. The unspoken beginning of the myth suggests that even before the triangle of relations with parents, an anxiety arises about the possibility of a child that might become *the other of the mother*, introducing the father to his mortality.

A similar image is sketched by Freud when he reconstructs the beginning of totemism, the early stage of human society, as he weaves the narrative of the primal myth, as the myth of the beginning of civilisation. He describes a cruel and jealous primal father who did not allow other males to approach females. In this depiction of the dawn of times, the patriarchal figure emerges as a terrible and cruel tyrant, "a violent and jealous father who keeps all the females for himself and drives away his sons".[26] While the conventional reading of the Oedipal story begins from the point of view of the son who desires his mother and wishes to murder his father, this text deals with the question of what was there before, what are the conditions that enabled the Oedipal narrative. Freud, who established the Oedipal narrative as a reflection of the child's inner world – the desire to kill the father and have sexual relations with the mother – begins with a story that opens a window into the world that preceded this Oedipal picture.

Following Darwin, Freud marks the beginning of civilisation in primitive human tribes, ruled by a dominant male who kept all the females for himself and expelled the sons. This historical situation existed, he explains, until

> One day the brothers who had been driven out came together, killed and devoured their father and so made an end of the patriarchal horde. United, they had the courage to do and succeeded in doing what would have been impossible for them individually.[27]

The "tumultuous mob of brothers", who collectively murdered the father, revealed in their actions

> the same contradictory feelings which we can see at work in the ambivalent father-complexes ... They hated their father, who presented such a formidable

---

26 Sigmund Freud. *Totem and Taboo: Some Points of Agreement Between the Mental Lives of Savages and Neurotics* (Translated by James Strachey. Routledge, [1912–1913] 2003), p. 164.

27 Sigmund Freud. *Totem and Taboo: Some Points of Agreement Between the Mental Lives of Savages and Neurotics* (Translated by James Strachey. Routledge, [1912–1913] 2003), p. 164.

obstacle to their craving for power and their sexual desires; but they loved and admired him too.[28]

Whereas, prior to the murder, the taboo prohibitions were imposed from outside, after the event, social organisation was founded:

> The dead father became stronger than the living one had been—for events took the course we so often see them follow in human affairs to this day. What had up to then been prevented by his actual existence was thenceforward prohibited by the sons themselves, in accordance with the psychological procedure so familiar to us in psycho-analyses under the name of 'deferred obedience'. They revoked their deed by forbidding the killing of the totem, the substitute for their father; and they renounced its fruits by resigning their claim to the women who had now been set free. inevitably corresponded to the two repressed wishes of the Oedipus complex. Whoever contravened those taboos became guilty of the only two crimes with which primitive society concerned itself.[29]

Out of a sense of guilt for the act of patricide, the primal horde rendered every murder a heinous act, and in order not to repeat the same atrocity, forbade all mating within the family. After satisfying the brother's aggressive desire for patricide, "the affection which had all this time been pushed under was bound to make itself felt", and the shared sense of guilt made "the dead father became stronger than the living one".[30] Following the murder, the brothers forbade themselves from what the father had denied them in his very existence declaring the prohibition against killing the totem animal and establishing exogamy. In doing so, they sought "to allay their burning sense of guilt" as "a kind of reconciliation with their father" in which, as Freud explains,

> The totemic system was, as it were, a covenant with their father, in which he promised them everything that a childish imagination may expect from a father—protection, care and indulgence—while on their side they undertook to respect his life, that is to say, not to repeat the deed which had brought destruction on their real father.[31]

Reflecting the way in which the repressed and the return of the repressed are intertwined, this psychic process becomes the emergence of social life. From the

---

28 Sigmund Freud. *Totem and Taboo: Some Points of Agreement Between the Mental Lives of Savages and Neurotics* (Translated by James Strachey. Routledge, [1912–1913] 2003), p. 166.

29 Sigmund Freud. *Totem and Taboo: Some Points of Agreement Between the Mental Lives of Savages and Neurotics* (Translated by James Strachey. Routledge, [1912–1913] 2003), pp. 166–167.

30 Sigmund Freud. *Totem and Taboo: Some Points of Agreement Between the Mental Lives of Savages and Neurotics* (Translated by James Strachey. Routledge, [1912–1913] 2003), p. 166.

31 Sigmund Freud. *Totem and Taboo: Some Points of Agreement Between the Mental Lives of Savages and Neurotics* (Translated by James Strachey. Routledge, [1912–1913] 2003), p. 168.

moment the father was murdered, the brothers were able to internalise his image, creating a mutual contract and obliging them to what will become paternal law. Overwhelmed with guilt, the ambivalence towards the father was repressed and the image of a protective and loving father served as the basis for a social system to emerge. While the pre-Oedipal narrative depicts a real father motivated by rage and jealousy, the Oedipal guilt arising after the murder, establishes the image of a good father, the protector and guardian of the law.

Anchoring the Oedipal flag at the forefront of the prehistoric, archaic and pre-Oedipal picture erases from the horizon the question of the maternal. Under this narrative, as I will argue, the 'return-of-the-repressed' structure that culti-vates paternal law as both an internal and a cultural symbol does not allow for a similar process to establish the 'law of the mother'. In the face of Oedipal totality, a double-layered matricide is eliminating the maternal from the realm of language.

Female Genealogy[32]

One of the main features that Freud highlights as characteristic of totem cultures is maternal inheritance. At various points in the text, he notes the priority of maternal inheritance and even adds that "the totem is as a rule inherited through the female line, and it is possible that paternal descent may originally have been left entirely out of account".[33] When he explores "the original nature of totemism", he explains that "originally ... Totems were inherited only through the female line".[34]

In his attempts to trace the 'origin', to understand the beginnings of social ex-istence, Freud is led to historical descriptions of matriarchal, or mother-centred societies, in which inheritance passed from the mother to her children and social power was held in the hands of women. In 1861 Bachofen presented the concept of pre-historical matriarchy that preceded today's known patriarchal societies. He described four historical stages of human development, the second of which was a matriarchal lunar phase with an early form of Demeter as the dominant de-ity. These societies were, according to Bachofen, social, political, cultural and philosophical systems in which women founded the family and agriculture, and in which inheritance passed via a matrilineal line.[35] Freud touches on the studies of Bachofen but does not explore further the "the institution of matriarchy", as a

32 Some of the following analysis was published in: Yael Pilowsky Bankirer, "A Birth without a Mother: The Paradoxical Myth of Patriarchal Origin to Monotheism in Freud." In: Giulia Pedrucci (ed.) *Maternità e monoteismi - Motherhood(s) and Monotheisms* (2020).

33 Sigmund Freud. *Totem and Taboo: Some Points of Agreement Between the Mental Lives of Savages and Neurotics* (Translated by James Strachey. Routledge, [1912–1913] 2003), p. 123.

34 Sigmund Freud. *Totem and Taboo: Some Points of Agreement Between the Mental Lives of Savages and Neurotics* (Translated by James Strachey. Routledge, [1912–1913] 2003), p. 124.

35 Johann J. Bachofen. *An English Translation of Bachofen's Mutterrecht (Mother Right) (1861): A Study of the Religious and Juridical Aspects of Gynecocracy in the Ancient World* (Lewiston, NY: Edwin Mellen, 2005).

clue into early human civilisation. Although he recognises matrilineal transmission as a central aspect of totemic culture, he does not attempt to discover other meanings inherent in it beyond the Oedipal explanation and moves to position the myth of the father's murder as the one event that precipitated all major historical manifestations.

What is transmitted from mother to daughter through the totem? What is held by mothers in the process of cultural formation and how is the social realm shaped in relation to the maternal? In an almost religious attempt to adhere to his one narration of origin, Freud frames matriarchy as a short historical period without any influence or significance on the forthcoming events. Matriarchy only existed, he concludes, for a short period of time in history, as a temporary gap between male rulers, until it was "replaced by the patriarchal organization of the family".[36] Despite its centrality in these cultures, Freud struggles to connect maternal inheritance to his structural theory.

Although recognising the existence of matrilineal heritage and despite acknowledging that such hereditary systems predominated in these early societies, Freud quickly moves to erase any meaning inborn to this historical phase by anchoring the role of such genealogical legacies in the desire of men. As he explains, passing of the totem name from mother to daughters is meant as an act against incest. Since sexual relations were only allowed outside the family structure of the clan, a matrilineal heritage is intended to limit the incestuous relationship of *the sons with their mothers*. Strangely enough, in the Freudian reconstruction, it is the desire of the sons and the father's ban against it, which provides the historical significance of maternal inheritance.

When matriarchal culture as a cardinal component of human development arises in the text, Freud closes the door on its theoretical meanings by providing a phallocentric interpretation of maternal inheritance: "These implications of totem prohibitions suggest that descent through the female line is older than that through the male, since there are grounds for thinking that totem prohibitions were principally directed against the incestuous desires of the son".[37] Under this interpretative framework, priority is once again granted to masculine desire, reducing the different meaning inherent to maternal genealogy through the father's desire and the Oedipal narrative – maternal heredity is nothing more than the father's way of forbidding the sons from sexual contact with the mother. Paternal law is used as an explanation covering the histories, symbolisms and myths hidden in matriarchate, and the relationship between mother and daughter is concealed by a patriarchal structure of relationship between men in which women can only function as objects.

36 Sigmund Freud. *Totem and Taboo: Some Points of Agreement Between the Mental Lives of Savages and Neurotics* (Translated by James Strachey. Routledge, [1912–1913] 2003), p. 167.

37 Sigmund Freud. *Totem and Taboo: Some Points of Agreement Between the Mental Lives of Savages and Neurotics* (Translated by James Strachey. Routledge, [1912–1913] 2003), p. 6.

According to Bachofen, after the formation of patriarchy, any memory of the ma-triarchate had to be repressed because every such encounter with matriarchal history, with the possibility of a different cultural heritage, undermines the eternity of the father's ruling. Thus, patriarchy is a cultural structure that is rooted in the fear of (m) otherness, specifically the dread of maternal power, which has led to the historical memory of this period to be forgotten and erased. Even in exploring the relationship with the mother-in-law, that is with the mother of the mother – maternal geneal-ogy and female history, Freud posits the incest taboo as a *theoretical* line that can-not be crossed. Just like the prohibition against incest, *the relationship with female heritage, lies in the desire of the father.* As Bachofen explains, any interface with maternal history, with the possibility of another cultural heritage, undermines the exclusivity of the father and opens the door to an alternative existence system, to difference. Thus, textual and theoretical encounters with the maternal – whether in the memory of matriarchal heritage or in the relationship with the mother – lead to the prohibition of incest, to the law of the father, leaving the maternal in the only position possible – of a desired object between men.

Freud's extensive preoccupation with the prohibition of incest seems to be-come a borderline in his own text, a repetitive reminder of that which must not be touched, of the impossibility of a theoretical exploration of the maternal. As he himself explains, "[h]is horror of incest insists that the genealogical history of his choice of an object for his love shall not be recalled".[38] Freud's conscious inten-tion was to say that the customary prohibition against contact with mothers-in-law is intended at the memory of incest and the necessity to forget the man's attitude toward his own mother, repressing the chain of psychic events that have made him fall in love with his wife. But, literally a Freudian slip, these words resonate in the text revealing the repression of female lineage in every theoretical encounter as well. Freud complies with the imperative and prohibition of incest turning his gaze from questions of how social relationships are shaped in relation to female genealogy, reminding himself that "[i]t is not right that he should see the breasts which suckled his wife".[39] Looking away not from the breast of his wife's mother but from the mother-daughter relationship itself, he is setting in its place the phal-lus, paternal law and the father's desire. If maternal inheritance is just a way for the father to prohibit his sons from having sexual relations with their mothers, female genealogy and heritage are reduced through the father's desire and the Oedipal narrative. While he describes at length the various prohibitions against incest, he also covers the emotional complexity inherent in these relationships, by replacing

---

38 Sigmund Freud. *Totem and Taboo: Some Points of Agreement Between the Mental Lives of Savages and Neurotics* (Translated by James Strachey. Routledge, [1912–1913] 2003), p. 18.

39 Sigmund Freud. *Totem and Taboo: Some Points of Agreement Between the Mental Lives of Savages and Neurotics* (Translated by James Strachey. Routledge, [1912–1913] 2003), p. 16. Freud here is quoting Crawley (Crawley, E. *The Mystic Rose*, London, 1902, p. 401), quoting Leslie (Leslie, D. *Among the Zulus and Amatongas*, Edinburgh, 1875, p. 141). It is interesting in relation to the repeated taboo.

it with paternal threat of castration. Those primary relationships with the maternal and matriarchal cultural worlds remain inaccessible.

Conducting a comprehensive reading of Freud's texts, Madelon Sprengnether identifies the maternal as a textual spectral dimension that occasionally emerges from between the lines.[40] When Freud formulates the Oedipal narrative, she explains, he establishes the mother as a passive object that is meant to fulfil libidinal impulses of either the child or the father, while erasing any theoretical thought that may lead the reader towards maternal desire and maternal subjectivity. This, she claims, is complemented by two other strategic movements – one idealising maternal devotion to her children and the other constantly reminds the readers of her castration and lack as a woman. These textual movements, which are interpreted by Sprengnether as unconscious attempts to evade maternal power, do not remain only on the level of the individual but are followed by Freud's readings of social and cultural development. As she explains in her analysis of *Totem and Taboo*, the Freudian myth of the primal horde erases the importance of matriarchy and ignores the cardinal role of maternal dimension in human history, thus removing her meaning not only from his theories of subject development but also from psychoanalytic understandings of human history. Repression of maternal dimension, Sprengnether argues, leaves a trail of evidence in Freud's texts — gaps, contradictions and textual incoherencies, which she identifies as a *'symptomatic text'*.

Positioning the mother as an object alone creates the textual movement as a closed system that gradually spirals into itself. While the text begins with a wide range of possible narratives, theoretical questions and fluid movement between different symbolic representations, the rich theoretical circles gradually narrow, and a single Oedipal story emerges. Although Freud opens with an exploration of maternal origin and structure, the textual narrative is shifted and maternal aspect is erased. Instead of an opening into a feminine legacy, matrilineality is, for Freud, a prohibition of fathers towards their sons, rooted in masculine desire. He does not continue his study into the legacy of matriarchal societies and repeatedly covers its traces in history by only adhering to one side of the Oedipal metaphor. In such narrative of origin, presenting a seemingly pre-political society, all women are envisaged as objects, a valuable token of exchange in the power struggle between men and the relationship that formulates the steering wheels of history is that of *sameness* – between father and son. The place of the mother – matriarchal legacy, the memory traces of matrilineal heritage, which according to historical evidence dominated the emerging totemic societies, and the meaning of these in the evolution of religion – are all buried in Freud's texts. This omission of maternal legacy in Freud writing is the bedrock of both the mother's absence and the portrayal of the mother *as* absence (a lack) in psychoanalytic theory.

---

40 Madelon Sprengnether. *The Spectral Mother: Freud, Feminism, and Psychoanalysis* (Ithaca: Cornell University Press, 1990); Madelon Sprengnether. "Reading Freud's Life." *Am. Imago* 52 (1995): 9–54.

Texts and Rituals

The Freudian myth of the cruel tyrant whose murder precipitated human culture is accompanied, as I have shown, by a closing textual movement that resists any reference to the maternal as part of the transition into social life. Although the text begins with the question of incest, it quickly proceeds by positioning the prohibition as a principle beyond which it is impossible to think. Freud begins the journey with a courageous attempt to explore the difficulty and complexity in the face of the maternal, but at the moment of truth, he places a forbidding father figure as the one unquestionable origin. As I will show, the sacrificial ritual described in the text is a central axis in this movement.

"The oldest form of sacrifice, then, older than the use of fire or the knowledge of agriculture, was the sacrifice of animals, whose flesh and blood were enjoyed in common by the god and his worshippers".[41] Freud analyse at length the ritual of the totem animal sacrifice, in which all members of the tribe gather to eat the flesh of the totem together, and provides a description of such a feast from the 4th century AD:

> The victim of the sacrifice, a camel, 'is bound upon a rude altar of stones piled together, and when the leader of the band has thrice led the worshippers round the altar in a solemn procession accompanied with chants, he inflicts the first wound … and in all haste drinks of the blood that gushes forth. Forthwith the whole company fall on the victim with their swords, hacking off pieces of the quivering flesh and devouring them raw with such wild haste, that in the short interval between the rise of the day star which marked the hour for the service to begin, and the disappearance of its rays before the rising sun, the entire camel, body and bones, skin, blood and entrails, is wholly devoured.'[42]

Freud follows to describe sacrificial rituals in different cultures; discusses the significance of killing kings and rulers; draws parallels between different human sacrifices of a religious nature and lays out the principles of the reincarnation of the sacrifice in later times and its expressions in mythological literature. As he goes through a range of meanings and interpretations, many cards are laid before the readers out of which only one Oedipal explanation is chosen. Juxtaposing all the rituals through the metaphor of circumcision to castration complex, Freud is anchoring the wealth of questions that arise in the text to the Oedipal narrative and to the relationship between father and son:

> Fear of castration plays an extremely large part, in the case of the youthful neurotics whom we come across, as an interference in their relations with their

---

41 Sigmund Freud. *Totem and Taboo: Some Points of Agreement Between the Mental Lives of Savages and Neurotics* (Translated by James Strachey. Routledge, [1912–1913] 2003), p. 155.

42 Sigmund Freud. *Totem and Taboo: Some Points of Agreement Between the Mental Lives of Savages and Neurotics* (Translated by James Strachey. Routledge, [1912–1913] 2003), p. 161.

father. The illuminating instance reported by Ferenczi (1913a) has shown us how a little boy took as his totem the beast that had snapped at his little penis. When our children come to hear of ritual circumcision, they equate it with castration. The parallel in social psychology to this reaction by children has not yet been worked out, so far as I am aware. In primæval times and in primitive races, where circumcision is so frequent, it is performed at the age of initiation into manhood and it is at that age that its significance is to be found; it was only as a secondary development that it was shifted back to the early years of life. It is of very great interest to find that among primitive peoples circumcision is combined with cutting the hair and knocking out teeth or is replaced by them, and that our children, who cannot possibly have any knowledge of this, in fact treat these two operations, in the anxiety with which they react to them, as equivalents of castration.[43]

Freud points out that the metaphor of sacrifice – wounding, cutting and eating the animal's flesh – is a central component of rituals in which the body is marked in order to be granted with social meaning. As he explains, "[a] notion of this kind lies at the root of all the blood covenants by which men made compacts with each other".[44] Quoting Robertson Smith, who wrote at length about sacrificial rituals and blood covenants, Freud marks the parallel between archaic and violent ceremonies and the Jewish ritual of circumcision.[45] The numerous quotes cited by Freud and the lengthy discussion of the totem sacrifice evoke in the text the image of circumcision as a symbolic motif for various sacrificial ceremonies.

Freud uses the ritual of circumcision to explain the cardinal role of the relationship with the father in various rituals as well as in the totemic animal sacrifice. "The original animal sacrifice" he writes, "was already a substitute for a human sacrifice—for the ceremonial killing of the father".[46] The cutting of the totem animal in the sacrificial ritual is replaced by the cutting of the male organ, and the solidarity bonds between those feasting from the animal's flesh gives way to the male brotherhood that is solidified by the circumcision ceremony.

The image of circumcision is sewn into the image of castration anchoring the cutting of(/off) the male penis and focusing on the relationship between father and son. Using the image of circumcision makes it possible to clearly mark the separation between the sexes produced in the ceremony and to portray social identity that is formed in it as a purely masculine. It allows Freud to distil the notion that "the

43 Sigmund Freud. *Totem and Taboo: Some Points of Agreement Between the Mental Lives of Savages and Neurotics* (Translated by James Strachey. Routledge, [1912–1913] 2003), p. 177. Footnote.

44 Sigmund Freud. *Totem and Taboo: Some Points of Agreement Between the Mental Lives of Savages and Neurotics* (Translated by James Strachey. Routledge, [1912–1913] 2003), p. 160.

45 Wiliam Robertson Smith. *Lectures on the Religion of the Semites* (First Series, London: The Fundamental Institutions, 1894).

46 Sigmund Freud. *Totem and Taboo: Some Points of Agreement Between the Mental Lives of Savages and Neurotics* (Translated by James Strachey. Routledge, [1912–1913] 2003), p. 176.

problems of social psychology, too, should prove soluble on the basis of one single concrete point—man's relation to his father".[47]

While Freud turns the gaze towards the relationship with the father, Kristeva lingers on to think about the abjected relationship with the maternal, which underlies various rituals, specifically that of circumcision. In her book *The Powers of Horror*,[48] she conceptualises *the abject* – a simultaneously mesmerising and repulsive aspect of the maternal that is rejected as a radical otherness in the process of subject formation. Kristeva explores the complexity of this relationship with the maternal as expressed in literary works, religion and in various cultures, and among other things, presents an analysis of the abject within Jewish tradition.

The mother's body, she explains, is a core element in the process of subject formation that prelude both culture and the relationship with the father as described by Freud. Identifying herself with the abject, the mother creates her own body as the boundary line through which the distinction between inside and outside, nature and culture, 'me' and 'not me' is made, as the subject forms his/her identity. The maternal body becomes *The Thing* that the (future) subjects are captivated by and frustratingly dependent on; a dimension that they must repudiate in order to salvage their subjectivity from the claws of otherness. The child gradually sheds the unbearable abjected with its inherent maternal images to create his/her separated identity, a process in which the subject's boundaries are gradually formed –between subject and object, between liquid and solid, between pure and impure, between self and other.

Analysing the logic of exclusion that constitutes the maternal abject in different cultures, she draws on various anthropological studies and especially the writing of Mary Douglas, who "seems to find in the human body the prototype of that translucid being constituted by society as symbolic system".[49] She analyses, among other cultures, the prohibitions of Judaism and the ritual of circumcision, which is based, according to her, on continuous rejection of the maternal through relentlessly proliferating laws of impurity. Unlike Christianity, in which an opening is left for identifying the source of impurity within, and thus, allowing a dialectical relation to the abject,[50] in Judaism, the impure is identified with the maternal and is constantly isolated through the engendering of more and more laws of impurity, which also cements the separation between the sexes. As she explains, Jewish law establishes the division between nature and culture through the exclusion of the feminine and maternal expressed in the ritual of circumcision:

---

47 Sigmund Freud. *Totem and Taboo: Some Points of Agreement Between the Mental Lives of Savages and Neurotics* (Translated by James Strachey. Routledge, [1912–1913] 2003), p. 182.

48 Julia Kristeva. *Powers of Horror: An Essay on Abjection* (New York: Columbia University Press, 1982).

49 Julia Kristeva. *Powers of Horror: An Essay on Abjection* (New York: Columbia University Press, 1982), p. 66.

50 She writes: "Christ, whose introjection by means of numerous communions sanctifies me while reminding me of my incompletion. Because it identified abjection as a fantasy of devouring, Christianity effects its abreaction. Henceforth reconciled with it, the Christian subject, completely absorbed into the symbolic, is no longer a being of abjection but a lapsing subject". p. 119

The body must bear no trace of its debt to nature: it must be clean and proper in order to be fully symbolic. In order to confirm that, it should endure no gash other than that of circumcision, equivalent to sexual separation and/or separation from the mother. Any other mark would be the sign of belonging to the impure, the non-separate, the non-symbolic, the non-holy.[51]

Kristeva specifically touches on the custom of circumcision and explains it is the first act of cutting, the primordial act (of murder) that establishes Jewish culture through separation from the mother. Circumcision is the original incision that resonates in all Jewish laws the mechanisms of separation from the feminine, creating the abject as the pivotal division between the pure and the impure:

[W]hat the male is separated from, the other that circumcision carves out on his very sex, is the other sex, impure, defiled. By repeating the natural scar of the umbilical cord at the location of sex, by duplicating and thus displacing through ritual the preeminent separation, which is that from the mother, Judaism seems to insist in symbolic fashion—the very opposite of what is "natural"—that the identity of the speaking being (with his God) is based on the separation of the son from the mother. Symbolic identity presupposes the violent difference of the sexes.[52]

For Freud, similar to Kristeva, circumcision is a metaphor that incorporates the core of the ritual act. The image of cutting holds within it a dense conglomerate of what takes place in the transition to culture. However, while Freud insists on the primacy of castration arising from the image of circumcision, Kristeva listens to the cut of the maternal. For her, culture is rooted in the conflicted torment with the abject, which is identified with the mother, through which the subject is drawn to a constant return to the archaic dyad in order to relive the primary cutting that is at the same time both the death of the subject and his/her birth. The same archaic cut is reflected in the Jewish ceremony in order to draw the boundary line, remove the maternal and create the separation between the sexes.

The textual *vanishing of the maternal* can be identified in Freud's description and analysis of the animal sacrifice. Pointing out the ambivalent feelings in relation to the totem, Freud explains that

[i]n spite of the ban protecting the lives of sacred animals in their quality of fellow-clansmen, a necessity arose for killing one of them from time to time in solemn communion and for dividing its flesh and blood among the members of the clan.[53]

51 Julia Kristeva. *Powers of Horror: An Essay on Abjection* (New York: Columbia University Press, 1982), p. 102.
52 Julia Kristeva. *Powers of Horror: An Essay on Abjection* (New York: Columbia University Press, 1982), p. 100.
53 Sigmund Freud. *Totem and Taboo: Some Points of Agreement Between the Mental Lives of Savages and Neurotics* (Translated by James Strachey. Routledge, [1912–1913] 2003), p. 159.

In this event, all the members of the tribe participate in the killing of the sacred animal, in the act of murder, which is lamented together afterwards. The prohibition against killing the totem transforms into a festive event on this day in which all members of the tribe violate the taboo and as Freud describes, only the participation of the entire clan enables the killing of the sacred animal whose life was immune to harm. The shared act allows them to bear the guilt and generate the feelings of closeness that form the social basis of the tribe, and through which they are bound to each other in a sense of shared destiny. This communal eating of the flesh creates "the mutual dependence existing between one another and their god".[54] The eating and drinking together establishes the social structure of shared commitment. As Freud explains, "the participation in the same substance establishes a sacred bond between those who consume it when it has entered their bodies".[55]

For Freud, the sacrificial ritual expresses an ambivalent set of feelings that tells the story of the totem's origin from the father figure. "Psycho-analysis has revealed" he explains, "that the totem animal is in reality a substitute for the father"[56] and therefore complex feelings towards the father surface during the ritual. The strict prohibition against killing the animal and the celebration that accompanies the totem feast indicate the "ambivalent emotional attitude" that arises in the father-son relationship. At the totem murderous feast, feelings of rage and jealousy towards the father are expressed but the act eating, incorporating pieces of the animal also reflects the desire to resemble him, to swallow his image and identify with him. After eating the totem – and murdering the father – "the affection which had all this time been pushed under was bound to make itself felt".[57] The brothers are then able to take upon themselves the father's law, pledging not to harm or kill the totem and establishing the incest taboo. Thus, out of the shared experience of guilt and regret and in response to their shared destiny in the communal identification with the father in the act of eating, social structure is established.

The description of the camel being sacrificed makes it possible to directly witness the intensity of the shared experience, to touch the ecstasy of the emotions involved in the brutal event where the clansmen mercilessly cut the animal and consumes its flesh, blood and bones. The animal is tied up within a circle of intensifying voices until a cut is made and the blood bursts out of the hardening body. Through this climax moment in which the body of the animal is cut, the living and bleeding wound serves to pour the budding of the social system. The description of the cut made in the flesh echoes the Jewish circumcision ceremony in which the

54 Sigmund Freud. *Totem and Taboo: Some Points of Agreement Between the Mental Lives of Savages and Neurotics* (Translated by James Strachey. Routledge, [1912–1913] 2003), p. 156.

55 Sigmund Freud. *Totem and Taboo: Some Points of Agreement Between the Mental Lives of Savages and Neurotics* (Translated by James Strachey. Routledge, [1912–1913] 2003), p. 159.

56 Sigmund Freud. *Totem and Taboo: Some Points of Agreement Between the Mental Lives of Savages and Neurotics* (Translated by James Strachey. Routledge, [1912–1913] 2003), p. 163.

57 Sigmund Freud. *Totem and Taboo: Some Points of Agreement Between the Mental Lives of Savages and Neurotics* (Translated by James Strachey. Routledge, [1912–1913] 2003), p. 166.

child is held or tied and the circle of voices and singing around him grows louder. It vividly captures the moment of the cut, when the blood bursts out, and the subject's identity is formed as part of the group. As Freud explains, performing the act of cutting together establishes the bond of guilt between the tribesmen and, "[t]his bond is nothing else than the life of the sacrificial animal, which resides in its flesh and in its blood and is distributed among all the participants in the sacrificial meal".[58] The same emotional turbulence is also present in the ritual of circumcision in which the baby's entering into the realm of society and the legacy of Jewish masculine identity are similarly formed through a cut, involving a wound, and vulnerability.

Freud describes the *Totem Feast* as an "integral part of the totemic system"[59] that both drives and perpetuates its structure. A repeated occurrence of the feast bestows clan members their identity and shapes their relationship to each other and to their totem. Through this repeated act, the tribe members revisit and reenact the moment of birth of their civilisation and the act of murder, which, according to Freud, is fundamental to social life. Freud explains the power of communal eating, the social significance hidden in this act of shared dining. Through the communal meal, the clan members create a kinship that "can be acquired and strengthened by food which a man eats later and with which his body is renewed",[60] and through which they become one physical unity, "expressing a conviction that they were of one substance".[61]

While the textual conscious movement focuses on the ambivalent attitude towards the father as the root of the totem feast, the maternal and specifically breastfeeding emerges from beneath the surface. Freud explains that a sense of kinship sharing "bone and flesh" is different from the basic "fact that a man is a part of his mother's substance, having been born of her and having been nourished by her milk".[62] Despite Frued's use of negation, *the breastfeeding imagery* emerges in the text from the ritual description as an organising motif through which social relationships is established in the ritual – the shared meal is based on the mother nourishing her children, feeding them with her milk, and renewing their bodies with parts from her own body.

The Hebrew word "feast" or "dine together" (*lisod*), which also means "to nurse" allows a glimpse into that etymological bifurcation incorporated by maternal breastfeeding. A relationship of physical dependency that involves care and nourishing has a similar meaning as shared eating and drinking, pointing again to the origin of kinship in primary maternal images. This connection is also expressed

---

58 Sigmund Freud. *Totem and Taboo: Some Points of Agreement Between the Mental Lives of Savages and Neurotics* (Translated by James Strachey. Routledge, [1912–1913] 2003), p. 160.

59 Sigmund Freud. *Totem and Taboo: Some Points of Agreement Between the Mental Lives of Savages and Neurotics* (Translated by James Strachey. Routledge, [1912–1913] 2003), p. 154.

60 Sigmund Freud. *Totem and Taboo: Some Points of Agreement Between the Mental Lives of Savages and Neurotics* (Translated by James Strachey. Routledge, [1912–1913] 2003), p. 157.

61 Sigmund Freud. *Totem and Taboo: Some Points of Agreement Between the Mental Lives of Savages and Neurotics* (Translated by James Strachey. Routledge, [1912–1913] 2003), p. 157.

62 Sigmund Freud. *Totem and Taboo: Some Points of Agreement Between the Mental Lives of Savages and Neurotics* (Translated by James Strachey. Routledge, [1912–1913] 2003), p. 157.

in the details of the ritual itself and in the way in which the description of blood in the text echoes the act of maternal breastfeeding: the bound camel is placed on the altar, and even before the eating of the flesh begins, the blood bursts from the body of the animal and the tribe leader drinks it with ecstasy and desire. The emotional forces surrounding the anticipation, the thirst (for blood or milk) and the ritual ecstasy, echo the first moment of drinking milk from the mother's breast. Freud explains that in various ceremonies, the blood – or its substitute, wine – is the heart of the communal bond, leading the readers to the father-son relationship, but the textual description of the blood bursting out of the camel's body, resonates the primal experience of the milk coming out of the mother's breasts.

"The ethical force of the public sacrificial meal rested upon very ancient ideas",[63] Freud writes. Indeed, the image of breastfeeding sits at the basis of intimacy established through shared eating. Although emphasising the core of kinship in becoming "one substance"[64] and despite his exploration of that "ancient" image, Freud skips maternal breastfeeding and hastens to draw attention to the identification with the father in the killing and eating of the totem animal. He turns his gaze to the Oedipal narrative explaining that when the totem is consumed, swallowed and internalised, both poles of the ambivalent attitude towards the father – murderous and identificatory – can be expressed and resolved.[65] Just as identification with the father and incorporation of his image is the resolution of the conflictual attitude towards him, so is eating of the totem constitutes the solution that establishes paternal image from which the social order sprouts.

This is, in fact, the Freudian totem. In the myth he portrays, the images of the father oscillate between being a cruel and persecuting tyrant and being a victim of the brother's rage. The relationship towards the totem consists of a circular movement of projections and introjections that echoes Klein's conceptualisation of the primary relationship with the mother. Her descriptions of the schizoid-paranoid polarisation between the 'good breast' and the 'bad breast', representing the split in the maternal image, which is sometimes experienced as nourishing and at other times as threatening and dangerous. When the infant struggles to bear the experience of rage and frustration within, they attempt to deal with the anxiety, by using phantasies of splitting, projection and introjection, in which maternal images oscillate between nourishing and persecuting. Thus, when the infant finds it difficult to bear the anxiety of the destructive forces coming from outside, he/she internalises the overflow of projections in order to experience the mother's breast as abundant, satisfying and loving. From its earliest days, the baby has been engaged in such

63 Sigmund Freud. *Totem and Taboo: Some Points of Agreement Between the Mental Lives of Savages and Neurotics* (Translated by James Strachey. Routledge, [1912–1913] 2003), p. 182.
64 Sigmund Freud. *Totem and Taboo: Some Points of Agreement Between the Mental Lives of Savages and Neurotics* (Translated by James Strachey. Routledge, [1912–1913] 2003), p. 157.
65 Sigmund Freud. *Totem and Taboo: Some Points of Agreement Between the Mental Lives of Savages and Neurotics* (Translated by James Strachey. Routledge, [1912–1913] 2003), p. 183.

a circular struggle of projection and introjection of the destructive forces, which produce polarisation between love and hate in his or her inner world.[66]

Splitting is prominent in Freud's description of the relationship with the father, in the contrast between the violent and cruel tyrant figure before the murder and the loving and protective father figure after the hunger and the anger have been satisfied in the murderous feast. Just as in Klein's theory of the primary dyadic relationship, the tribesmen express a behaviour that oscillates between violent outbursts of hatred towards the totem animal and feelings of guilt and remorse reflected in their reconciliatory and reparative efforts. The ritualistic killing of the totem animal, accompanied by feelings of anger and hatred, allows the clan members to develop the image of the good, caring and loving father within them. As Klein explains, after feeding from the breast, when the infant is full and satisfied, the image of the good breast can grow within.

Both the projection-introjection cycles and the splits characterising Freud's primal myth echo the early attitude towards the mother's breast and the emotional flux arising in the archaic dyad. A maternal image of breastfeeding thus serves as an unconscious framework in the text and Freud indeed uses words such as "blood", "flesh", "body" and "milk" to describe kinship shared relation with the totem. He describes feelings of closeness and intimacy, the desire to suckle and swallow, the experience of dependency and the oral aggression expressing anger and frustration. All these characterises the early relationship towards the mother in breastfeeding but are nonetheless used in the text to describe the complex relationship with the father. Maternal breastfeeding becomes the textual unconscious image underlying the descriptions of the ritual which is then framed under a masculine structure that marks the beginning of paternal law.

Maternal images and emotional conflicted attitude towards the mother create the conditions upon which the myth of patricide and the Oedipal metaphor is built. As Silverman points out in writing about circumcision, the rite "erases female motherhood while conferring uterine fertility onto men".[67] By using maternal symbolism, the pattern of identification between men in the ceremony is born as a replacement for the maternal. Highlighting the envy of maternal reproductive capacity, Silverman describes the way an inability to recognise conflicted feelings in the relationship with the mother leads to a melancholic identification with her – an appropriation of maternal qualities while erasing the conflicted relation to their origin.

A similar analysis is conducted by Róheim for *the covenant of the pieces*– the biblical ceremony between God and Abraham in Genesis 15. During the ceremonial covenant Abraham severs livestock into two pieces to allow a beam of light to pass between them. As Róheim elaborates, the image of the passing between

---

66 Melanie Klein. "Notes on Some Schizoid Mechanisms." *Int. J. Psychoanal.* 27 (1946): 99–110.
67 Eric Kline Silverman. "Circumcision and Masculinity: Motherly Men or Brutal Patriarchs?" In: Harry Brod and Shawn Israel Zevit (eds.) *Brother Keepers: New Perspectives on Jewish Masculinity.* (Harriman, TN: Men's Studies Press, 2010), p. 55.

the two parts of the body, and the creation of the protective bond through this cutting and separating, echo the image of birth, allowing two male characters in the text, God and Abraham, to 'give birth' to their covenant, cultivating maternal primary qualities such as intimacy, fertility, care and protection.[68] By appropriating maternal fertility and birth qualities in the ceremony, the male covenant grants Abraham the ability to reproduce and procreate. As in the ritual of circumcision, male kinship – close bonds of care and intimacy, grow out of a psychic process of both repudiation and appropriation – identification and denial – of the maternal. The creation of the masculine circle in the ceremony is based on the appropriation and reconstruction of characteristics of the primary relationship with the mother: the cutting of the foreskin replaces the cutting of the umbilical cord; wine replaces blood; eating together and then speaking replace the act of breastfeeding.

"Through the mouth that I fill with words instead of my mother whom I miss from now on more than ever, I elaborate that want, and the aggressivity that accompanies it, by saying". Kristeva writes.[69] Whereas Freud explains the conflictual feelings arising in the ritual of the totem sacrifice as a representation of the attitude towards the father, Kristeva marks them as a reflection of the drama that accompanies the subject's relationship to the mother's body. Going back to the maternal, she shows that, in fact, both the prohibition against eating from the totem and its murderous feast are attempts to work through the conflict towards the mother. The frustrating relationship with the mother's body, she explains, is manifested in the totemic ritual that reasserts the separations on which culture is founded. Freud describes the birth of the social subject through the ritual and Kristeva uses Lacanian terms to draw on his interpretation explaining that, if the imaginary register envelops the subject in an unbearable frustrating relations, expressed in the whole-body image the sacrificial act, by cutting the body and shattering its wholeness, allows for the symbolic order to be established. In the painful absence of the maternal – represented by the totem animal – words can begin to grow as its substitute and symbolic signification. Through identification with the pain of the animal and out of the experience of loss, verbal representation can appear. Thus, through the cutting of the body, a transition is created to the symbolic field, allowing representation in language.

The cutting of the animal body lays out a matrix of binary oppositions organised in language: inside and outside (through the act of swallowing), matter and spirit, human and divine, pure and impure, solid and liquid. For Kristeva, however, this cutting is not that of the male body, (as in circumcision and castration - or at least not only about that), but rather a more primal cutting deeply rooted in the relationship with the mother. The ritual of eating the totem recapitulates the primary drama that takes place in the subject's world in relation to the

---

68 Géza Róheim. "The Symbolism of Subincision." *Am. Imago* December 6, no. 4 (1949): 321–328.
69 Julia Kristeva. *Powers of Horror: An Essay on Abjection* (New York: Columbia University Press, 1982), p. 41.

mother's body. The food is abominable, she explains, because it blurs the boundary between nature and culture, between the self and non-self, between inside and outside. Oral aggression expressed in the ritual stems from the frustrating relationship with maternal breast which introduces the subject to early experiences of separation and deprivation – a primary cutting before the threat of castration is coupled with the paternal function. The totem animal represents the maternal oral object and the prohibition against harming and eating the animal is associated with the prohibition of incest. In other words, for Kristeva, the prohibition against eating the totem reflects the primary moments of separating the speaking subject from maternal body, distinguishing nature from culture through the abjection of the mother's body in which aggressive swallowing creates the conditions for detaching from it.

The animal's body is consumed in the ritual, devoured by the clansmen until it disappeared entirely, and nothing remains of it, but the digestion of its flesh both creates to and conceals images of the mother's body. This communal eating enables expression of conflicted feelings inherent to the relationship with the maternal and allows internalisation of its symbolism. Yet, once created, this representation, must also be repressed and disappear under a phallocentric language. Within a language that is based on the prohibition of incest, there is no room for images arising from the intimate relationship with the maternal. Any return to a dimension that touches on the maternal, must be repressed and covered with the characteristics of the paternal function. Thus, the ritual establishes the separation from maternal body, but at the same time covers the images originating from it. Although returning to an archaic confrontation with the abjected maternal body, it is enveloped by the symbolic function and the image of the father.

As if obeying the incest taboo, Freud rejects any interpretation that preserves the memory of the relationship with the mother. In the previous chapter, I pointed out Freud's strong opposition to theoretical attempts to expand the concept of castration to include the loss of maternal breast.[70] Lou Andreas-Salomé and others have argued that every interruption of the continuum in the infant's world, any detachment from the breast made by the mother is experienced by the infant as a cutting, a loss of a part of his/her body. If the process of entering the symbolic is enabled through the experience of loss, through the breaking of the whole-body image, the act of breastfeeding is the dimension through which this transition is made possible. The threat of castration in the child's inner world recapitulates the cutting experience arising from the detachment from the breast, and the ambivalent attitude towards the father echoes the emotional conflict towards the mother. The textual movement repeats a similar structure in which the journey to get to the bottom of the simmering image beneath the totem feast, turns the gaze from the maternal to the Oedipal narrative linking the attributes emerging from the image of breastfeeding to the complex relationships between fathers and sons.

70 See Chapter I, pp. 59–60.

A Foreclosed Murder

Freud describes the way the historical traces of the taboo outline the formation of transactional exchange and trade relations. In the past, the word taboo, he explains, inhabited two opposite meanings: "the sacred and the unclean—was originally one and did not become differentiated until later".[71] The distinction we make today between the holly and the demonic, did not exist in the early stages of taboos, " 'Taboo' is itself an ambivalent word", he remarks, "and the prohibitions of taboo are to be understood as consequences of an emotional ambivalence".[72] The tabooed totem initially signified both divinity and corporality and included as a sort of transitional entity both the transcendent and material aspects at the same time.

The roots of totemic ritual represented in the past both the intimacy of shared meal with the deity and the absorption of the divine. The meaning of sacrifice, Freud explains, "—the sacred act par excellence … —originally had a somewhat different meaning, however, from its later one of making an offering to the deity in order to propitiate him or gain his favour".[73] Initially, it was not an act of exchange with the gods—a surrender and renunciation to gain protection, refuge, or assistance. Originally, the sacrifice itself was a conflicted act of both hostility and appeasement among believers in their relationship with their gods in which "sacrifice was nothing other than 'an act of fellowship between the deity and his worshippers'", and in which "[t]he god shared the animal sacrifices with his worshippers".[74] "As time went on", Freud continues, "the animal lost its sacred character and the sacrifice lost its connection with the totem feast; it became a simple offering to the deity, an act of renunciation in favour of the god".[75] Describing the transformation that took place over the years from the totem to the other deity, Freud elaborates on the split that gradually evolved in the divine, in which the images of gods shifted from the physical to take the form of the spiritual, and the sacrifice became a bodily representation fundamentally opposed to the divine transcendent aspect. In this process of separating between the sacred and the impure, between matter and the transcendent, "the animal lost its sacred character and … became a simple offering to the deity, an act of renunciation in favour of the god".[76] The same animal that initially contained both the divine and corporal aspects gradually

71 Sigmund Freud. *Totem and Taboo: Some Points of Agreement Between the Mental Lives of Savages and Neurotics* (Translated by James Strachey. Routledge, [1912–1913] 2003), p. 78.

72 Sigmund Freud. *Totem and Taboo: Some Points of Agreement Between the Mental Lives of Savages and Neurotics* (Translated by James Strachey. Routledge, [1912–1913] 2003), p. 78.

73 Sigmund Freud. *Totem and Taboo: Some Points of Agreement Between the Mental Lives of Savages and Neurotics* (Translated by James Strachey. Routledge, [1912–1913] 2003), p. 154.

74 Sigmund Freud. *Totem and Taboo: Some Points of Agreement Between the Mental Lives of Savages and Neurotics* (Translated by James Strachey. Routledge, [1912–1913] 2003), p. 155.

75 Sigmund Freud. *Totem and Taboo: Some Points of Agreement Between the Mental Lives of Savages and Neurotics* (Translated by James Strachey. Routledge, [1912–1913] 2003), p. 174.

76 Sigmund Freud. *Totem and Taboo: Some Points of Agreement Between the Mental Lives of Savages and Neurotics* (Translated by James Strachey. Routledge, [1912–1913] 2003), p. 174.

split into an oppositional binarism in which the animal becomes equated to matter, radically objectified in a way that could be traded as part of transactional exchanges with the deity, and whose sacrifice enabled a God in its more familiar form. This process facilitated the movement from a god to God, giving rise to the concept of divinity as a transcendental representation opposed to material dimension, a God who overcame "the animal side of his own nature",[77] distancing "*himself*" from the earthly, the material and the feminine.

Freud depicts this process as part of the transition to patriarchy,

> God Himself had become so far exalted above mankind that He could only be approached through an intermediary—the priest. At the same time divine kings made their appearance in the social structure and introduced the patriarchal system into the state.[78]

Alongside this movement, gradually splitting between the divine and the material, an ability to trade and engage in exchanges solidified as well: "With the establishment of the idea of private property sacrifice came to be looked upon as a gift to the deity".[79] The sacrificial ritual marks the beginning of an exchange relations between humans and gods in which sacrificing the body enables to tear it from its' transcendent aspect reducing it to a corporality that can be traded, the sacrifice of which at the same time elevated God to "his" inaccessible transcendence.

Deploying the binary opposites in the sacrificial ritual is not only the mark of a relationship of exchange with God but also the creation of the binary structure through which the maternal becomes identified with corporality. The transition into the symbolic in the subject's world becomes possible, according to Kristeva, through a process in which the mother's body is abjected – expelled, murdered and sacrificed – enabling the formation of a fertile ground upon which meanings can be created in language.

While describing this process, and without delving into the depth of the conflict with the maternal, Freud uses the emotional richness arising from the primary dyadic relationship in order to impart exclusivity and primacy to the Oedipal paternal relationship. This Freudian trajectory mirrors the ritual, re-enacting it in a textual movement. He draws from the forces and images that emerge in the relationship with the mother to establish them in the relationship with the father. Portraying an Oedipal picture of an ongoing struggle between fathers and sons, in which the mother serves as an object of desire alone, he obscures any trace of the intensity of feelings: of dependency, rage and love in the relationship with the maternal that

77 Sigmund Freud. *Totem and Taboo: Some Points of Agreement Between the Mental Lives of Savages and Neurotics* (Translated by James Strachey. Routledge, [1912–1913] 2003), p. 175.

78 Sigmund Freud. *Totem and Taboo: Some Points of Agreement Between the Mental Lives of Savages and Neurotics* (Translated by James Strachey. Routledge, [1912–1913] 2003), p. 174.

79 Sigmund Freud. *Totem and Taboo: Some Points of Agreement Between the Mental Lives of Savages and Neurotics* (Translated by James Strachey. Routledge, [1912–1913] 2003), p. 160.

might have been part of his allegory of the social subject emergence. He does not touch on the complex emotions stemming from the relationship with the maternal, expressed in the murderous feast of the totem, but explains them within the framework of the relationship with the father, refusing an exploration of maternal images such as *birth* and *breastfeeding* resonating in the text. The maternal disappears, and the relationship with the mother is repudiated, but the images, hidden in plain sight continue to move through the text and serve to establish the basis for language. Thus, the picture drawn by Freud is fundamentally rooted in both the use of maternal function and the denial of its significance in establishing culture.

Through the textual repression of the emotional richness and conflicts in relation to the maternal, fixating them solely into the paternal, the mother is robbed of the possibility of becoming a subject. Mirroring the ritual, Freud establishes his theory in the text through a web of binary oppositions – the separation between body and mind, matter and spirit, as well as between man and woman, solidified upon entering the symbolic realm. The social subject (both male and female) can only identify him/herself through the Oedipal, leaving the maternal associated with the corporeal abject. In Kristeva's words, in the Freudian theory, "the Other no longer has a grip on the three apices of the triangle where subjective homogeneity resides; and so, it jettisons the object into an abominable real, inaccessible except through jouissance".[80]

The image of circumcision, as it emerges in the text, is positioned to provide an answer to maternal breastfeeding and female fertility. An infantile experience of vulnerability, hunger and dependency in the text is understood and solved by placing the male genitalia as an organising axis through which the child can be symbolically nourished. Freud summons this image precisely at the textual moment in which a discussion of the mother goddesses emerges, serving as a reminder of the danger inherent in maternal power. Laying out cycles of incarnation of the father-son relationship in historical sequence, he also briefly touches on female deities. Within the circular description, which oscillates between "the son's sense of guilt and the son's rebelliousness",[81] feminine divinities emerge for which Freud finds it difficult to find a place in the historical continuum. As he writes, "I cannot suggest at what point in this process of development a place is to be found for the great mother-goddesses".[82]

In the face of the possibility that maternal goddesses might have played a role in cultural development, Freud hastens to posit the metaphor of circumcision, bringing the discussion back to the ritual, to the father-son relation and interrupting the exploration of maternal power. Elaborating the threat posed to anyone who

80 Julia Kristeva. *Powers of Horror: An Essay on Abjection* (New York: Columbia University Press, 1982), p. 9.
81 Sigmund Freud. *Totem and Taboo: Some Points of Agreement Between the Mental Lives of Savages and Neurotics* (Translated by James Strachey. Routledge, [1912–1913] 2003), p. 176.
82 Sigmund Freud. *Totem and Taboo: Some Points of Agreement Between the Mental Lives of Savages and Neurotics* (Translated by James Strachey. Routledge, [1912–1913] 2003), p. 173.

worships or remains loyal to the goddesses, Freud connects the image of circumcision to the notion of castration as a reminder of the bitter fate of god figures such as Athis, Adonis and Tammuz, who were "youthful divinities [who] enjoying the favours of mother goddesses".[83] In this way, he reminds readers (and perhaps more accurately, himself) of the danger inherent in "committing incest with their mother in defiance of their father".[84] These young male deities, who remained faithful to the maternal goddesses, who recognised and worshipped maternal power, lived, as Freud interprets, a short life, and were subjected to punishments that echoes castration. Thus, when the maternal power and nourishment arise in the text, when a window is opened to the mother's role in the historical process of cultural development, when Freud encounters the power of female motherhood and the dependency relationship embedded in it, he positions the image of circumcision as a key that eliminates the conflict and reminds us of the intensity of the threat of castration.

Different interpretations of the totem emerge in the text and a wide range of theories are laid out. However, the image of circumcision narrows multiple possibilities to focus on the centrality of castration anxiety and the totality of paternal realm. The cutting of the male genital organ signifies the central symbolic axis through which social life is formed and through which subjects assume their identity. While laying out in front of the readers a wealth of theories, modes of thinking and interpretations to the origins of totemism, towards the end of the text, after describing the sacrificial ritual, Freud, insists on the parallel between the totem and the father, emphasising the Oedipal meanings of the ritual. Instituting a knot between circumcision and castration he confines a range of theoretical possibilities to the Oedipal narrative, and the male lineage.

In response to maternal images in the text, the image of circumcision appears casting additional cover to eliminate maternal roots. This manoeuvre preserves the primal relationship with the mother as an archaic memory or image through which the subject's social identity grows, while, at the same time, obscuring the traces of the maternal and appropriating the drama of the conflicted relation towards her through the Oedipal attitude towards the father. Thus, the emotional complexity remains buried under the veil of a ritual that is simultaneously tied to castration as a taboo against approaching the maternal. Although the "cut" originates in the conflicted relationship with the mother, it is converted through the image of circumcision to become a paternal legacy that forbids access to the maternal realm.

Perhaps we can understand the way in which the image of breastfeeding constitutes an external envelope that organises the relationship with the totem (and the father) by using the concept of Foreclosure.[85] When Freud repudiates the

---

83 Sigmund Freud. *Totem and Taboo: Some Points of Agreement Between the Mental Lives of Savages and Neurotics* (Translated by James Strachey. Routledge, [1912–1913] 2003), p. 177.

84 Sigmund Freud. *Totem and Taboo: Some Points of Agreement Between the Mental Lives of Savages and Neurotics* (Translated by James Strachey. Routledge, [1912–1913] 2003), p. 177.

85 Foreclosure is a psychic mechanism Lacan described in the development of psychotic conditions and as an explanation for the Freudian term *Verwerfung*, meaning repudiation. In contrast to neurotic

maternal – the relation with which is not only conflicted and thus repressed but also denied and undergo a Foreclosure, a *Verwerfung* – maternal images return to embrace the text from the outside. In this way, the image of maternal breastfeeding serves as the basis for identification with the father figure and provides the structure of closeness created in the totemic ritual through the act of eating. The repeated cycle of projections and introjections that characterises the relation to the totem stems from an ambivalent relationship with the mother that is denied and thus return from without as an organising image.

This conceptualisation of the foreclosed maternal also makes it possible to mark the difference between the aftermath of the ambivalence in the relationship with the father, and the conflicted emotions in the relationship with the mother. As Amber Jacobs points out, the return of the repressed is what befalls in relation to phantasies of patricide – the murder of the father – which, are repressed, but then reappear in language and culture as the law of the father. The conflict in relation to the maternal, on the other hand, is not repressed but undergoes foreclosure: maternal dimension is rejected, denied, eliminated and disappears without any possibility of returning; Matricide, the murder of the mother does not receive expression within the realm of language and the symbolic. Jacobs points out that the Oedipal myth is not only the founding myth of psychoanalysis but also the only myth through which meaning is given, and through which the subject can enter into language.[86] The exclusivity of the Oedipal myth prevents it from becoming a part of a vast and inexhaustible mosaic of other myths, she explains; a totality that also causes it to lose its complexity and movement. By isolating the story of Oedipus as the founding, constitutive and sole myth of psychoanalysis, a range of alternative mental structures is denied and the possibility of touching on other aspects and other understandings of the Oedipal myth itself disappears.

In Freud's narrative for the development of culture presented in *Totem and Taboo*, the Oedipal myth is inflated and positioned as an origin, a pre-Oedipal aetiology, anchoring the formation of society in a specific history focused on the relationship with the father. This fixation of prehistory in the structure of the relationship with the father alone obscures the range of structures, questions and emotions associated with maternal relationship, and positions the Oedipal structure as a monolithic, timeless and all-embracing truth. This movement raises questions, following Jacobs' words, regarding the gap between the return of the repressed that occurs in the relationship with the father, which returns as a significant component in the foundation of culture and what is not possible for the relationship with the

---

structure in which the signifier is repressed and pushed into the unconscious, producing a gap in the chain of signifiers that will manifest as a symptom, in Foreclosure, the process of signification itself is eliminated, creating a different structure of the chain of signifiers. The signifier that undergoes Foreclosure does not arise from the unconscious but returns from the outside, creating the psychotic symptoms of hallucinatory states.

86 Amber Jacobs. *On Matricide: Myth, Psychoanalysis, and the Law of the Mother* (New York: Colombia University Press, 2007).

mother. If, as Freud so accurately describes, the phantasy of patricide constitutes the beginning of a creative process, through which the image of the good father is internalised establishing 'paternal law' and the internal structure of the superego, what happens in the parallel process in relation to *Matricide* – the murder of the mother? The conflicted eruptive emotions in relation to the mother, feelings of dependency, rage, and matricidal phantasies towards her do not give rise to a similar process, and *a law of the mother* does not receive recognition to become part of the social system. When it comes to matricide, it is possible, to trace a 'double murder' that drives a wedge in the return of the repressed process, repudiating the mother beyond the boundaries of language and culture. The mother is not only repressed but also denied rejected and negated; when it comes to psychoanalysis, the maternal is foreclosed, abolished to the realm of forgetfulness and can only be identified with 'absence' and 'nothingness'. While the Oedipal myth of the 'murder of the father' acts as an essential component of the process of human development and "as a powerful metaphor at the root of culture, the 'murder of the mother' is thrown into the abyss of oblivion and its lost traces can only echo 'nothingness'".[87]

"The memory of the first great act of sacrifice thus proved indestructible, in spite of every effort to forget it",[88] Freud writes. The many attempts to repress the primordial act of murder, upon which culture grew, failed and, time after time, the forgotten image arises from the depths of the unconscious. The sacrificial rituals that are repeated in different forms in many cultures recreate the same mythical tragedy, reminiscent of an "original sin", a terrible act that has been forgotten, but traces of this elimination process, according to Freud, "must inevitably have left ineradicable traces in the history of humanity; and the less it itself was recollected, the more numerous must have been the substitutes to which it gave rise".[89] Indeed, the repeated Oedipal story of the murder of the father is a substitute for an earlier, more primal murder whose roots penetrate deep into the depths of the human psyche and return throughout the annals of humanity, namely, the murder of the mother. Yet, the traces of this Matricide is repeatedly blurred in the transition to culture.

Kristeva and the "Doubling" of the Maternal

The narrowing of the theoretical discussion on matricide indicates the transparency of this concept for psychoanalysis itself in which the separation from the mother and her radical othering is perceived as vital elements in the subject's development. Matricide, Kristeva explains, "is a vital necessity, the sine-qua-non condition of our individuation". According to her, it is the basis for our becoming speaking

---

87 Yael Pilowsky Bankirer. "'I Really was the Mummy' the Double Act of Matricide." *Conversations* (in Hebrew) 3, no. 2 (2022): 176.

88 Sigmund Freud. *Totem and Taboo: Some Points of Agreement Between the Mental Lives of Savages and Neurotics* (Translated by James Strachey. Routledge, [1912–1913] 2003), p. 176.

89 Sigmund Freud. *Totem and Taboo: Some Points of Agreement Between the Mental Lives of Savages and Neurotics* (Translated by James Strachey. Routledge, [1912–1913] 2003), p. 180.

subjects, and yet she traces the footsteps of the maternal to explore the intricacies of this pre-lingual dimension.[90] In revisiting Freud's *Totem and Taboo*, she recounts the story of the primal horde, the events leading to the formation of culture and the starting point of language and representation.[91] As she reveals, the aspects that Freud delves into regarding the paternal function, which prohibits and separates, conceal beneath it another, even more primal dimension – the dual, ambivalent relation towards the mother; an under-spoken realm, revealing glimpses of other possibilities for psychoanalysis, "other thoughts of Freud, from which he will not draw any conclusions, that allow one to progress in another direction".[92]

When Freud portrays the profane/sacred ambivalence as relating only the paternal pole, he neglects what Kristeva refers to as "the other side of the religious phenomenon", an aspect "that Freud points to when he brings up dread, incest…" but "nevertheless disappears during the final elucidation of the problem".[93] He discusses at length the taboo of incest, she explains, but in the end, he declares the primordial murder of the father as the mythical event that founds religion, leaving the question of incest and the maternal merely as a background for cultural development. The economy of the subject described by Freud in the text also contains another aspect omitted from sight. The Freudian argument, which hastens to conclude by "substituting the father for the totem animal in the formula for totemism",[94] neglects the other, maternal aspect.

Contrary to the paternal pole that Freud extensively explores, Kristeva illuminates the other side, the hidden and elusive, maternal dimension. As she demonstrates, the origin of religion and culture is deeply embedded in the relationship with the mother, emerging from an experience of "imprecise boundaries" in which there are no separations between self and other, pleasure and pain, subject and object, and in which "pain is born out of an excess of fondness and a hate that, refusing to admit the satisfaction it also provides, is projected toward an other".[95] Her understandings draw on both Freud's texts and Lacan's theory, but in contrast to them, she argues that the body precedes the gaze and that without the body there would be no reflection in the mirror and no words. For her, both the process of becoming a speaking subject and the beginning of culture originate earlier, in the dyadic relationship with the maternal, through the encounter with the abject.

90 Julia Kristeva. *Black Sun: Depression and Melancholia* (New York: Columbia University Press, 1987). pp. 27–28.
91 Julia Kristeva. *Powers of Horror: An Essay on Abjection* (New York: Columbia University Press, 1982).
92 Julia Kristeva. *Powers of Horror: An Essay on Abjection* (New York: Columbia University Press, 1982), p. 60.
93 Julia Kristeva. *Powers of Horror: An Essay on Abjection* (New York: Columbia University Press, 1982), p. 57.
94 Sigmund Freud. *Totem and Taboo: Some Points of Agreement Between the Mental Lives of Savages and Neurotics* (Translated by James Strachey. Routledge, [1912–1913] 2003), p. 152.
95 Julia Kristeva. *Powers of Horror: An Essay on Abjection* (New York: Columbia University Press, 1982), p. 60.

Kristeva coins the term 'abject' to articulate the mechanism of rejection (of the mother's body) in the process of subject formation, the revolt against that which gave us our own existence. The abject, identified with the mother's body, is an ambivalent dimension of both attraction and repulsion, of enchantment and violent expulsion. It is an aggressive uprising against parts of the self that continue to provoke the subject, to charm and arouse him/her; against an aspect that is both craved for and suffocating, desired and impossible. The abject signifies what is expelled from the body, rejected and turned into an 'other': Spit, blood, milk, urine, faeces, puss and vomit – these vital products are essential to preserve life, but that life cannot bear. It is the way to know the self through the non-self; to recognise the ego through the otherness that has been removed from the 'I'; through eliminating an other.

In this process of self-formation, the mother's body functions as the boundary line that teaches the child to distinguish between inside and outside, nature and culture, 'I' and 'non-I'. The mother, as the caregiver of the child, teaches him/her to recognise the products of his/her body as an external essence, through using her own body, identifying herself with what has been secreted, with the abject that has been removed. The mother's body becomes something that the (future) subject is captivated by and frustratingly dependent on, the dimension that he or she must reject in order to save himself or herself from the abject and to become autonomous. Even before the separation between subject and object is established, the infant learns to cope with the frustration inherent in the encounter with the mother's body through the process of abjection, defending him/herself against a disturbing ambivalent experience through repeatedly marking a boundary line that expels the abject to produce a separated subject. It is the ongoing psychic process of excretion of the abject, the liquid, the impossible which is anchored in the maternal body image and becomes separated through the drawing of boundaries which will gradually sharpen: between self and other, between inside and outside, between liquid and solid, between pure and impure, between nature and culture.

The abject simultaneously constitutes and threatens the self. It provides an encounter with an otherness within, which repeatedly overwhelms the subject. That abjected part which is excreted from the body, exiled and repressed, does not cease to threaten the integrity and coherence of the self, and therefore the subject is continuously guarding against it by delineating the border. Due to the difficulty of addressing this aspect of the abject, according to Kristeva, culture is based on repeated abjection of the maternal. Various societies go to great lengths to eliminate and control women's power. Wherever taboos are present, "ritualization of defilement is accompanied by a strong concern for separating the sexes, and this means giving men rights over women". The laws of impurity, religious prohibitions, and taboos in various societies are designed to protect against female power which "becomes synonymous with a radical evil that is to be suppressed".[96] Even when women are positioned as submissive objects, more and more defences are required

---

96 Julia Kristeva. *Powers of Horror: An Essay on Abjection* (New York: Columbia University Press, 1982), p. 70.

to domesticate them and ward off their threat. The ambiguous and blurred boundaries associated with the abjected maternal, pose a danger to symbolic order as a system of differences created through binaries pivoting around the axis of gender.

According to Kristeva's analysis, the need to guard against maternal power is not a direct result of paternal law or prohibition but rather a product of the generative maternal power; of her procreation and maternal creativity which at the same time enables the creation of culture and threatens it. While Freud analyses both the murder taboo and the incest taboo as products of paternal law, Kristeva leads to another possibility rooted in the relationship with mother's body. The taboos that underlie culture echo the initial process that takes place even before the law of the father and are embedded in the primary encounter with the maternal. Following Lévi-Strauss, she marks the "confrontation with the ab-ject"[97] as the primary origin through which every social system, every symbolic and linguistic ability is cast. But unlike him, she does not investigate social structure but leads the readers to the libidinal economy of the subject indicating the ways in which the taboos hinder the unpleasant and fascinating encounter with the abject.[98] For her, this pre-linguistic and chaotic experience, characterised by emotional duality and ambivalence leads to the formation of these taboos in order to separate between inside and outside and between pleasure and pain, which would later be constituted as external taboos under paternal law.

Kristeva marks the primary relationship to the mother's body as a prototype on the basis of which other relationships are formed. This impossible psychic possession holding an incessant and ambivalent tension creates the preliminary conditions for the emergence of representation. The prohibition against incest has its origins, long before the father, in the frustrating relationship to the mother's body, against which an archaic cutting is established, a primary separation which is not yet castration and certainly not symbolic, but it establishes a first prototype for boundary drawing. At a time in which the separation between self and other is not yet formed, the subject defends him/herself against those primary experiences of pain mixed with pleasure through abjection. This cutting, taking place in the infant's psyche, remains an archaic memory, even after being repressed by paternal taboo prohibitions.

The difficulty of bearing the abject, Kristeva explains, is expressed in a Freudian psychoanalytic theory, which is attempting to gloss over maternal otherness and is quick to fetishise any lack as a missing object, phallus or male organ, thus covering

---

97   Julia Kristeva. *Powers of Horror: An Essay on Abjection* (New York: Columbia University Press, 1982), p. 42.

98   Lévi-Strauss emphasised the structural aspect of the prohibition on incest. He saw it as a basic characteristic of any human society, through which the mechanism of exchange between different families, societies and cultures is established. The prohibition on incest does not allow the base units (the family) to act as an Autarkic economy and facilitate the involvement of other units (families). In this way, a symbolic system of exchange (and trafficking of women) is created, on the basis of which the entire social structure is formed.

the tensions inherent to the maternal. From this perspective, we can think both about Freud's 'cuts' in the text when discussing the question of incest and about the coupling he makes between circumcision and castration. Similar to the economy of the subject, every encounter with the maternal brings with it the threat to the ability to conceptualise a psychoanalytic theory as a closed and coherent system. Thus, the gaze turns towards paternal law, and the mother is positioned as an object. The textual response reveals itself as an almost ritualistic process, separating the pure from the impure and positioning the maternal as an object of desire, an external dimension of otherness.

Any attempt to open a theoretical discussion in which the mother is neither an object of desire for the father, nor an object of satisfaction for the child evokes the same impossible experience that Kristeva attributes to the encounter with the maternal abject. Freud himself describes a similar anxiety response to the maternal in his *Das unheimlich assay*. As he details "the most uncanny thing of all", is in fact, "a transformation of another phantasy which had originally nothing terrifying about it at all, but was qualified by a certain lasciviousness—the phantasy, I mean, of intra-uterine existence".[99] In these words, Freud describes the horror that arises in the encounter with the maternal; a terror that grows – as he himself shows – not because of paternal prohibition and castration anxiety but out of that primary experience in relation to blurred boundaries of the maternal, the helplessness and dependency, due to what Kristeva calls the "abject encounter with feminine sex".[100]

In both Freud's and Lacan's conceptualisation of the Oedipal complex, the emphasis is placed on the father and the role of paternal law to illuminate the way into language. In Kristeva's scenario, the father remains as the third who echoes the voices produced in the primary dyad between mother and child. While Freud identifies the transition to language and symbolic representation through paternal law, Kristeva opens a door to an earlier relational field within which the law is formed: the relationship with the maternal. Building on Freud's outlining of the ambivalence towards the father which underlies social structure, Kristeva leads to a previous ambivalence through which the attitude towards the father is created, in reproducing a 'multiplication' of that relationship and transferring it into the symbolic array. She describes the primary experience of frustration, an ambivalent battle, saturated with anxieties and threats towards the (m)other which constantly returns from within; repeated need to reject and guard against the abject; a legality that emerges in the cuts and rhythms of the body – all these constitute, for her, the emotional richness of the relationship with the maternal, which later serve as the paradigmatic model for every encounter, social relations and paternal law; the turbulence through which language itself is formed.

99 Sigmund Freud. "The Uncanny." In: James Strachey (ed.) *The Standard Edition of the Complete Psychological Works of Sigmund Freud* 17 (1919). London: The Hogarth Press and the Institute of Psycho-Analysis, 1955. p. 243.

100 Julia Kristeva. *Powers of Horror: An Essay on Abjection* (New York: Columbia University Press, 1982), p. 164.

According to Kristeva, the incest taboo – paternal prohibition – guards against that return of the abject that threatens the subject's existence, but it does so by establishing a boundary line, another cut that mirrors the archaic movement in the face of the maternal. Incest prohibition, she explains, "throws a veil over primary narcissism and the always ambivalent threats with which it menaces subjective identity".[101] Recreating a similar movement at the level of the symbolic, the prohibition performs both a cover and a repetition in relation to the maternal. Anchored in paternal function, the taboo comes to the aid of the subject to draw another boundary and protects against the abject through creation of the maternal as an external to the symbolic, placing women as objects of desire in the world of men. Thus, with the entry of paternal third, the law of the father, the separation between the subject and the object is cast into the symbolic order. However, in this way, the ancient murder of the mother remains buried under a veil that can only speak of the murder of the father.

Maternal Love[102]

The narrative described by Freud opens with the conflict – rejection, shame and love – inherent in the relationship with the mother, but then receives one answer: its origin lies in paternal prohibition. Questions inherent to the maternal, reflected through the prohibition of incest, are no longer the product of a complex relationship between the child and the mother, but a necessary consequence of the father's threat of castration and paternal law. As Kristeva explains, the focus on the father skips over a whole range of earlier complex relationships, splitting off the maternal dimension, which remains solely physical, bodily and inaccessible, while the Oedipal relationship emerges as the first stage of culture. Emphasising only one side of the Oedipal triangle this prism covers – rather than discovers – the many complexities and questions that exist within the richness inherent in the maternal vertex.

Kristeva's analysis expands the Oedipal conflict, turning the gaze to its maternal apex and anchoring the emerging ambivalent emotions in the relationship with the mother. Her description focuses not only on the abject and the difficulty in the face of maternal power but also explores the significant part of maternal love in the transition to culture. According to her, paternal law alone is not enough to defend against incest and murder, love is vital in this transition and the identification with maternal love is necessary in order to allow a transition into language. Without the possibility of bearing that love in our inner world, we would all be left engulfed in the actual body of the mother, and only the rebirth of the maternal within the paternal function allows the entry of the third. As she explains, this process requires

101 Julia Kristeva. *Powers of Horror: An Essay on Abjection* (New York: Columbia University Press, 1982), p. 63.
102 Parts of this subchapter were also published in Hebrew in MA'ARAG: The Israel Annual of Psychoanalysis. Yael Pilowsky Bankirer, "The Mother's Name of the Father: On Names and Subjectivity." *MA'ARAG Israel Ann. Psychoanal.* 11 (2024): 19–40.

passing through the identification with the mother, with both her love and her desire, that is, with maternal subjectivity.

In order to explore the buds of language, Kristeva turns to the early relationship with the mother portraying within it the creation of a triangular space in maternal ability to hold the gap, to maintain a dialectical movement, between the semiotic and symbolic. Whereas for Freud and Lacan the child is torn from the maternal (by the father) and is transferred into the symbolic, for Kristeva, this transition into language is not solely based on castration anxiety but also on surplus and pleasure derived from maternal love. As she argues, although the possibility to speak is rooted in the separation from maternal body in the absence of which language is generated, the conditions that allow representation emerge from maternal body itself. What is required is not only severance from the physical body but also the prospect of carrying the body image into language. In other words, the transition to the symbolic is not a violent act of negating the body, of detaching from it, but rather a process that establishes the body image in language through the semiotic and through maternal love.[103]

The semiotic layer is a pre-lingual field that contains within it the movement, emotion and linguistic rhythm. It is intrinsically close to the physical dimension and is created from it like a dance movement that precedes the array of signifiers, the symbolic layer. The impulses and movements of the body shape the sounds, melodies and feelings, pouring them into the linguistic system. The semiotic dimension is the integration of various modes in which the body is rooted in language. According to Kristeva, the subject is in constant tension between the semiotic and the symbolic, between the pre-linguistic space, where impulses lie, the layer that produces the body's movements, and the space of symbolic representations, the system of signifiers. The dialectical movement between these two layers, as she reminds psychoanalysis, is what allows the subject to acquire language. The gap created in the subject's inner world provides the conditions for generating linguistic substitutes through verbal representations, as words continue to be created in an attempt to bridge the gap that they themselves produce.

Kristeva describes the process of subject-formation as a continuous becoming, through this dialectical movement between the semiotic and the symbolic. In contrast to the familiar conception of coherent and stable subjectivity, she introduces a 'subject in process' to psychoanalytic theory, a subjectivity that is an unstable continuous transformation.[104] Her understandings make it possible to think of subjectivity not in absolute terms but as a multi-faceted, dynamic entity inherently incorporating conflicts and contradictions. Emerging from the encounter with the

103 Julia Kristeva. *Tales of Love* (New York: Columbia University Press, 1987a).

104 Julia Kristeva and Toril Moi. *The Kristeva Reader* (New York: Columbia University Press, 1986); Julia Kristeva. "Women's Time." In: C. Zanardi (ed.) *Essential Papers on the Psychology of Women* (New York: New York University Press, 1990), pp. 374–400; Julia Kristeva. "The Speaking Subject Is Not Innocent." In: Barbara Johnson (ed.) *Freedom and Interpretation: The Oxford Amnesty Lectures.* (New York: Basic Books, 1993), pp. 147–174.

mother's body and its pre-linguistic semiotic realm, the subject continues to form through moving between the body and the possibility of carrying an image.

This process begins, as Kelly Oliver interprets Kristeva's theory, in the mother's inner world, in her desire and love. The mother's phantasy of an other – any third beyond the child – opens a triadic space within the relationships with the child. Love, for Kristeva, is the ability to bear and hold the tension between the physical and the symbolic, to maintain the gap that will open the door to the entrance of that third. Through this love, the space between the vertices of the Oedipal triangle is preserved and the three-dimensional structure is formed, into which the father of the law will later enter. In this process, the child internalises the mother's longing for an other, identifies with her desire and is therefore able to release his/her grip of the actual body in order to identify with an image from her inner world.[105]

For Oliver, the transition to the symbolic, and to paternal law, is rooted in the possibility of moving from the mother's body to an identification with her desire through her love. The imaginary father, representing all the objects of the mother's love (men, women, books, work, social life, etc.), introduces a third dimension into the dyad even before the entry of the actual father. The maternal function always contains within it a third through which the child's relational world begins in the inner world of the mother. While, for Freud, the law of the father performs a cutting of the maternal in order to transfer the child from the mother's body into language, Oliver, following Kristeva, replaces this cutting with love and shows that the separation from the mother's body is preceded by a process of identification with maternal subjectivity, with her desire for a third, that later makes room for the entry of the father, thus creating the Oedipal structure.

When Freud explores the transition from the Darwinian brutal reality between men to social life in which fathers and their sons can sit together, describing the story of the primal horde of brothers murdering the father, he also lays out in a footnote Atkinson's theory that "found a less violent transition from the primal horde to the next social stage, at which numbers of males live together in a peaceable community".[106] Atkinson imagined a cycle of violence between fathers and sons, a never-ending murderous cycle and a struggle for power, in which "an ever-recurring violent succession to the solitary paternal tyrant, by sons whose parricidal hands were so soon again clenched in fratricidal strife". Portraying a story of jealousy and rage, and an endless war between men, Atkinson suggests that the transition to social life of peace could only happen through the mother's intervention. As he explains

> through the intervention of maternal love the sons—to begin with only the youngest, but later others as well—were allowed to remain with the horde, and

105 Kelly Oliver. "Kristeva's Sadomasochistic Subject and the Sublimation of Violence." *J. Fren. Franco. Phil.* 21, no. 1 (2013): 13–26.

106 Sigmund Freud. *Totem and Taboo: Some Points of Agreement Between the Mental Lives of Savages and Neurotics* (Translated by James Strachey. Routledge, [1912–1913] 2003), p. 165, footnote.

that in return for this toleration the sons acknowledged their father's sexual privilege by renouncing all claim to their mother and sisters.

without the mothers, "any new organization of society would be precluded".[107] While Freud's 'upper' text describes the contract between father and sons, the 'lower' text, the footnote, raises the possibility of exploring the role of the mother in the transition to peaceful social life. A similar idea is introduced by Juliet Mitchell, in her description of the mother's prohibitions and love in the mediation of sibling violence and excess-affection. This horizontal social axis between brothers and sisters, explored in her books "Siblings"[108] and "Fratriarchy", is governed by what she identifies as "the law of the mother" – the mother's key contribution to the psychosocial, prohibiting both violence and incest at the stage of new sibling arrival. "[M]ost of the world today operates upon patriarchal and patrilineal vertical family lines through what has been called the 'Law of the Father'" she writes, "...I argue ... that prior to that stage, the mother insists on the same prohibitions, but with different effects – she insists that there must be no incest or murder between her children, that is between the siblings".[109]

Mitchell's *law of the mother* echoes in Atkinson's description in which it is "through the intervention of maternal love",[110] and not due to paternal law, that the violence and incest are prevented. A similar argument can be found in Kristeva's writing, directing psychoanalytic theory to the power of maternal love and its significance in the transition to culture. Both of them uncovers – among other things – maternal role in the development of the ethical stance – *Thou Shalt Not Kill*. This movement is made possible by the mother's ability to hold within herself the relational bonds, both between father and son, and between siblings, holding love and thus enabling their connection in the budding of culture.

Although Kristeva is focused on the pre-Oedipal relationship between father and child and Mitchell is referring to the horizontal relations between siblings, they both emphasise, in my view, a similar struggle in which the child encounters a mother's other. Whether it is a new baby that will soon join the family or the realisation of the mother's 'third', the father, both traumatic situations encapsulate a challenge for the child – to deal with maternal subjectivity – the mother's desire and love for an other beyond him/her. In these new challenges for the child, it is the mother's love or in Mitchell's definition – the law of the mother, that allows this challenge to be faced without murder or incest, enabling the transition to social existence.

---

107 Sigmund Freud. *Totem and Taboo: Some Points of Agreement Between the Mental Lives of Savages and Neurotics* (Translated by James Strachey. Routledge, [1912–1913] 2003), p. 165.

108 Juliet Mitchell. *Siblings: Sex and Violence* (Cambridge: Polity Press, 2003).

109 Juliet Mitchell. *Fratriarchy: The Sibling Trauma and the Law of the Mother* (London and New York: Routledge, 2023), p. 4.

110 Sigmund Freud. *Totem and Taboo: Some Points of Agreement Between the Mental Lives of Savages and Neurotics* (Translated by James Strachey. Routledge, [1912–1913] 2003), p. 165.

The story outlined by Atkinson, hidden in the margins of the text, echoes Kristeva's theory as well as Mitchell's concepts of the budding of the psycho-social: it is maternal love that allows the transition from a violent Darwinian phantasy to social reality in which peace prevails. When Freud fastens his "upper text" description of the tyrannical pre-Oedipal father and his loving Oedipal counterpart, he overlooks maternal role linking together the various aspects of her love, bringing together father and son. This textual movement shifts the gaze from the origin of the Oedipal triangle in maternal subjectivity erasing the significance of the maternal vertex in the triadic relationship. Freud rejects Atkinson's arguments, explaining that he developed his theory because he "had no psycho-analytic hints to help him and ... was ignorant of Robertson Smith's studies".[111] According to him, it was patricide and the sons' experience of remorse and guilt that led them to "reconciliation with their father", and thus "[t]he totemic system was..., a covenant with their father, in which he promised them everything that a childish imagination may expect from a father—protection, care and indulgence".[112] Although he raises and discusses Atkinson's theory, in making this assertion, he closes the possibility of three-dimensional exploration of the foundation of social life, leaving the mother's role in the margins of the text.

Whereas the Freudian explanation of social life is reduced to the Oedipal, Kristeva asks to pause for a moment longer, adding further complexity to the Oedipal relationship.[113] She demonstrates that paternal love sprouts from maternal love and that the child's need for the mother's protection, care and love are, in fact, the foundation of social life and are later transferred or 'copied' into the father figure in the process of the formation of the totem. Thus, culture originates in maternal love, but at the same time, it is denied and cloned to another 'origin', in a way that leaves the mother as a spectral dimension beyond language.

Explorations of Maternal Subjectivity

When Freud describes the beginnings of culture and social structure, he cements the meaning of the totem in the father image erasing the mother's role in the pre-Oedipal. Alongside this image, other possibilities of genesis arise in the text, restoring the gaze at the maternal apex of the triangle. These theories emerge from between the lines of Freud's broad review, and although almost all of them are dismissed by him for various reasons in his efforts to substantiate his narrative of the origin of totemism, an alternative story of origin resonates through them.

One example is Frazer's psychological theory, following Spencer and Gillen's descriptions of the Arunta people in central Australia. According to Spencer and Gillen,

---

111   Sigmund Freud. *Totem and Taboo: Some Points of Agreement Between the Mental Lives of Savages and Neurotics* (Translated by James Strachey. Routledge, [1912–1913] 2003), p. 165.

112   Sigmund Freud. *Totem and Taboo: Some Points of Agreement Between the Mental Lives of Savages and Neurotics* (Translated by James Strachey. Routledge, [1912–1913] 2003), p. 168.

113   In *Tales of Love*, Kristeva calls this relationship: the imaginary or prehistoric father.

[t]he Arunta have a peculiar theory of conception and reincarnation. They believe that there are places scattered over the country ['totem centres'] at each of which the spirits of the dead of some one totem await reincarnation and enter the body of any woman who passes by the spot. When a child is born, the mother reports at which of these places she thinks it was conceived, and the child's totem is determined accordingly.[114]

On the basis of these descriptions, Frazer established a "theory of conception", which places the origin of the totem in the mother's desires.

Anything indeed that struck a woman at that mysterious moment of her life when she first knows herself to be a mother might easily be identified by her with the child in her womb. Such maternal fancies, so natural and seemingly so universal, appear to be the root of totemism.[115]

As Freud explains,

originally the woman believed that the animal, plant, stone or other object, with which her imagination was occupied at the moment when she first felt she was a mother, actually made its way into her and was later born in human form.

According to this understanding, the mother's inner world, her beliefs, desires and thoughts are expressed in the foundation of the totem, and in the beginning of social life, in which "the identity between a man and his totem would have a factual basis in his mother's belief".[116]

What was a woman in the totem culture thinking about in the moment she felt she was becoming a mother? What entered into her when she realised she was carrying a new baby? Touching upon the conditions that enable the formation of the Oedipal triangle, sketching the pre-Oedipal, the "before" moment, receives here a different answer to the question of 'origin', marking the formation of the 'third' even before the birth of the child, in the mother's fantasy, within the physical recognition of conception. Sensing movements inside her and fantasising about what has entered her body, the relationship with the 'father', the totem or the spirit of a third, emerges through the mother's subjectively. Thus, she links the various aspects of her life and connects her sexuality to her motherhood, her desires and sensations to the baby about to be born. Incorporating her pregnant body experience into the

114 Sigmund Freud. *Totem and Taboo: Some Points of Agreement Between the Mental Lives of Savages and Neurotics* (Translated by James Strachey. Routledge, [1912–1913] 2003), p. 133.

115 Sigmund Freud. *Totem and Taboo: Some Points of Agreement Between the Mental Lives of Savages and Neurotics* (Translated by James Strachey. Routledge, [1912–1913] 2003), p. 137. Freud is quoting from Frazer here: (James G. Frazer. *Totemism and Exogamy: A Treatise on Certain Early Forms of Superstition and Society* (London, 1910), p. 4).

116 Sigmund Freud. *Totem and Taboo: Some Points of Agreement Between the Mental Lives of Savages and Neurotics* (Translated by James Strachey. Routledge, [1912–1913] 2003), p. 136.

social realm, the mother weaves together the fantasy about the spirit that penetrated her with the fantasy about the child growing inside her, thus the body is carried as an open aspect to the symbolic, from which meanings are created and the beginning of the triadic relationship is cast.

Even before birth, even before the dyad between mother and child as two separate bodies, the mother's fantasy, incorporating the different aspects of her subjectivity provides the condition for establishing the triangular reality. Frazer's theory opens the possibility of exploring motherhood – conception, pregnancy, maternal-child relation – from the mother's point of view, touching the different ways in which her experiences, her subjectivity, create meanings. Whereas psychoanalysis explores the maternal through the eyes of the child, this possible fantasy opens the door to another perspective distilling the mother's apex in the Oedipal triangle. It enables an exploration of the way the connection between father and child is first established in the inner world of the mother-woman at the moment of fantasy of conception, in which the triangular space germinates, and in which the mother holds in one hand the fantasy for the child and in the other her desire for a third.

Encountering the inner world of mothers, in his fascinating investigations, Freud works on two opposing fronts simultaneously. With one hand he opens the door to a discussion of matriarchal cultures, the connection between the maternal and female sexuality, and the importance of the mother's inner world for the growth of the relationship between father and son, but with his other hand he covers the possibility of looking at these questions. He refers to Frazer's theory of conception as "remarkable" and advocates that it was in fact an expression of the "ignorance of the process by which men and animals reproduce their kind; and, in particular, ignorance of the part played by the male in fertilization".[117] He explains that if this was true, "totemism would be a creation of the feminine rather than of the masculine mind: its roots would lie in 'the sick fancies of pregnant women'". These are rooted, according to him, deep in the irrationality of a woman's mental-hormonal system, in "maternal imaginations" and "sick desires" of the pregnant woman. The encounter with the mother's inner world quickly leads him away from the open psychoanalytic discourse to the use of biological terms, through which he covers the cultural and social meanings of maternal subjectivity, imprisoning the mother in her corporal body.

The possibility that the totem represents the mother's feelings opens the door to understanding of desire as a process, and as a dimension which involves movement. Rather than a concept of desire which is focused solely on an object, this narrative contains a generative-desire that holds within it an array of evolving relationships. Maternal desire encapsulates a triangular space, maintaining the ongoing relationship between father and son/daughter. The theory of conception emerging in the text provides an opening into a view of pregnancy as a representation of the

---

117 Sigmund Freud. *Totem and Taboo: Some Points of Agreement Between the Mental Lives of Savages and Neurotics* (Translated by James Strachey. Routledge, [1912–1913] 2003), p. 167.

gap carried by the mother, which Kristeva describes, between the corporeal and symbolic. While the perception of motherhood through the eyes of the child leads to the collapse of images of pregnancy into a hermetic dyad – the baby and its part-objects, a look from the inner world of mothers reveals that it is a triangular space, linking sexuality and motherhood, desire and procreation, father and child, body and spirit.

Although the maternal at its very core – from pregnancy to motherhood – is a triangular space par excellence, under a concept that refuses to incorporate maternal subjectivity, to tie together her desire and her parenting, it remains as a dimension that contains within it a hermetic relationship, under a two-dimensional model of subject and object. Under this model, the mother-woman can only alternate between being a container for the child and being a container for the father. As part of the social structure projected onto the mother, Iris Young explains, there is also a split between a *woman's sexuality* and her *motherhood*.[118] The difficulty to integrate mothers' parental existence with their sexual existence is rooted in a social and cultural ambiance that creates the totality of maternal love and deny woman of being perceived as whole subjects. Women, while breastfeeding, are required to desexualise their pleasure and the sensuality of their lactating breasts and when they think of themselves as sexual beings, they must deny that their breasts could nourish.

A prism that also holds the mother's inner world makes it possible to rethink a triadic structure in a different way to the familiar Oedipal view, which frames the mother as an object for the child.[119] Even before paternal entry, as Oliver explains, the maternal function contains the buds of the triangular space, with the mother holding in one hand the connection with her child and in the other her desire for the third. Maternal subjectivity contains a triangular space, and a triadic structure of desire – always beyond two. While the maternal inner world may open to a multidimensional space of relationships, in the absence of maternal subjectivity, this space collapses into a dyadic structure – in which pregnancy, childbirth and motherhood remain solely biological – detached from the enveloping images in the symbolic, from their inherent sexual desire and from the realm of experience that accompanies them.

The encounter with the maternal confronts the subject, according to Kristeva, with the fluidity and blurred boundaries that underlie culture, constantly introducing the subject to the disintegration of the coherent experience that he/she seeks to stabilise as 'I'. According to her, in a culture based on separation from the feminine, the only way to maintain language is to allow the mother to do her job, to stand in the middle, holding the gaps that require her own repression. The taboo on incest grows as a law that protects from any contact with that threatening aspect

118 Iris Young. *Throwing like a Girl and Other Essays in Feminist Philosophy and Social Theory* (Ann Arbor: University of Michigan, 2002(1990)).

119 Alison Stone. "Against Matricide: Rethinking Subjectivity and the Maternal Body." *Hypatia* 27, no. 1 (2012): 118–138.

and is positioned as a necessary basis for the existence of language and culture. For Kristeva, the maternal world must remain the foundation from which culture grows but at the same time an inaccessible dimension. In order to preserve the existing order and language, the mother must not only create for her children the gap into which the third will enter, the paternal function, but also take upon herself the abject thus leaving herself outside the boundaries of the symbolic. Her role is to separate the child from her body and place herself in the interim so that she/he can identify with the father and become a subject in language. While the mother is identified with the abject, the father will assume the role of liberator of the subject, leading him/her to autonomy.

Jessica Benjamin puts her finger on this split – explored in the next subchapter – between the regressive and dangerous mother and the authoritative liberating father rethinking the Oedipal 'riddle'. In her book *Bonds of Love*, she analyses the Oedipal narrative as one that is missing its purpose of encountering otherness and remains captive of a one-dimensional perception of relationships based on dominance.[120] While Kristeva focuses on separation from the mother as a necessary step in the process of becoming a subject, Benjamin questions whether the world of the maternal must disappear: Why is it that one culture must be destroyed? She asks.

> Why must one civilisation bury the other? Why must the struggle between maternal law and paternal law end in unilateral defeat rather than in a tie? Why must a patriarchal father supersede and depose the mother? if the struggle between paternal and maternal power ends in paternal victory, the outcome belies the victors claim that the loser, the mother, is too dangerous and powerful to coexist with. Rather it would seem that the evocation of women's danger is an age-old myth which legitimate her subordination.[121]

Impossible Dependency

The difficulty and paradoxes inherent in the encounter with maternal subjectivity are articulated differently in Kristeva's and Benjamin's conceptualisations. According to Kristeva, within a patriarchal culture that denies maternal subjectivity, the mother's inner world is both essential and impossible. On the one hand, maternal phantasies and fantasies about the moment of conception and about the 'third', are necessary for holding the gap through which language is generated. Only through maternal subjectivity and desire, the three vertices of the Oedipal triangle can meet and the father encounters his children. But on the other hand, maternal subjectivity creates a rapture undermining both existing patriarchal order and the structure of separated subjectivity. For Kristeva, language is fundamentally

---

120 Jessica Benjamin. *The Bonds of Love: Psychoanalysis, Feminism, and the Problem of Domination* (New York: Pantheon Books, 1988).
121 Jessica Benjamin. *The Bonds of Love: Psychoanalysis, Feminism, and the Problem of Domination* (New York: Pantheon Books, 1988), p. 156.

constructed not only through detachment from the mother's body but also through erasing its memory, and therefore any reminder of its existence undermines the unity of the speaking subject.

While Kristeva conceptualises the difficulty of encountering the maternal within a patriarchal culture, Benjamin challenges the binarism and analyses the Oedipal solution from an intersubjective perspective. Her conceptualisation unfolds a three-dimensional space in which recognition of dependency plays a vital role in any relationship. The primary dependency in the relationship with the mother is a challenge that can lead the child to a multidimensional space of relationships in which there is a constant movement between being a subject and being an object. This relational field in which the mother desires an other beyond the dyad can open the door to the development of a complex sense of self that embraces a triadic experience beyond the dichotomy of sameness and otherness.

The encounter with maternal subjectivity awakens the challenge of dependency and opens the possibility for a structure that is not based on negation; that entails a recognition of the fluidity of the subject's experience and the inherent inseparability of our existence. Both Kristeva and Benjamin welcome the fundamental gaps and tensions in the conflicting relationship with the mother. Kristeva envisions a movement in which the gap is replaced by language as an endless fountain of words covering her absence. For Benjamin, the developmental process is not a linear line from dependence to independence, from symbiosis to autonomy, from being immersed in the mother's body to creating a barrier and separation through words, but rather a two-way movement across a spectrum. A developing ability to hold the gaps might allow, according to her, a fluid movement – beyond creating separations through language – dismantling of binary meanings within language, and recognising the blurred boundaries between self and other, an inherent inter-dependency. Autonomy, she writes is not the process of separation but rather the ability to recognise our dependency.

According to Benjamin, the Oedipal myth, as conceived in the psychoanalytic tradition, contains a paradox from which the gaze has been diverted. The Oedipal is an ongoing riddle that challenges the child with the question of difference and multiplicity, yet, the solution of this riddle, the way it is described by Freud, in which the child resolves castration complex by identifying with the father – is missing its mark. While presenting the child with the challenge of recognising difference, and opening a multidimensional space of relationships, the solution entails negating the maternal and establishing a relationship of dominance over woman. The father in this solution – in all its forms – always represents difference and separation and is set in a privileged position compared to the mother. In this solution, in order to consolidate an autonomous identity, the maternal and the possibility of identifying with the mother must be renounced. It is the father who saves the child from regression. It is his authority that protects against irrationality and symbiosis associated with the mother, defending both the boy and the girl from being swallowed in the maternal primal world. Whereas paternal power is associated with development and growth, the maternal aspect is associated with the primitive world and her power remains a seductive danger threatening the subject. For Benjamin, the privilege of the male position and the other side of the coin – the devaluation of the mother – undermines the possibility inherent in the Oedipal narrative: an encounter with difference. The interpretation of the Oedipal complex as we know it perpetuates a one-sided version of individuation that does not bring balance between different psychic forces and does not achieve the goal it has set for itself when it closes the door to the encounter with the maternal otherness.

The polarisation between women and men in the Freudian Oedipal model grows, according to Benjamin, from the assumption that the baby must be freed from the initial unity with the mother and escape identification with her. The mother-baby dyadic relationship represents dependency, irrationality and symbiosis and is placed in contrast to values of freedom and autonomy that underlie Western society. Analysing the Freudian myth in *Totem and Taboo*, she emphasises that

> In the most common version of the Oedipal model, the existence of the most archaic dangerous father is completely obscured and the split between the good and bad father is instead reformulated as the opposition between a progressive Oedipal father and a regressive archaic mother.[122]

The maternal becomes a siren that seduces the subject back to be swallowed by an undifferentiated regressive realm. The relationship with the mother becomes a threat and danger to the liberation of the subject and only the Oedipal father and the identification with him assigns the child to the psychic path towards subjectivity, rationality and separateness. As she points out, the Oedipal solution assumes the child must break free from the world of motherhood in order to position himself or herself as a subject in language. They must renounce any identification with the mother in order to salvage themselves from a primitive state of unity, symbiosis and narcissism.

Psychoanalysis, Benjamin argues, developed a limited, almost 'autistic' model of the primary relationship between mother and baby. The infant is described as a closed system, passive and self-absorbed, that expresses a defensive attitude toward the world. She criticises theories (such as Mahler's), which portray the process of separation and individuation as a transition from a primary state of symbiosis with the mother – an undifferentiated oneness in which the infant is engulfed in the mother's body – towards a state of separation in which the individual operates independently. Under this perception, autonomy implies independence, and the developmental process is a unidirectional movement away from dependency. This image depicts the relationship with the mother as the paradigmatic model of dependency and as an opposition to autonomy that is defined as self-sovereignty and separateness. Only by severing the connection with the maternal can the subject position himself or herself as autonomous. This paradigm also contains the

122 Jessica Benjamin. *The Bonds of Love: Psychoanalysis, Feminism, and the Problem of Domination* (New York: Pantheon Books, 1988), p. 146.

assumption that maternal primary dimension is fundamentally bodily, impulsive, and irrational, and that the transition to separateness is a movement toward intelligent existence, reflecting – but also reproducing – the dichotomies that identify the maternal with the physical, primitive, emotional and irrational.

The mother is often described in psychoanalysis as an object for satisfying the physical needs of the baby. The relationship with her is often spoken about in biological terms – the breast serves as nourishment, the contact with the baby's skin relieves physical tension, and the mother's feelings for her children are an expression of hormonal turbulence (as described by Winnicott in conceptualising *"primary maternal preoccupation"*).[123] The primary relationship is depicted in terms of immediacy and physicality, framing the mother-baby dyad as a bodily mechanism, thereby erasing its symbolic meanings.

Benjamin portrays a different picture presenting her understanding of autonomy not as independence and separateness, but rather, as the ability to bear the constant tension inherent in relation to the other. Her relational perspective depicts the entire process of development as taking place within a relationship, as a dialectical movement between *self-expression* and *recognition* of others. While the Freudian psychoanalytic model sees the subject as a closed system desiring external objects, Benjamin describes a reciprocal process of change in the presence of an other. The tension that occurs in the encounter with another subject is a condition for both self-expression and recognition of others, constituting the basis for development and growth. But when the tension cannot be held, she explains, the psyche gives up the dialectical attitude in favour of a perception of oppositions. Polarity produces a binary perception that cannot grasp two alternating dimensions of reality and create mental integration between them. This collapse of tension sets the stage for a relationship of domination in which there is a split between the two poles – one side is idealised, and the other is given an inferior value.

In order to explain this polarising split, Benjamin uses Hegel's *master-slave paradox* opening it to the question of subjectivity and the need for recognition that arise already within the initial dyad with the mother. Already in this early relationship, the subject seeks to influence the (m)other, both to receive her approval and recognition and in order to position herself/himself as self-expressing independent subject. As in any relationship between two subjects, there is a constant tension between the two opposing needs: recognition and self-expression. With self-expression simultaneously reflecting both dependency (on the mother's recognition) and autonomy (separating from her) the subject is born, from his/her very beginning, into a dialectic movement between these two poles. It is the gaze of the (m)other that confirms the existence of the self as having agency, and autonomy, and therefore in order to express his/her separateness, the subject must recognise his/her dependency on the (m)other and his/her need to receive recognition from her.

123 Donald W. Winnicott. "Primary Maternal Preoccupation" [1956]. In: *Through Paediatrics to Psycho-Analysis* (Routledge, 1984), pp. 300–305.

Freud, like Hegel, depicts the necessary break of tension in the encounter with the other since, for him, the subject always fights to dominate the other and does not give up the phantasy of superiority except in a state of submission, and therefore the tension will always increase and develop into a one-sided state of control. Freud's answer to the question of otherness, like Hegel's, fundamentally assumes human aspiration for omnipotence leading to an aggressive and unbalanced relationship, and to a closed system based on opposites. Polarisation is created, the dialectical movement collapse, and parts of the subject are projected onto the other in order to create splits: good and bad, matter and body, upper and lower, dominant and controlled, active and passive, man and woman. Contrary to this fragmented state, in which both sides are positioned as opposing and separate tendencies, Benjamin presents an alternative of a blurred boundary line and constant tension. She explains that in an ideal situation, the paradox remains in a state of tension, in a dynamic movement between recognition and self-expression, a dialectical frame that continues to hold its internal contradiction. The subject does not reach a state of total liberation or total surrender, recognising his/her dependency on the other, their need for recognition and strive to express themselves with the growing emotional perception that recognition of self and recognition of the other are intertwined: autonomy contains dependency.

For Benjamin, the developmental challenge inherent to the *mutual recognition paradox* can be seen in the early dyad relationship with the mother. Its first buds emerge when the mother recognise her baby as separate yet connected; as part of her but as a different from her, an other. Benjamin describes the feeding moments when the emotional storm intensifies, the baby's crying and his/her body twitches, the attempts to attach the baby's mouth to the nipple, and the gradual relaxation that occurs when breastfeeding begins and the milk flows. She then describes the silence, the familiar alert gaze of the baby at his/her mother's face, which, for Benjamin is a moment of recognition. It is a contradictory mix of connection and separateness, of similarity and difference. The pleasure that the mother derives from the child's existence includes at the same time her connection to him/her and his/her existence as separated from her.

The crisis emerges, she explains, with the beginning of mutual recognition in the relationship with the mother, in which the child's aspiration for autonomy and self-expression cannot exist without recognising the mother as a separate subject, who is also capable of self-expression. Outlining the mother-child challenge that arises with the realisation of dependency on the maternal, she brings to the foreground the way in which separation and vulnerability are tied together. Being similar to him/her, the mother is also a subject, and she too can distance herself and express herself as separated from him/her. She is able to detach the breast from his/her mouth and can desire and choose an other beyond him/her. This is a developmental challenge that involves recognising the mother's subjectivity and her existence as her ability to love, desire and choose a third beyond the dyadic relationship.

When Freud encounters the possibility of opening maternal subjectivity in the text, when the question of origin leads him to the inner world of the mother, he narrows the triadic space by shifting his gaze away from her and clinging to the phallus. Thus, when the mother's fantasy about the moment of conception emerges in the text, as an opening to a triangular space of relationships that passes through maternal subjectivity, Freud closes the possibility of looking at the relationship with her by shifting all desire to the paternal pole, reducing motherhood and the image of pregnancy to biological terms. Pointing to the physiology of conception, hormones and to the role of the male in fertilization, he explains that no meaning can be found in those maternal "imaginations" beyond being a physical product of hormonal fluctuations of pregnancy. When pregnancy remains solely bodily, it is disconnected from maternal fantasies and phantasies inherent to it, bypassing the triangular structure woven by the inner world of the mother. In this way, the maternal can only be understood as a vessel for her child's needs, her sexuality cannot be engaged with, and the triangular space shrinks into a relationship between the father and the son/daughter – competing for the same object.

What can be so unbearable about Frazer's theory of conception that necessitates Freud's heavy artillery of maternal negation? This theory shows, as Freud writes, that "the ultimate source of totemism would be the savages' ignorance of the process by which men and animals reproduce their kind; and, in particular, ignorance of the part played by the male in fertilization".[124] This third of the mother, bringing in the symbolic from the realm of her "sick fancies", is experienced as a sort of patricide, an omnipotence parthenogenetic phantasy that violently excludes the father.[125] In Freud's theoretical framework there is no reconciliation of the contradiction between maternal symbolic otherness and the role of "male fertilization". In other words, for psychoanalysis, maternal f/phantacy cannot escape an omnipotent imagery realm of the phallic mother, falling back to the power struggle in which maternal monster must be erased and negated.

While for Freud, as well as for Kristeva, maternal power must be repudiated, Benjamin reminds psychoanalysis that omnipotence and loss of tension are two sides of the same coin. Kristeva describes the early mother-infant relationship as a frustrating dyad in which the (future) subject is constantly threatened by the omniums maternal, confronting the subject with its vague boundaries, its inseparability. Benjamin, on the other hand, articulates the struggle as a relational challenge of carrying the dependency inherent to the conflicted needs for both self-expression and mutual recognition. For both, the paradoxical experience originates at the beginning of life with the encounter with the maternal. However, contrary to Kristeva, who emphasises maternal threat to the subject's existence as a talking creature, Benjamin describes the difficulty as a challenge through which an understanding of difference can develop. In intersubjective terms, maternal subjectivity opens the

124 Sigmund Freud. *Totem and Taboo: Some Points of Agreement Between the Mental Lives of Savages and Neurotics* (Translated by James Strachey. Routledge, [1912–1913] 2003), p. 137.

125 I'd like to thank Tali Artman Partock for her thoughtful remark about the parthenogenetic phantasy imbedded in the maternal phantasy of conception.

door to a multidimensional relationship that is not based on negation but rather on the recognition of difference.

In order to explore the triangular relationship within the maternal, Benjamin distinguishes between two intertwined models of a third that play a role in the early relationship with the mother.[126] Moments of recognition and connection in the dyad between mother and child are identified by her as *the one in the third* – these moments originate in non-verbal first experiences of shared gaze, and responsive movement that involve emotional encounter and recognition of mutuality. This shared third, sprouting from the dyad, has a transitional and playful quality in the sense that it has no single origin or a fixed and absolute meaning. Capturing a transcendent movement, as Benjamin writes, this "co-created third has the transitional quality of being both invented and discovered. To the question of 'Who created this pattern, you or I?', the paradoxical answer is 'Both and neither' ".[127]

The more familiar understanding of the third—the father or the other of the mother—Benjamin names *the third in the one*, explaining that the two elements of the third are entangled with each other, in constant tension arising from the paradox of recognition. Without *the one in the third*, she argues, the more familiar understanding of the third, *the third in one* – or, to put it simply, the Other – collapses into what she calls a complementary relationship – a relationship between two in which only submission or dominance is possible. The ability to recognise the other of the other (or mother's other) – the intimacy from which the subject is excluded, essentially depends on the ability to experience *the one in the third* – a shared experience of creating a third from which others are excluded. A dialectical movement between these dimensions of the 'third' is necessary for creating and continuing to hold a triangular space.

Using this perspective, Benjamin demonstrates that the movement between the *third in the one* and *the one in the third* is necessary in order to hold the tension of a triangular space in which maternal subjectivity plays a vital role. Without recognising the mother as a subject, external and with desire, the child can never become a separated subject. Recognition of the mother as a subject with separate and independent abilities opens the space for the third to enter the inner world of the child, as it contains the possibility that the gaze of the mother transcends beyond the maternal-child space, and her f/phantasy of otherness allows a place for the existence of a third beyond the child. This process of understanding that in the mother's world there are other entities or relationships from which the child is excluded, that she is not merely an object for fulfilling his/her needs, requires a shared experience of creating a third in which the child's self-expression is recognised. The child faces his/her dependency on the mother, who also has needs and desires beyond the dyadic relationship, and therefore experiences conflicting emotions in

---

126 Jessica Benjamin. "Beyond Doer and Done to: An Intersubjective View of Thirdness." *Psychoanal. Q.* 73 (2004): 5–46.

127 Jessica Benjamin. "Beyond Doer and Done to: An Intersubjective View of Thirdness." *Psychoanal. Q.* 73 (2004): 5–46, 18.

an endless movement between self-expression and mutual recognition. Just as the child can separate from the mother, so too the mother is able separate from him/her and express her/his independence, and therefore, with the recognition of her as a subject, the triangular space opens, and the child subject is led into a triadic relational field and into the beginning of the Oedipal challenge.

Going back to *Totem and Taboo* and to Frazer's theory of conception, it is possible to recognise that even before the baby is born, pregnancy is a triangular concept that challenges the monadic understanding of the Oedipal, not only for the child but for the father as well. Pregnancy is an image for the ability to create a third in any dyad, an image of an other for the mother, that ignites feelings of exclusion. Just as the father is the third for the child, so is the child a third for the father, challenging every "dyadic" relationship with maternal subjectivity. The mother's love, her desire and choice beyond any dyadic relation, introduces not only the child but also the father to the mother's subjectivity – opening their relationship to the challenge of a 'third in the one' – the other of the mother, and to an experience of dependency.

How is it that from being the subject holding both other poles, whose subjectivity is fundamental for the emergence of a triangular space, the mother becomes excluded, rejected, repressed and repudiated as a subject? Benjamin answers this question explaining that when it is impossible to bear the tension in the encounter with the (m)other, and the inherent dependency is denied, the dialectical movement is broken, and a relationship of domination is formed. When the subjectivity of the other cannot be tolerated, the subject struggles to position himself or herself as totally separated, and every reminder of dependency becomes impossible. The relationship develops into a power struggle in which the tension is broken, the two-way movement disappears and oppressive relationships are formed. The recognition of dependency is, according to Benjamin, the most significant challenge that needs to be faced in the Oedipal structure. However, often the difficulty of bearing the experience of vulnerability in relation to the (m)other, and the inherent tension, lead to a defence mechanism of split, in which many unwanted elements are projected onto the maternal, establishing a relationship of oppression and dominance.

When the dialectic tension between self-expression and recognition is broken, the subject finds it difficult to receive recognition from the other, and thus to express himself or herself as autonomous, creating an intensifying cycle of repeated splitting, polarising between object and subject, control and submission. The inability to contain the paradox inherent in the relationship between the self and the other, the difficulty of bearing the tension, leads to a struggle in which the subject seeks to destroy the subjectivity of the other striving for an independent (impossible) existence.

A description of a triangular space, arising in the text from Frazer's theory of conception, leads to a 'symptomatic' textual structure – fragmented, interrupted and splits, in what seems like a struggle to engage with the challenges hidden in this theory. Through the fantasy of the mother about the spirit of a 'third', which begins long before birth, the woman connects the vertices of the Oedipal triangle, opening a triadic space in which the son/daughter and the father meet via maternal subjectivity. However, the Oedipal solution emerging in the text, which hierarchically splits between the sexes, leaving the mother only as an object, misses the potential for its inherent theoretical development.

The Totem Ceremony as a Transitional Space

When questions of origin that Freud raises lead him to the subjectivity of the mother, he reduces the triadic space by turning his gaze to the Oedipal narrative in a way that leaves her solely as an object. Thus, when the mother's fantasy about her pregnancy appears in the text as an opening into a triangular space of relationships, Freud closes this theoretical exploration through the reduction of its symbolic aspects to biological language. He reminds the readers of the physiology of conception, and the role of the male in fertilisation explaining that no meaning can be found in these "maternal imaginations" apart from the "sick desires" of hormonal pregnancy. Switching from symbolic multilayered language to physiology, pregnancy is disconnected from the fantasies, phantasies and desires inherent to maternal subjectivity, skipping the triangular connection created in the inner world of the mother. In this way, the mother remains as a container for her children's needs, her sexuality is split from her motherhood and the triangular space is reduced to a relationship between two – the father and the child – competing for the same object.

Maternal subjectivity is negated in a similar way throughout the text. When Atkinson's theory raises the possibility of maternal love playing a role in the relationship between fathers and sons, at the emergence of social life, the possibility of observing the way maternal subjectivity connects the three vertices of the Oedipal triangle, opens for a moment. However, Freud leaves this possibility in the margins of the text, in a footnote, and in the 'upper' layer places the image of the father and the struggle between the sons and their father over the women in the tribe. This textual movement eliminates the significance of maternal love and desire, and once again leaves the woman as a mere object in the world of the men around her. The separation between a woman's sexuality and parenthood flattens the triangular space, takes away the mother's ability to choose, and represses the power inherent in her nurturing. It makes it possible to omit the experience of dependency and thus cannot hold the tension inherent in the triadic space. As Benjamin shows, this Oedipal solution represses the challenge inherent in the triangular relationship, and instead of encountering the question of difference, it turns into a power struggle of dominance.

This is also the case when the place of maternal deities in human development arises in the text. When a window opens for the exploration of maternal power and the complexity of the relationship with her, Freud conjures up the image of circumcision attaching it to castration anxiety. Clinging to the male phallus seems to be an answer to the image of maternal breastfeeding and to any encounter with the mother in which dependency arise. This answer positions the mother as an object of desire for the father and as a needs-fulfilling object for the baby, eliminating the connection between these dimensions in her inner world. It places the prohibition of incest as a blanket taboo for any possibility of opening the door to maternal subjectivity. The cut that emerges from this image, cuts away the maternal, yet shifts the gaze from the complex relationship with the mother to the wrath of the father, and cements it as a primary answer beyond which it is impossible to step.

Splitting between subject and object, as Benjamin explains, is also intrinsically related to the psychic ability to move between fantasy and reality. A state of omnipotence – and domination – is created by 'destroying' or 'eliminating' the other, striving to liberate the subject in reaching a state of independence. It is a grandiose psychic position in which recognising an external and real other is denied. In the early relationship with the mother, she explains, the infant encounters the challenge to recognise a reality that is beyond his or her control, to understand that the mother is also a subject in the world and therefore is outside the infant's control. He/She must give up, on the one hand, the possibility of magical control over the mother, and on the other hand, her existence as a grandiose entity controlling him/her. The result of this process entails a state of constant tension in which the subject develops an ability to bear his/her dependency on the mother and at the same time preserves the desire for self-expression and recognition from her. This continuous tension is a dialectical relational position in which the split of domination and submission is avoided.

In order to explain the psychological process that enables a dialectical psychic stance, Benjamin uses Winnicott's conceptualisations of *transitional spaces* and what he calls *the use of an object*.[128] This paradoxical transitional space of blurred boundaries between the inside and the outside and between the self and the other is a creative field that constitutes an intermediate zone of experience, between fantasy and reality. While at the beginning of life, the child experiences the world as part of his/her inner world under his/her control, the transitional space is essential in the process of recognising the object outside his/her grasp, understanding the object as a real entity external to the self. For Benjamin, the transitional space is not just an intermediate stage through which the child distinguishes between inside and outside, reality and fantasy, but an inter-psychic realm that constantly mediates the encounter with the other. This area of ambiguous boundaries between separateness and symbiosis, between fantasy and reality is an essential dimension in order to maintain the paradoxical tension that exists in the encounter between two subjects.

The use of the object, for Benjamin, develops from the challenge faced by the subject to place the object outside his or her control. The process by which this ability to (creatively) use an object passes through the phantasy to destroy the object. When the subject succeeds in 'murdering' the parent in phantasy, but they survive in reality, the ability to use the object germinates by recognising their external existence. When the object is destroyed internally but survives externally, the child can begin to recognise reality, the other's independent existence, his/her otherness.

---

128 Donald W. Winnicott. "The Use of an Object." *Int. J. Psycho-Anal.* 50 (1969): 711–716.

This challenge opens the door to enjoying a relationship of mutual recognition between two different people with a shared experience.

For Freud, like Benjamin, the developmental path goes through renouncing omnipotence and recognising reality. The subject develops through her/his inability to control the external world, through an acceptance of a reality beyond the subject. In order to explain the significance of this process in the cultural and social development, Freud draws a parallel to the mental structure of the individual. As he explains,

> If we may regard the existence among primitive races of the omnipotence of thoughts as evidence in favour of narcissism, we are encouraged to attempt a comparison between the phases in the development of men's view of the universe and the stages of an individual's libidinal development. The animistic phase would correspond to narcissism both chronologically and in its content; the religious phase would correspond to the stage of object-choice of which the characteristic is a child's attachment to his parents; while the scientific phase would have an exact counterpart in the stage at which an individual has reached maturity, has renounced the pleasure principle, adjusted himself to reality and turned to the external world for the object of his desires.[129]

According to this explanation, the process that takes place in the totem sacrificial ritual moves the members of the tribe, or alternatively, the subject, from a state of primary narcissism and omnipotence to the beginning of the second stage, religion – a state in which the subject is willing to transfer part of control to the father, the law, while relinquishing the desire for the mother. This process solidifies through the sacrificial ritual in which the consumption of the animal body – which according to Freud represents the father – enables an internal image of the good and caring father to emerge.

As Freud explains, the father does not disappear in this process but rather the relationship with him is demonstrated within a metaphorical ritual space in which rage and aggression can be expressed. By internalising the father figure, the ability to symbolise develops, and paternal law becomes as an external reality shared by the tribesmen. Through the contained act of murdering the imaginary father, paternal function is established, and the subject enters the symbolic and the realm of language. The sacrificial act (or rather cut) breaks the imagery body that is phantasised as wholesome, thus, creating a rapture through which the matrix of opposites initiates language. The killing of the animal, the imaginary father figure, enables an external dimension of law and an internal dimension of morality to grow, and the prohibition of incest becomes the foundation upon which culture is formed.

129 Sigmund Freud. *Totem and Taboo: Some Points of Agreement Between the Mental Lives of Savages and Neurotics* (Translated by James Strachey. Routledge, [1912–1913] 2003), p. 105.

Returning to the parallels between the psychological development of the individual and the development of culture, Freud outlines the Oedipal solution inherent in the ritual of the totem sacrifice. Through the act of cutting in the ceremony – reviving the image of circumcision and castration anxiety – the sons give up the omnipotent position, give up the desire to 'have it all', and identify with the father. Having expressed their ambivalent attitude in the ceremony, while at the same time being reminded of castration, they are ready to obey the imperative forbidding incest and give up the mother. For Freud, the ritual provides the transitional space that allows the tribesmen to confront the conflictual relationship with the father and develop the ability to identify with him. Expressing aggression and rage, killing the father in phantasy allows the sons to accept his existence as the basis of cultural reality that entails renunciation of the mother and acceptance of the law as an external reality.

But what if the sacrificial ritual does not express only the ambivalent attitude towards the father but also, as Kristeva outlines, the conflictual feelings towards the mother? The father, who returns as an internal structure of the law becomes the foundation of society and culture, but what becomes of matricide in the ritual and how does that translate into a gendered dichotomy? The ritual, which is fundamentally based on the image of maternal breastfeeding, expresses a conflictual emotional array formed in the primary relationship with the mother. It recreates the frustration and ecstasy inherent in the relationship with the mother's body and expresses the dependency and helplessness that reverberates in the primary dyad. If the transitional space allows for a movement from omnipotence to recognition of self-partiality by being able to 'kill' the objects in phantasy and their survival in reality, in the ritual the father indeed survives as an external aspect of the law, but the maternal disappears. From this moment on, the incestuous taboo is established as an impenetrable dimension that does not allow contact with the inner world of the mother. From then on, the complex relationship with her can no longer be opened, and the maternal aspect is identified with material body that is abjected, cut off, swallowed and disappears. As Benjamin explains, when the object does not survive the subject's attacks, an omnipotent attitude and relationship of dominance develop.

While Freud outlines the Oedipal answer in which psychological development progresses from an omnipotent position through relinquishing the mother and identifying with the father, Benjamin shows that this 'solution' is more of the same: transferring the relationship of domination to another arena, to the relations between the sexes. The split between the parents is created – the mother disappears, and the father receives the unlimited power inherent in the phallus. The maternal aspect is erased from the discourse – as well as from the text – while the paternal is idealised. As Freud describes it, "[a]tonement with the father was all the more complete since the sacrifice was accompanied by a total renunciation of the women".[130]

---

130 Sigmund Freud. *Totem and Taboo: Some Points of Agreement Between the Mental Lives of Savages and Neurotics* (Translated by James Strachey. Routledge, [1912–1913] 2003), p. 179.

The initial relationship with the mother remains as a memory of dependency, of symbiotic absorption in the mother's body, a regressive dimension that stands in stark contrast to the ideal of autonomy made possible by the relationship with the father. In the ritual, as described in the text, a split is created – the maternal body remains as a casual and meaningless substance, the feminine is identified with the earthly and the physical, while the masculine with the sublime, and the law of the father becomes the guiding light for culture itself.

Freud's Sphinx Riddle

The meaning of the word 'taboo', Freud explains, can be understood through its opposite that "in Polynesian is 'noa', which means 'common' or 'generally accessible'".[131] The taboo is, in fact, the subject's encounter with something beyond his/her daily routine, with otherness, difference or novelty that evoke a mixture of excitement, curiosity and anxiety. An experience that harbours the conflict of encountering otherness beyond the self, presenting the subject with a developmental challenge to recognise his/her own partiality and renounce omnipotence.

From Benjamin's perspective, the Oedipal solution – described in the text as an outcome of the ritual – does not eliminate omnipotence but rather channels it into polar relations between the sexes. Instead of developing a genuine encounter with the (m)other, recognising self-partiality, and acknowledging dependency and difference, the Oedipal solution portrayed by Freud, in which the child identifies with the father and the mother disappears, flattens subjectivity through sameness, centred around the male genital organ. As she explains, the Oedipal narrative, although describing a developmental challenge of recognising difference, of understanding subjectivity within a triadic space, is in fact, avoiding its mark: "the idea of phallic monism is clearly at odds with the acceptance of difference that the Oedipus Complex is supposed to embody", she writes. "It denies the difference, between the sexes or rather it reduces difference to 'absence', to lack".[132] The father "enjoys a privileged position above the mother. Her power is identified with early primitive gratifications that must be renounced while the father's power is associated with the development and growth". This split dichotomy that Benjamin describes, and the devaluation of femininity, "undermines precisely what the Oedipus Complex is purported to achieve: difference, erotic tension and the balance of intrapsychic forces. The Oedipal model illustrates how one-sided version of individuation undoes the very difference that it purports to consolidate".[133] The fracture described in the ritual organises the binary split between the sexes and produces the relationship

131 Sigmund Freud. *Totem and Taboo: Some Points of Agreement Between the Mental Lives of Savages and Neurotics* (Translated by James Strachey. Routledge, [1912–1913] 2003), p. 21.
132 Jessica Benjamin. *The Bonds of Love: Psychoanalysis, Feminism, and the Problem of Domination* (New York: Pantheon Books, 1988), p. 166.
133 Jessica Benjamin. *The Bonds of Love: Psychoanalysis, Feminism, and the Problem of Domination* (New York: Pantheon Books, 1988), p. 159.

between men and women as a relationship of domination between male subjects and female objects.

The Oedipalisation occurring in the ritual, differentiating between the corporeal and the transcendental, also propels the binary and hierarchical relationship between the sexes. When there is no room for recognising dependency, oppressive relationships of domination are established, characterised by the gendered splitting between subject and object. The emotional tension inherent to the relationship with the maternal is repressed, the mother's role is devalued, her desire erased, and she becomes inaccessible except through the male phallus, as an object of desire. The ritual does not work through the conflictual relations but creates a sharp social split between subject and object, between domination and submission and between the corporeal-maternal and the symbolic-paternal. The same phallus, which was supposed to represent difference, stands as a monadic principle through which the attitude to the world and to otherness is mediated, via a binary separation of the haves and the have nots.

Such a process of splitting, which gradually intensifies, can be seen throughout the text. Freud opens the text with a wide range of theories, thoughts and questions. He brings examples from different cultures exploring many customs in different places. He unfolds before the reader a multitude of theoretical analyses and uses clinical case studies in order to search for the link between the development of the individual and the advancement of culture and social life. Touching on a wide range of theories through nominalist, sociological and psychological perspectives, the encounter with the maternal arises in various ways. Gradually, the various possibilities to open new directions of inquiry are sealed by placing the maternal as an object, reducing difference under a phallic super-signifier, and fixing it onto the Oedipal narrative. When the ritual of the totem sacrifice and the image of circumcision arise in the text, the possibility of opening a window into the inner world of the mother disappears. The textual movement gradually changes its character from a deconstructive inquiry, which delves inward to excavate multiple layers, to a reconstruction process, establishing a single hermetic Oedipal theory. In this textual movement, the theoretical richness gives way to the Freudian myth about the origin of culture, and the opening tone is replaced by a sharp and clear narrative. Instead of the multiple archaeological findings emerging in the text, a coherent narrative is established as a single phallic structure.

Benjamin describes the rift created through repudiation of the inherent dependency in the relationship with the (m)other. Then, the dialectical tension between self-expression and recognition collapses, creating a split that denies the complexity of emotions. The Freudian solution of the Oedipal phase understands relationships as a complementary intersection between the two opposites of self and other: active and passive, domination and submission. The subjectivity of the (m)other disappears, swallowed by the totality of the One and the subject is positioned as liberated. Benjamin emphasises the fact that through the Oedipal solution, the child's ability to identify with the mother is lost, thereby sealing off an encounter with otherness and the possibility of mutual recognition. Instead of allowing dialectical movement in the encounter with otherness, domination is created under the guise of renunciation of omnipotence. Although faced with the challenge of difference in the relationship with the mother, maternal function is erased and covered by paternal function, leaving only one option for subjectivity – identification with the father.

Using Benjamin's theory, and her elaboration on the paradox of dependency hidden in the encounter with the other, it is possible to delve into the inter-subjective difficult encounter with the mother. In the *riddle of the Sphinx* Oedipus is introduced to the question of dependency: *what walks on four feet in the morning, two in the afternoon and three at night?*, she asks him. This creature with wings, a body of a lion and head of a woman, who threatens to overthrow Thebes under her power, is a feminine image standing in the way of Oedipus. She is neither human nor an animal, neither man nor woman. She wants nothing for herself but introduces Oedipus to the complexity of the encounter with otherness inherent in the feminine and maternal dimensions, to the blurring of boundaries that reside in the unconscious. In her riddle, she reminds Oedipus of his partiality, his mortality, his dependency, the place he came from and to which he is headed. Oedipus answers the riddle with the help of logic and reason, the tools of the ego and banishes the monster back into the depths of the unconscious, without realising that the legs he was asked about were indeed his own; the same legs that were tied together as a child when he was sent by his parents to his death. These legs, a phallic symbol of potency on which he walks is a temporary illusion for men, since, in the beginning of life, as well as in the end, their weakness reveal his dependency.

Freud is called upon to solve an Oedipal 'riddle' of his own, and he indeed opens the book with a search for the mother, the question of incest, opening the door to different theories that explain the process of subject-formation and the beginning of culture. Commencing his theoretical journey in the relationship with the (m)other, the question of incest appears as the central axis into which Freud wishes to dive. Like the riddle of the Sphinx in Oedipus's story, the book opens with a question concerning relations of dependency. But the narrative that Freud outlines after describing the ritual portrays the primal father as a "violent and jealous father who keeps all the females for himself and drives away his sons as they grow up".[134] The incest taboo, the prohibition on relationship with the maternal is then positioned as a primary dimension of pre-cultural life. Even before social reality was established, even before the subject entered language, the father forbade contact with the women keeping them to himself. This narrative retroactively erases the power of the mother, bypassing the experience of dependency on her – for the sons, for the father, for the social – and introduces her as a mere object from the very beginning. Maternal subjectivity is repressed and the possibility of opening the complex relationship with her disappears as the taboo on incest is disconnected

134 Sigmund Freud. *Totem and Taboo: Some Points of Agreement Between the Mental Lives of Savages and Neurotics* (Translated by James Strachey. Routledge, [1912–1913] 2003), p. 164.

from the relationship with her and displaced as an eternal boundary line that has always prevailed through the unlimited power of the father.

As Benjamin explains, when dependency cannot be acknowledged, it becomes difficult to bear the tension, and the relationship is redirected towards a relationship of dominance through splitting. This mechanism arises in the text and reaches its climax, in the ceremony of the totem sacrifice in which the animal body is cut, giving way to social life through a split between the sexes. The Oedipal solution described in response to this rapture contains a similar fracture: erasing the possibility of identification with the mother and positioning women as objects for the father.

In the picture Freud portrays, the change emerging from the Oedipal challenge is not recognition of difference, but rather the closure of the door that allows identification with the mother. The taboo on incest is not only a prohibition on sexual relation but also a prohibition on the internal – both psychic and theoretical – existence of the maternal; a prohibition on touching the complexity of that relationship, and on identification with the mother. Just as the child is denied access to the maternal forces within him/her, to an inner dimension of nourishment and creativity, and to identification with the mother, so too psychoanalysis is denied the possibility of touching on the complexity of this relationship and their meanings.

When Freud solves the *'riddle of origin'* by placing the image of the cruel prehistoric father as desiring and dominating the female, he too, like Oedipus, bypasses the challenge posed by the 'riddle'. He ignores the possibility of encountering the powerful and ambivalent experience facing the mother and her cardinal role in the formation of culture. If the conscious text posits the answer to the prohibition of incest as a result of the father's rage and victorious power, the maternal is simmering in the textual unconscious, a spectral dimension that Freud refuses to touch.

Chapter 3

The Jewish Key-fossil

Between war, censorship and book-burning
his image was drawn to Moses.
His tongue burnt sealing letters
ignited by pens and cigars
stamped by the hand that shoved in
burning coal.

Sometimes he almost caught her.
In galloping graphomania
haunted words of hunted people
a rose worm-letter hidden between
the lines.
The same creature that
feasted on his O's and his I's
and his tongue.

The unspoken scorched
ulcers in his mouth
an inconsolable thirst crawled up to his throat
as once again the hourglass
was shuttered into a silent wall
and once again bending over
picking pieces of glass and sand
from the ground.

For a split-second, the future was possible:
to step down from the mountain
or to leave the desert behind
or touch water
with his overstretched hands.
It was still possible

DOI: 10.4324/9781003394334-4

even when he already knew:
the last grain of sand will return to its ashes
right at the entrance of that wretched land
slipping
from between his fingers.
        (Sand and Soil, *Between Our Tongues*)[1]

In a letter to Arnold Zweig about the writing of *Moses and Monotheism*, Freud explains: "Faced with the new persecutions, one asks oneself again how the Jews have come to be what they are and why they have attracted this undying hatred. I soon discovered the formula: Moses created the Jews".[2] Placing Judaism and the Jewish people on the psychoanalytic couch, Freud analyses in this work the Jewish neurosis, exploring the phenomenon of antisemitism and reconstructing the origin of the Jewish people.

My explorations into Freud's work can be outlined through the three chapters of this book: in the first chapter, *In Her Shadow: Three Case Studies* I analyse Freud's theory through case studies and the realm of the subject, the second chapter *Totem and Taboo: Phantasies of Origin* looks into Freud's understandings of the social and cultural dimensions. This third chapter, *The Jewish Key-fossil*, delves into Freud's text *Moses and Monotheism* and analyses his understanding of religion and the history of the Jewish people. In this book, Freud redraws the beginning of the Jewish people through the Oedipal event of the murder of the great father anchoring the origin of Judaism in an earlier Egyptian monotheism. Using psychoanalysis, he weaves a convoluted narrative about the beginning of the Jewish people trying to explain the Jewish 'racial resilience' throughout history and the way it is tied to the development of monotheism in general. Linking the text with his writing in *Totem and Taboo*, written 25 years earlier, Freud binds together the development of the individual, with the process of culture formation and the beginning of the Jewish people, uniting them all through an Oedipal narrative.

Unlike texts analysed in previous chapters, in which circumcision appears as a turning point in the text, an image that diverts the gaze away from the relationship with the mother to castration anxiety and the relationship with the father, in this text, Freud marks circumcision as a key-fossil from its very beginning. In his reading into ancient Jewish texts, he recognises circumcision as an ambivalent textual fossil that can be used to trace the conflicts in the historical narrative of the Jewish people, unveiling the locations where an otherness has been repressed. This understanding of circumcision as a *Leitfossil* – which I have used throughout my analysis in this book – positions the image of circumcision as an ambivalent textual *Archimedean point*, which at the same time touches an origin and covers it up.

---

1 Yael Pilowsky Bankirer. *Between our Tongues* (in Hebrew) (Tel-Aviv: Catharsis Publishing, 2023).
2 Sigmund Freud and Arnold Zweig. *The Letters of Sigmund Freud and Arnold Zweig* (Ed. Ernst L. Freud. New York: Harcourt, Brace & World, 1970). p. 91.

Through this metaphor, Freud traces the contradictions and gaps in biblical texts, the places where anxiety surges and petrification occurs, and in which the narrative freezes and the hidden truth peeks from underneath the surface. However, Freud, too, as I will show, does not remain merely an observer of these circles of obliterations covering the trauma. In his search for the truth, he vehemently rejects stories about Moses' childhood and Jewish maternal legacy, demonstrating another series of erasures in his own text. Gradually drawn into fascination with the monotheistic ideas, the resilience of the Jewish people and the strength of the great man, Moses, he reconstructs Jewish history in accordance with a monadic narrative in which others are once again erased.

Moses, an Egyptian: Freud's Historical Reconstruction

In *Moses and Monotheism*, Freud unfolds the most profound discussion of circumcision. Exploring biblical sources, historical texts, their commentaries and interpretations, he marks circumcision as a key-fossil, a *Leitfossil*, in tracing the answers to the question of how the Jewish people and monotheism came into being. As he writes: "Here we may once again call on the evidence afforded by circumcision, which has repeatedly been of help to us, like, as it were, a key-fossil".[3] In order to reach the 'historical truth' and bring it to light, he turns to that Jewish signifier, circumcision, which constitutes a conflictual and terrifying *unheimlich* element. Due to its being, according to Freud, the paradigmatic sign of trauma and repression, it serves him as a sort of litmus test for identifying an unresolved conflict in the history of the Jewish people.

In order to weave the reconstructed story of the origin of Judaism and monotheism, Freud presents his own interpretation of biblical texts, legends and well-known folktales. Identifying gaps in the text, repetitions and contradictions he challenges the presented story and exposes – as an archaeologist using the excavated remains and fossils – the hidden truth beneath the surface. As he explains, distortions in the text are created by opposing forces working simultaneously, some of which attempt to preserve the 'historical truth', while others seek to conceal it. Just as unconscious conflict creates a symptom, so does these conflicting forces are revealed within a text as "gaps, disturbing repetitions and obvious contradictions have come about—indications which reveal things to us which it was not intended to communicate".[4] Conflicting attempts to both reveal and conceal resurface in the text as distortions of the truth, thus, allowing the observant reader, who employ 'hermeneutics of suspicion' to embark on the path of tracing its original footsteps.[5]

---

3 Sigmund Freud. "Moses and Monotheism, Three Essays." In: James Strachey (ed. & trans.) *The Standard Edition of the Complete Psychological Works of Sigmund Freud* 23 (1939) (London: The Hogarth Press and the Institute of Psycho-Analysis, 1964), p. 39.

4 Sigmund Freud. "Moses and Monotheism, Three Essays." *The Standard Edition of the Complete Psychological Works of Sigmund Freud* 23 (1939), p. 43.

5 Ricoeur, Paul. *Freud and Philosophy: An Essay on Interpretation.* (D. Savage, Trans.). New Haven, CT: Yale University Press, 1970.

Freud identifies in circumcision such element of distortion of origin, of a compromise emerging out of an ambivalent struggle between concealing and revealing. According to him, it is a key-fossil emerging from a conflict that he identifies in biblical texts. Tracing the contradictions, gaps and linguistic discrepancies about circumcision within these texts, he uses various historical evidence as well as psychoanalysis to understand whether the narratives he encounters are precious 'gemstone', pointing to the truth, or an insignificant piece of 'rock' that should be erased. By tracing the distorted trajectories of the circumcision-fossil, Freud identifies beneath the stones a different origin or rather, an origin of difference, through which the entire Jewish narrative is turned upside down.

"[I]f one allows oneself to be carried away by the ... arguments which I have put forward here" Freud writes, "if one sets out to take the hypothesis seriously that *Moses was an aristocratic Egyptian*, very interesting and far-reaching prospects are opened up". Naming the first essay "Moses an Egyptian", Freud presents a hypothesis that undermines the way the history of the Jewish people has hitherto been told. If this possibility is true, he continues, then we might be able

> to obtain a grasp of the possible basis of a number of the characteristics and peculiarities of the laws and religion which he [Moses] gave to the Jewish people; and we shall even be led on to important considerations regarding the origin of monotheist religions in general.[6]

In order to substantiate his conclusions, he makes two thought-provoking arguments. First, he reanalyses the name 'Moses' pointing out that "his name was derived from the Egyptian vocabulary".[7] As he explains following J. H. Breadster, "[i]t is important to notice that his name, Moses, was Egyptian. It is simply the Egyptian word 'mose' meaning 'child' ... [and] is not uncommon on the Egyptian monuments".[8] Secondly, Freud explains that the legend regarding the birth and early life of Moses does not conform to the accepted pattern – which Otto Rank has described in his studies – of the myth of the birth of the hero. Then, "all at once we see things clearly", he concludes, "Moses was an Egyptian—probably an aristocrat—whom the legend was designed to turn into a Jew. And that would be our conclusion".[9]

While, in the first essay, Freud asks readers to look at the possibility that Moses is of Egyptian descent, in the second essay he opens with this assumption, naming the essay "If Moses was an Egyptian...". This hypothesis, initially put forward as a

---

6 Sigmund Freud. "Moses and Monotheism, Three Essays." *The Standard Edition of the Complete Psychological Works of Sigmund Freud* 23 (1939), p. 16. Emphasis added.

7 Sigmund Freud. "Moses and Monotheism, Three Essays." *The Standard Edition of the Complete Psychological Works of Sigmund Freud* 23 (1939), p. 17.

8 Sigmund Freud. "Moses and Monotheism, Three Essays." *The Standard Edition of the Complete Psychological Works of Sigmund Freud* 23 (1939), p. 8.

9 Sigmund Freud. "Moses and Monotheism, Three Essays." *The Standard Edition of the Complete Psychological Works of Sigmund Freud* 23 (1939), p. 15.

playful fantasy, later becomes a cornerstone on which the 'historical truth' is built. In this text, Freud puts together the pieces of the puzzle to present a complete historical reconstruction of the origin of the Jewish people, Judaism and monotheism. As he gathers the signs hidden in biblical texts and follows the clues revealed by the discrepancies about circumcision, Freud seeks to discover the meaning hidden beneath the surface. Lifting the *Leitfossil* of circumcision, he searches for the answer to the question of its origin: where did circumcision come from? – to which one surprising answer is put forward – the custom of circumcision came to the Jews from Egypt. "It is true", he writes,

> that the Biblical account contradicts this more than once ... These, however, are distortions, which should not lead us astray; later on we shall discover the reason for them. The fact remains that there is only one answer to the question of where the Jews derived the custom of circumcision from—namely, from Egypt.[10]

Freud's arguments are based on findings in Egyptian mummifications, descriptions found on tomb walls, as well as on the accounts of historians such as Herodotus and biblical scholars such as Edward Meyer, who identify that circumcision was practised by Indigenous Egyptians. Why did Moses, he asks, if he was indeed a Jew who had just liberated his people, "impose on them a troublesome custom which even, to some extent, made them into Egyptians and which must keep permanently alive their memory?"[11] If the custom was common in Egypt and Moses was indeed a Jew, it is inconceivable that during the struggle for the liberation of Jews he would also impose a custom that strengthened and preserved Egypt in their memory. After all, it was known to them that circumcision was practised in Egypt. In order to mark the difference of the Jewish people and their distinction from other peoples, it would have made sense to choose a sign that will differentiate them. This contradiction leads Freud to conclude that Moses was not a Jew but an Egyptian and thus, the origin of the Jewish religion is rooted in an earlier monotheism that prevailed in Egypt. If Moses was indeed Egyptian, Freud explains, then the religion given to the Jews, which is named after him – *Mosaic religion* – "was the Egyptian one".[12]

Freud traces the signs of the first monotheistic religion back to the 18th Dynasty in ancient Egypt, to the reign of King Amenophis IV. During this period, when Egypt became a world empire, Pharaoh Amenophis IV (Akhenaten) established the religion of Aten –

---

10 Sigmund Freud. "Moses and Monotheism, Three Essays." *The Standard Edition of the Complete Psychological Works of Sigmund Freud* 23 (1939), pp. 26–27.

11 Sigmund Freud. "Moses and Monotheism, Three Essays." *The Standard Edition of the Complete Psychological Works of Sigmund Freud* 23 (1939), p. 27.

12 Sigmund Freud. "Moses and Monotheism, Three Essays." *The Standard Edition of the Complete Psychological Works of Sigmund Freud* 23 (1939), p. 18.

a strict monotheism, the first attempt of the kind, so far as we know, in the history of the world, and along with the belief in a single god religious intolerance was inevitably born, which had previously been alien to the ancient world and remained so long afterwards.[13]

In many ways, Freud explains, Egyptian monotheism resembled Judaism. Its characteristics included worship of one god, rejection of human attributes of the one god, exclusion of magic and sorcery, and dismissal of the idea of an afterlife. The root of both religions is a rigorous monotheism, which celebrates the exclusivity of a universal One God.

However, in Egypt this tradition was short-lived. The Egyptian people revolted against the rigid monotheistic demands, and even before Akhenaten's death, the belief in Aten religion crumbled, and people returned to polytheistic worship of multiple deities:

> The glorious Eighteenth Dynasty was at an end and simultaneously its conquests in Nubia and Asia were lost. During this gloomy interregnum the ancient religions of Egypt were re-established. The Aten religion was abolished, Akhenaten's royal city was destroyed and plundered and his memory proscribed as that of a criminal.[14]

Moses, according to Freud, was "an aristocratic and prominent man, perhaps in fact a member of the royal house", a privileged and high-ranking man who was also "a convinced adherent of the new religion, whose basic thoughts he had made his own".[15] During this period of the collapse of Aten religion, being desperate and broken, he sought to revive the monotheism he believed in and continue its path. He placed hopes in an oppressed Semitic tribe, liberated these people from slavery and created a new nation for the continuity of the monotheistic faith.

In Freud's reading of biblical and historical sources, he identifies a split – two figures of Moses and two gods that differ from each other both in name and in nature, a conflict that cannot be settled into a single coherent narrative. In order to bridge the gaps and contradictions in these descriptions, he turns to Ernst Sellin's hypothesis that "Moses, the founder of their religion, met with a violent end in a rising of his refractory and stiff-necked people, and that at the same time the religion he had introduced was thrown off".[16] Similar to the Egyptian people, the new nation, the Israelites, struggled with the rigorous demands of monotheism and, in a

---

13 Sigmund Freud. "Moses and Monotheism, Three Essays." *The Standard Edition of the Complete Psychological Works of Sigmund Freud* 23 (1939), p. 20.
14 Sigmund Freud. "Moses and Monotheism, Three Essays." *The Standard Edition of the Complete Psychological Works of Sigmund Freud* 23 (1939), p. 24.
15 Sigmund Freud. "Moses and Monotheism, Three Essays." *The Standard Edition of the Complete Psychological Works of Sigmund Freud* 23 (1939), p. 28.
16 Sigmund Freud. "Moses and Monotheism, Three Essays." *The Standard Edition of the Complete Psychological Works of Sigmund Freud* 23 (1939), p. 36. Over time, Sellin changed his mind. Freud knew this fact yet continued to adhere to his conclusion regarding the historical event of Moses' murder.

wild uprising, murdered Moses. Over the years, the murder was repressed, leaving nothing but a forgotten guilt-inducing collective memory. However, centuries later, another event occurred: the people who left Egypt allied themselves with a neighbouring Semitic tribe in Midian and the fierce and wild god of these tribes, a god called *Yahweh*, became their national god. As a result, the new god merged with the old one and the figure of Moses – his actions, personality and history – were attributed to a Midianite priest, who was also called Moses. Seeking to preserve the memory of Egypt and monotheistic tradition, the descendants of Moses the Egyptian, the Levites, insisted on maintaining the custom of circumcision that signified the Egyptian religion and the legacy of their leader. The Semitic people, who sought to expand the reign of their god, *Yahweh*, agreed, according to Freud, to the compromise made in the Kadesh, in which two separate peoples became one, two figures of Moses were united, the divergent paths were hidden and the act of murder repressed.

Freud reconciles in this way the contradictions revealed in the texts, explaining the conflicting descriptions of Moses' personality, as well as the split in the name and characteristics of the Jewish god – *Adonai* [Lord] and *Yahweh*. Initially, he argues, after the unification, the newly formed religion was not a rigid monotheistic tradition, and its characteristics were not much different from those of the surrounding polytheistic peoples. However, over time, the repressed memory of the previous '*true*' belief, originating in Egyptian monotheism, simmered and emerged until it gained enough strength, awarding *Yahweh* with the spiritual attributes of the Egyptian monotheistic One God. The new religion transformed into a rigorous Jewish monotheism, and the memory of Moses returned as the Jewish leader, who liberated the people from slavery in Egypt.

Freud's reconstructed story recasts both the history of Moses, the history of the Jewish people and the development of monotheism. In this narrative, Judaism preceded by an earlier monotheism, an Egyptian monotheism, and the Jewish people began with the murder of Moses, an Egyptian leader who freed them from oppression. In Freud's textual reconstruction, circumcision constitutes a basic link in the chain of evidence, and a cornerstone in arriving at his conclusions. It is the "key-fossil", as he explains, that reveals textual inconsistencies, leading to the 'historical truth' about the Egyptian roots of Judaism.

While the second essay in the book is a historical reconstruction and hardly touches on psychoanalytic theory, in the third essay, Freud seeks to weave into this narrative the psychoanalytic evidence that will support it. This third text, completed by Freud after fleeing to England following the rise of Nazism in Vienna, links the historical reconstruction of the origins of Judaism to the Oedipal narrative centred on the ambivalence towards the father, patricide and the son's feelings of guilt. Using psychoanalytic concepts, Freud parallels the development of religion, specifically Judaism, with a repressed neurosis that repeatedly returns to the historical trauma that birthed it, attempting to touch it, while, simultaneously, concealing it. Drawing on analogies from the clinical world as well as his theories of psychosexual development, he illustrates the Oedipal conflict hidden beneath the neurotic symptom of religion. As he explains, just like in the psyche of the individual sub-ject, early trauma that has been repressed and forgotten in the history of Judaism remains simmering beneath the surface in a sort "incubation period", in which the conflict is seemingly forgotten, and life goes on as usual. However, the truth and the historical conflict emerge years later from the depth of the unconscious, return-ing from repression. Thus, the monotheistic truth remained hidden for many years, during which Judaism behaved in its practices similar to other local polytheistic religions, in which "no sign was to be detected of the monotheist idea, of the con-tempt for ceremonial or of the great emphasis on ethics",[17] until, after a long period of latency,

> this tradition of a great past which continued to operate (from the background, as it were), which gradually acquired more and more power over people's minds and which in the end succeeded in changing the god Yahweh into the Mosaic god and in re-awakening into life the religion of Moses that had been introduced and then abandoned long centuries before.[18]

The development of the Jewish religion is linked in this text not only with the development of the individual but also with things Freud wrote 25 years earlier, in *Totem and Taboo*, establishing the Jewish narrative as a specific case of the theory he created about the origins of religion and culture in general. In this way, the events of the Jewish people and the development of monotheism are entwined into Freud's theories and circumcision serves as a key-concept through which Freud returns to the conflict between father and son binding all threads together under the Oedipal narrative–the individual, Judaism, society and culture.

Freud, a Jew: The Historical Context of Writing

Freud wrote the text between 1934 and 1938, towards the end of his life and during the historical period of pre-World War II, in the midst of Jewish persecution and antisemitism. The text incorporates passages and preliminary notes in which Freud lays out his dilemmas in writing and adds personal testimonies of the historical re-ality in which the essays were written. One can observe – and much has been writ-ten on it – the intertwining of Freud's writings in this particular book with his life, his Jewishness, and the historical context in which the text was written. Despite his attempts to maintain a clean and separate investigation of his research, the echoes of his reality at the time reverberate throughout the text: his descriptions of mono-theism are intertwined with questions of his own Jewish identity, his own history is woven into the reconstruction of Moses' life, and the distortions he finds within

---

17 Sigmund Freud. "Moses and Monotheism, Three Essays." *The Standard Edition of the Complete Psychological Works of Sigmund Freud* 23 (1939), p. 67.
18 Sigmund Freud. "Moses and Monotheism, Three Essays." *The Standard Edition of the Complete Psychological Works of Sigmund Freud* 23 (1939), p. 70.

biblical texts lead to a folded structure and distortions in his own text. Indeed, if there ever is one, *Moses and Monotheism* is not a contained scientific research and is inseparably linked to its writer and to the circumstances of its writing.

In *The Interpretation of Dreams*, Freud describes a story he heard from his father (Jacob Freud) when he was a child:

> 'When I [Sigmund's father] was a young man,' he said, 'I went for a walk one Saturday in the streets of your birthplace; I was well dressed, and had a new fur cap on my head. A Christian came up to me and with a single blow knocked off my cap into the mud and shouted: "Jew! get off the pavement!"' 'And what did you do?' I asked. 'I went into the roadway and picked up my cap,' was his quiet reply.[19]

Hearing about this event as a child, left a strong imprint on Freud: "This struck me as unheroic conduct on the part of the big, strong man who was holding the little boy by the hand",[20] he writes. This description reflects the grim antisemitic reality of the time, which, even if was not daily, its presence had been entrenched and clearly had a profound influence on Freud's thinking and writing. As Chasseguet-Smirgel writes,

> [t]o be a Jew of the diaspora, living in the conditions that reigned at the end of the nineteenth century and the first third of the twentieth century, as Freud did, and not to experience ambivalent feelings with regard to Judaism, would be purely and simply to escape the laws governing the human psyche.[21]

Despite his secular beliefs and his affiliation with the European enlightenment movement, Freud's Jewish identity during this European period had a profound impact on his worldview and was undoubtedly inextricably connected to the narrative at the centre of *Moses and Monotheism*.

Freud indeed testifies to his complex relationship with Judaism. In the preface to the Hebrew translation of *Totem and Taboo*, he states that,

> [n]o reader of the Hebrew version of this book will find it easy to put himself in the emotional position of an author who is ignorant of the language of holy writ, who is completely estranged from the religion of his fathers—as well as from every other religion—and who cannot take a share in nationalist ideals, but who has yet never repudiated his people, who feels that he is in his essential nature a

---

19 Sigmund Freud. *The Interpretation of Dreams* (translated by Strachey, SE. 4–5 London: The Hogarth Press and The Institute of Psycho-Analysis 1954 [1900]), p. 218.

20 Sigmund Freud. *The Interpretation of Dreams* (translated by Strachey, SE. 4–5 London: The Hogarth Press and The Institute of Psycho-Analysis 1954[1900]), pp. 218–219.

21 Janine Chasseguet-Smirgel "Some Thoughts on Freuds Attitude During the Nazi Period", *Psychoanal. Contem. Though.* 11 (1988): 249–256. p. 256.

Jew and who has no desire to alter that nature. If the question were put to him: 'Since you have abandoned all these common characteristics of your country men, what is there left to you that is Jewish?' he would reply: 'A very great deal, and probably its very essence.' He could not now express that essence clearly in words; but some day, no doubt, it will become accessible to the scientific mind.[22]

Even though he distanced himself from religion analysing it as a neurotic process, the threads woven by his psychoanalytic theory around cultural development, and the history of Jewish religion cannot be disconnected from his life as a Jew during this European reality in which the text was written.

Freud wrote *Moses and Monotheism* over the course of four years, in a pre-World War II European reality, during which time he was forced to emigrate from Austria to England. As many critics have already illuminated, the text bears witness not only to the historical reality in which it was written but also to Freud's ambivalence regarding his Jewish identity. It consists of three essays of different lengths, two prefaces at the beginning of the third essay and a third introduction in the middle of this essay, many internal summaries and repetitions of repetitions. Such deviations from the rules of writing are uncharacteristic to Freud's other writings, and he himself points them out in his familiar apologetic tone.[23] Not only is it filled with hesitations and repetitions, but it was also printed in parts: the first and second essays were published in 1937 in the journal *Imago*. The third part, although written earlier, was rewritten and published only after Freud was forced to emigrate to England, in 1938, and shortly before his death. The entire text converges into itself in a kind of distortion, whose origins can be explained, as the editors of the Hebrew translation write,

> by the circumstances in which the book was written: the long period of writing—four years and perhaps more—during which he repeatedly changed it, and the grave external circumstances of the political events in Austria, which culminated in its occupation by the Nazis and Freud's forced emigration to England.[24]

Not only the textual structure is evidence of the difficulties and conflicts that surrounded the writing process, but the content written therein also testifies to the circumstances in which the text was created, amidst the upheaval in Europe.

---

22 Sigmund Freud. *Totem and Taboo: Some Points of Agreement Between the Mental Lives of Savages and Neurotics* (Translated by James Strachey. London: Routledge, [1912–1913] 2003), preface to the Hebrew translation. The preface to the Hebrew edition was written in Vienna in 1930 and was first published in German in 1934.

23 Sigmund Freud. "Moses and Monotheism, Three Essays." *The Standard Edition of the Complete Psychological Works of Sigmund Freud* 23 (1939), p. 103.

24 Introduction of the editors to the Hebrew translation, Yitzhak Binyamini and Rakefet Zalashik, Resling, p. 13.

In fact, it is possible to quote Freud's psychoanalytic formulation regarding histori-cal reconstruction, in relation to his own text:

> Long-past ages have a great and often puzzling attraction for men's imagination. Whenever they are dissatisfied with their present surroundings—and this hap-pens often enough—they turn back to the past and hope that they will now be able to prove the truth of the unextinguishable dream of a golden age.[25]

As part of the historical reconstruction, Freud also reimagines the course of Moses' life, creating his character as a "great man" who leads the Jewish people into the desert.[26] Freud's Moses was an Egyptian man, a charismatic and idealistic leader who sought to continue the Egyptian monotheistic tradition and, thus, freed the repressed people from slavery and oppression. Throughout the essays, Freud is fascinated by the figure of Moses asking:

> How is it possible for a single man to evolve such extraordinary effectiveness that he can form a people out of random individuals and families, can stamp them with their definitive character and determine their fate for thousands of years?[27]

In this question, one can hear Freud's enchantment with the power of the "great man" and his acknowledgement of the exceptional impact Moses have had on him.

Indeed, Freud was fascinated by the figure of Moses throughout his life. He admits, referring to Michelangelo's statue of Moses in the Church of San Pietro in Rome, that he never experienced such a powerful influence from any sculpture, and in a letter to Edoardo Weiss regarding this masterpiece, he confesses: "Every day for three lonely weeks of September, 1913 [a slip for 1912], I stood in the church in front of the statue".[28] Freud stood in front of Michelangelo's Moses every day, for many hours, scribbling sketches and writing down its details, and then published anonymously as *The Moses of Michelangelo* in the journal *Imago*. In this text, Freud attempts to decipher Michelangelo's intention in creating the statue of Mo-ses, holding the stones of the covenant under his right arm. According to Freud's interpretation, Michelangelo

---

25 Sigmund Freud. "Moses and Monotheism, Three Essays." *The Standard Edition of the Complete Psychological Works of Sigmund Freud* 23 (1939), p. 71.

26 Freud also refers to his father in the eyes of himself as a child (described in the quote from *The Interpretation of Dreams*) by using this phrase "the big man".

27 Sigmund Freud. "Moses and Monotheism, Three Essays." *The Standard Edition of the Complete Psychological Works of Sigmund Freud* 23 (1939), p. 107.

28 Sigmund Freud. "The Moses of Michelangelo." In: *The Standard Edition of the Complete Psychological Works of Sigmund Freud* 13 (1914) (London: The Hogarth Press and the Institute of Psycho-Analysis, 1955), p. 210.

has modified the theme of the broken Tables; he does not let Moses break them in his wrath but makes him be influenced by the danger that they will be broken and makes him calm that wrath, or at any rate prevent it from becoming an act.[29]

In contrast to the familiar interpretation of the statue in which Moses is about to smash the Tablets in rage, Freud presents an alternative understanding in which Moses masters the storm of his emotions in order to preserve the Tablets, embraces them into his arm and does not succumb to rage. With this reading, Freud gave new meaning to Michelangelo's intentions, attributing Moses what was for him "the highest mental achievement that is possible in a man, that of struggling successfully against an inward passion for the sake of a cause to which he has devoted himself".[30]

This essay on Michelangelo's Moses was written at a time when Jung abandoned Freud's ranks and has been read by some scholars, as evidence of his own anger at his betrayal. According to this interpretation, Freud's deep identification with the figure of Moses is rooted in the experience of a father realising the unfaithfulness of his people who abandoned the way of God and created a different idol for themselves, forsaking their religion in exchange for a golden calf. Thus, an Oedipal narrative is resurfacing as a central motif in Freud's life, as he was drawn to the statue of Moses as a sort of working through the intensity of the relationship between father and son. He too, like Moses, gazes down from the mountain at the child he nurtured and feels the soar of his betrayal; And he too, strives to master his wrath, focusing his attention on the mission he is devoted to – his psychoanalytic theory.

Yosef Hayim Yerushalmi, in his book *Freud's Moses: Judaism Terminable and Interminable*, provides an alternative interpretation to Freud's fascination with Michelangelo's Moses.[31] For him, Freud identifies not with the father but with the son who feels guilty for betraying his father and the Jewish tradition. Analysing Freud's writing of *Moses and Monotheism* at the end of his life, at the age of 78, Yerushalmi explains his preoccupation with the story of Moses as a renewed dialogue with his father and with Jewish history. "In 1891", Yerushalmi writes,

on Freud's thirty-fifth birthday, his father presented him with an unusual gift. He had rebound in leather the Philippsohn Bible that Sigmund had studied in his childhood and now gave it to him with an elaborate Hebrew inscription that he had composed.[32]

---

29 Sigmund Freud. "The Moses of Michelangelo." In: *The Standard Edition of the Complete Psychological Works of Sigmund Freud* 13 (1914), p. 233.

30 Sigmund Freud. "The Moses of Michelangelo." In: *The Standard Edition of the Complete Psychological Works of Sigmund Freud* 13 (1914), p. 233.

31 Yosef Hayim Yerushalmi. *Freud's Moses: Judaism Terminable and Interminable* (New Haven: Yale University Press, 1991).

32 Yosef Hayim Yerushalmi. *Freud's Moses: Judaism Terminable and Interminable* (New Haven: Yale University Press, 1991), p. 71.

In this dedicated inscription, Yerushalmi continues, Freud's father expressed a "dramatic call to return to the Bible, to the originally shared values with the father, 'a memorial and a reminder of love'".[33] This letter, Yerushalmi argues, offers a rereading of Freud's preoccupation with Moses throughout his life, a prism that captures the intensity of guilt that surges in relation to his father's Jewish legacy. Towards the end of his life, at the age of 78, Freud returned, in his own way, to deal with both the collective as well as the private Jewish history, listening to his father's "dramatic call to return" to the Bible, the shared values of Jewish tradition. Yerushalmi reveals in the writing of *Moses and Monotheism*, a renewed connection between Freud's Judaism and his theory, portraying psychoanalysis as a "Jewish science". According to him, in writing the book, engaging with Jewish history and the Bible, Freud returns to what was repressed throughout his life, initiating a dialogue with the ghost of his dead father. The repressed collective patricide, the murder of Moses, resurfaces in its personal form in Freud's life, as he strives to atone, in the twilight of his life, for the original sin and reconnect with the legacy of his father, with Judaism and with his Jewish heritage.

Indeed, it is impossible to draw a clear boundary between the text that Freud wishes to lay before readers as 'historical truth' and his own life; between the history of the Jewish people about which he writes and the specific circumstances in which Jews were living in Europe at the time of writing. While writing about Moses who "had lost his country" and "saw all his hopes and prospects destroyed", but "was not prepared to abjure all the convictions that were so dear to him",[34] Freud begins his investigation in the shadow of war with a reality of escalating antisemitic violence, and with psychoanalysis facing the Church's scrutiny. As he explains,

> We are living in especially remarkable period. We find to our astonishment that progress has allied itself with barbarism ... If our work leads us to a conclusion which reduces religion to a neurosis of humanity and explains its enormous power in the same way as a neurotic compulsion in our individual patients, we may be sure of drawing the resentment of our ruling powers down upon us ... It would probably lead to our being prohibited from practising psycho-analysis.[35]

As Freud relates, the anxiety about the forces of destruction enveloped the writing process:

> I was living under the protection of the Catholic Church, and was afraid that the publication of my work would result in the loss of that protection and would

33 Yosef Hayim Yerushalmi. *Freud's Moses: Judaism Terminable and Interminable* (New Haven: Yale University Press, 1991), p. 74.

34 Sigmund Freud. "Moses and Monotheism, Three Essays." *The Standard Edition of the Complete Psychological Works of Sigmund Freud* 23 (1939), p. 28.

35 Sigmund Freud. "Moses and Monotheism, Three Essays." *The Standard Edition of the Complete Psychological Works of Sigmund Freud* 23 (1939), pp. 54–55.

conjure up a prohibition upon the work of the adherents and students of psycho-analysis in Austria.[36]

Through the veil of threats and violence surrounding his Jewish identity on the one hand, and psychoanalysis on the other, Freud choses to write the third essay of the text not in order to publish it, but in order to shelve the book and wait for the days when it could be brought to light.[37] As he explains,

> I shall not give this work to the public. But that need not prevent my writing it … It may then be preserved in concealment till someday the time arrives when it may venture without danger into the light, or till someone who has reached the same conclusions and opinions can be told: 'there was someone in darker times who thought the same as you!'.[38]

Only after moving to England, he felt safe enough to publish the entire text.

The story of Moses, who "[i]n this predicament he found an unusual solution",[39] in bringing monotheism to light, is intrinsically connected to Freud's own seeking, despite destructive forces, to birth the text into the world, even if that means hiding it for a while before it can be published. This essay was written in a long process that tormented Freud, as he testifies, "like an unlaid ghost". Faced with rising waves of antisemitism on the one hand and the forces of castrating Church on the other, Freud courageously insists to give expression to that piece of truth that was revealed to him.[40] Like Akhenaten who believed in Ma'at (truth and justice), and like Moses after him, who remained faithful to the monotheistic religion with "a heroic attempt to combat destiny",[41] Freud does not compromise, and when the right time comes, he dares "to take the plunge" and makes his work public, reviving the forbidden and the repressed.[42] Returning from the depths of the repressed unconscious

---

36 Sigmund Freud. "Moses and Monotheism, Three Essays." *The Standard Edition of the Complete Psychological Works of Sigmund Freud* 23 (1939), p. 57.

37 In fact - rewrite and link to the previous two papers on the subject. The third essay had already been written two years earlier.

38 Sigmund Freud. "Moses and Monotheism, Three Essays." *The Standard Edition of the Complete Psychological Works of Sigmund Freud* 23 (1939), p. 56.

39 Sigmund Freud. "Moses and Monotheism, Three Essays." *The Standard Edition of the Complete Psychological Works of Sigmund Freud* 23 (1939), p. 28.

40 "I have made yet another attempt to get the difficulty out of the way, by telling myself that my fears are based on an over-estimation of my own personal importance: that it will probably be a matter of complete indifference to the authorities what I choose to write about Moses and the origin of monotheist religions. But I feel uncertain in my judgement of this". p. 71.

41 Sigmund Freud. "Moses and Monotheism, Three Essays." *The Standard Edition of the Complete Psychological Works of Sigmund Freud* 23 (1939), p. 28.

42 Sigmund Freud. "Moses and Monotheism, Three Essays." *The Standard Edition of the Complete Psychological Works of Sigmund Freud* 23 (1939), p. 57.

"a portion of the eternal truth which, long concealed, came to light at last and was then bound to carry everyone along with it".[43]

As World War II loomed and anti-Jewish sentiments surged in Europe, Freud found it imperative to bring to light a truth that disturbed his rest. When echoes of war and waves of hatred were interwoven, Jews were also "the others", second-class citizens, whose rights were limited and the image of the circumcised Jew was perceived, as Geller explains, as castrated and feminine.[44] Exploring the gendered aspect of the European antisemitic ambience of that time, Geller analyses the emotional intensity and the drive for writing the essay as stemming from a desire to cast the Jewish (feminised) image in a different light, in an attempt to portray Jewish monotheism as masculine, and to revive the image of Moses through an opposition to the feminine image of the Jew.

Further to this analysis, Boyarin suggests that Freud's focus on the Oedipal narrative and the father–son rivalry, not only as a product of fear of the feminine perception of the Jew in Europe but also due to the need to repress his own homoerotic tendencies. As he explains, at the end of the 19th century, an antisemitic discourse emerged in Europe, which also linked the image of the passive, pale and weak Jewish man to homosexual orientations. Within this cultural reality, and in response to the intimate relationship Freud had with Fliess, his theoretical focus on essentially heterosexual Oedipal masculinity unconsciously intended to erase and hide his homoerotic desires, replacing the image of a "feminised male, father-desiring, pathic, hysterical Jewish queer" with "an active, phallic, mother-desiring, father-killing, 'normal' (that is, gentile) man".[45]

Thus, in the text, the figure of Moses evolves into the archetype of "the great man", the masculine hero, whose greatness reaches "divine proportions", and his charisma attracts followers.[46] He is described as an Egyptian leader "an aristocratic and prominent man, perhaps in fact a member of the royal house ... He was undoubtedly aware of his great capacities, ambitious and energetic".[47] He demonstrated impressive ability in battles such as his "victorious military actions as an Egyptian general in Ethiopia", expressing his "decisiveness of thought, the strength of will, the energy of action". As Freud explains, "[o]ne must admire him, one may trust him, but one cannot avoid being afraid of him too".[48] Binding Moses's image

43 Sigmund Freud. "Moses and Monotheism, Three Essays." *The Standard Edition of the Complete Psychological Works of Sigmund Freud* 23 (1939), p. 129.

44 Jay Geller. "A Paleontological View of Freud's Study of Religion: Unearthing the "leitfossil" Circumcision." *Mod. Juda.* 13, no. 1 (1993): 49–70.

45 Daniel Boyarin. "Freud's Baby, Fliess's Maybe: Homophobia, Antisemitism, and the Invention of Oedipus." *GLQ: J. Gay Lesb. Stud.* 2, no. 2 (1995): 115–147, 139.

46 Sigmund Freud. "Moses and Monotheism, Three Essays." *The Standard Edition of the Complete Psychological Works of Sigmund Freud* 23 (1939), p. 110.

47 Sigmund Freud. "Moses and Monotheism, Three Essays." *The Standard Edition of the Complete Psychological Works of Sigmund Freud* 23 (1939), p. 28.

48 Sigmund Freud. "Moses and Monotheism, Three Essays." *The Standard Edition of the Complete Psychological Works of Sigmund Freud* 23 (1939), pp. 109–110.

with that of God and providing him all the same qualities included in the image of the Jewish god, Freud also acknowledge other masculine traits that portray him as "domineering, hot-tempered and even violent".[49] Apparently, he explains,

> some of the character traits which the Jews included in their early picture of their God—describing him as jealous, severe and ruthless—may have been at bottom derived from a recollection of Moses; for in fact it was not an invisible God but the man Moses who brought them out of Egypt.[50]

In difficult times, Freud explains, "there is a powerful need for an authority who can be admired, before whom one bows down, by whom one is ruled and perhaps even ill-treated". This basic human need for a hero, a "great man" in times of trouble stems, according to Freud, from the "longing for the father felt by everyone from his childhood onwards, for the same father whom the hero of legend boasts he has overcome … who but the father can have been the 'great man' in childhood?" The longing for a father as a heroic saviour beats in the heart of every child, as Freud writes, particularly in difficult times, for the father is the great man of our childhood.[51]

Just as the Jewish people in their difficulties needed a father and followed Moses, so did Freud, at a time of crisis in which the image of the feminine inferior Jew was fuelling European antisemitic emotions, created that legendary figure of Moses, as a powerful and masculine Egyptian prince. In a time when Freud was forced to emigrate from his country, to leave his home, the land where he grew up since childhood, he too raised his head upwards searching for a paternal figure and thus portrayed the image of Moses as a "great man", in a reconstruction of history that at the same time, erases traces of his childhood, his vulnerability and particularly, as I will show, his dependence on the women around him.

The Hero Archetype

Freud reconstructs Moses' early life through the myth of the hero, which, as he shows, referring to Rank's writing, also characterises legends and myths such as those of "Oedipus, Kama, Paris, Telephos, Perseus, Heracles, Gilgamesh, Amphion and Zethos, and others".[52] Rank's studies, which Freud admits were written with his encouragement and guidance, reveal that the typical pattern in myths and legends

---

49 Sigmund Freud. "Moses and Monotheism, Three Essays." *The Standard Edition of the Complete Psychological Works of Sigmund Freud* 23 (1939), p. 41.

50 Sigmund Freud. "Moses and Monotheism, Three Essays." *The Standard Edition of the Complete Psychological Works of Sigmund Freud* 23 (1939), pp. 32–33.

51 Sigmund Freud. "Moses and Monotheism, Three Essays." *The Standard Edition of the Complete Psychological Works of Sigmund Freud* 23 (1939), pp. 109–110.

52 Sigmund Freud. "Moses and Monotheism, Three Essays." *The Standard Edition of the Complete Psychological Works of Sigmund Freud* 23 (1939), p. 11.

about the birth of various heroes presents the hero as having "two families", two sets of parents. The first family into which the protagonist is born is privileged and royal, while the second, the one in which he grows up, is a simple and humble one. However, in the case of Moses, according to Freud's analysis, the narrative was distorted when "some later and clumsy adapter of the material of the legend found an opportunity for introducing into the story of his hero Moses something which resembled the classical exposure legends marking out a hero",[53] in a way that created a reversal – the first family is the modest one and the second is the Egyptian royal one.

When presented with the need to reconcile two different families, Freud solves the riddle by deleting one of them, which he calls "humble" ('inferior' in the Hebrew translation), explaining that due to the need to attribute Moses' origins to the Jewish people, the author clumsily reversed the narrative – anchoring his origin from the Jewish people and his growing up in the royal family. "If we have the courage to recognize this assertion as universally true" he writes, "and as applying also to the legend of Moses", we will conclude that the first family into which Moses was born – the Jewish family – is fictitious, and the second, the one in which he grew up – the Egyptian royal family – is the real one, and "then all at once we see things clearly: Moses was an Egyptian".[54]

"When a people's imagination attaches the myth of birth which we are discussing to an outstanding figure", Freud concludes, "it is intending in that way to recognize him as a hero and to announce that he has fulfilled the regular pattern of a hero's life". In this way, he interprets the legend of Moses' two families using the reality principle, as a late invention of a "clumsy adapter", who sought to place Moses as the hero of the Jewish people, concluding that the legends of his childhood are nothing more than a textual ploy designed "to create a patent of nobility for the hero, to raise his social standing".[55] Emphasising the Oedipal pattern of the myth expressing the way in which children perceives their parents – or in fact, the way sons perceive their fathers – at the beginning of life through idealisation (and therefore as royal): "the source of the whole poetic fiction is what is known as a child's 'family romance', in which the son reacts to a change in his emotional relation to his parents and in particular to his father".[56]

Freud is referencing myths and legends to understand the 'historical truth', the hidden meaning at their origin. Searching for the reasons that led to the creation of the myth, with an emphasis on the reality principle, he tones down the echoes of

53   Sigmund Freud. "Moses and Monotheism, Three Essays." *The Standard Edition of the Complete Psychological Works of Sigmund Freud* 23 (1939), p. 14.

54   Sigmund Freud. "Moses and Monotheism, Three Essays." *The Standard Edition of the Complete Psychological Works of Sigmund Freud* 23 (1939), p. 15.

55   Sigmund Freud. "Moses and Monotheism, Three Essays." *The Standard Edition of the Complete Psychological Works of Sigmund Freud* 23 (1939), p. 13.

56   Sigmund Freud. "Moses and Monotheism, Three Essays." *The Standard Edition of the Complete Psychological Works of Sigmund Freud* 23 (1939), p. 12.

symbolic layers in which two different families can represent different phantasies and in which the question of being either real or false is immaterial. In myth, in fact, an interpretation can follow different and even contradicting meanings arriving from the unconscious. As Jung explains, when interpretation of mythical stories can only follow the pattern of the personal unconscious and material reality, symbolic meanings are lost, and the creative forces of the psyche erased.

Jung's theoretical implications and those of his followers are based on archetypal patterns, the use of symbolic language, myths and dreams to preserve creative movement, deepening the gaze into the human psyche's ambiguity and its inherent contradictions, which cannot be translated into a single interpretation. According to him, mythology, legends and dreams unfold a wide range of symbolic meanings that not only describe the inner world but also facilitate movements in the human psyche. Symbols are a message, an opportunity for change, opening a potential for growth that always remains 'pregnant' with other and different meanings. In Jungian theory, myths are not only representations of unconscious contents but also a movement that contains a strong energetic potential of creative and destructive effects that drive the human.[57] This psychic movement is based on those formless energies that Jung called archetypes – patterns of a priori intuition, of pre-mental perception directing and characterising human existence. Archetypes are not accessible to perception unless they appear in consciousness in the form of images or symbols, as experienced in dreams or through mythologies. Jung investigated myths and dreams understanding them as an expression of the deeper layers of the human unconscious—what he referred to as the *objective psyche* or the *collective unconscious*. Alongside the contents of the personal unconscious, he sought to characterise the healing power of the psyche and the trends of development and integration rooted in the deeper layers of the collective unconscious. He argued that due to the activation of psychic images at this layer, mythical stories have an important power for both inspiration and destruction, for growth and war, for healing and annihilation.[58]

An archetypal reading of the heroic myth of Moses teaches that in legends and myths, the image of a king often represents *collective consciousness*. The king as the earthly incarnation of God, ruling through his laws, relying on God's authority in the material world, represents the accepted and conscious aspect of collective law. The seat of the king is the seat of the law, cultural constraints, rules and conventions. It is also the area opposing change, responsible for maintaining the status quo. The birth of the hero reflects a new motif emerging into the world with the promise of change, and therefore stands in conflicting relationships with the king and collective consciousness. The child born into the royal family is in fact born

57 Carl, G. Jung. "Symbols of Transformation." Vol. 5, In: R.F.C. Hull, Michael Fordham Gerhard Adler (eds.) *Collected Works* (New York: Princeton University Press, 1967), pp. 1–404.

58 Carl, G. Jung. "The Archetypes and the Collective Unconscious." Vol. 9, In: R.F.C. Hull, Michael Fordham Gerhard Adler (eds.) *Collected Works* (New York: Princeton University Press, 1967), pp. 1–66.

into this conflict and, as Freud shows, poses a threat to the continuity of existing law which therefore often provokes the wrath of the father, the king. Symbolising the conflict that arises at birth, the new force arriving into the world brings with it the winds of change.

While the royal family represents aspects of the law, the simple and humble family, residing closer to nature and taking care of the child – according to various myths of the hero – represents a psychic area distanced from authority and the light of consciousness, the unconscious. This psychic realm that is close to nature's primal richness and to treasures, which Jung also refers to in his descriptions of the *Great Mother* archetype. If the father represents the illuminated areas of collective consciousness, the mother archetypal image resides in more distanced areas of the psyche, more shadowy, blurred and perhaps terrifying for our consciousness, the other side of which is, of course, its wealth and transformative potential. The child in the myth of the hero, despite being born into the world of the law, grows far from the collective consciousness, far from the demands of culture and remains close to that primal realm that has access to the treasures of the unconscious, to elements of creativity inherent to the maternal world. In the various myths the hero is saved and fed by a woman, sometimes female animals, symbolising the key to the creative dimension of the self, to transformations that necessitate the far-hidden maternal aspect of the psyche.

The biblical story and other Jewish legends describe the maternal and the feminine strength that protected Moses in his early life. He was born, according to the biblical narrative, against the backdrop of the Israelites' enslavement in Egypt, culminating in Pharaoh's decree to throw the new born sons into the Nile. Hoping to save their son, his parents kept him safe and hidden for three months and when that was no longer possible his mother Jochebed, placed Moses in a basket upon the Nile and sent his sister Miriam to watch over him from afar. Pharaoh's daughter saw him,[59] heard his cries and, in her compassion, drew him from the water, "named him Moses, saying, 'I drew him out of the water'", and brought him to the palace to be raised there.[60]

In his analysis of the hero myth and reconstruction of Moses' life, Freud is suspicious of the story about Pharaoh's daughter, writing that "it is absurd to attribute to an Egyptian princess a derivation of the name from the Hebrew" and that the name Moses is "simply the Egyptian word 'mose' meaning 'child'".[61] As he explains, the name Moses leads directly to the solution, to the one origin that lies underneath, 'answering' the question of the two families of origin in the myth: Moses was an Egyptian. In Freud's interpretation, the biblical stories of Moses' early childhood – his birth to a Jewish woman, his rescue by his mother and sister, and being drawn

---

59 According to the *midrash*, she was Batya, the daughter of Pharaoh, who is mentioned in the Book of Chronicles.

60 Exodus, II, 10.

61 Sigmund Freud. "Moses and Monotheism, Three Essays." *The Standard Edition of the Complete Psychological Works of Sigmund Freud* 23 (1939), p. 8.

from the water by Pharaoh's daughter are marked as false narratives that should be erased. These parts of the biblical text, which highlight the dependence on the feminine and the maternal and emphasise the vulnerability that characterises the beginning of the hero's life, are obliterated in Freud's reconstruction.

The name given to him by Pharaoh's daughter, Moses, (in Hebrew: *Moshe*), is indeed a familiar Egyptian name, meaning the child, as Freud points out. But, it is precisely this fact that transforms his name into a palimpsest, containing a hidden layer of meaning, in which the Hebrew and Arabic names encounter each other at the moment the child is saved and drawn from the water. The point of divergence is also the point of encounter – a second birth in which the child's (Mose) Egyptian life begins by recognising his past: being drawn from the water (literally meaning: Moshe). Under the hands of Pharaoh's daughter, a different reconciliation of the two families emerges, one that does not require the erasure of one to preserve the other – otherness is intertwined – and Moses, the Jewish child drawn from the water, is also the Egyptian child. Moses, due to his Egyptian name, Mose, can be introduced into the palace and be accepted by the Pharaoh as an Egyptian child, but it is precisely this palimpsest of a name that both reveals and conceals the origin of his otherness and the subversive action of Pharaoh's daughter against her father's commands.

The double meaning embedded in the name is not a sign of Moses' Egyptian origin alone but rather a testimony of a feminine ability to contain difference. It shows the courage, strength, resourcefulness of Pharaoh's daughter and other women in Moses' early life, demonstrating the inclusive nature of the maternal realm in which two different elements can co-exist. The name Moses – perhaps like circumcision – does not necessarily have to be a sign of separation but rather a symbol of connection and an opening to the other. Freud, echoing the Pharaoh's command that all Jewish boys should be thrown into the Nile, demands a decision of one origin. While the masculine perspective, both of Pharaoh's and Freud's, does not identify the various meanings arising from Moses' name, Pharaoh's daughter opens the door to a dialogue between the Egyptian royal household and Moses' Jewish family. Introducing Moses into her father's palace as Mose and at the same time preserving his legacy as a Jewish child (Moshe), she manages to raise him simultaneously as both a Jewish child and an Egyptian prince. Pharaoh's daughter's ability lies in carrying a complex, multidimensional picture that simultaneously holds the two meanings in his name. Indeed, she finds a way, the legend continues, to keep his relationship with his Jewish mother and, although he is raised at the king's court, under his control and laws, Pharaoh's daughter, wisely and courageously, finds the way to provide him with nourishment from Hebrew sources, enabling him proximity to his mother, Jochebed.

Thinking about this act in Jungian terms, Pharaoh's daughter can be seen as the bridging aspect between the two symbolic families. Raising the hero as a royal, she also brings him back to the bosom of the other family, allowing him maternal nourishment from the other dimension, or rather from the dimension of otherness, and thus, enabling a continued connection with psychic maternal treasures. The dialogue and cooperation between Hebrew and Egyptian women stand in a striking contrast to the 'masculine' relationship between the two peoples, introducing a hybrid motive into the binarism in which Freud seeks to choose a single 'historical truth'.

In his lecture *Freud and the Non-European*, Palestinian-American intellectual Edward Said argues that in the way Freud depicts Moses' Egyptian origin, he establishes the monotheistic Jewish identity by referring to the Egyptian other. "[I]n excavating the archaeology of Jewish identity", he explains, "Freud insisted that it did not begin with itself but, rather, with other identities (Egyptian and Arabian)".[62] Freud's text does indeed point to the always intertwined identities, outlining the way in which otherness is essentially inherent to any identity. However, while with one hand he identifies this hybrid core, with his other hand Freud specifically attacks the narratives that allow this dialogue to exist, thus, both repeating and reproducing in the text the process in which one identity is erased in the face of the other. Selecting one 'true' identity for Moses, he deletes the only narrative in which a dialogue takes place between the peoples, represented by the feminine and the maternal.

While the biblical narrative emphasises maternal presence in Moses' early life, Freud directs the gaze to descriptions of his characteristics as a "great man", denying his childhood, his vulnerability as an oppressed Jew and his dependency on the maternal: he was not born into a Jewish family, he was not placed in a basket by his mother and was not drawn from the Nile by Pharaoh's daughter. As he explains, "the interpretation of the *myth of exposure* which was linked with Moses necessarily led to the inference that he was an Egyptian whom the needs of a people sought to make into a Jew".[63] Using the clues he gathered in analysing the myth of the hero with an emphasis on the principle of reality, he presents a different narrative about his childhood, portraying Moses as an Egyptian prince, a royalty from the very beginning. "The Jews possess a copious literature apart from the Bible", he writes,

> in which the legends and myths are to be found which grew up in the course of centuries round the imposing figure of their first leader and the founder of their religion, and which have both illuminated and obscured it.[64]

Separating truth from false in his reconstruction of Moses' life, Freud selects the stories that are consistent with his image of the "great man", casting aside as false those that might indicate dependency and vulnerability.

While in the 'birth legend' of Moses, the power that protects the newborn from death is feminine and maternal, Freud delineates his masculinity, vehemently

---

62 Edward Said. *Freud and the Non-European* (London: Verso, 2003). p. 44.
63 Sigmund Freud. "Moses and Monotheism, Three Essays." *The Standard Edition of the Complete Psychological Works of Sigmund Freud* 23 (1939), p. 17. Emphasis added.
64 Sigmund Freud. "Moses and Monotheism, Three Essays." *The Standard Edition of the Complete Psychological Works of Sigmund Freud* 23 (1939), p. 32.

opposing the possibility of dependency even in his early life. As he explains, Moses' characteristics throughout his life are "decisiveness of thought, the strength of will, the energy of action ... part of the picture of a father—but above all the[his] autonomy and independence of the great man".[65] In contrast to the story of Moses' Jewish origin, as part of an oppressed and enslaved people, Freud builds his image as a noble and respected Egyptian prince – above all independent and separated. Faced with the dependence on women described by Jewish texts, he brings forth the Oedipal narrative, shifting the focus to his relationship with the father. Only one legend from his childhood may contain "fragments of trustworthy tradition" – the time "when Pharaoh had taken him in his arms and playfully lifted him high in the air, the little three-year-old boy snatched the crown from the king's head and put it on his own". This amusing myth connotes the father-son relationship in a narrative that, according to Freud, exclusively and repeatedly shaped his life.[66]

Freud vividly presents the conflict between father and son emerging with the birth of the hero. He describes the beginning of the hero's life as being born into this struggle with the father and tells of the legend in which Pharaoh's rage arose against Moses, who took off the royal crown and placed it on his head. As in the myth of the hero, the child was "rescued despite his father's evil intention",[67] and, thus, Moses' life began with a conflict with the Egyptian king. In Jungian words, being born into the Pharaoh's command to throw all newborn male into the Nile, the Hero's archetypal Journey begins with the conflict in relation to this process of transformation. The hero, and in this case Moses, is born into danger, threatened by the aspect of the law, seeking to preserve things as they are. Confronted with this danger, it is often the maternal that protects the child from the wrath of the father, and it is the women around Moses, both Jewish and Egyptian, that cooperate to protect him and save his life. His mother places him in a basket, his sister watches over him from afar, and Pharaoh's daughter draws him from the water and brings him into the king's palace, undermining her father's decree. A Jungian analysis of the myth reveals that the waters are a maternal aspect that does not drown Moses but keeps him alive as a baby in amniotic fluid within the womb. Under the care of the women, the basket floating in the water, like an embryo in the womb, is a representation of pregnancy, the containing and transformative aspects of the maternal.

Describing this symbolic picture, Freud writes that "[t]he exposure in a casket is an unmistakable symbolic representation of *birth*: the casket is the womb, and the

---

65 Sigmund Freud. "Moses and Monotheism, Three Essays." *The Standard Edition of the Complete Psychological Works of Sigmund Freud* 23 (1939), pp. 109–110.

66 Sigmund Freud. "Moses and Monotheism, Three Essays." *The Standard Edition of the Complete Psychological Works of Sigmund Freud* 23 (1939), p. 32.

67 Sigmund Freud. "Moses and Monotheism, Three Essays." *The Standard Edition of the Complete Psychological Works of Sigmund Freud* 23 (1939), p. 32.

water is the amniotic fluid".[68] This portrayal, of baby Moses in the basket floating on the water, even according to Freud's description, resembles pregnancy rather than childbirth, yet Freud calls it "birth". According to him, this is not a symbol of protection and envelopment by the mother, but rather a symbol of separation and detachment. Maternal abandonment had to be reversed by the author, he explains, in a textual inversion which is "somewhat violently twisted. From being a way of sacrificing the child, it was turned into a means of rescuing him". Without pausing the textual movement, Freud inverts (back) maternal images in the myth of rescuing and protection to a picture of neglect and abandonment, which he presents as a legend of exposure.[69]

Throughout the discussion, Freud avoids referring to the childhood story of Moses – as it is commonly called – the story of his rescue, narrating it as "legend of exposure" and abandonment. He refers to Moses as "the child exposed in the Nile after his birth",[70] and to the mother placing him in the basket as an act of abandonment, "exposure in the water".[71] In his brief reference to Moses' childhood legends, before dismissing them as untrue, Freud describes maternal heroism as acts of betrayal. Although the mythological narrative portrays heroic acts of women saving the child, Freud shifts the gaze away from their strength, compassion and courage, in textual erasures that reveal, in fact, his own difficulty in dealing with this aspect of Moses' life – his vulnerability and dependency.

From a Jungian perspective, we can listen to the myth of Moses' childhood and the symbolic meanings in the hero archetype as reflecting a developmental process of moving between the two families. In Freud's Oedipal description, which focuses on the relationship between father and son emphasising the strength and independence of the hero, the symbolic function of the maternal as well as the "humble family" is omitted. Freud ignores these parts not only as those who saved and protected Moses in his early life but also as a cardinal aspect of "the hero" as a symbol. Contrary to this conceptualisation, the archetypal pattern of the hero can be interpreted through incorporating maternal images and understanding the two families as an ability for dynamic movement within the psyche – between regression and progression, between the conscious and the unconscious, between adapting to the world's demands and listening to inner voices within the self. Rather than grasping on external achievement, the hero archetype represents the ability to move between

---

68 Sigmund Freud. "Moses and Monotheism, Three Essays." *The Standard Edition of the Complete Psychological Works of Sigmund Freud* 23 (1939), p. 12.

69 Sigmund Freud. "Moses and Monotheism, Three Essays." *The Standard Edition of the Complete Psychological Works of Sigmund Freud* 23 (1939), p. 15.

70 Sigmund Freud. "Moses and Monotheism, Three Essays." *The Standard Edition of the Complete Psychological Works of Sigmund Freud* 23 (1939), p. 13.

71 Sigmund Freud. "Moses and Monotheism, Three Essays." *The Standard Edition of the Complete Psychological Works of Sigmund Freud* 23 (1939), p. 15.

these two dimensions, two different aspects, two different families the encounter with which propels the human psyche to become 'a hero'.

While according to Freud "[a] hero is someone who has had the courage to rebel against his father and has in the end victoriously overcome him",[72] this analysis argues that heroism is a dynamic process that entails constant transformation; an inward movement and not only a fighting ability; a reflexive dialogue that constantly touches shadow areas and remote parts of the psyche. The other side of the hero myth emphasises not only bringing change to the world but also the parallel movement of internal transformation from which growth and development occur. The hero is the one who can move between the two dimensions, and thus, the myths of heroes often provide them with two sets of parents. The royal family represents the authority, paternal function, collective consciousness and the law, while the simple family, represents remote aspects of the psyche, and opens the door to encounter with the creativity and transformation residing in the depths of the unconscious. The possibility of encountering these two psychic elements – represented by the existence of two sets of parents – creates a dynamic movement that draws from psychic 'treasures' that exist in both worlds. Only the movement between the two worlds enables heroism – it is the ability to develop a dialogue between the two psychic dimensions, represented by the two families, that creates a hero.

Erich Neumann, a Jungian analyst elaborated on the various aspects of the maternal in the psyche and has written lengthily about the image of the *Great Mother*, the *Fear of the Feminine* and patriarchal anxiety at the core of masculine monotheism.[73] As he explains, in a culture that cannot touch the maternal aspect, the earth is separated from its spiritual motif and the gaze is carried upward, toward the sky. The denial of our dependency on the mother, the inability to recognise her impact on psychic and cultural development, has caused a split between the earth and the sky. While the heaven became the exclusive source of male light, spiritual awareness and objectivity, the earth grew dark, material and static and was identified with the non-meaningful-feminine.[74]

According to Neumann's description, monotheistic religions were founded upon such a split perception. The earth absorbed into it the negative projections that blackened it, whereas the skies were cleansed and covered with the clear light of God, the Supreme Ruler. While Freud sketches the establishment of monotheistic religion as the product of the conflicted relationship with the father, Neumann explains that the split between heaven and earth, between the material and the spiritual, between the masculine and the feminine, that govern monotheism – all

---

72 Sigmund Freud. "Moses and Monotheism, Three Essays." *The Standard Edition of the Complete Psychological Works of Sigmund Freud* 23 (1939), p. 12.
73 Erich Neumann. *The Great Mother; an Analysis of the Archetype* (New York: Pantheon, 1955).
74 Erich Neumann. *The Fear of the Feminine: And Other Essays on Feminine Psychology* (Princeton: Princeton University Press, 1994). pp. 165–226.

stem from the fear of the feminine. He turns back the gaze to that archetypal earthly aspect that has been repressed with the creation of a single heavenly god and argues that the conflict that cries out from the depths in the formation of the masculine god is not that of the father's murder, but rather that of a culture that attempts to subdue the earth and strives to repress the maternal.

Such fear to encounter the power of motherhood and its significance brings Freud to lift his gaze upwards in fascination with the mighty father, erasing any meaning inborn to the relationship with the mother. While Freud redraws the life of Moses, he deletes from it his childhood, the dependency on women in his life, shifting the textual gaze to Moses' greatness and masculine heroic abilities. Portraying him as active (rather than passive), independent and autonomous (rather than dependent on the woman around him), as a royalty, noble and respected (rather than an oppressed Jew), Freud erases the maternal aspect, his early life, his Jewishness and lifts his eyes to the heavens, to be swept by the power of the "great man" Moses, and the monotheistic promise he carries with him. As he shifts his gaze from the relationship with the mother to the relationship with the father, he sketches the image of Moses as a powerful hero, dismissing the legends of his childhood, emphasising his military successes, the independence of the "great man", enlightened and masculine, introducing the spirituality of monotheism.

Perhaps like Moses, who stood on the threshold before the Promised Land but could not reach it, Freud, too, led psychoanalysis to the premises of challenging patriarchy when he opened the door to the recognition of otherness at the core of identity. Yet, at the same time, he himself remained engrossed in a father's realm without the ability to reach other dimensions. Due to the difficulty of touching the maternal – moving between the two dimensions – he remained imprisoned in the desert of a repeated paternal complex. Conceptualising Moses as a hero following the path of an earlier rigid father, he skips the experience of dependency and oppression of Israelite slavery in Egypt. Positioning Moses as an Egyptian prince, he skips his early life and his dependence on maternal strength to survive. While his gaze is lifted upwards to the light and the masculine, he neglects the encounter with maternal symbolic meanings which are then fossilised in the text.

Textual Fossils

When Freud identifies the 'origin' of monotheism in Egypt, he announces that for the first time in history, a new way of thinking was founded. It was not just another religion that came into the world, but a revolutionary worldview that "introduced something new, which for the first time converted the doctrine of a universal god into monotheism—the factor of exclusiveness".[75] Akhenaten's religion "increased

---

75 Sigmund Freud. "Moses and Monotheism, Three Essays." *The Standard Edition of the Complete Psychological Works of Sigmund Freud* 23 (1939), p. 22.

little by little to ever greater clarity, consistency, harshness and intolerance".[76] It included strong and uncompromising opposition to the existence of other gods, and to any ritual worship of material representations, resisting those gods who had ruled Egypt before – the god Amun and Osiris, the god of the dead, whose work revolved around the intense preparation for the afterlife. Pharaoh Amenophis IV was so hostile to all memory of the previous Egyptian deity that

> the king changed his name, of which the proscribed name of the god Amun formed a part. Instead of 'Amenophis' he now called himself 'Akhenaten'. But it was not only from his own name that he expunged that of the detested god: he erased it too from every inscription—even where it occurred in the name of his father, Amenophis III.[77]

Akhenaten was jealous and hostile to every bit of memory of the existence of other gods:

> Throughout the kingdom temples were closed, divine service forbidden, temple property confiscated. Indeed, the king's zeal went so far that he had the ancient monuments examined in order to have the word 'god' obliterated in them where it occurred in the plural.

Not only did Akhenaten erase the memory of the past, but he also abandoned the capital, "the Amun-dominated city of Thebes" to build a new royal capital, "which he named Akhetaten (the horizon of the Aten)".[78]

In addition to describing the intolerance of the new religion, Freud also sketches the connection between the rigid nature of monotheism and the imperialistic conquest that began to emerge in Egypt during this period. Monotheistic exclusivity, as Freud claims, is intrinsically linked with the imperialism that arose and turned the Egyptian Pharaoh into the ruler of a world empire:

> The political conditions in Egypt had begun at this time to exercise a lasting influence on the Egyptian religion. As a result of the military exploits of the great conqueror, Tuthmosis III, Egypt had become a world power: the empire now included Nubia in the south, Palestine, Syria and a part of Mesopotamia in the north. This imperialism was reflected in religion as universalism and monotheism. Since the Pharaoh's responsibilities now embraced not only Egypt but

---

76 Sigmund Freud. "Moses and Monotheism, Three Essays." *The Standard Edition of the Complete Psychological Works of Sigmund Freud* 23 (1939), p. 22.

77 And so, he added to himself the name of the new god – Aten. Sigmund Freud. "Moses and Monotheism, Three Essays." *The Standard Edition of the Complete Psychological Works of Sigmund Freud* 23 (1939), p. 23.

78 Sigmund Freud. "Moses and Monotheism, Three Essays." *The Standard Edition of the Complete Psychological Works of Sigmund Freud* 23 (1939), pp. 34–35.

Nubia and Syria as well, deity too was obliged to abandon its national limitation and, just as the Pharaoh was the sole and unrestricted ruler of the world known to the Egyptians, this must also apply to the Egyptians' new deity.[79]

Freud explains the beginning of monotheistic thought as one that grew out of an imperialist worldview characterised by rigidity and exclusivity. Just as the dominion of Akhenaten spread, with his name glorified beyond the borders of Egypt, so did the emergence of the monotheistic god who was "a single father-god of unlimited dominion".[80] Alongside the construction of the new religion, Akhenaten determined to erase any reminder of previous religious reality. With the establishment of God, it became necessary to glorify him, or more precisely "to wipe out the traces of earlier religions".[81] In order to establish the belief in one god, it was necessary to "make room" for that universal, singular and invincible god, and to prove his power by erasing and destroying other gods or alternative ways of idolatry.

In describing the growing monotheism in Egypt, it seems that Freud, similarly to Akhenaten is fascinated and mesmerised by its characteristics. He is in awe of the power of the belief in a single God and the idea of exclusivity:

With *magnificent* inflexibility he resisted every temptation to magical thought, and he rejected the illusion, so dear to Egyptians in particular, of a life after death. In an *astonishing presentiment of later scientific discovery,* he recognized in the energy of solar radiation the source of all life on earth and worshipped it as the symbol of the power of his god. He boasted of his joy in the creation and of his life in Ma'at (truth and justice).[82]

Monotheism, Freud continues in fascination, gives its followers priceless and unique possessions, and Akhenaten was captivated by the intoxicating power of the new monotheistic religion, which was

a more highly spiritualized notion of god, the idea of a single deity embracing the whole world, who was not less all-loving than all-powerful, who was averse to all ceremonial and magic and set before men as their highest aim a life in truth and justice. (*ma'at*)[83]

79 Sigmund Freud. "Moses and Monotheism, Three Essays." *The Standard Edition of the Complete Psychological Works of Sigmund Freud* 23 (1939), p. 32.

80 Sigmund Freud. "Moses and Monotheism, Three Essays." *The Standard Edition of the Complete Psychological Works of Sigmund Freud* 23 (1939), 84.

81 Sigmund Freud. "Moses and Monotheism, Three Essays." *The Standard Edition of the Complete Psychological Works of Sigmund Freud* 23 (1939), p. 44.

82 Sigmund Freud. "Moses and Monotheism, Three Essays." *The Standard Edition of the Complete Psychological Works of Sigmund Freud* 23 (1939), p. 59. emphasis added.

83 Sigmund Freud. "Moses and Monotheism, Three Essays." *The Standard Edition of the Complete Psychological Works of Sigmund Freud* 23 (1939), p. 50.

Holding a high spiritual level, a moral core and "such advances in intellectuality", as Freud explains, "have as their consequence that the individual's self-esteem is increased, that he is made proud —so that he feels superior to other people who have remained under the spell of sensuality".[84] According to him, the particular characteristics of this one god "enabled the people of Israel to survive all the blows of fate and that kept them alive to our own days".[85] The monotheistic idea was held by the people

> as a precious possession and, in turn, … kept them alive by giving them pride in being a chosen people: it was the religion of their primal father to which were attached their hope of reward, of distinction and finally of world-dominion.[86]

In writing the text Freud joins the legacy of Moses, following Akhenaten, bringing to light a 'historical truth' which had had, as he explains, an "overwhelming effect on men because it is a portion of the eternal truth which, long concealed, came to light at last and was then bound to carry everyone along with it".[87] In this process of returning from the repressed

> each portion which returns from oblivion asserts itself with peculiar force, exercises an incomparably powerful influence on people in the mass, and raises an irresistible claim to truth against which logical objections remain powerless: a kind of 'credo quia absurdum'.[88]

Just as Akhenaten, and later Moses, believed deeply in the idea of truth and in the moral power of the single God, so was Freud uncompromisingly seeking that truth hidden beneath historical distortions, searching to uncover that piece of history, to place it before our eyes in all its glory.

The journey for the discovery of this truth entails, as Freud himself shows, the erasure of the 'false' past, resisting other possibilities and a constant struggle to preserve the "exclusivity" of the one truth. Despite seeing and even explaining this movement in the history of monotheism, Freud, too, engages in a similar restoration process of a concealed truth, operating a textual system of erasures, negations and resistances to previous ways. Just as Akhenaten was trying to create the new religion by destroying the memory of the old ones, Freud constructs the new

---

84 Sigmund Freud. "Moses and Monotheism, Three Essays." *The Standard Edition of the Complete Psychological Works of Sigmund Freud* 23 (1939), p. 115.

85 Sigmund Freud. "Moses and Monotheism, Three Essays." *The Standard Edition of the Complete Psychological Works of Sigmund Freud* 23 (1939), pp. 50–51.

86 Sigmund Freud. "Moses and Monotheism, Three Essays." *The Standard Edition of the Complete Psychological Works of Sigmund Freud* 23 (1939), p. 85.

87 Sigmund Freud. "Moses and Monotheism, Three Essays." *The Standard Edition of the Complete Psychological Works of Sigmund Freud* 23 (1939), p. 129.

88 Sigmund Freud. "Moses and Monotheism, Three Essays." *The Standard Edition of the Complete Psychological Works of Sigmund Freud* 23 (1939), p. 85.

narrative by erasing biblical narratives that tell an alternative story. Immediately after describing Akhenaten violent erasures in Egypt, he turns to Jewish texts to identify distorted trends and "bring to light fresh fragments of the true state of things lying behind them".[89] He uses the sign of circumcision to differentiate between the various stories, classify them into those that lead to the core of truth and others whose "trustworthiness has been severely impaired by the distorting influence",[90] which must be erased in order to reveal the 'truth' about the history of the Jewish people.

Freud returns several times in the text to the circumcision performed by Joshua upon entering the Land of Israel. According to him, this event is a 'fossil' folding within it two contradicting threads: if circumcision was indeed customary and accepted in Egypt, this act – Joshua circumcising the people – whose purpose was to unite them under a sign that would separate them from others, reveals itself as problematic. Embodying contradicting forces in relation to their Egyptian past – circumcision is an attempt to separate from that past, while, simultaneously connecting to it. As Freud explains, this custom "to some extent, made them into Egyptians and ... keep permanently alive their memory of Egypt",[91] but this is the very same custom through which Joshua sought "to 'roll away the reproach [i.e. contempt] of Egypt'".[92] In order for the Egyptian origin that flows through their veins to be forgotten, Freud concludes, the umbilical cord of Egyptian memories must be erased from the pages of history and "every trace of Egyptian influence was to be disavowed".[93]

Circumcision emerges here again as an ambivalent sign that attempts to disconnect from the past by repeating it, when striving to bring about a new beginning that is liberated from the shackles of the past, is marked by a repetition that reveals the same history that it seeks to erase. When Freud discovers the ambivalent function of circumcision, he is striving to correct the historical injustice, exposing, once and for all, a purely separated truth, but he, too, in his uncompromising desire to disconnect from "distorting influence of tendentious purposes",[94] and bring the 'historical truth' to light, repeats the act of erasure – which connects it again to the very thing he wants to forget, leaving traces in the text. Like Akhenaten in his monotheistic ventures to oppose and exalt the existence of other

---

89 Sigmund Freud. "Moses and Monotheism, Three Essays." *The Standard Edition of the Complete Psychological Works of Sigmund Freud* 23 (1939), p. 42.
90 Sigmund Freud. "Moses and Monotheism, Three Essays." *The Standard Edition of the Complete Psychological Works of Sigmund Freud* 23 (1939), p. 27 footnote.
91 Sigmund Freud. "Moses and Monotheism, Three Essays." *The Standard Edition of the Complete Psychological Works of Sigmund Freud* 23 (1939), p. 27.
92 Sigmund Freud. "Moses and Monotheism, Three Essays." *The Standard Edition of the Complete Psychological Works of Sigmund Freud* 23 (1939), p. 35.
93 Sigmund Freud. "Moses and Monotheism, Three Essays." *The Standard Edition of the Complete Psychological Works of Sigmund Freud* 23 (1939), p. 44.
94 Sigmund Freud. "Moses and Monotheism, Three Essays." *The Standard Edition of the Complete Psychological Works of Sigmund Freud* 23 (1939), p. 27.

gods, and like the biblical texts that distort and fold to hide, Freud too approaches the craft of finding the truth using the same tools that only repeat the same thing he wishes to erase.

Freud particularly marks two biblical narratives as untrue. The first is the story of the circumcision of Moses or his son performed by Zipporah in the desert. The second is the origin of circumcision in the ancestral lineage of patriarchs and the significance of Jewish heritage emerging from this historical narrative. According to Freud, these are two distorted pieces of evidence that were invented to create "a decisive blow against the Egyptian origin of the custom of circumcision",[95] which had to be violently erased at all costs. He calls these narratives "distortions, which should not lead us astray",[96] and "a particularly clumsy invention",[97] designed to mislead and confuse us.

1. Zipporah and the Flesh

The key-fossil, circumcision, leads to the story of Zipporah, Moses' wife, and to the vague verses in the Bible, in which either Moses or their son are circumcised by her in the desert.[98] In this story, when Moses is given the mission to lead the Israelite out of Egypt, he leaves his place of stay with Jethro along with Zipporah and his two sons. On the way, when an angel appears and threatens death, Zipporah saves Moses (or her son) by performing circumcision; afterwords, she repeats the verse: "Truly you are a bridegroom of blood to me!" ... "A bridegroom of blood by circumcision".[99]

This biblical narrative, which demonstrates both the strength and resourcefulness of a mother, enrages Freud. "It is only as a deliberate denial of the betraying fact that we can explain the puzzling and incomprehensibly worded passage in Exodus [iv, 24-6]", he writes. God was "angry with Moses because he had neglected circumcision, and his Midianite wife saved his life by quickly carrying out the operation(!)".[100] One can sense Freud's anger in writing about Zipporah holding a sharp stone in front of the male organ. He does not call Zipporah by her name but refers to her as "his Midianite wife". His uneasiness is expressed in rhetoric that includes words such as "betraying", "deliberate denial", "puzzling and incomprehensibly worded passage" and "distorting influence of tendentious purposes". He places an exclamation mark after the word operation (so it is in the German origin),

---

95 Sigmund Freud. "Moses and Monotheism, Three Essays." The Standard Edition of the Complete Psychological Works of Sigmund Freud 23 (1939), p. 44.

96 Sigmund Freud. "Moses and Monotheism, Three Essays." *The Standard Edition of the Complete Psychological Works of Sigmund Freud* 23 (1939), p. 26.

97 And so, he added to himself the name of the new god – Aten. p. 45.

98 Is it a threat to Moses' life or to her son's? The answer to this question is not clear, and the interpretations of this verse in the Bible do not provide a definitive answer.

99 Exodus 4: 24–26.

100 Sigmund Freud. "Moses and Monotheism, Three Essays." *The Standard Edition of the Complete Psychological Works of Sigmund Freud* 23 (1939), p. 44.

referring of course to the performance of circumcision by Zipporah: "operation!". Seemingly, this narrative could have supported the reconstruction that Freud argues for, contributing to the biblical evidence that Moses the Midianite was forced to mark circumcision on his body as part of the compromise achieved in Kadesh. Freud's objection, therefore, arises not due to the contradiction revealed in the text, but because of the encounter with the woman-mother, and her resilient action. The "betrayal" that Freud finds difficult to bear in these lines is not the concealment of Moses' Egyptian origin, but rather maternal cutting, her appearance as a subject beyond her role of containing and nourishing the child; her ability to cut – the umbilical cord, the breast from the baby's mouth, and in this case – the foreskin.

The dependency on maternal "cutting" abilities is vital, as the biblical text teaches, not only for the survival of the child but also for that of father, and for establishing the new religion. Maternal subjectivity integrates the ability to nourish and protect with the ability to cut and separate. However, the complexity of this maternal movement awakens in Freud a defensive response – erasing of the maternal, clinging to the phallus, insisting on the exclusivity of the relationship with the father. He points out the lack of clarity of these biblical verses, referring to them as "puzzling and incomprehensibly worded passage" with the aim to deliberately deny the truth about the origin of circumcision. He does not stop to listen to Zipporah's voice and does not attempt to decipher her vogue repeated words, as he often does when encountering an unclear massage. He portrays her speech as feminine, irrational words of a mother speaking from her hysterical cord.

In analysing Zipporah's story, Bonna Devora Haberman highlights maternal sacrifice. Linking it to the story of the Akeda, the binding of Isaac, she points out the fact that Sarah, Isaac's mother is not mentioned in the chapter, and her death is only revealed at the beginning of the following chapter.[101] As she explains, Zipporah's actions show maternal sacrifice within a culture that is fascinated by the spiritual realm but terrified of the body. While Moses refuses to attend to the body, Zipporah opposes the split between love of God and earthly love and courageously performs the act of circumcision that Moses is unable to do. However, from this moment on, she also disappears from the text. Like Sarah, who is found dead after the Akeda, Zipporah is erased from the text after her brave act of circumcision. According to Haberman, her words speak of the sacrifice of a mother, for her disappearance in a culture sharply separating between matter and spirit. While Zipporah touches the body, Moses can lift his eyes to the heavens. The corporeal dimension is projected onto women who are identified with body and matter, excluded from the spiritual and the symbolic. Her words, "a bridegroom of blood to me!", Haberman explains, is a cry of reproach and pain for maternal sacrifice that does not receive recognition.

Freud's attempts to separate the 'historical truth' from the evidences that "should not lead us astray" are intrinsically manifested as a textual neurotic movement that repeatedly separates the sublime and what he recognises as meaningless matter,

---

101 Bonna Devora Haberman. "Foreskin sacrifice - Zipporah's Ritual and the Bloody Bridegroom." In: Elizabeth Wyner Mark (ed.) *The Covenant of Circumcision: New Perspectives on an Ancient Jewish Rite* (London: Brandeis series on Jewish Women, 2003). pp. 18–29.

splitting off an (m)otherness. The two characteristics that he identifies in Egyptian monotheism and later in Jewish monotheism – the opposition to the creation of material figures of God, and the rejection of the idea of an afterlife – both stem from the struggle against materiality and sensuality and constitute the essence of the linear progress he wishes to sketch. This transition from practicing "magic and sorcery" to "the heights of sublime abstraction" constitutes, for him, the greatest challenge both in individual development and in cultural growth. In both the intrapsychic and the sociocultural levels, Freud outlines a consistent developmental trajectory in which "sensuality is gradually overpowered by intellectuality and that men feel proud and exalted by every such advance".[102] This is described as the transition from a polytheistic faith, which has not yet completed its development from ancient totem religion and is still bound by the impulse to sublime monotheism, which triumphed over sensuality and developed the intellectual ability for abstract thinking.

The monotheistic effort to move beyond bodily instinct and matter is at the same time, as Freud himself reveals, a gender struggle, which, while seeking to "overcome" the physical body, also projects this aspect onto the feminine, erasing the maternal in favour of the paternal:

> [T]he matriarchal social order was succeeded by the patriarchal one—which, of course, involved a revolution in the juridical conditions that had so far prevailed … But this turning from the mother to the father points in addition to a victory of intellectuality over sensuality—that is, an advance in civilization, since maternity is proved by the evidence of the senses while paternity is a hypothesis, based on an inference and a premiss. Taking sides in this way with a thought-process in preference to a sense perception has proved to be a momentous step.[103]

Identifying motherhood with the immediate, sensory and material, Freud posits the paternal as the transcendent counterpart, a dimension of intellect thinking, capable of overcoming its physical element. The text gradually establishes a hierarchical conception of cultural progress from matriarchy to patriarchy, linking the primitive and inferior with the feminine, maternal and bodily, and placing the pinnacle of morality in moving towards the spiritual:

> An advance in intellectuality consists in deciding against direct sense-perception in favour of what are known as the higher intellectual processes—that is, memories, reflections and inferences. It consists, for instance, in deciding that paternity is more important than maternity, although it cannot, like the latter, be established by the evidence of the senses, and that for that reason the child should bear his father's name and be his heir. Or it declares that our God is

102 Sigmund Freud. "Moses and Monotheism, Three Essays." *The Standard Edition of the Complete Psychological Works of Sigmund Freud* 23 (1939), p. 118.
103 Sigmund Freud. "Moses and Monotheism, Three Essays." *The Standard Edition of the Complete Psychological Works of Sigmund Freud* 23 (1939), pp. 113–114.

the greatest and mightiest, although he is invisible like a gale of wind or like the soul.[104]

Thus, Freud attaches the intellectual to the paternal and designates the transition to patriarchy as a victory of reason over physical and emotional impulses, of science over sensuality. The desire to bring to light the moral truth inherent in monotheism becomes embedded in Freud's text in his attempts to divert the gaze from the maternal dimension towards the paternal. The fascination that builds up from the renunciation of the impulse and the disconnection from the physical body is intrinsically connected with the textual shift away from the maternal in the legends of Moses' childhood towards the masculine independence of the "great man". His textual movement erases Moses' childhood as well as Zipporah's story – all of which elaborate the basic relationships of dependency that characterise human existence in relation to the mother.

Whereas the text marks the body as a treacherous prison of temptation, for Merleau-Ponty, it is precisely this partiality of 'the flesh', its specific location, dependency and desire, that enables the body to perceive the world. Introducing the concept of 'the flesh', Merleau-Ponty explains that the deprivation of the body and its partial position is the axis that mediates the interface with the world. It is the excess created by the chiasmatic interface with otherness in relation to the bodily physical identity, that produces the gap, (écart) in which the subject remains between corporeal and ideal, between being an object and being a subject. The 'fleshiness' of the body is a limited, vulnerable and penetrable quality that allows an interface with the world and with various objects within it because it, too, is made of similar material.[105]

When our hands touch one another, he explains, they are simultaneously touching and being touched, both capable of sensing, and wanting to touch but also being the object, being touched, sensed and perceived. They are not capable, however, of being in both positions at the same time. Rather, they oscillate between the different states, changing their experience between being a touched object and being a touching subject. This is, for Merleau-Ponty, the chiasmatic nature of the 'flesh', which is not limited to touch but can be expanded to include sight and other senses, highlighting the paradoxical core of perception. Thinking in terms of sight, Merleau-Ponty emphasises that the view of any object is always made from within the field in which the gaze itself is also an inseparable part, and therefore, may not only see but also be seen. Thus, this "seen" situated position is never completely separated from the object it wishes to perceive. Through the way these chiasms of touch and sight are intertwined, we create our position as subjects in the world by being objects within it.

104 Sigmund Freud. "Moses and Monotheism, Three Essays." *The Standard Edition of the Complete Psychological Works of Sigmund Freud* 23 (1939), pp. 117–118.
105 Maurice Merleau-Ponty, *Phenomenology of Perception*. Translated by D. Landes. London: Routledge, 2012.

If perception is the result of intimate relations with the world, then the perceiving body shapes and influences what is perceived, and things do not reach consciousness in isolation, in their abstract and objective sense, but are created within the human-world interaction through a dynamic and two-way web of relations. Although many of Freud's psychoanalytic concepts support this worldview in theorising the body, instinct and desire as an integral part of subjectivity, his textual movement in *Moses and Monotheism* gradually sharpens the splits between body and spirit. As Freud is drawn into the intricacies of monotheistic questions, he emphasises the separation from the body as a "peak" of morality introduced by monotheism through the ability to transcend and control the body. As he explains, while the earlier, polytheistic religions were "very close to primitive phases [of development]" the new monotheism "has risen to the heights of sublime abstraction". The "difference in spiritual and intellectual level" between the old and the new religion manifests itself in firmly opposing materialism and sensuality, and a "harsh prohibition against making an image of any living or imagined creature".[106] This prohibition against making an image of God, he continues, and "the compulsion to worship a God whom one cannot see",[107] had a "profound effect" on the development of culture, "[f]or it meant that a sensory perception was given second place to what may be called an abstract idea—a triumph of intellectuality over sensuality or, strictly speaking, an instinctual renunciation, with all its necessary psychological consequences".[108]

The chiasmatic encounter with the world sketched by Merleau-Ponty is not a harmonious movement without conflicts, but rather, a complex experience that encounters the world from its physical partiality, from its inherent deprivation and dependency on the environment. Seeking to grasp an external and absolute truth, to encompass the material world through consciousness, and to separate between the body and the mind, is a perpetual and impossible attempt to escape the essence of our paradoxical perceptual existence. The textual difficulty of encountering this 'fleshy' element – the partiality of the self, its ambiguous boundaries, and dependency on otherness (particularly motherness) – leads to repeated attempts to escape from the question of materiality by erasing the maternal. When Freud places the sign of the covenant as the mark of entry into transcendence, he also identifies the mother with that corporeal dimension, and while raising his gaze to the Oedipal relationships, he is drawn into a cycle of erasures, which interestingly leads to the disappearance of the stories about the relationship with the mother. Just as Akhenaten erases the memory of other gods, different ways of worshipping and various ceremonial representations, so does Freud erase from the text those stories that

---

106 Sigmund Freud. "Moses and Monotheism, Three Essays." *The Standard Edition of the Complete Psychological Works of Sigmund Freud* 23 (1939), p. 19.

107 Sigmund Freud. "Moses and Monotheism, Three Essays." *The Standard Edition of the Complete Psychological Works of Sigmund Freud* 23 (1939), p. 113.

108 Sigmund Freud. "Moses and Monotheism, Three Essays." *The Standard Edition of the Complete Psychological Works of Sigmund Freud* 23 (1939), p. 133.

open the door to a different worldview and alternative ways of being – particularly the maternal, dependency and the question of the body. As he describes Moses following Akhenaten in their adherence to monotheism, he too is increasingly drawn by an effort to touch a transcendent dimension of 'truth'.

Thus, the text tirelessly strives to position Freud's research as separated from its writing context: the truth about Moses' Egyptian origin from Freud's Jewish origin; the truth of Moses's masculine independency from the truth about the feminine image of Jews in Europe; monotheistic spirituality from the physical pain of the ill body of the writer. As Freud shows circumcision is a sign of separation from the other, that at the same time brings back to the other as evidence of trauma, of the erasure that occurred – returning again to the aching body, from which it seeks to escape.

2. Patriarchs and Matriarchs

The second narrative that Freud questions in his reconstruction of the 'historical truth' about the origin of the Jewish people relates to the narrative of circumcision in the stories of the Jewish patriarchs. Using circumcision as a sign of both separation/connection from/with Egypt, he replaces one stone with another:

> And here was the opportunity for a decisive blow against the Egyptian origin of the custom of circumcision: Yahweh, it was said, had already insisted on it with Abraham and had introduced it as the token of the covenant between him and Abraham. But this was a particularly clumsy invention. As a mark that is to distinguish one person from others and prefer him to them, one would choose something that is not to be found in other people; one would not choose something that can be exhibited in the same way by millions of other people.[109]

According to Freud, this "clumsy invention" in the stories of the patriarchs is intended to erase the Egyptian origin of circumcision, to conceal Judaism's origin in Egypt, and to forget the memory of the murder, yet it remains a distorted sign indicating the truth that hides beneath the surface. The attempt to erase the past through the creation of "the legends of the patriarchs of the people—Abraham, Isaac and Jacob",[110] meant to position circumcision as a formative event that took place even before they immigrated to Egypt, as an identifying mark of the ancient Jewish dynasty.

Whereas for Freud circumcision is meant as a boundary line through which the distinction from the other is marked, a closer look at the narratives of circumcision in the stories of the patriarchs reveals a more intricate system of identity formation not simply grounded in the separation from others. In it, the sign of the covenant

---

109   Sigmund Freud. "Moses and Monotheism, Three Essays." *The Standard Edition of the Complete Psychological Works of Sigmund Freud* 23 (1939), pp. 44–45.

110   Sigmund Freud. "Moses and Monotheism, Three Essays." *The Standard Edition of the Complete Psychological Works of Sigmund Freud* 23 (1939), p. 44.

operates not as an act of separation but rather as a mark of partiality within difference. The origin of Jewish heritage in the ancestral lineage creates a more complex system of relationships that includes not only fathers and sons but also the mothers and matriarchal lineage: although Abraham circumcised all males in his household, only Isaac, because he was Sarah's son, continued the Jewish lineage. These stories bring back to the foreground maternal transmission practised in Judaism, highlighting the fact that it is not the sign of circumcision alone that determines Jewish identity but rather the mother. As the stories of the patriarchs reveal, the covenant of circumcision signifies the relationship or perhaps the wound between fathers and sons within a broader system of relationships that includes the mothers.

Freud completely ignores maternal heredity customary in Judaism – which is passed through the mother – and describes the Jewish monotheistic identity as transmitted from father to son. According to his analysis "the archaic heritage of human beings comprises not only dispositions but also subject-matter—memory-traces of the experience of earlier generations".[111] The monotheistic idea is passed down from generation to generation through those psychic traces of memory that remain engraved in the psyche of the individual: "the psychical precipitates of the primaeval period became inherited property which, in each fresh generation, called not for acquisition but only for awakening".[112] Connecting the origin of monotheism to his writing in *Totem and Taboo*, Freud anchors the historical memory from which monotheism was born, in an event that preceded the beginning of human civilisation, the murder of the ancestor that was repeated again, according to him, in Jewish history, with the murder of Moses. Bound by the forces of 'truth', the monotheistic idea is passed down from generation to generation as a transhistorical heritage that originates in this act of patricide, providing an ontological explanation for human development. It is not a product of any particular reality, or a result of intimate interpersonal relationships, and not a derivative of bodily heredity – paternal or maternal, but is transmitted as an ideational legacy, latently present and recurring throughout history, manifesting in an Oedipal trauma which shapes the fate of all humanity.

This transmission, which is neither matrilineal (transmitted by the mother to her daughters) nor patrilineal (passed on by the father to the sons) but rather *ultrapatrilineal*: an inheritance passed from father to son through the memory traces of the Oedipal trauma. Within this perspective, the covenant of circumcision emerges as a sign through which the Oedipal narrative and castration anxiety are given an all-embracing eternal status. They become a sign through which this *transhistorical inheritance* is transmitted, as a marker that separates those who carry the traces of the traumatic memory from others who do not hold within them the memory-traces of the archaic event. It serves as a symbol that distinguishes those whose memory of the patricidal event flows through their veins and others whose world is not

111 Sigmund Freud. "Moses and Monotheism, Three Essays." *The Standard Edition of the Complete Psychological Works of Sigmund Freud* 23 (1939), p. 99.
112 Sigmund Freud. "Moses and Monotheism, Three Essays." *The Standard Edition of the Complete Psychological Works of Sigmund Freud* 23 (1939), p. 132.

shaped by this repressed prehistoric truth. As Freud describes, this separation from the uncircumcised other is the beginning of a power struggle, a hierarchical system in which only one can win:

> Our findings may be thus expressed in the most concise formula. Jewish history is familiar to us for its dualities: two groups of people who came together to form the nation, two kingdoms into which this nation fell apart, two gods' names in the documentary sources of the Bible. To these we add two fresh ones: the foundation of too religions—*the first repressed by the second but nevertheless later emerging victoriously behind it,* and two religious founders, who are both called by the same name of Moses and whose personalities we have to distinguish from each other. *All of these dualities are the necessary consequences of the first one: the fact that one portion of the people had an experience which must be regarded as traumatic and which the other portion escaped.*[113]

As Freud explains, a schism is created between two that eventually unite, but this reunion is not harmonious; rather, it involves a violent struggle in which one engulfs the other. Portraying in this way the historical narrative of the origin of the Jewish people and the relationship between monotheism and other religions, Freud's words resonate in the text, a 'Freudian slip' that echoes the two sexes. Perhaps the circular relationship towards an other portrayed in the text, discovering the roots of identity in an otherness, is first and foremost that of the gendered other. We can read the unconscious meaning of these words as portraying the gendered struggle between the two parts of the people – one of which has experienced the trauma of circumcision and the other did not undergo the traumatic cut. Prior to its being an act of separation from other peoples, circumcision is a cut creating a defining barrier within Judaism itself – between the circumcised men and those Jews who did not undergo the traumatic cut: Jewish women.

Marking circumcision as an act of cutting and separation, Freud is repeating a similar split between the sexes. In contrast to the stories of the patriarchs in which two ways of inheritance coexist, the movement between two different narratives is gradually erased in the text and only one 'survives'. Alongside this textual movement, the meaning of circumcision as an image is gradually evolving to become not only a symbol of past trauma but also a symbol of being chosen and a promise for the future. In this way, it transforms from being a marker of the conflict that pertains to the past, to become the proclamation of victory and the future power to come. The Jewish people, Freud explains, find a solution to the conflict that permeates them, by appeasing the historical injustice of patricide through their love for God and their service to 'him'. Not only do they worship God, but they also

---

113 Sigmund Freud. "Moses and Monotheism, Three Essays." *The Standard Edition of the Complete Psychological Works of Sigmund Freud* 23 (1939), p. 52. emphasis added.

become his favourite, the chosen people, transforming the traumatic memory into a valuable possession. As he goes on to describe,

> they are inspired by a peculiar confidence in life, such as is derived from the secret ownership of some precious possession, a kind of optimism: pious people would call it trust in God. We know the reason for this behaviour and what their secret treasure is. They really regard themselves as God's chosen people, they believe that they stand especially close to him; and this makes them proud and confident. ... If one is the declared favourite of the dreaded father, one need not be surprised at the jealousy of one's brothers and sisters, and the Jewish legend of Joseph and his brethren shows very well where this jealousy can lead.[114]

It is the experience of being chosen by the father, Freud explains, that creates a sense of an inner secret and confidence in the son making him feel superior to others, just as Joseph, wearing the coat of many colours, felt superior to his brothers. However, Jacob's love for Joseph is bound up with the historical narrative that exists in the stories of the patriarchs in which the sons are connected to their fathers and are chosen through the love of their mothers. Jacob's intense love for Rachel, Joseph's mother, her love for her son and the fact that she brought him into the world after many years of infertility, are intimately connected to the question of being chosen by the father. As in the story of Joseph, so it is in the other patriarchs' narratives – those of Isaac and Jacob who were chosen to continue the Jewish dynasty – in which choosing them over their siblings was a result of the patriarchs' relationship with the mother. Isaac was the son of Sarah, Abraham's beloved wife, who was also born after many years of infertility. Jacob, the younger and favoured son of Rebecca, received his father's blessing with the help of his mother through the deceit of being the firstborn.[115] In both cases, the biblical narrative unfolds a complex human story in which the choosing of the sons, the continuation of the legacy and the love of the father grows out of the relationship with the mother. Although circumcision is also marked on the bodies of both Ishmael (Abraham's son From Hagar) and Esau (Isaac's eldest son), Jewish continuity is given to Isaac and later to Jacob because of their relationship with their mothers.

If Freud focuses his gaze on the relationship between father and son, on transhistorical Oedipal male-only inheritance, the stories of the patriarchs and the matriarchs add another, third vertex to the question of being chosen – that of the mother. In these stories, the inheritance through which Jewish monotheism is transmitted

---

114 Sigmund Freud. "Moses and Monotheism, Three Essays." *The Standard Edition of the Complete Psychological Works of Sigmund Freud* 23 (1939), p. 106.

115 Commentators put forward different versions of Jacob's birthright even though he was not the biological firstborn. In the first version, he 'buys' it legitimately (even if it is possible to criticise the circumstances under which the purchase was made). In the second version, he cheats and manipulates his father, with the help of his mother. Either way, he gains primacy because of God's promise to his mother, Rebecca.

takes place in the particular lives of matriarchs and patriarchs, as a result of complex family relationships, reflecting a particular, local and human choice. While Freud regards circumcision as an absolute sign of identity through separation from the other, in these stories the concept of circumcision is reintroduced under a different worldview in which it is but one factor within a multidimensional field, a sign that, in fact, represents partiality.

The solution to the question of circumcision emerging from the story of the patriarchs provides an alternative perspective on the contradiction Freud identifies between the presence of circumcision as a sign of separation from other peoples and its marking on the non-Jewish bodies of the Egyptians. The third vertex of the Oedipal triangle introduced by these stories, the role of the mother in Jewish legacy, bridges the gap that Freud identifies as contradiction, outlining a dialectical process of inheritance that requires the existence of two parents: both the mother and the father. The fact that circumcision is not exclusive to the Jewish people reveals the significance of mothers in determining the continuation of Jewish lineage through which the sign of the covenant, circumcision, will pass on to be carried on the male body. Freud outlines circumcision through a narrow prism that erases maternal heredity and its importance, as the sole signifier for separation and difference, which grows out of the archaic trauma promising victory and being chosen by the father. While he aims to modify the distorted evidence in biblical texts, a closer look allows one to observe the philosophy inherent to these stories – an identity structure that is not created by erasing otherness, but rather, through a dialogue with them; a dialectical and dynamic movement that also challenges the absolute boundaries between self and other. It requires recognition of female genealogy alongside the male one and the role of women and mothers in passing Jewish identity to the next generation. Through this worldview circumcision is no longer a stable symbol of separation from the other, but in fact, a clue to the particularity, contingency and complexity of continuity – which is always hybrid and emerges from the relationship with the other.

Faced with this description of two transmission narratives – maternal and paternal – which cannot fuse but are also not separated from each other, remaining in a dynamic coexistence, Freud presents a different narrative, leaving no room for the existence of two side by side: *two become one*. The text demonstrates a sequence of struggles at the end of which the other is erased in order to "make room" for the one: Akhenaten erases the signs of the previous Egyptian god; Egypt after the time of Akhenaten rejected Aten religion, and the people banned its memory "as that of a criminal"[116]; the Jewish people, who left Egypt with Moses, violently murdered him and renounced the religion he founded, and then sought to erase the memory of the murder; the ancient Egyptian God, gradually overcame the Midianite Yahweh until he "victoriously overcome him",[117] and eliminated his memory;

---

116 Sigmund Freud. "Moses and Monotheism, Three Essays." *The Standard Edition of the Complete Psychological Works of Sigmund Freud* 23 (1939), p. 24.

117 Sigmund Freud. "Moses and Monotheism, Three Essays." *The Standard Edition of the Complete Psychological Works of Sigmund Freud* 23 (1939), p. 12.

the biblical texts, as Freud concludes, operate according to a similar structure seeking to erase the signs of Egypt in the Jewish religion, and only the traces of circumcision leads to their Egyptian past. Endless cycles of violent cuts and erasures, deletions upon deletions, a struggle to free oneself from the past, from the other, in a relentless pursuit to place one clear and separated 'truth'.

Freud is indeed aware of this structure and describes the psychic process of these repeated struggles, but he himself does not escape the circle of erasures. As he explains, an 'historical truth' that has been repressed due to its traumatic component, returns – sometimes after a long period of latency – from the depths of the unconscious confronting the subject, or alternatively, the people, as an undeniable truth, in which, "[n]ot until later does the change take place with which the definitive neurosis becomes manifest as a belated effect of the trauma".[118] The same is true in the process of monotheism and the development of Mosaic religion, when

> this tradition of a great past which continued to operate (from the background, as it were), which gradually acquired more and more power over people's minds and which in the end succeeded in changing the god Yahweh into the Mosaic god and in re-awakening into life the religion of Moses that had been introduced and then abandoned long centuries before.[119]

In this way, Freud links individual neurosis with the development of religion and the process of culture formation in general, describing them all as the outcome of trauma re-emerging with renewed intensity. This process, as he shows, involves a struggle that "ends often enough in a complete devastation or fragmentation of the ego or in its being overwhelmed by the portion which was early split off and which is dominated by the trauma".[120] In the case of the individual, "an identification with the father in early childhood … is repudiated, and even overcompensated, but in the end establishes itself once more".[121] In the case of the Jewish people, monotheism returns "after a long period of latency, taken hold of by them [the people], preserved by them as a precious possession and, in turn, itself kept them alive by giving them pride in being a chosen people".[122] And in the course of this historical development, "Matriarchy was succeeded by the re-establishment of a

118 Sigmund Freud. "Moses and Monotheism, Three Essays." *The Standard Edition of the Complete Psychological Works of Sigmund Freud* 23 (1939), p. 77.

119 Sigmund Freud. "Moses and Monotheism, Three Essays." *The Standard Edition of the Complete Psychological Works of Sigmund Freud* 23 (1939), p. 70.

120 Sigmund Freud. "Moses and Monotheism, Three Essays." *The Standard Edition of the Complete Psychological Works of Sigmund Freud* 23 (1939), p. 78.

121 Sigmund Freud. "Moses and Monotheism, Three Essays." *The Standard Edition of the Complete Psychological Works of Sigmund Freud* 23 (1939), p. 125.

122 Sigmund Freud. "Moses and Monotheism, Three Essays." *The Standard Edition of the Complete Psychological Works of Sigmund Freud* 23 (1939), p. 85.

patriarchal order",...[123] and "sensuality is gradually overpowered by intellectuality" in the process.[124]

Despite outlining the way in which the repressed and the return of the repressed are intertwined, and even though Freud shows that the elimination never succeeds and that the repressed aspect always returns demanding its place, the text itself does not escape the circle of erasures. The textual solution to the question of two different narratives is answered by obliteration. When he erases the story of the patriarchs and dismisses the description of Zipporah circumcising Moses (or her son) in the desert, he fails to bear a gap, a contradiction emerging in the text and a more intricated and multifaceted picture. Although he recognises that the solution that psychoanalysis strives for is "to reconcile with the rest those portions of the ego that have been split off by the influence of the trauma",[125] he uses the same currency and the text manifests a similar structure of deleting those other voices in the pursuit to establish the one dimension that eventually comes to light.[126]

When it is impossible to bear the gaps and contradictions, or the dialectical movement between two different dimensions, the encounter with the other becomes a traumatic experience that reproduces a violent act of deletions. Like Akhenaten and Moses before him, Freud remained fascinated by the possibility of presenting a single truth that would answer all questions. It seems that in the course of the textual movement, the search for an otherness gradually gives way to the possibility of placing a single, uniform historical reconstruction. Behind its pretension of making space for otherness, a fascination of the morality of the new religion emerges, the traces of which can be found in Oedipal psychoanalysis and the relationship with the father. While speaking out against biblical distortions and the repression of a historical truth about the origin of the Jewish religion in otherness, Freud himself almost maniacally engages in the process of erasing the evidence in the text that opens the door to a different worldview, which brings back to the body and to dependency on the maternal.

When Freud negates the story of the patriarchs, he wants to bring to light the piece of Egyptian heritage in Jewish history, but by repeating the same violent structure itself, he places the sign of circumcision as the sole and exclusive factor through which an identity is marked as separation from the other. The erased narratives highlight the vital role of mothers in the continuation of the covenant lineage and their significance to Jewish identity, as well as to the idea of identity in general.[127] Under this phallocentric gaze, two possibilities cannot exist together and

123 Sigmund Freud. "Moses and Monotheism, Three Essays." *The Standard Edition of the Complete Psychological Works of Sigmund Freud* 23 (1939), p. 83.

124 Sigmund Freud. "Moses and Monotheism, Three Essays." *The Standard Edition of the Complete Psychological Works of Sigmund Freud* 23 (1939), p. 118.

125 Sigmund Freud. "Moses and Monotheism, Three Essays." *The Standard Edition of the Complete Psychological Works of Sigmund Freud* 23 (1939), p. 77.

126 Sigmund Freud. "Moses and Monotheism, Three Essays." *The Standard Edition of the Complete Psychological Works of Sigmund Freud* 23 (1939), p. 68.

127 A detailed discussion of this question is described by Shaye Cohen in his writings: Shaye J. D. Cohen. *The Beginnings of Jewishness: Boundaries, Varieties, Uncertainties* (Berkeley: University

the relationship with otherness is formed under a structure of erasures – either erasing the memory of the Egyptian father or a complete repetition of it; either a radical separation or a complete monolithic unity; either negating otherness or complete swallowing of it into the world of the one. The absence of the third, maternal vertex in the Oedipal triangle leaves heredity and historical movement as a neurotic repetition – that Freud himself speaks of – a chain of sameness between father and son, violent erasure and total repetition of the past, two that are but one – mono (theism).

The Archive of Circumcision

In order to delve into the philosophical and psychoanalytic potential inherent in the covenant of circumcision as a sign of partiality, I will briefly turn to Derrida's theoretical thinking. Perhaps like Freud, Derrida began to engage with the question of Judaism towards the end of his life.[128] As Gideon Ofrat writes, Derrida's theoretical projects stem from an identity crisis from which a deconstructive array of identities erupts in the form of writing.[129] It is a process that moves (or perhaps keeps immigrating) from the autobiographical to the hermeneutic and theological, along which Judaism remains an open wound, carrying a constant unresolved quest for a remedy to heal the subject's identity rift: the unbridgeable gap between humans and their being.

In his book *Archive Fever*, Derrida turns to Freud's writings, examining the psychoanalytic archive through the works of Yosef Hayim Yerushalmi: *Freud's Moses: Judaism Terminable and Interminable* and *Zakhor: Jewish History and Jewish Memory*.[130] He weaves together Freud's Judaism and psychoanalysis, as two projects rooted in the paradoxes of the archive. An archive, he explains, contains two components,

> the principle according to nature or history, there where things commence-physical, historical, or ontological principle-but also the principle according to the law, there where men and gods command, there where authority, social order are exercised, in this place from which order is given-nomological principle.[131]

---

of California Press, 2001); Shaye J.D. Cohen. "A Brief History of Jewish Circumcision Blood." In: Elizabeth Wyner Mark (ed.) *The Covenant of Circumcision: New Perspectives on an Ancient Jewish Rite* (London: Brandies University Press, 2003); Shaye J. D. Cohen. *Why Aren't Jewish Women Circumcised?: Gender and Covenant in Judaism* (Berkeley: University of California Press, 2005).

128 Derrida died in 2004, among his most recent books that touched on Judaism: Jacques Derrida, and Eric Prenowitz. "Archive Fever: A Freudian Impression." *Diacritics* 25, no. 2 (1995): 9–63; Jacques Derrida (1993). Circumfession (G. Bennington, Trans.). In: G. Bennington (ed.) *Jacques Derrida* (pp. 3–315). Chicago: The University of Chicago Press.

129 Gideon Ofrat. *The Jewish Derrida* (New York: Syracuse University Press, 2001).

130 Yosef Haim Yerushalmi. *Zakhor: Jewish History and Jewish Memory* (Seattle: University of Washington Press, 1996); Yerushalmi, *Freud's Moses*.

131 Jacques Derrida, and Eric Prenowitz. "Archive Fever: A Freudian Impression." *Diacritics* 25, no. 2 (1995): 9.

The Archive is a space in which a vast amount of material is collected, inhabiting various components, but also the place where a common marking is created, coordinating the different components into a synchronous system in which heterogeneity is gathered under a uniform sign. Thus, it is not only the place of preservation of the collected material or the events that took place, of the past. The structure of the archive, Derrida argues, also produces the archival content by its very appearance and attitude to the future: while recording the event, it also establishes it, propelling it forward.[132]

This dual effect of the act of preservation creates a two-way movement that, on the one hand, nostalgically wishes to protect the past, providing it with an eternal place of refuge and memory and on the other hand, uses the law to position that past, employing mechanisms of control and authority that, while establishing the memory of the remains, also determines what will be forgotten. The archive contains within it the violence of classification, separation, recording and cutting that violates its natural flow and determines the form of continuity in a process, which is constantly haunted by the forgotten otherness of what is not being archived. The assemble of the archive, Derrida explains, repeatedly fails to truly grasp that piece of the past and is always haunted by its absence, the remnant, by the 'other' aspect.

The desire to remember that constitutes the archive – the desire to capture once and for all the entirety of human memory, is also what constantly brings it closer to oblivion. Derrida recognises this as the structural contradiction folded within the very existence of the Archive, its fundamental paradox and the origin of the violence it entails – a violent structure which is nothing more than the other side of its excessive eagerness to preserve. Thus, Archive Fever, as Derrida articulates it, is the death instinct intertwined with the desire to revive the past; the attempt to bring back to life what is always already dead in which an effort to touch the beating heart of the origin ends up crossing into the realm of death.[133] The urge for preservation itself grows out of the desire to prevent the possibility of absolute forgetfulness, of death and absence, yet, precisely through such excess desire to revive, that the Freudian death drive – the urge for death, and destruction – is revealed. It is precisely the desire to preserve, through which the archive fever is manifested with full force – that inexhaustible desire to halt and capture life allows death to creep in.

Psychoanalysis, Derrida explains, reveals human memory as an archival project which is similarly based on its dual nature. The subject is always struggling to grasp the pieces of memory that will forever elude the attempts to reach them. Although psychoanalysis theoretically recognises such archival structure, it often becomes itself a restoration project that repeats the same thing to which it opposes. The therapeutic process of trying to reach a semblance of memory that has been

---

132 Jacques Derrida, and Eric Prenowitz. "Archive Fever: A Freudian Impression." *Diacritics* 25, no. 2 (1995): 15.

133 Gish Amit. *What is the Desire of the Archive?* (in Hebrew, Tel-Aviv: Haaretz Books, 2006).

repressed and forgotten is fuelled by the burning desire to uncover the truth and the hidden past, to reach an origin. Despite understanding that the past is always already lost and thus, destined to evade, it continues to move forward with a belief that even if it is unreachable, somewhere, an origin does indeed exist, and psychoanalysis will uncover its impressions from the depths of repression.[134]

In his analysis of the history of Judaism, Freud recognises a similar structure, articulating it in his own words: "[t]he effects of traumas are of two kinds, positive and negative", he writes.

> The former are attempts to bring the trauma into operation once again—that is, to remember the forgotten experience or, better still, to make it real, to experience a repetition of it anew ... to revive it ... We summarize these efforts under the name of 'fixations' to the trauma and as a 'compulsion to repeat'.[135]

The obsessive return to the wounded origin is a neurotic attempt to touch, revive and repair the past, but "[t]he negative reactions follow the opposite aim: that nothing of the forgotten traumas shall be remembered and nothing repeated. We can summarize them as 'defensive reactions'".[136] With one hand the neurotic subject seeks to reveal the past, but with the other, he/she covers and pushes it into the depths of repression. The death drive to erase and destroy the memory of the past is ambivalently weaved with the desire to uncover it, and the conflictual intertwining is revealed in a neurotic symptom, in the *archive fever* and, as Freud shows, in the history of the Jewish people.

While pointing to the conflict that ossified the memory of the past, Freud approaches the task of repairing injustice, bringing to light the wounded origin that has been forgotten. In his research-historical-psychoanalytic project of *Moses and Monotheism*, he aims to look beyond the distorted lenses to reveal, as he explains, the 'historical truth':

> It is worth specially stressing the fact that each portion which returns from oblivion asserts itself with peculiar force, exercises an incomparably powerful influence on people in the mass, and raises an irresistible claim to truth against which logical objections remain powerless: a kind of 'credo quia absurdum', This remarkable feature can only be understood on the pattern of the delusions of psychotics. We have long understood that a portion of forgotten truth lies hidden in delusional ideas, that when this returns it has to put up with distortions and misunderstandings, and that the compulsive conviction which attaches to the delusion arises from this core of truth and spreads out on to the errors that

134 Gish Amit. *What is the Desire of the Archive?* (in Hebrew, Tel-Aviv: Haaretz Books, 2006).
135 Sigmund Freud. "Moses and Monotheism, Three Essays." *The Standard Edition of the Complete Psychological Works of Sigmund Freud* 23 (1939), p. 75.
136 Sigmund Freud. "Moses and Monotheism, Three Essays." *The Standard Edition of the Complete Psychological Works of Sigmund Freud* 23 (1939), p. 76.

wrap it round. We must grant an ingredient such as this of what may be called *historical truth.*[137]

An otherness that haunts the text returns from oblivion in this process – an un-archived dimension, of *'historical truth'* that precedes, as Freud explains, the *'material truth'*. According to Freud, 'historical truth', unlike 'material truth', returns from the repressed with some distortion, although the word distortion itself, *entstellung*, as he explains, has a double meaning. It not only signifies a change in form – innovation and addition but also a return, a folding of the old – a defensive entanglement seeking to preserve the core of truth within. The fossil of circumcision that Freud identifies in Jewish texts was created, according to him by such folding, a petrification that guards a precious part of the past that might have been lost by forces of destruction, in an attempt to save the 'historical truth' that lies beneath.

Thus, Freud explains, religion itself – the belief in God – "contains the truth—but the *historical* truth and not the *material* truth".[138] The idea of the one great God is nothing more than a distorted yet "completely justified memory", evoked by the fact that in the history of mankind, in ancient times, there was "a single person who was bound to appear huge at that time and who afterwards returned in men's memory elevated to divinity".[139] The existence of a paternal ancestor is the 'historical truth' that lies beneath the 'material truth' of religion and belief in god. The father's return as religion is an expression of the paradox inherent in human psyche, reflecting the violence of every archive that distorts 'truth' while trying to preserve it. As Freud writes, "To the extent to which it is distorted, it may be described as a delusion; in so far as it brings a return of the past, it must be called the truth".[140]

Freud distinguishes between 'material truth' and 'historical truth', embarking on a journey to narrow the gap between them, to bring them closer to each other. But Freud's investigation itself is an archive project, and the more he wishes to get closer to the truth, the more it eludes him, and the death drive is forcefully expressed. It is, according to Derrida,

> the principle of the internal division of the Freudian gesture, and thus of the Freudian concept of the archive, is that at the moment when psychoanalysis formalizes the conditions of archive fever and of the archive itself, it repeats the very thing it resists or which it makes its object.[141]

---

137 Sigmund Freud. "Moses and Monotheism, Three Essays." *The Standard Edition of the Complete Psychological Works of Sigmund Freud* 23 (1939), p. 85.
138 Sigmund Freud. "Moses and Monotheism, Three Essays." *The Standard Edition of the Complete Psychological Works of Sigmund Freud* 23 (1939), p. 129.
139 Sigmund Freud. "Moses and Monotheism, Three Essays." *The Standard Edition of the Complete Psychological Works of Sigmund Freud* 23 (1939), p. 129.
140 Sigmund Freud. "Moses and Monotheism, Three Essays." *The Standard Edition of the Complete Psychological Works of Sigmund Freud* 23 (1939), 130.
141 Jacques Derrida, and Eric Prenowitz. "Archive Fever: A Freudian Impression." *Diacritics* 25, no. 2 (1995): 57.

Freud's attempt to return to what has been forgotten, to touch the traumatic past, to revive it, is an example of Derrida's *mal de archive*, for his desire to revive also manifest the death drive that ossifies the past, erasing parts of that history into oblivion. The outcome of this *mal* is an archive that cannot but partially and violently testify to the origin it seeks to capture.

Like the biblical texts, Freud's text, *Moses and Monotheism*, spirals in a distortion. The intensity with which he seeks to expose the truth creates distortion, textual gaps, repetitions and internal contradictions. Similar to the process that Freud identifies in biblical texts, in his text too, circumcision is revealed as a fossilised sign. As Derrida explains, circumcision is often hastily attributed to castration, yet that very word itself, is a fossilised mark, a litmus paper unveiling textual conflict, ambivalence and indecisiveness, inherent to the act of archiving.[142] Circumcision is a "singular and immemorial archive",[143] as he writes, a paradigmatic sign for the act of archiving itself, containing within the ambivalently ossified intertwining of death and life instincts simultaneously desiring to preserve and to erase, to remember and to forget, reveal and conceal. The violence involved in the sign circumcision, as an archiving act is expressed in the classification and cataloguing inherent to it, that always also excludes its otherness. Engraving of identity, the sign of covenant on the baby's skin is fixing in him both his past and his future, his legacy and fate, even before he can speak or choose his path, it is inscribed on his skin with an excess desire, stamping his body – his sexual male organ – with the mark of the archive.

As Derrida explains, Yerushalmi (in his book *Freud's Moses*), is metaphorically circumcising Freud after his death, bringing him and psychoanalysis, into the Jewish covenant. Similarly, I argue, in a repetitive circularity, Freud's archival project of *Moses and Monotheism* strives for renewed circumcision of Moses under the Oedipal mark. As he endeavours to bring the truth to light, he reconstructs Jewish history and archives Moses' life according to the psychoanalytic Oedipal pattern that, as he explains, enables us to fill in the gaps in our knowledge of that primordial period.[144] Imprinting the mark of psychoanalysis into the text, the Oedipal narrative is retroactively engraved on Moses' body. With excess desire of an archival project, Freud links in his writing the development of the individual, the history of monotheism and the establishment of a culture under the Oedipal super-signifier. Just as Yerushalmi brings Freud into the Jewish covenant, circumcising him after his death, so too does Freud circumcise Moses after his death, inscribing onto him the sign of the Oedipal and psychoanalytic covenant. Removing Moses away from the feminine and maternal circle that surrounded him, according to the narratives,

142 Jacques Derrida, and Eric Prenowitz. "Archive Fever: A Freudian Impression." *Diacritics* 25, no. 2 (1995): 54.

143 Jacques Derrida, and Eric Prenowitz. "Archive Fever: A Freudian Impression." *Diacritics* 25, no. 2 (1995): 22.

144 Sigmund Freud. "Moses and Monotheism, Three Essays." *The Standard Edition of the Complete Psychological Works of Sigmund Freud* 23 (1939), p. 84.

during his childhood, Freud positions the figure of Moses within a renewed history and legacy – as a hero with a vision who introduced spirituality to the people, continuing the previous masculine dynasty for the sake of future generations. With the use of words – the covenant of the word (circumcision) and words of writing – he performs the archival act of circumcision, which retroactively reconstructs history and through the engraving of words of paper, cutting off its (m)otherness.

Archiving and (M)otherness

As Freud moves toward grasping the one truth that has come to light, he too, as a part of Western culture and modernity, follows an idea of the lost origin in an attempt to restore it. Gradually, the text shifts from *searching* for the roots of the Jewish people to *a reconstruction* of the historical narrative in which the *Great Father* is positioned as an all-embracing beginning. "I have no hesitation in declaring", he writes, "that men have always known (in this special way) that they once possessed a primal father and killed him".[145] He binds this genesis with words he had written 25 years earlier, in *Totem and Taboo*, and with the conclusive words with which he ended the book: "'in the beginning was the Deed' [the murder of the father]".[146] Thus, placing the Oedipal narrative at the centre of human existence, Freud links this origin not only to the beginning of Jewish religion but also to the life of the individual and to culture development in general.

In this process, progressing throughout the text, Freud gradually lays aside the psychoanalytic understanding about the archive structure, – the death drive of *mal de archive* – and the paradoxical core that he himself point out at the heart of Jewish monotheism. Like the Jewish history he describes, he clings with enchantment to the goal of his own archival project, and its promise for unity and wholeness – to discover the one origin of the Jewish people and to lay psychoanalytic revelation of the Oedipal narrative at its core. In an attempt to correct "distortions", a monotheistic belief is slowly catching up with him too, and he presents an all-embracing origin to human existence.

The nature of the text gradually changes throughout the book, and Freud's epistemological stance undergoes transformation. Whereas, at the beginning of the first essay, he wishes to start a thought experiment, wondering about the origin of the Jewish people, at the end of the third essay he explains that his research shed light "on the question of how the Jewish people have acquired the characteristics", and on the question of "how it is that they have been able to retain their individuality till the present day".[147] Moving from the search for an origin to a fascination with

---

145 Sigmund Freud. "Moses and Monotheism, Three Essays." *The Standard Edition of the Complete Psychological Works of Sigmund Freud* 23 (1939), p. 101.

146 Sigmund Freud. *Totem and Taboo: Some Points of Agreement Between the Mental Lives of Savages and Neurotics* (Translated by James Strachey. Routledge, [1912–1913] 2003), p. 187.

147 Sigmund Freud. "Moses and Monotheism, Three Essays." *The Standard Edition of the Complete Psychological Works of Sigmund Freud* 23 (1939), pp. 136–137.

"the peculiar religious genius of that people",[148] he also moves form questioning the narrative about the life of Moses to narrating the impact of his greatness. Bringing the 'historical truth' to light is wrapped in an almost religious fascination with the perseverance and mental strength of the Jewish people, in an enchantment with Moses' greatness and with the "spiritual progress" of monotheism.[149]

Freud's epistemological position undergoes transformation throughout the book in which, at the beginning of the writing, he labels the text "a novel",[150] providing it with an intermediate status between truth and fiction, but at the end, he positions the text as a scientific "study" that has revealed the core 'historical truth' of the Jewish people. Throughout the first essay, and at the beginning of the second essay, Freud asks his readers to accompany him on a thought experiment about Moses' Egyptian origins, a theoretical journey that begins with the hypothesis, "if Moses was an Egyptian".[151] By the end of the second essay the question word "if" is dropped and Freud refers to his writing as "purely historical study".[152] In the course of this second essay, he distances himself from any psychoanalytic explanation and only collects the historical materials. At the beginning of the third essay, he writes:

I begin with a résumé of the findings of my second study on Moses, the purely historical one. Those findings will not be submitted here to any fresh criticism, since they form the premiss to the psychological discussions which start out from them and constantly go back to them.[153]

What was once a hypothesis requiring proof becomes the historical basis for Freud's psychological analysis that will follow in the third essay, incorporating them into his psychoanalytic study. Linking the findings concerning the history of the Jewish people to the mental reality of the neurotic subject and the development of the individual, Freud connects these discoveries to what he wrote 25 years earlier in *Totem and Taboo*, to the beginning of human development and to the establishment of culture in general. Thus, the different threads are wrapped together, establishing the Oedipal narrative into the ultimate "historical truth". The primordial truth of the murder of the father comes to light as an all-embracing truth encapsulating the

148 Sigmund Freud. "Moses and Monotheism, Three Essays." *The Standard Edition of the Complete Psychological Works of Sigmund Freud* 23 (1939), p. 65.
149 Sigmund Freud. "Moses and Monotheism, Three Essays." *The Standard Edition of the Complete Psychological Works of Sigmund Freud* 23 (1939), p. 118.
150 "It was apparently during the summer of 1934 that Freud completed his first draft of this book, with the title: The Man Moses, a Historical Novel" Strachey notes (Sigmund Freud. "Moses and Monotheism, Three Essays." *The Standard Edition of the Complete Psychological Works of Sigmund Freud* 23 (1939), p. 3).
151 Sigmund Freud. "Moses and Monotheism, Three Essays." *The Standard Edition of the Complete Psychological Works of Sigmund Freud* 23 (1939), p. 17.
152 Sigmund Freud. "Moses and Monotheism, Three Essays." *The Standard Edition of the Complete Psychological Works of Sigmund Freud* 23 (1939), p. 52.
153 Sigmund Freud. "Moses and Monotheism, Three Essays." *The Standard Edition of the Complete Psychological Works of Sigmund Freud* 23 (1939), p. 59. footnote.

individual psychic reality, the development of culture and religion, the beginning of Judaism, and the transcendence of monotheism.

The epistemological transition from question to answer is a movement from opening up new possibilities inherent in the biblical and Jewish text to marvelling at the newly created narrative, a transition from the deconstruction of textual 'distortions' to the reconstruction of the one 'true' narrative. In an attempt to correct injustice, restoring from oblivion the hitherto unspoken otherness of the past, Freud becomes lost in a promise of the future inherent in the act of archiving. Captured by the same fascination that he warns against, he is enchanted by the possibility of bringing all under psychoanalytic roof: the individual, the Jewish people, religion and culture. Believing that he has discovered a hidden piece of the past and bringing it out into the light, he gradually turns his gaze to its promise for the future and is swept away by the power of the historical truth that has returned from the repressed. The focus of the book abandons the thought experiment about Moses' Egyptian origins, the origin of monotheism and the Jewish religion, and moves away from the attempt to sketch the connection between religion and neurosis. The textual gaze is carried with excitement towards the greatness of Moses, the perseverance and survival of the Jewish people and the spiritual power of monotheism.

Freud's fascination with the "great man", Jewish rigidity and monotheistic spirituality resonates in Derrida's thought about the question of Judaism. For him, the conflictual realm of Judaism is marked by a complex movement towards singularity that remains relentlessly haunted by its otherness, continually grappling with the wounded paradox of the archive. Thus, according to him, rigid monotheistic ideas of Oneness repeatedly confront the subject with the paradox of otherness. This paradox of subjectivity per se, which can be highlighted through Jewish ideas – or perhaps through the idea of being Jewish – can demonstrate the paradox of otherness and subjectivity: the more the subject wishes to differentiate himself/ herself and be identical to himself/herself, the more he/she is forced to deal with his/her inherent self-identity crisis.

Such movement is apparent in the text in which the fascination with monotheistic spirituality gradually gravitates towards a cycle of splits into opposite pairs: paternal-maternal; delayed-immediate; spiritual-corporeal, striving to hold and archive the former while erasing the other. Derrida reminds us – following Freud in fact – of the spectral nature of any archival system which is always haunted by more and more meanings inherent to its excluding structure. Each sign is haunted by the ghost of its opposite and other meanings that are silenced under the cloak of total unity of signifier and signified. According to Derrida the attempt to archive, to gather the past under one roof, is always haunted by its otherness, and the more it seeks to wrap itself in a single truth, the closer it is to its complete opposite.

Just as Judaism, as marked by Derrida, is a circular movement that touches its otherness, so it is in the Freudian text in which an attempt to capture a spiritual and abstract truth, gradually becomes an empty monument. As it strives to touch on divine spirituality, the structure of the text spirals into itself, turns repetitive until circumcision emerges as a container without content, an empty sign. While Freud repeatedly invokes circumcision as an image that signifies separateness, morality, wholiness and supremacy of the monotheistic Jewish religion, it is also revealed in the text as a sign that "has made a disagreeable, uncanny impression", due to recalling "a portion of the primaeval past which is gladly forgotten",[154] a terrifying, petrifying image, simultaneously revealing and concealing its opposite.

As Freud draws closer and closer to spirituality, the text remains fragmented and full of contradictions and discontinuities, just like the fossilised stones he himself reveals in the biblical texts, circumcision becomes a monument in his own text: bringing back the corporeal, the particular and the maternal. While the textual descriptions strive to create a phallogocentric picture that draws a linear evolutionary line from the inferior to the advanced, from the corporeal and the maternal to the transcendent, moral and spiritual, the structure of the text itself moves inwards in an obsessive circularity, and like a rolled-up card resists alignment. As Freud lifts his head towards the heavens, the Oedipal transhistorical truth, the textual distortions are pointing to the particular circumstances surrounding the process of writing the text, to the loss of Freud's own home, and perhaps also to the physical pain he experienced during these later years of his life.[155]

"[F]rom that time on the Jewish religion was to some extent a fossil", Freud writes.[156] Acknowledging the petrifying power of the sign of the covenant, the uncanny anxiety evoked by circumcision, he also recognises the fossilised character of Judaism in compulsively repeating a similar pattern. Freud identifies the trauma and paradoxes in Jewish religion, that interrupt its movement of life, but with the inertia of an archival project, he repeats a similar movement in his text. In his reconstruction, Judaism is a reincarnation of a previous monotheism, and God is the reincarnation of a great father, who was murdered in Jewish history, repeating an earlier murder in human history, before civilisation, the one he envisioned in *Totem and Taboo*. In a similar chain of sameness, Freud places psychoanalysis behind monotheistic Judaism. Moses resurrected "and behind him the returned primal father of the primitive horde, transfigured and, as the son, put in the place of the father",[157] with each structure replaced by a similar one: Freud stands behind Moses the "great man", incarnating Akhenaten and each incarnation is repeated through the principle of sameness and thus cannot escape its inherent repetition, a

---

154 Sigmund Freud. "Moses and Monotheism, Three Essays." *The Standard Edition of the Complete Psychological Works of Sigmund Freud* 23 (1939), p. 91.

155 In 1923, at the age of 67, Freud got ill with oral cancer (he smoked cigars for most of his life). He underwent over 30 treatments for the disease, including the part removal of his upper jaw. He suffered from severe pain during his last years until, in 1939, unable to bear the incessant pain caused by the disease, he asked his personal physician to put an end to his suffering.

156 Sigmund Freud. "Moses and Monotheism, Three Essays." *The Standard Edition of the Complete Psychological Works of Sigmund Freud* 23 (1939), p. 88.

157 Sigmund Freud. "Moses and Monotheism, Three Essays." *The Standard Edition of the Complete Psychological Works of Sigmund Freud* 23 (1939), p. 89.

compulsive system in which only a fossilisation indicates the otherness that moves beneath the surface.

While Freud marks the origin of monotheism in greatness, imperialism and conquest, the texts that he deletes connect the narrative to its complete opposite, linking the development of monotheism to vulnerability, to the experience of dependency, inferiority and slavery and perhaps most of all – to the maternal. Discovering the truth, the one essence of otherness hidden beneath textual distortions, Freud's archiving textual movement repeats a similar pattern in which an otherness or rather a motherness is erased. The more Freud seeks to enhance the masculine image of Moses, to position him as a "great man" characterised, above all by autonomy, the more the text is fossilised with distortion, folding within precisely its otherness – experiences of dependency of vulnerability, of being oppressed and enslaved, with the image of the feminised Jew is buried underneath the sequence of erasures, which are focused on maternal figures whose strength and actions saved Moses' life. Behind the textual emphasising of a sublime chain of great paternal leaders, emerges an otherness, anchored in Freud's own reality: the oppressed and enslaved Jew, the feminised Jew – inferior rather than transcendent, dependent rather than autonomous. Underneath the all-encompassing transcendence of the Oedipal father narrated in the text, a very particular reality is revealed: the conditions in which the text was written – bringing back to the maternal, to the body, to dependency.

Textual Melancholy

Throughout the essay, Freud seems to be oscillating in and out in relation to the biblical figure of Moses – drawing closer and then farther away. At times, one can feel his inspiration with the almost divine figure he depicts, and at other moments the reader can sense his identification with him. "Under the necessity of his disappointment and loneliness", Freud writes, "he [Moses] turned to these foreigners and with them sought compensation for his losses. He chose them as his people and tried to realize his ideals in them".[158] In Freud's reconstruction, Moses turned to the Semitic people in his "disappointment and loneliness" after his homeland "had nothing more to offer him—he had lost his country", and in a time when "he saw all his hopes and prospects destroyed".[159] As he explains, "[t]he Jews with whom he departed from his country were to serve him as a superior *substitute* for the Egyptians he had left behind".[160]

Freud writes these words in a reality in which he is about to be exiled from his homeland and forced to emigrate from Vienna to England. It seems that the character of the protagonist, Moses is interwoven with that of the writer – he too

---

158 Sigmund Freud. "Moses and Monotheism, Three Essays." *The Standard Edition of the Complete Psychological Works of Sigmund Freud* 23 (1939), p. 60.

159 Sigmund Freud. "Moses and Monotheism, Three Essays." *The Standard Edition of the Complete Psychological Works of Sigmund Freud* 23 (1939), p. 28.

160 Sigmund Freud. "Moses and Monotheism, Three Essays." *The Standard Edition of the Complete Psychological Works of Sigmund Freud* 23 (1939), p. 30, emphasis added.

sought to save something that could no longer grow on the land that betrayed him. He too, when he was cut off from his home, from his land, from his life – about to be exiled or worse – sought to hold on to one idea, one ideal, one truth and bring it to light.

Writing about loss and melancholy, Judith Butler points to the experience of loss as one that confronts the subject with his/her dependency. Beneath the linguistic system through which the self is established as separated from the other, as an autonomous individual, lies an inherent experience of interdependency on an other that is radically revealed with loss. The process of mourning, she explains, requires recognition of the situated and open structure of the subject: being bound by the other in a dependency that disintegrates the self without the other. These aspects of blurred boundaries of the self in relation to the other exist before the loss, but the absence highlights them, making them noticeable. Thus, every process of mourning, agreeing to let go of what has been lost, is also a sort of surrendering to transformation, to a process of involuntary change the results of which are never known in advance. It is an experience of dissolution that brings with it the pain inherent in recognising the subject's basic state of dependency. The subject's preconceptions collapse, dismantling their self-separateness and highlighting their fundamental interdependence state of existence.

When there is no possibility of mourning, as Butler continues, when dependency is repudiated, the fracture of loss leads to an experience of rage and frustration, followed by a chain of responses – both internal and external reactions, intrapsychic and intersubjective – aimed at denying the loss.[161] Rage, destruction and violence are products of unprocessed grief, of loss that cannot be mourned. Reconstructing the Freudian understanding of melancholy and bereavement, Butler conceptualises the melancholic reaction to loss as a foreclosure of a love object that the subject denies ever having loved. "Never having loved and never having lost" becomes the structural relation to the lost object, which is then incorporated in its entirety into the ego. According to this "never-never" theoretical framework, the subject not only represses the pain of losing the love-object but also denies ever having loved him or her and thus – he or she were never lost.[162] Not only the experience of loss itself (I have never lost) is denied but also every existence that preceded it is erased (I never loved). Every memory and every historical relic must be erased and denied.

When mourning is forbidden to the extent that recognition of any love that might have been must be repudiated, the ego finds a way to preserve the lost object in the form of identification. It incorporates the prohibited love-object, swallowing it in its entirety identifying with the lost object and thus becoming the person that 'was never loved and thus was never lost'.[163] As Butler explains, when it is not possible

161 Judith Butler. "Violence, Mourning, Politics." *Stud. Gend. Sexual.* 4 (2003): 9–37.
162 Judith Butler. "Melancholy Gender—Refused Identification", *Psychoanal. Dial.* 5 (1995): 165–180, esp. p. 171.
163 Butler ("Melancholy Gender—Refused Identification", 1995) presents this as a theory of gender in which gender identity is (at least partly) a foreclosure of a denied same-sex-love. Butler follows

to recognise the dependency in the relationship, the fracture leads to melancholic structure in which the lost part is internalised and incorporated into the ego. Butler conceptualises identifications of the ego, at least partly, as foreclosure, as an act of negation in which the subject is enveloped from the outside to incorporate the repudiated object, shaping his/her psychic structure. That lost object on which the subject is dependent on and for which it is impossible to mourn grows as an aspect of the self, swallowed into the ego. The prohibition on mourning simultaneously leads to denial of the loss (I have never lost), and to a melancholic incorporation of the lost object, that appears in the form of identification that constitutes the subject's identity.

The melancholic state brings with it incessant attempts to deny that the object was loved (never having loved) and to erase all memory and hint of its existence. As Freud himself shows in *the ego and the id*,[164] a forbidding, rigid and punishing internal superego grows as a result of an external prohibition, a forbidding environment that restricts both the object and the possibility of mourning for its loss. Yet, the formation of the internal structure of the rigid superego is not a mimetic process, according to Butler. It is not an internalised external prohibition in its simple sense, in which the subject behaves as harshly as he or she was treated, but rather a result of an impossibility of processing and mourning the loss, which leads to rage and frustration and to the creation of a punitive internal structure. As she explains, the rigid prohibition is not directed only internally but also towards any memory of these relationships in the world. The system of prohibitions that is formed, not only denies the existence of the lost object in the subject's internal world but also revolting against any external mention that could evoke a similar effect.[165] Any trace of the existence of the lost object must be denied, inside and

---

Freud's discussions in 'Mourning and Melancholia' and 'the Ego and the Id' to rethink melancholy as a process of preserving love objects that are lost but cannot be mourned. Under unspoken laws of heteronormative culture in which homoerotic feelings must be denied, the subject responds in an act of repudiating the lost object while at the same time preserving it by integrating what had to be renounced into the ego in its entirety. The prohibited lost object becomes a structural part of the ego and the subject can preserve what is forbidden for love as part of his or her identity. This way, homoerotic desire manifest itself as gender identity when a subject that can neither love nor mourn their same-sex-loved-lost-objects internalise this primary loss in the form of melancholic identification: becoming a man/a woman.

164 Sigmund Freud. "The Ego and the Id". In: James Strachey (ed. & trans.) *The Standard Edition of the Complete Psychological Works of Sigmund Freud* 19 (1923), pp. 1–66. London: The Hogarth Press and the Institute of Psycho-Analysis, 1961.

165 The superego is one of the structures in Freud's structural model apart from the ego and the id. This is the structure responsible for internalising cultural values and parental demands, traditionally referred to as the moral aspect of the psyche in which conscience resides. The superego can be harsh and punishing and can arouse feelings of guilt and inferiority whenever the subject deviates from accepted moral values. Lacan constructs three levels of its structure: the Superego (the real) is that vengeful and punishing entity that bombards the ego with impossible demands; The Ego-Ideal (the imaginary) is the aspect with which the ego is identified as an ideal self-image; The Ideal Ego (symbolic) is the gaze of the Other through which I observe myself and through which I direct my behaviour. Jacques Lacan, *The Seminar Book I. Freud's Papers on Technique, 1953–54* (New York: Nortion; Cambridge, 1988).

outside, and thus, the subject moves from passivity to activity, from dependency to prohibition, from pain to violence, leaving the imprints of their own inability to mourn on others as well. Transferring the distress and hardship to others is "an egalitarian act", as Butler explains, that forces the environment to feel a similar melancholic loss, the same impossible experience. This is the connection that Butler highlights between mourning or its inability and violence, between loss and acts of rage and destruction. Thus, she explains, the difficulty of bearing an experience of loss and pain can easily become a venture of erasing otherness, stemming from the inability to bear an inherent dependency.

Butler's analysis of mourning and its political implications can be discussed at length. One of its far-reaching theoretical implications is her emphasis that prohibition is not just a response to internal desire (the super-ego controlling the id) but mainly relates to the difficulty of containing loss and cultural tolerance of mourning. Building on Butler's insights, paternal law – with its various derivatives – originates, at least partly, in a loss that cannot be contained, and for which there is no permission to mourn. In this way, both the renunciation of the beloved object and the prohibition against it become components of the ego. The need and desire are not eliminated but rather incorporated in reverse to become a tool of the subject, as an aspect of his or her ego structure, preserving the conflict and using it again and again to declare the self as separated and independent from it.

As Freud indeed demonstrates in the text, that forbidden truth, the loss that must be denied, eventually returns from the repressed, rising back from the depths of the unconscious by way of 'compromise' and 'substitution'. "Since the path to normal satisfaction remains closed to it by what we may call the scar of repression", Freud writes, "somewhere, at a weak spot, it opens another path for itself to what is known as a substitutive satisfaction".[166] Thus, the distorted return of the repressed is expressed in the new religion, which was repressed but did not disappear until its distorted return. The ecstasy of devotion to a single god captivates the hearts of the people because it represents what was once repressed and then returned. As he writes,

> the idea of a single god produced such an overwhelming effect on men because it is a portion of the eternal truth which, long concealed, came to light at last and was then bound to carry everyone along with it.[167]

The belief in a single god and its ability to reach people's hearts is rooted in the repressed. The fascination with the divine reveals a primal libidinal experience but also, Freud argues, hides its origin. When the repressed returns, he explains, it is important to remember that "[t]heir distinguishing characteristic, however, is the far-reaching distortion to which the returning material has been subjected as

166 Sigmund Freud. "Moses and Monotheism, Three Essays." *The Standard Edition of the Complete Psychological Works of Sigmund Freud* 23 (1939), p. 127.
167 Sigmund Freud. "Moses and Monotheism, Three Essays." *The Standard Edition of the Complete Psychological Works of Sigmund Freud* 23 (1939), p. 129.

compared with the original",[168] that is, the repressed does not return in its original form but in a certain distortion in relation to reality. Explaining the distortion manifested in the return of the repressed in the image of God, Freud also points his readers to the 'historical truth': "in primaeval times there was a single person who was bound to appear huge at that time and who afterwards returned in men's memory elevated to divinity".[169] The people cling strongly to the image of the one God, and to monotheistic religion because it is a "substitute" for that ancient memory of the murder of the great father – and in the Jewish case – of the murder of Moses allowing a solution to both feelings of guilt and of longing. However, in order to illustrate the process of the return of the repressed, Freud lays out to the reader the story of a young girl who "has reached a state of the most decided opposition to her mother. She has cultivated all those characteristics which she has seen that her mother lacked, and has avoided everything that reminded her of her mother".[170] Why does Freud use an example of difficult feelings towards the mother figure to illustrate the return from the repressed of the murdered father? This textual slip reveals Freud's repressed otherness, a spectral (m)otherness repeatedly resurfacing from the depths of the textual unconscious.

Going back to Butler's analysis, it is possible to identify Freud's textual erasures as a symptom of the impossibility of mourning. When it is impossible to recognise dependency on the maternal, when there is no space to mourn the loss of homeland, when the feminine identification of the Jew in Europe must be denied,[171] the conflict returns from the unconscious as part of the ego's prohibiting function. Thus, while seeking to correct injustice caused by denying the past, Freud uses a similar erasing currency and launches a series of deletions in which the defensive structure of "never having loved and never having lost" can be identified. Thus (never-never) he erases Moses' experience of dependency on the women and mothers who saved his life as a child; Thus (never-never) he turns his gaze away from the lost land and the aching body and looks up to Jewish heavenly spirituality, marking as the peak of morality; Thus (never-never) he repudiates oppression and hardship of Moses as a Jew in Egypt, portraying him as a great Egyptian prince.

"For a man who no longer has a homeland, writing becomes a place to live", Theodor Adorno writes.[172] Just as Moses created Jewish monotheism as a "substitute" for his losses, so does Freud in writing the book, creates a substitute for the harsh reality during these years, towards the end of his life. When the body betrays, during a reality in which the umbilical cord of homeland has been severed,

168 Sigmund Freud. "Moses and Monotheism, Three Essays." *The Standard Edition of the Complete Psychological Works of Sigmund Freud* 23 (1939), p. 127.
169 Sigmund Freud. "Moses and Monotheism, Three Essays." *The Standard Edition of the Complete Psychological Works of Sigmund Freud* 23 (1939), p. 129.
170 Sigmund Freud. "Moses and Monotheism, Three Essays." *The Standard Edition of the Complete Psychological Works of Sigmund Freud* 23 (1939), p. 125.
171 See references to Daniel Boyarin's and Joe Geller's analysis in the subchapter "Freud, a Jew".
172 Theodor W. Adorno. *Minima Moralia: Reflections from Damaged Life* (London: Verso, 1978). p. 51.

Freud finds a substitute in writing. This archival project was a writing process that emerged, as Freud describes, beyond his control, tormenting him "like an unlaid ghost".[173] Tracing the beginnings of monotheism and rewriting the life of Moses, he connects Judaism with the findings of psychoanalysis, fixing all under the Oedipal supra-structure and under the rigidity of the father. Just as Moses lost his land but "in this predicament he found an unusual solution",[174] he too is able to substitute the loss with heavenly spirituality; in the place of physical and emotional pain, he positions intellectual research in which instead of inferiority and oppression for Jews, he portrays the greatness of their historical father, Moses the Egyptian, whose inferiority and slavery is erased. As a fundamental part of this textual movement Freud removes the experience of primary dependency, into which a subject is born, the relationship with the mother.

When Freud negates the story of Zipporah circumcising her son, he wishes to conceal the life-saving power of the maternal, to deny the mother's ability to cut and to obscure the inherent dependency in relation to her. When he relocates the Jewish idea of being chosen and the legacy of circumcision from the story of the patriarchs, he reclaims monotheistic masculine inheritance as a trans-historical essence, erasing once again the significance of the maternal in a complex transmission of the Jewish legacy that requires (at least) two: fathers and mothers. When he redraws the life of Moses, he erases those testimonies that tell of the heroism and courage of women and mothers at the beginning of his life and strives to portray the hero as emerging solely from Oedipal relations with the father. Thus, the difficulty in recognising dependency leads to a cascade of erasures that aim to narrow and conceal that dimension of vulnerability – a cascade that begins with the denial of dependency and ends with identifying women and mothers with body and matter. The emerging textual structure – encapsulating both monotheism and psychoanalysis – is formed in response to a denied loss and thus is organised around sharp separations – between body and soul, matter and spirit, woman and man – that conceal basic human interdependency, loss and vulnerability.

In 1938, as waves of antisemitism rise in Europe, when Freud is forced to emigrate from his home, when he is about to be exiled from his land, he finds a way to sever Moses' umbilical cord as well. At a time when his body is weak and aching, Freud produces his last essay in order to claim: "never having loved and never having lost". Striving to eliminate the trauma and the pain, he clings to a monotheistic tradition that was handed down from father to son, interpreting Judaism as a transhistorical dimension of law marked by the covenant of circumcision. Bound by the Oedipal narrative and psychoanalysis, the father figure inflates as a primordial origin that simultaneously shapes the development of the individual and human history as a whole.

---

173 Sigmund Freud. "Moses and Monotheism, Three Essays." *The Standard Edition of the Complete Psychological Works of Sigmund Freud* 23 (1939), p. 103.
174 Sigmund Freud. "Moses and Monotheism, Three Essays." *The Standard Edition of the Complete Psychological Works of Sigmund Freud* 23 (1939), p. 28.

Discussion

In the Footsteps of Freud: Reflections on Motherhood and Circumcision

Maternal Triangular Space

Following the 'key-fossil' of circumcision in Freud's texts allowed me to identify the way wounds of masculinity are interwoven into questions of the maternal. Indeed, Freud recognises this image – circumcision – as symbolising the conflicted separation from the other in the process of forming an identity, but it is gradually revealed that this 'other' is first and foremost, a mother. Identifying this metaphor as an ambivalent marker that simultaneously connects and separates subjects from their otherness, Freud has provided the prism into his own texts, uncovering a conflictual dimension and illustrating the way matricide is repeated at the root of psychoanalytic theory.

Encountering vulnerability and partiality inherent to the relationship with the maternal, Freud is responding, throughout his writing, with an apotropaic attachment to the male genitalia, turning the gaze of readers to the paternal pole of the Oedipal triangle which, in juxtaposing circumcision and castration, also aligns the penis and the phallus. In the face of maternal subjectivity, a textual anxiety is revealed, a petrification in which theoretical thinking is reduced to a system of binary oppositions pivoting around the male organ. Leaping straight to the relationship with the father, Freud connects the various layers of his theory – the individual, the cultural and the historical, weaving together subject formation and the emergence of societies around the Oedipal narrative as a transhistorical existence that precedes any particular reality. Anchoring the Oedipal metaphor at the root of both subjectivity and social development, Freud portrays one origin embedded in the intergenerational trauma of patricide: the murder of the father.

Although circumcision is portrayed as the hallmark of this intergenerational trauma of patricide, demonstrating the transhistorical connection to the mighty father, it also leaves a wounded trail of evidence within Freudian texts. The omission of maternal subjectivity – encompassing not only the mother's ability to nourish but also her ability to cut and separate – and the emotional complexity in relation to it, leaves behind the image of circumcision as a textual *Leitfossil*, a living dimension that has been petrified, remaining as a trace of ossified memory for the conflict

DOI: 10.4324/9781003394334-5

that lies beneath. In all the texts analysed, with their range of contexts – individual, socio-cultural, and historical – this image emerges as a conflictual key-fossil, both revealing and concealing that what is engraved onto the body of the male baby is linked to the conflicted relationship towards the mother, and what is cut off symbolises, in various ways, matricide.

The leap from vulnerability to the portrayal of the mighty father, erasing the mediating role of the maternal, is consistent from the very beginning of Freud's writing. "At early stages the human organism is incapable ...", he writes without mentioning the mother, "[i]t is brought about by extraneous help, when the attention of an experienced person has been drawn to the child's condition ... the original helplessness of human beings is thus the primal source of all moral motives".[1] This early remark of Freud's (already in 1895, in *The Project*), is typical to his erasure of the maternal vital role in relation to the helplessness and dependency of the human subject. This sentence and many similar others demonstrate his characteristic omission of the maternal in relation to human vulnerability and lack.

Even when Freud's writings touch on the maternal, he rarely explores the complexities inherent to this relationship or deeply examines motherhood in his writings. He does not delve into the pre-Oedipal relationship between mother and baby, does not impart substantial emotional significance to the intricacies inherent to it, and emphasises the Oedipal challenges as the psychic complexities responsible for the bulk majority of mental development. Most of the times in which the maternal is addressed, it is described through language of biology, in a way that incarcerates the mother as receptive physicality with no symbolic value and no identity as a subject.

Freud bases his conceptualisations of femininity, of women's development and of motherhood in an attempt to create a parallel to his familiar theory of the male subject development, positioning its core structure around the Oedipal axes of penis envy and castration. In his essays "The Dissolution of the Oedipus Complex",[2] "Some Psychological Consequences of the Anatomical Distinction between the Sexes",[3] and later in "On Female Sexuality"[4] and "Femininity",[5] he outlines a process by which the girl internalises her castration, realises her lack (of male organ)

1 Sigmund Frued. "Project for a Scientific Psychology." In: James Strachey (ed. & trans.) *The Standard Edition of the Complete Psychological Works of Sigmund Freud*, Volume 1 (1895), pp. 295–397. London: The Hogarth Press and the Institute of Psycho-Analysis, 1953.

2 Sigmund Freud. "The Dissolution of the Oedipus Complex." In: James Strachey (ed. & trans.) *The Standard Edition of the Complete Psychological Works of Sigmund Freud*, Volume 19 (1924), pp. 171–180. London: The Hogarth Press and the Institute of Psycho-Analysis, 1961.

3 Sigmund Freud. "Some Psychological Consequences of the Anatomical Distinction between the Sexes." *Int. J. Psycho-Anal.* 8, no. 2 (1927): 133–142.

4 Sigmund Freud. "Female Sexuality." *Int. J. Psychoanal.* 13 (1932): 281–297.

5 Sigmund Freud. "New Introductory Lectures on Psycho-Analysis." In: James Strachey (ed. & trans.) *The Standard Edition of the Complete Psychological Works of Sigmund Freud* 22 (1933), pp. 1–182. London: The Hogarth Press and the Institute of Psycho-Analysis, 1964.

and relinquishes her 'masculine' qualities to develop a mature female sexuality that is passive, gentle and maternal.

Conditioning normal development on the ability to accept and internalise the social and cultural limitations derived from biology, Freud anchors psychosexual subjectivity of both sexes in their anatomical differences: in order to become a man or a woman, one must internalise the symbolic meanings of the genitals and create a psychical connection between biological sex and gender role. In this way, he conceptualises femininity, through the recognition of the anatomical differences between the sexes, as secondary – a sort of masculine development that has lost its path. Masculine subjectivity, according to this model, is the default developmental path, while the girl – who prior to the realisation of castration grows as a 'boy' – will acquire her feminine subjectivity by shedding her 'masculine' qualities and accepting the reality of being castrated.

As he explains, up to the age of three the girl "is a little boy", and therefore, like the male boy, she exhibits traits of activity, potent aggression and desire, which continue to develop until the moment when she internalises her lack and being castrated. The transition to identification with the mother and the development of femininity, according to Freud, means recognising castration and accepting the passive role devoid of desire and aggression. In order to develop mature and normal femininity, the girl must abandon the phantasy of identifying with the father, abandon active and aggressive clitoral sexuality, and switch to receptive and passive vaginal sexuality. As part of this process, she must get rid of the remnants of masculinity – potency and desire – that accompanied her at the beginning of her development. The realisation of castration gradually leads her to abandon the wish for a penis and replace it with a desire for pregnancy, specifically, the birth of a son, who becomes a substitute for lack of male organ. As Freud emphasises, it is not the transition to motherhood per se that is significant for a woman, but rather, mothering a male child through which her desire for a phallus is fulfilled.

This is, of course, a simplistic description that reflects not only Freud's worldview but also the spirit of the time, which is jarring to more recent conceptions of gender and sexuality. Developments in psychoanalysis over more than a century have allowed new readings and expansions of the Freudian theory with an emphasis both on his recognition of sexual polymorphism, and on his descriptions of sexuality in which desire can be directed towards both sexes. Yet, despite advancing his theory into a more complex thinking, the maternal remains "everywhere and nowhere", to quote Lisa Baraitser,[6] reflected in the absence of psychoanalytic discourse about maternal subjectivity. As Anat Palgi-Hecker explains in her book, psychoanalysis understands mothers, following the prevailing cultural perception, as an object for the baby.[7] The mother is the first object of attachment for the baby, she is the first object of desire, she is the means of nourishment, the holding

---

6 Lisa Baraitser. *Maternal Encounters: The Ethics of Interruption* (London: Routledge, 2008).

7 Anat Palgi-Hecker. *From I-mahut to Imahut* (in Hebrew, Tel-Aviv: Am Oved, 2005).

container, the frustrating function, the admiring gaze; she is the safe base from which the child can separate and walk away but she is never conceptualised as a subject, and her only repetitive purpose is her material existence, her presence as an object for the child.

Feminist psychoanalytic writings that challenge these perceptions have gradually opened the door to dismantling the monolithic model of motherhood and to thinking about maternal subjectivity. Karen Horney, already back in the early 20th century, voiced a sharp critique of Freud's theory of femininity.[8] Questioning traditional psychoanalytic discourse, she claims it is the fruit of a patriarchal culture that cowers from exploring basic components of female sexuality such as motherhood, breastfeeding, and physical sensations originating in the vagina and uterus. Her feminist analysis of Freudian theory conceptualises it, in a sense, as a limited thought process whose blind spot is projected onto women.

Horney puts forward a theory that challenges the idea of 'penis envy', presenting its parallel idea of womb envy. Feminine ability to become pregnant, to bear children, to give birth and to breastfeed, produces in men, according to Horney, an inherent envy. This sense of inferiority in the face of female life-giving ability unconsciously pushes men on one hand to social and cultural productivity and on the other hand to ceaselessly diminish and objectify women. Castration anxiety, she explains, the fear of the father, is masking a more primal and deep anxiety of the mother. Repressed feelings of inferiority and conflict towards the mother are the main reason for the cultural marginalisation of women as well as the reason for overlooking the maternal within the Freudian theory.

Whereas for Freud femininity is secondary, a mis-development of the default male subjectivity, Horney symbolically turns the theoretic bowl upside down, and asks psychoanalysis to acknowledge female sexuality and motherhood not as a product of female castration and penis envy but as a natural and essential growth rooted in the female body. As she explains, the desire for a child, female sexual pleasure, and even the satisfactions of motherhood are primary physiological attributes, rather than secondary to penis envy as Freud claims (and as developed by Deutsch).[9] Vaginal sensations do not arise from the interface with the penis but rather exist in the body prior to any encounter with men, as a primary predisposition. The reason that female sexuality and motherhood have hitherto been perceived as a secondary product of penis envy lies, according to her, in the centrality of male thinking and the difficulty in recognising female sexuality and motherhood.

Horney's criticism was taken another step further by Clara Thompson who began a process – which still continues in feminist psychoanalytic thinking – of liberating

---

8 Karen Horney. "On the Genesis of the Castration Complex in Women." *Int. J. Psycho-Anal.* 5 (1924): 50–65; Karen Horney. "The Flight from Womanhood: The Masculinity-Complex in Women, as Viewed by Men and by Women." *Int. J. Psycho-Anal.* 7 (1926): 324–339.

9 Helena Deutsch. *The Psychology of Women; A Psychoanalytic Interpretation.* Vol. 1 (New York: Grune & Stratton, 1944); Helena Deutsch. *The Psychology of Women; A Psychoanalytic Interpretation.* Vol. 2. Motherhood. (New York: Grune & Stratton, 1945).

women from the shackles of the female body, or rather, from the social chains of their bodies, shifting from biological language to social conceptualisation.[10] Penis envy, she explains, is in fact symbolic – women envy the power that men hold in society, and thus, it is an envy of the phallus rather than the penis. When girls and women learn where social power is located, and begin to understand the conditions for social recognition, they are gradually exposed to the privilege of being male.

Years later, in the 1970s, Mitchell made a similar claim about Freudian theory, reconceptualising it under a cultural category.[11] Freud, she explains, is not properly understood by feminist psychoanalysis. While he is interpreted as talking about positivism and biology, his theories should be understood as portraying the process of subject development under a specific, western and patriarchal culture. His intention is not to explain mental reality as it develops "in nature" but rather to describe the way in which sexual representations become gender-signified in culture. This conceptualisation brought with it a renewed understanding of Freud's writing about the structure of the psyche of women (and men) in Patriarchy. It also allowed an exploration of the internalised unconscious structure within which representations of femininity and masculinity are organised as binary and hierarchical. Mitchell's understandings bridged between feminism and psychoanalysis by allowing Freud's words about women to be used – not to define femininity, but to describe the culture in which we live, and the oppressive structures internalised within it. In this sense, Mitchell's theory also mediates between object-relations approaches that dominated Britain and the post-Lacanian theories that developed in France, which aimed to re-read Freud as a paradigm of language.

Janine Chasseguet-Smirgel similarly reformulated concepts underlying Freudian theory such as 'penis envy', the 'primal scene', and the 'Oedipal complex', providing a cardinal role to the relationship with the mother.[12] For both sexes, according to her analysis, the primary relationship with the mother provokes an experience of dependency and inferiority. Human babies are born in a state of immaturity and are therefore completely dependent on the power of the mother, a relationship that leads to the creation of a strong inner image of maternal power. In response to maternal power, as she explains, both boys and girls turn to the father in search of his salvaging power. Through these understandings, a rereading can be conducted in which both penis envy and the Oedipal identification with the father are no longer a product of paternal abundance but rather a result of the difficulty in encountering maternal strength. This powerful maternal image exists, according to Chasseguet-Smirgel, not only in the subject's inner world but also as a social

10 Clara Mabel Thompson, "Towards a Psychology of Women." *Pastoral Psychol.* 4, no. 34 (1953): 29–38.
11 Julliet Mitchell. *Psychoanalysis and Feminism: Freud, Reich, Laing, and Women* (New York: Pantheon Books, 1974).
12 Janine Chasseguet-Smirgel. "Freud and Female Sexuality—The Consideration of Some Blind Spots in the Exploration of the 'Dark Continent'." *Int. J. Psychoanal.* 57 (1976): 275–286.

principle through which culture is formed: an imagery that constitutes the unconscious collective basis that shapes society and its attitude towards women.

These theories and others explored throughout the book, touch on the significance of the conflict and relationship with the mother, as expressed in various dimensions of culture. Shifting the attention to the theoretical and psychical possibilities inherent to maternal realm as well as to the linguistic images that can grow from it, psychoanalytic feminist thinking is gradually developing a knowledge base opening into the world of motherhood, seeking to understand, name and conceptualise maternal subjectivity.

Joan Raphael-Leff conceptualises maternal subjectivity starting from the very beginning of pregnancy.[13] For her, the mother's psychological experience during this period is expressed as a widening of the emotional range, particularly, the ability to contain uncertainties, and an extended tolerance for ambivalence. The process of becoming a mother means letting go of the familiar sense of self as a separated subject, and developing what she coins as 'placental paradigm' – a sense of being stemming from the image of placental reciprocal encounter. Similar to Bracha Lichtenberg Ettinger's *matrixial borderspace*, and to Luce Irigaray's description of the placenta-uterine, as a flexible boundary between two, she seeks to render an image of the subject's growth and development at the point of encounter – for the mother as well as for the baby. Raphael-Leff is careful not to portray the relationship between the two, (mother and child), as an idyllic, anxiety-free bubble and outlines the concept of *'primary maternal persecution'* as an expression of maternal ambivalence toward her children, and as an idea that echoes Winnicott's concept of *'primary maternal preoccupation'*. Whereas Winnicott's depiction of the mother's totality, almost psychotic, ideal reduces maternal subjectivity to her biological and instinctive essence, she allows a gap between mother and baby – bringing in an emphasis on the mother's emotional and psychological experience, which involves different aspects: ambivalence, an experience of helplessness and feelings of persecution in the face of the baby's incessant demands.

The ability to touch on the complex, ambivalent experience of the mother is also evident in Rozsika Parker's writing, emphasising the often invisible link between the personal and the political in motherhood, particularly recognising the role of culture in shaping a split maternal image and producing an experience of guilt.[14] Motherhood inherently contains an ambivalent experience, conflicting intense emotions that must be repressed in a culture that denies maternal subjectivity. These unprocessed conflicts give rise to feelings of guilt, anxiety and shame in the

---

13 Joan Raphael-Leff. *Psychological Processes of Childbearing* (London: Chapman & Hall, 1999); Joan Raphael-Leff. *The Dark Side of the Womb: Pregnancy, Parenting and Persecutory Anxieties* (London: Anna Freud Centre, 2015); Joan Raphael-Leff. "Psychoanalysis and Feminism." *Brit. J. Psychother.* 12 (1995): 84–88; Joan Raphael-Leff. "Pregnancy—Procreative Process, The 'Placental Paradigm', and Perinatal Therapy." *J. Amer. Psychoanal. Assn.* 44 (1996): 373–399.

14 Rozsika Parker. *Torn in Two: The Experience of Maternal Ambivalence* (London: Virago Press, 2005).

mother. Despite the theoretical recognition of the conflictual nature of maternal role, the mother's subjectivity is still a blind spot for psychoanalysis, which creates a monolithic, universal and faceless figure of the mother, often blaming her and not releasing her from her position as an object.

Acknowledging the way in which motherhood is constructed, in both culture and psychoanalysis as an object for the child, Parker embarks on a journey of rethinking motherhood, focusing on maternal ambivalence. According to her, integrating these complex feelings can pose a developmental challenge for the mother through which a capacity to tolerate conflicting emotions can grow. Motherhood enhances the ability to bear ambivalence and therefore expands the emotional complexity from which the mother's curiosity towards her children emerge; an ability to listen and recognise her children's emotional nuances, while renouncing omnipotent phantasies to know all their needs in advance. On the other hand, Parker explains, when these experiences are not contained and do not receive cultural recognition, severe feelings of guilt can be triggered leading to splits in both the parenting experience and in the way a mother perceives her children.

Parker uses conceptualisations of French feminist theorists arguing that our culture is imprisoned by the idealisation of the primary relationship with the mother, of primary narcissism: the lost paradise, the omnivorous womb, the yearning for perfect unity. This idealisation of the primary relationship is fraught with obstacles for the mother whose emotional experience is interpreted as a symptom of maternal – and thus more generally, women's – inability to separate. Standing on the ridge between phantasy of unity and aspiration for autonomy, mothers are accused of overprotection on the one hand and neglect on the other. The maternal role forged on this thin borderline is doomed to fail.

Escaping this dichotomy and breaking the cycle of shame, lies, for Parker, in freeing mothers from the omnipotent phantasy of perfection, through dismantling the social perception projected onto them. Finding maternal voice requires fostering a discourse about maternal subjectivity that goes beyond the dyadic relationship between mother and baby, through an analysis that includes the social and cultural context, that is, the triangular encounter between mother, baby and "a third" – father/culture.

It is interesting to recognise that culture, as well as psychoanalysis, tend to think of motherhood in hermetic and dyadic terms—as a relationship between two, in which there is no third and thus describe the relationship with the third (the father) as negating the primary dyad. Motherhood is perceived as a closed dyad between the mother and the baby and therefore the role of the father is to tear the child away from the mother and transfer him or her from this two-dimensional relationship to the multidimensional space of culture. Although maternal subjectivity, as I have shown, is both the budding and maintenance of any triadic space, it is repeatedly portrayed as a terrifying danger to it, and as an opposition to "a third", reducing its inherent triangular space to its dyadic, immediate, bodily attributes.

Thinking about motherhood in these terms represents, in fact, the cultural split between female sexuality and motherhood, denying its imminent triadic structure, in which a mother's parenthood is inherently linked to her sexuality, and in which the relationship with the child and the relationship with the father/third are always interwoven. Recognising the various elements intertwined in the mother's inner world, her ability to choose, her desire and her movement between the different dimensions of her subjectivity, shows that it is only within the mother's inner world that the father and the child first encounter one another. As Kristeva explains, it is the mother's fantasy of the third beyond the dyad with the child that creates the space for the father to enter his or her (the child's) world. Similarly, it is the mother's fantasy about the child that will be born that brings the child into the father's world and allows him to know his children. The triangular image is created within maternal subjectivity, which lays the foundations for the beginning of a triadic space.

As I have pointed out in my analysis, maternal subjectivity, the inner world of the mother, in which female sexuality and motherhood are carried together, summons re-examining of terminology used to describe the relationship with the mother as a hermetic dyad between two. Although it is a triadic relationship par-excellence, the language used to describe the maternal collapse into biology and remain binary. The mother's sexual desire and love for the child/father are both encapsulated within the structure of maternal subjectivity which is inherently open to bringing in a third. Only through her subjectivity: desires, fantasies, and phantasies can the triangular relationship emerge. Through her love, the other two poles of this triangle encounter each other, and the father can learn to love his children, and through her aggression (i.e. her ability to cut) they both begin to encounter partiality in the realisation that there is always an other.

The symptomatic structure of Freud's texts reveals the difficulty of allowing this triangular space to exist. Maternal subjectivity links maternal sexuality and motherhood, and contains within it an otherness beyond the dyadic relationship, becoming the entrance into a multidimensional field of participants who can never be separated from each other. Thus, maternal subjectivity holds a dual position that on one hand is necessary for the creation and maintenance of the triangular system, of social life and of language but it is also a place in which every subject encounters its partiality. Indeed, only through the mother's inner world can the three poles of the Oedipal triangle encounter one another, yet, maternal subjectivity, as a continual process of creating thirds, is challenging any monadic idea of subjectivity, dismantling the notion of oneness. While the mother connects children to their father, she also maintains the gap between them, a space of doubt and ambivalence within which otherness will continue to grow.

A woman's pregnancy – as an image – is at the same time a reminder of her sexuality, of the existence of the father in her life, and of her motherhood, of the relationship with her children. While conventional views reduce pregnancy to a dyadic image, the recognition of the mother's inner world, her f/phantasies about conception, turns the image of pregnancy into a triangular space in which her sexual desire and love for the child are packed together. Only through her subjectivity can the three vertices of the triangle encounter each other: only through the mother's gaze can the child encounter his or her father and only through her desire can the father encounter his son/daughter. This image of pregnancy, as Freud reveals through his discussion of Frazer's theory of conception, encapsulates not just a triangular space but always an excess of desire, that undermines the totality of the father's realm, presenting an openness into endless possibilities of 'others' that might be the father. Indeed, as Kristeva points out, the structure of the maternal in relation to the father – as well as language – is characterised by duality. On one hand, her subjectivity is the place from which the triangular space emerges – and only through her inner world can the father encounter his children, but at the same time, her subjectivity always holds a gap of doubt, since the mother's most intrinsic loyalty is not devoted to the father but rather to the process of creating thirds itself, to the playful and creative movement inherent in it. This is perhaps one main reason for the impossibility of maternal subjectivity: while the mother brings the son or daughter closer to their father with her love, she also makes sure to leave a distance between them, a space of doubt and ambivalence within which other thirds will grow.

Skipping maternal subjectivity, the inability to bear the mother's inner world, flattens the image of pregnancy from being a triangular space and cements it as a paradigmatic model for a hermetic dyad that has no room for a third. Under a patriarchal concept of pregnancy – which cannot hold together the mother's sexuality and parenthood – pregnancy remains a dimension that contains within it an intimate hermetic relation between two. This can be recognised in psychoanalytic (both clinical and theoretical) understanding of pregnancy as the hallmark of a dyad that will later be raptured by the entrance of the father. In this view, the mother's body is a source of nourishment and protection for the child, enveloping him/her away from the outside world, sealing the maternal-child dyad as a primary, archaic, harmonious unity.

The Wound

Re-encountering the mother in all these texts not only awakens the paradoxes of subjectivity but also dismantles the textual narratives one by one. Layers of matricide are explored, anxieties in the relationship with the mother and concepts such as *The Primal Scene* and *The Phallic Mother* open to their other theoretical possibilities. These textual moments, in which the maternal comes back from her position of absolute otherness, reveal additional questions, connecting the text to its excluded parts – to vulnerability, to the body, to the wounds of identity, and blurring the familiar boundaries between self and other, subject and object. Theories Freud begins to unfold relating to female genealogy, to the question of incest and to the role of the maternal at the origin of civilisation – provide a gateway into a renewed discussions not only about (the absence of) maternal subjectivity but also in relation to other questions of subjectivity and partiality. The encounter with the maternal dimension evokes in the text the paradoxes that underline the subject's coherent identity and brings to the foreground a range of alternative ways of thinking both within psychoanalytic theory and within language and culture.

One concept that can be re-imagined through this rereading is circumcision itself. A trail of testimonies is left in the text that makes it possible to look at the 'wound' not in parallel to castration and thus as an aspect projected onto the feminine (the female lack), but as the product of an encounter with otherness which is not swallowed into the world of the one; as an opening to recognition of the partiality of the self. If maternal pole can be embraced, circumcision emerges as a symbol for partiality in the encounter with otherness, signifying the gap and the paradoxes inherent to the question of identity. Whereas the conscious textual movement introduces circumcision as a gateway to pairs of opposites that underlie culture, in which the other is erased in the attempt to archive the One, from a psychoanalytic position, every system is forever haunted by the ghosts of its inherent otherness, and thus, it is always bound by the contradictions of its spectral nature.

This paradox of identity is portrayed by Derrida particularly in relation to Judaism and to the pain marked by circumcision.[15] Writing about experiences of alienation, exile, and ontological non-identity, as the wounded components of Judaism, he depicts the paradox of identity that accompanies the yearning for completeness and differentiation. Judaism (like any identity), according to him, is a paradoxical movement, circumscribing around the core of its *mal de archive*, inherent to central ideas such as 'severe monotheism' and the 'chosen people'. In other words, the Jewish strive to identify with the idea of being chosen, and the monotheistic insistence on One God, ascending to reach a transcendental dimension of uniformity and holiness – are bound to continually encounter its opposite: partiality, fragmentation and absence. It is precisely the desire to reach wholeness that brings back the hole confronted by the wounded paradox of the archive, with multiplicity and otherness that remain beyond the self, marking the subject's partiality.[16]

Just as identity is a hyperbolic process that keeps returning to its opposite, so might the narratives erased in Freud's texts open the door to circumcision as a signifier of the gap that accompanies the (masculine) subject's experience. Perhaps the wound engraved by the father is the parental pain, paternal in its shade – but one that characterises parental role in general – facing an inability to determine the child's future. Marking a long-standing legacy on the baby's skin, bringing him into the masculine-Jewish covenant, also reveals that the question of that baby's future and identity remains open like a wound. Despite 'knowing better', wishing to determine their path and choose their future, parents must recognise the short length of their arms and contain the gap between intention and fulfilment; between the desire for the child to grow up with a particular identity and the possibilities which, despite paternal law and legacy, remain open; Despite the aspiration to determine their future and connect them to the past, they may follow their own.

15 Jacques Derrida. *Monolingualism of the Other or the Prosthesis of Origin* (Stanford, CA: Stanford University Press, 1998).
16 Jacques Derrida. *Of Hospitality*, Edited by Anne Dufourmantelle (Stanford, CA: Stanford University Press, 2000).

This gap of being parents that lay out the world before their children but are none-the-less limited in leading them in predetermined ways, can introduce a re-imagining of circumcision as signifying masculine partiality. This wound transmitted from father to son is marking the partiality of patriarchal legacy since Jewish identity – and perhaps all identity – goes through the mother. Despite the desire to portray an endless cycle of repeated sameness transmitted from father to son, the third pole of the triangle, the mother, constantly introduces an otherness that challenges its totality and prevents self-identity. The question of Jewish identity, transmitted through the mother, introduces the father to his fundamental partiality – to the dependency on another dimension, maternal. Thus, it is gradually revealed that the other side of the coin of the masculine covenant is the painful gap that arises from the encounter with an (m)otherness. Rather than being a mark of masculine genealogy which is established through breaking the initial bond with the mother, it can be interpreted as a signifier of the pain inherent in the triadic relationship and the dependency on her.

This other side of the masculine pendulum, uncovering conflicted areas of vulnerability, dependency and anxiety, is explored in the analysis throughout the book, and shown, for example, in the stories of the patriarchs. Diving into the biblical stories of the mothers and fathers of Judaism – negated by Freud as untrue – reveals the complicated way through which (Jewish) identity is transmitted. The stories portray a different inheritance system that grows out of the particular lives and relationships that include the maternal pole, in which circumcision is neither a sufficient condition nor a necessary condition for the continuation of Jewish identity. Jewish legacy, passed on through the mother, is always interwoven within its particular narratives, repeatedly proving the centrality of maternal subjectivity for the continuation of identity. While Freud refers to circumcision as a sign of identity established through separation from the other, a revival of the erased stories in the text reveals that it is, in fact, the wounded mark of incompleteness, marked on the male (fore)skin as the sign of the partiality of patriarchal legacy, transmitted from father to son.

When maternal subjectivity can be woven into the textual narrative, when it is possible to bear the gaps and contradictions the image of circumcision can carry with it new meanings. Being but one factor within a multidimensional field of relationships and no longer signifying absolute separation, this masculine wound can be envisioned as the mark of a break in the idea of oneness, bringing with it the pain of partiality and lack, inherently exposed vis-à-vis the (m)other.

The No-Thing and the Name of the Mother

The image of circumcision is a prism into a Freudian textual movement driven by a psychoanalytic search for the truth, which is nonetheless, gradually spiralling into an archiving act that is focused on excluding its surplus, its residue of the maternal. Throughout the texts, Freud is projecting the wound, the 'absence' and the lack onto the mother, portraying her as a necessary object for the subject to enter into the world of language and culture but her subjectivity stays beyond the border of language, and she never receives words for herself. Psychoanalysis is devoted to the search for subjectivities, but the maternal disappears or remains only as a stem from which culture grows and language originates, as an abject for the subject. Incarcerating the mother outside the borders of subjectivity, language and culture, her name remains – to quote Hélène Cixous – written in white ink.[17]

This process is portrayed in language, in which, etymologically, the *mother* is formed through the process of creating an *other*. In Hebrew, the word for motherhood *imahut*, holds a similar complexity echoing the process of abjection that occurs with the birth of the subject. The word motherhood – *imahut* contains within it the process of birthing the subject while abjecting the maternal. The 'non/un' (translated to Hebrew as – *i*) is the removal, the rejection, the renunciation of what is not the essence (translated to Hebrew as – *mahut*). The subject and the essence (*mahut*) is reborn each time out of the negation of what it is not (*imahut*), the mother.

Under the Oedipal structure, subjectivity means the negation of motherhood, and the maternal is marked by an 'absence', as a radical otherness and as nothingness. Freud is indeed preoccupied with the 'nothing' of the mother, encouraging his male young patients to internalise the phallic power of the male organ by recognising the feminine lack. Through the coupling of the phallus with the male organ, women are excluded and silenced, framed by feminine stereotypes of having nothing; produced as the negation of that masculine ideal. However, as Bion writes, the *no-thing* – which interestingly can also be translated to Hebrew as motherhood (*i-mahut*) – is not nothingness but an element in psychic life that can give birth to things and create meanings.[18] As he explains, the *no-thing* is an essential component of the psyche that manifests itself as absence, as a lack devoid of physical substance, but also as a space whose essence cannot be encompassed, as a sort of *imahut*, (non-essence) that seeks to be impregnated, receive something into it, change and grow. As Michael Eigen elaborates,

> [i]t points to a general characteristic of mental life as such–its intangibility, invisibility, immateriality, or spacelessness. It also points to "specific no-things," which may function as mental aches akin to hunger or gaps that call for accretions of meaning. Meaning itself is a no-thing, not a thing.[19]

Eigan describes the process in which the no-thing, holding multiplicity, shrinks into nothingness. When the no-thing is denied – when 'no-things' are treated as objects or as nothingness – the creative space inherent to it collapses, and in the case of the maternal, we lose the ability to think, to imagine, to understand its various

17 Hélène Cixous. "The Laugh of the Medusa." *Signs* 1, no. 4 (1976): 875–893.
18 Wilfred Bion. *Transformations* (London: Heinemann, 1965).
19 Michael Eigen. *Psychic Deadness* (London and New York: Routledge, 2004), p. 45.

meanings beyond the mother's corporality. "When words are used to evacuate rather than to build meaning", he explains, "meaning is murdered. No-thing is murdered insofar as it is treated as an object. The realm of experiencing as such is lost or aborted: physical things or thoughts as things are substituted for the evolution of experience."[20] The growth movement of the no-thing collapses when the no-thing (or *imahut*) is denied, negated, or becomes a thing. "If persecutory feelings are strong" Bion writes, "the constant conjunction of elements can lead to a naming of the conjunction with intent to contain it, rather than to mark it for investigation".[21] When the subject is petrified with fear of the no-thing, thinking seeds are replaced by a language that denies the gap and erases it.

When it is impossible to contain the gaps, vulnerability and partiality brought forward by the maternal, the lack is projected onto the mother, and she is reduced to be understood as an object, as a mere corporeal dimension, or, in fact, as a representation of nothingness. Within the Oedipal structure, the gaze is directed towards the paternal phallus, erasing the traces of the mother and positioning her as the inverse of his name: she lacks the male organ and thus signifies lack, 'absence', or nothing.

In a language that must deny matricidal (and other) feelings towards the mother – dependency, anger, guilt, anxiety and identification – in the process of separation from her, the process of separation is accelerated and accompanied by defence mechanisms of fragmentation and malignant denial until the mother is erased and the traces of the murder itself disappear. This structure is revealed in the analysis of Freud's texts, in which the conscious narrative, the Oedipal essence, emerges through an erasure of the maternal. These wounded textual moments bring about the collapse of the no-thing of the maternal, into nothingness. When it is not possible to mark the movement of separation, the dependency and partiality – and internal absence – exposed by the maternal, the 'absence' is projected onto the mother, and she is reduced to a corporal representation of nothingness. Under the Oedipal structure, the gaze is shifted to the paternal pole, and traces of the mother are erased by positioning her as nothing and as the opposite of all essence. Aligning the penis and the phallus, and juxtaposing between circumcision and castration, creates the conditions that necessitate any symbolic essence to pass through the male genital organ, and while lacking male genitalia, the mother is marked as its opposite, as 'absence'.

In order for the no-thing not to collapse into nothing, it is necessary to understand the double layers of matricide and to distinguish between the process of separation from the mother and the inability to mark it. Matricide does not stem from the movement of separation itself, from the rejection of the mother, from the emotional ambivalence towards her, or from the painful process of mourning her absence; instead, it is embedded in the need to conceal the traces of the gaps and emotions inherent to this relationship. The double act of matricide creates language that is

20 Michael Eigen. *Psychic Deadness* (London and New York: Routledge, 2004), p. 47.
21 Wilfred Bion. *Transformations*. (London: Heinemann, 1965), p. 99.

born out of the erasure of its own traces and the denial of the mourning process that generates words. As I described elsewhere, while patricide and ambivalence towards the father take up a significant role and contain various meanings in both psychoanalysis and culture,

> when it comes to matricide, there is often a 'double murder' that repudiates the process of the return of the repressed, propelling the maternal beyond the bounds of language. She becomes not only repressed but also denied; the mother is foreclosed and exiled to the realm of nothingness.[22]

When marking the gaps is impossible, as Eigen explains,

> [a]ctual murder is substituted for thoughts of murder. That is, the capacity to think about murderous feelings is killed off. Instead of learning from experience, one kills experience or rather kills the capacity to support experiencing. Actual psychic murder is substituted for meeting oneself and others.[23]

Naming according to Lisa Baraitser is a process of framing in language an 'open structure'. She quotes Deleuze explaining that "an individual acquires a true proper name as the result of the most severe operations of depersonalization".[24] To be named is to open ourselves to the multiplicities that pervade us, to the intensities that run through our whole being. It is a process of extreme alienation due to fixing an excess of otherness into a word that will – gradually and maybe violently – stick to us, narrowing an inherent gap, and making the strange familiar. Under a colonising gaze, in which subjectivity and otherness are envisioned as two opposite poles, the mother must give herself to the child, in all her classic positions: other, holder, feeder, mirror, object, abject and lack. This is the reason that, for Baraitser, to be named as a mother is a command to silence. "To mum", she writes, "is to mime, to act without words. The actors in such silent plays were called mummers".[25] Indeed, under a framework of subjectivity that incarcerates the maternal within the marginal position of radical otherness, the word mother is silencing mothers under the image of nothingness. The name of the mother echoes in this interpretation the double layers of matricide, that is, not only the separation from the mother but also, the inability to mourn it, or provide it with meanings within language. Instead of contemplating an internal lack, encountering partiality and speaking of loss, the lack is projected onto the mother, and she is named as nothing.

22 Yael Pilowsky Bankirer. "'I Really was the Mummy' the Double Act of Matricide." *Conversations* (in Hebrew) 3, no. 2 (2022): 157.
23 Michael Eigen. *Psychic Deadness* (London and New York: Routledge, 2004), p. 47.
24 Lisa Baraitser, "Mum's the Word: Intersubjectivity, Alterity, and the Maternal Subject." *Stud. Gend. Sex.* 9, no. 1 (2008): 88.
25 Lisa Baraitser, "Mum's the Word: Intersubjectivity, Alterity, and the Maternal Subject." *Stud. Gend. Sex.* 9, no. 1 (2008): 86–110, p. 87.

However, if subjectivity and otherness do not stand on different poles opposing each other, if otherness is a perpetual movement within subjectivity and subjectivity is a continuous creation within otherness than to 'mother' is to em-other, to impart with "otherness" to constantly open ourselves to otherness. Perhaps through this Bionian dialectic of the concept no-thing, we can begin to understand the complexity of the mother's name and listen to its subtle murmurs entailing a promise not to commit to one single narrative. I guess I want to suggest that if to name is to encounter otherness, making the strange familiar, the name mother is the ultimate signifier for the process of making the familiar strange. Marking the maternal as a no-thing rather than nothing can open the door for exploration of maternal subjectivity within the linguistic realm. It transpires that like the maternal, the multiplicity characterising no-things is a constant dialectical movement towards the thing and its essence, enabling it but at the same time continually dismantling it. Similar to the no-thing, the maternal resists the consolidation of words into oneness – a thing, or even a meaning. Operating in two directions simultaneously, the mother both supports the creation of new meanings in language and undermines it, leaving a playful gap within words, ceaselessly deconstructing the coherent stance of the subject, and challenging it with otherness. To name and explore the mother as a no-thing, is to acknowledge the maternal as an endlessly pregnant concept that describes the creative potential in a dual position in relation to language, maintaining a gap from any essence (*imahut*). Or to use English, a potential to make the familiar into an other, to em-other; to mother is a commitment to find the otherness within the one.

Like "no" in no-thing, (and the *i* in *imahut*) the maternal signifies the countermovement in relation to the thing and the essence, as well as the dialectical continual movement in relation to the other. While the mother is essential in the creation of subjectivity, she also undermines its oneness, opposing an Oedipal stance that declares only one narrative, one meaning and one name-of-the-father. The mother's position is a structure laden with conflicts and multiple meanings, that deconstructs in order to build and builds in order to deconstruct, loyal not to any particular meaning but to the transformative process of creation itself.

References

Abraham, Nicolas and Torok, Maria. *The Wolf Man's Magic Word: A Cryptonymy*. Translated by Nicholas Rand. Minneapolis: University of Minnesota, 1986.

Adorno, Theodor W. *Minima Moralia: Reflections from Damaged Life*. London: Verso, 1978, p. 51.

Aron, Lewis. "The Internalized Primal Scene." *Psychoanal. Dial.* 5 (1995): 195–237.

Azoulay, Ariella and Ophir, Adi. "We Don't Ask 'What Does It Mean' but 'How Does It Work': An Introduction to a Thousand Plateaus." *Theor. Critic.* (in Hebrew), 17 (2000): 123–131.

Bachofen, Johann J. *An English Translation of Bachofen's Mutterrecht (Mother Right) (1861): A Study of the Religious and Juridical Aspects of Gynecocracy in the Ancient World*. Lewiston, NY: Edwin Mellen, 2005.

Baraitser, Lisa. "Mum's the Word: Intersubjectivity, Alterity, and the Maternal Subject." *Stud. Gend. Sexual.* 9, no. 1 (2008a): 86–110.

Baraitser, Lisa. *Maternal Encounters: The Ethics of Interruption*. London: Routledge, 2008b.

Benjamin, Jessica. *The Bonds of Love: Psychoanalysis, Feminism, and the Problem of Domination*. New York: Pantheon Books, 1988.

Benjamin, Jessica. "An Outline of Intersubjectivity: The Development of Recognition." *Psychoanal. Psychol.* 7 (1990): 33–46.

Benjamin, Jessica. "The Story of I: Perspectives on Women's Subjectivity." *Can. J. Psychoanal.* 1 (1993): 79–95.

Benjamin, Jessica. "Sameness and Difference: Toward an 'Overinclusive' Model of Gender Development." *Psychoanal. Inq.* 15 (1995): 125–142.

Benjamin, Jessica. *Shadow of the Other*. New York & London: Routledge, 1998.

Benjamin, Jessica. "Beyond Doer and Done to: An Intersubjective View of Thirdness." *Psychoanal. Q.* 73 (2004): 5–46.

Bettelheim, Bruno. *Symbolic Wounds: Puberty Rites and the Envious Male*. Glencoe, IL: Free Press, 1954.

Bion, Wilfred. *Transformations*. London: Heinemann, 1965.

Bloch, Maurice. *From Blessing to Violence: History and Ideology in the Circumcision Ritual of the Merina of Madagascar*. Cambridge: Cambridge University Press, 1986.

Bloch, Maurice. *Prey into Hunter: The Politics of Religious Experience*. Cambridge: Cambridge University Press, 1992.

Bonnigal-Katz, Dorothée. "From Medusa to Kronos: The Fragile Illusion of the Maternal Phallus." *Psychoanal. Cult. Soc.* 25 (2020): 114–121.

Boothby, Richard. *Freud as Philosopher: Metapsychology after Lacan.* New York: Routledge, 2001.

Borch-Jacobsen, Mikkel. *Freud's Patients: A Book of Lives.* London: Reaktion Books, 2022.

Boyarin, Daniel. *A Radical Jew: Paul and the Politics of Identity.* Berkeley: University California Press, 1994.

Boyarin, Daniel. *Unheroic Conduct: The Rise of Heterosexuality and the Invention of the Jewish Man.* Berkeley: University of *California* Press, 1997.

Boyarin, Daniel. "Freud's Baby, Fliess's Maybe: Homophobia, Antisemitism, and the Invention of Oedipus." *GLQ: A Journal of Gay and Lesbian Studies*, 2, no. 2 (1995): 115–147.

Boyarin, Jonathan and Daniel, Boyarin. "Self-Exposure as Theory: The Double-Mark of the Male Jew." In: D. Battaglia (ed.) *Rhetorics of Self-Making.* Berkeley: University of California Press, 1995. pp. 16–42.

Butler, Judith. "Melancholy Gender—Refused Identification." *Psychoanal. Dial.* 5 (1995): 165–180.

Butler, Judith. "Violence, Mourning, Politics." *Stud. Gend. Sexual.* 4 (2003): 9–37.

Burton, Roger V. and Whiting, John W.M. "The Absent Father and Cross-Sex Identity." *Merrill-Palmer Q. Behav. Develop.* 7 (1961): 85–95.

Cixous, Hélène. "The Laugh of the Medusa." *Signs* 1, no. 4 (1976): 875–893.

Corbett, Ken. *Boyhoods: Rethinking Masculinities.* New Haven, CT: Yale University Press, 2009.

Chasseguet-Smirgel, Janine. "Freud and Female Sexuality—The Consideration of Some Blind Spots in the Exploration of the 'Dark Continent'." *Int. J. Psycho-Anal.* 57 (1976): 275–228.

Chasseguet-Smirgel, Janine. "Some Thoughts on Freud's Attitude During the Nazi Period." *Psychoanaly. Contemp. Though.* 11 (1988): 249–265.

Cohen, Shaye J.D. *The Beginnings of Jewishness: Boundaries, Varieties, Uncertainties.* Berkeley: University of California Press, 2001.

Cohen, Shaye J.D. "A Brief History of Jewish Circumcision Blood." In: Elizabeth Wyner Mark (ed.) *The Covenant of Circumcision: New Perspectives on an Ancient Jewish Rite.* London: Brandies University Press, 2003. pp. 30–42.

Cohen, Shaye J.D. *Why Aren't Jewish Women Circumcised?: Gender and Covenant in Judaism.* Berkeley: University of California Press, 2005.

Crapanzano, Vincent. "Rite of Return." *Psychoanal. Stud. Soc.* 9 (1981): 15–36.

Deleuze, Gilles and Félix Guattari. *Anti-Oedipus: Capitalism and Schizophrenia.* Minneapolis: University of Minnesota, 1983.

Deleuze, Gilles. *Two Regimes of Madness.* New York: Semiotext, 2006.

Deleuze, Gilles. "I have Nothing to Admit." *Semiotext(e)* II, no. 3 (1977): 111–116.

Derrida, Jacques. *Circumfession* (G. Bennington, Trans and G. Bennington (Ed.)). Chicago: The University of Chicago Press, 1993.

Derrida, Jacques. "Archive Fever: A Freudian Impression." *Diacritics* 25, no. 2 (1995): 9–63.

Derrida, Jacques. *Monolingualism of the Other or the Prosthesis of Origin.* Stanford, CA: Stanford University Press, 1998.

Derrida, Jacques. *Of Hospitality.* Edited by Anne Dufourmantelle. Stanford, CA: Stanford University Press, 2000.

Deutsch, Helena. *The Psychology of Women; A Psychoanalytic Interpretation.* Vol. 1, New York: Grune & Stratton, 1944.

Deutsch, Helena. *The Psychology of Women; A Psychoanalytic Interpretation*. Vol. 2. Motherhood: New York: Grune & Stratton, 1945.

Durkheim, Émile. *Incest: The Nature and Origin of the Taboo*. New York: Lyle Stuart, Inc., 1963.

Eigen, Michael. *Psychic Deadness*. London and New York: Routledge, 2004.

Evans, Fred and Leonard Lawlor. *Chiasms: Merleau-Ponty's Notion of Flesh*. Albany: State University of New York, 2000.

Frazer, James G. *Totemism and Exogamy: A Treatise on Certain Early Forms of Superstition and Society*. London: Macmillan, 1910.

Freud, Sigmund and Ferenczi, Sándor. *The Correspondence of Sigmund Freud and Sándor Ferenczi* Volume 1(1993): 1908–1914. Cambridge, MA: The Belknap Press of Harvard University Press, 25: 1–571.

Freud Sigmund and Zweig, Arnold. *The Letters of Sigmond Freud and Arnold Zweig*, Translated Elaine Robson-Scott and William Robson-Scott. Ernst L. (ed.) New York: Harcort Brace & World, 1987.

Freud, Sigmund. "Project for a Scientific Psychology." In: James Strachey (ed. & trans.) *The Standard Edition of the Complete Psychological Works of Sigmund Freud*, Volume 1 (1895), pp. 295–397. London: The Hogarth Press and the Institute of Psycho-Analysis, 1953.

Freud, Sigmund. "The Aetiology of Hysteria." In: James Strachey (ed. & trans.) *The Standard Edition of the Complete Psychological Works of Sigmund Freud* 3 (1896): 187–221. London: The Hogarth Press and the Institute of Psycho-Analysis, 1953.

Freud, Sigmund. "The Interpretation of Dreams." In: *The Standard Edition of the Complete Psychological Works of Sigmund Freud*, vol. 4–5. (1900): 1–627. London: The Hogarth Press and The Institute of Psycho-Analysis, 1954.

Freud, Sigmund. "Delusions and Dreams in Jensen's 'Gradiva'." In: James Strachey (ed. & trans.) *The Standard Edition of the Complete Psychological Works of Sigmund Freud* 9 (1907): 7–95. London: The Hogarth Press and the Institute of Psycho-Analysis, 1959.

Freud, Sigmund. "Analysis of a Phobia in a Five-Year-Old Boy." In: James Strachey (ed. & trans.) *The Standard Edition of the Complete Psychological Works of Sigmund Freud* 10 (1909): 1–150. London: The Hogarth Press and the Institute of Psycho-Analysis, 1955.

Freud, Sigmund. "Leonardo Da Vinci and a Memory of his Childhood." In: James Strachey (ed. & trans.) *The Standard Edition of the Complete Psychological Works of Sigmund Freud* 11 (1910): 57–138. London: The Hogarth Press and the Institute of Psycho-Analysis, 1957.

Freud, Sigmund. "Totem and Taboo: Some Points of Agreement Between the Mental Lives of Savages and Neurotics." Translated by James Strachey. London: Routledge, 2003, 1912–1913.

Freud, Sigmund. "The Moses of Michelangelo." In: James Strachey (ed. & trans.) *The Standard Edition of the Complete Psychological Works of Sigmund Freud* 13 (1914): 209–238. London: The Hogarth Press and the Institute of Psycho-Analysis, 1955.

Freud, Sigmund. "Introductory Lectures on Psycho-Analysis." In: James Strachey (ed. & trans.) *The Standard Edition of the Complete Psychological Works of Sigmund Freud* 16 (1917): 241–463. London: The Hogarth Press and the Institute of Psycho-Analysis, 1963.

Freud, Sigmund. "From the History of an Infantile Neurosis." In: James Strachey (ed. & trans.) *The Standard Edition of the Complete Psychological Works of Sigmund Freud* 17 (1918): 1–124. London: The Hogarth Press and the Institute of Psycho-Analysis, 1955.

Freud, Sigmund. "The Uncanny." In: James Strachey (ed. & trans.) *The Standard Edition of the Complete Psychological Works of Sigmund Freud* 17 (1919): 217–256. London: The Hogarth Press and the Institute of Psycho-Analysis, 1955.

Freud, Sigmund. "Medusa's Head." In: Neil Hertz (ed.) *Writings on Art and Literature.* Stanford, CA: Stanford University Press, 1997, 1922.

Freud, Sigmund. "The Ego and the Id." In: James Strachey (ed. & trans.) *The Standard Edition of the Complete Psychological Works of Sigmund Freud* 19 (1923): 1–66. London: The Hogarth Press and the Institute of Psycho-Analysis, 1961.

Freud, Sigmund. "The Dissolution of the Oedipus Complex." In: James Strachey (ed. & trans.) *The Standard Edition of the Complete Psychological Works of Sigmund Freud* 19 (1924): 171–180.London: The Hogarth Press and the Institute of Psycho-Analysis, 1961.

Freud, Sigmund. "Negation." In: James Strachey (ed. & trans.) *The Standard Edition of the Complete Psychological Works of Sigmund Freud* 19 (1925): 233–240. London: The Hogarth Press and the Institute of Psycho-Analysis, 1961.

Freud, Sigmund. "Some Psychological Consequences of the Anatomical Distinction between the Sexes." *Int. J. Psycho-Anal.* 8 no. 2 (1927): 133–142.

Freud, Sigmund. "Female Sexuality." *Int. J. Psychoanaly.* 13 (1932): 281–297.

Freud, Sigmund. "New Introductory Lectures on Psycho-Analysis." In: James Strachey (ed. & trans.) *The Standard Edition of the Complete Psychological Works of Sigmund Freud* 22 (1933): 1–182. London: The Hogarth Press and the Institute of Psycho-Analysis, 1964.

Freud, Sigmund. "Moses and Monotheism, Three Essays." In: James Strachey (ed. & trans.) *The Standard Edition of the Complete Psychological Works of Sigmund Freud* 23 (1939): 1–138. London: The Hogarth Press and the Institute of Psycho-Analysis, 1964.

Freud, Sigmund. *Papers on Technique, 1953–54.* New York: W.W. Norton, 1988.

Geller, Jay. "A Paleontological View of Freud's Study of Religion: Unearthing the 'Leitfossil' Circumcision." *Mod. Jud.* 13, no. 1 (1993): 49–70.

Geller, Jay. "The Godfather of Psychoanalysis: Circumcision, Antisemitism, Homosexuality, and Freud's 'Fighting Jew'." *J. Am. Acad. Relig.* 67, no. 2 (1999): 355–386.

Gilbert, H. Herdt. *Guardians of the Flutes: Idioms of Masculinity.* New York: McGraw Hill, 1981.

Gilbert, H. Herdt. "Fetish and Fantasy in Sambia Initiation." In: Gilbert H. Herdt (ed.) *Rituals of Manhood: Male Initiation in Papua New Guinea.* Berkeley: University of California Press, 1982. pp. 44–98.

Gilman, Sander. *The Case of Sigmund Freud: Medicine and Identity at the Fin de Sidcle.* Baltimore: Johns Hopkins University Press, 1993a.

Gilman, Sander. *Freud, Race, and Gender.* Princeton: Princeton University Press, 1993b.

Gish, Amit. *What is the Desire of the Archive?* (in Hebrew), Haaretz Books, 2006.

Gollaher, David. *Circumcision: A History of the World's Most Controversial Surgery.* New York: Basic Books, 2000.

Goettner-Abendroth, H. *Matriarchal Societies. Studies on Indigenous Cultures across the Globe.* New York: Peter Lang, 2012.

Graf, Max. "Reminiscences of Professor Sigmund Freud." *Psycho-Analy. Quar.* 11: 465–476. 1942.

Haberman, Bonna Devora. "Foreskin Sacrifice - Zipporah's Ritual and the Bloody Bridegroom." In: Elizabeth Wyner Mark (ed.) *The Covenant of Circumcision: New Perspectives on an Ancient Jewish Rite.* London: Brandeis Series on Jewish Women, 2003. pp. 18–29.

Herman, Judith Lewis. *Trauma and Recovery: The Aftermath of Violence - from Domestic Abuse to Political Terror.* New York: Basic Books, 1992.

Hiatt, Lester Richard. "Indulgent Fathers and Collective Male Violence." In: Ariane Deluz and Suzette Heald (eds.) *Anthropology and Psychoanalysis: An Encounter Through Cultures*. London: Routledge, 1994. pp. 171–183.

Horney, Karen. "On the Genesis of the Castration Complex in Women." *Int. J. Psycho-Anal.* 5 (1924): 50–65.

Horney, Karen. "The Flight from Womanhood: The Masculinity-Complex in Women, as Viewed by Men and by Women." *Int. J. Psycho-Anal.* 7 (1926): 324–339.

Irigaray, Luce. *Speculum of the Other Woman*. Translated by Gillian C. Gill. Ithaca: Cornell University Press, 1985a.

Irigaray, Luce. *This Sex Which Is Not One*. Ithaca, NY: Cornell University Press, 1985b.

Irigaray, Luce. *Marine Lover of Friedrich Nietzsche*. Translated by Gillian C. Gil. New York: Colombia University Press, 1991.

Irigaray, Luce. *An Ethics of Sexual Difference*. Translated by Gillian Gill and Carolyn Burke. Ithaca: Cornell University Press, 1993.

Irigaray, Luce. *I Love to You: Sketch of a Possible Felicity in History*. Translated by Alison Martin. New York: Routledge, 1996.

Jacobs, Amber. *On Matricide: Myth, Psychoanalysis, and the Law of the Mother*. New York: Colombia University Press, 2007.

Jentsch, Ernst. "On the Psychology of the Uncanny". 1906. Translated by Roy Sellars, *Angelaki: Journal of the Theoretical Humanities* 2, no. 1 (1995): 7–16.

Jonte-Pace, Diane. *Speaking the Unspeakable: Religion, Misogyny, and the Uncanny Mother in Freud's Cultural Texts*. Berkeley: University of California Press, 2001.

Jung, Carl G. "The Archetypes and the Collective Unconscious." Vol. 9, In: R. F.C. Hull and Michael Fordham Gerhard Adler (eds.) *Collected Works*. New York: Princeton University Press, 1967. pp. 1–66.

Jung, Carl G. "Symbols of Transformation." Vol. 5, In: R. F.C. Hull and Michael Fordham Gerhard Adler (eds.) *Collected Works*. New York: Princeton University Press, 1967. pp. 1–404.

Kitahara, Michio. "A Cross-Cultural Test of the Freudian Theory of Circumcision." *Int. J. Psychoanal. Psychother.* 5 (1976): 535–546.

Klein, Melanie. "Mourning and Its Relation to Manic-Depressive States." *Int. J. Psychoanal.* 21 (1940): 125–153.

Klein, Melanie. "The Oedipus Complex in the Light of Early Anxieties." *Int. J. Psychoanal.* 26 (1945): 11–33.

Klein, Melanie. "Notes on Some Schizoid Mechanisms." *Int. J. Psychoanal.* 27 (1946): 99–110.

Kristeva, Julia. *Desire in language: A semiotic approach to literature and art*. New York: Columbia University Press, 1980.

Kristeva, Julia. *Powers of Horror: An Essay on Abjection*. New York: Columbia University Press, 1982.

Kristeva, Julia. *Tales of Love*. New York: Columbia University Press, 1987a.

Kristeva, Julia. *Black Sun: Depression and Melancholia*. New York: Columbia University Press, 1987b.

Kristeva, Julia. "Women's Time." In: C. Zanardi (ed.) *Essential Papers on the Psychology of Women*. New York: New York University Press, 1990. pp. 374–400.

Kristeva, Julia. "The Speaking Subject Is Not Innocent." In: Barbara Johnson (ed.) *Freedom and Interpretation: The Oxford Amnesty Lectures 1992*. New York: Basic Books, 1993. pp. 147–174.

Lacan, Jacques. "The Function and Field of Speech and Language in Psychoanalysis." In: *Écrits: A Selection*. Trans. Alan Sheridan. London: Tavistock, 1977. pp. 30–113.

Lacan, Jacques. *Feminine Sexuality: Jacques Lacan and the ecole freudienne*. Edited by J. Mitchell & J. Rose. New York: Norton, 1982.

Lacan, Jacques. *The Seminar. Book III: The Psychoses.* New York: Norton, 1993[1955–1956].

Lacan, Jacques. *The Seminar XX, Encore: On Feminine Sexuality, the Limits of Love and Knowledge*. Edited by Jacques-Alain Miller. New York: W.W. Norton & Co., 1998.

Lacan, Jacques. "The Mirror Stage as Formative of the Function I as Revealed in Psycho-analytic Experience." *Écrits* (The First Complete Translation in English), Trans. Bruce Fink, New York and London: W. W. Norton, 2006[1949]. pp. 75–81.

Lang, Andrew. *Social Origins*. London: New York and Bombay 1903.

Lang, Andrew. *The Secret of the Totem*. London: New York, 1905.

Laplanche, Jean. "The Theory of Seduction and the Problem of the Other." *Int. J. Psycho-analy.* 78 (1997): 653–666.

Layard, Jhon. *Stone Men of Malekula*. London: Chatto & Windus, 1942.

Lévi-Strauss, Claude. *Totemism*. Boston: Beacon, 1963.

Lichtenberg Ettinger, Bracha. "Matrix and Metramorphosis." *Troub. Arch.*, Special issue of *Differences*, 4, no. 3 (1992): 176–208.

Lichtenberg Ettinger, Bracha. "The Feminine/Prenatal Weaving in the Matrixial Subjectivity as Encounter." *Psychoanaly. Dial.* VII, no. 3 (1997): 363–405.

Lichtenberg Ettinger, Bracha. "Matrixial Gaze and Screen: Other than Phallic and Beyond the Late Lacan." In: Laura Doyle (ed.) *Bodies of Resistance*. Evanston, IL: Northwestern University Press, 2001. pp. 103–143.

Lichtenberg Ettinger, Bracha. "Matrixial Trans-subjectivity." *Theor. Cul. Soc.* 23 (2006): 2–3.

Lichtenberg Ettinger, Bracha. "The Sublime and Beauty beyond Uncanny Anxiety." In: F. Dombois, U. M. Bauer, C. Marais and M. Schwab (ed.) *Intellectual Birdhouse. Artistic Practice as Research*. London: Koening Books, 2012. pp. 115–128.

Mc'Lennan, John. "The Worship of Animals and Plants". Part I, *The Fortnightly Review* 6 (1869): 407–427.

Meltzer, Donald. *Sexual States of Mind*. Perthshire, Scotland: Clunie, 1973.

Merleau-Ponty, Maurice. *Phenomenology of Perception.* Translated by D. Landes. London: Routledge, 2012.

Meyer, Eduard. *Die Israeliten und ihre Nachbarstamme*, Leipzig: J.C. Hinrichs'sche Buch-handlung, 1906.

Mitchell, Juliet. *Psychoanalysis and Feminism: Freud, Reich, Laing, and Women*. New York: Pantheon Books, 1974.

Mitchell, Juliet. *Siblings: Sex and Violence*. Cambridge: Polity Press, 2003.

Mitchell, Juliet. *Fratriarchy: The Sibling Trauma and the Law of the Mother*. London and New York: Routledge, 2023.

Moi, Turil and Kristeva, Julia. *The Kristeva Reader*. New York: Columbia University Press, 1986.

Neumann, Erich. *The Great Mother; An Analysis of the Archetype*. New York: Pantheon, 1955.

Neumann, Erich. *The Fear of the Feminine and Other Essays on Feminine Psychology*. Princeton, NJ: Princeton University Press, 1994.

Ofrat, Gideon. *The Jewish Derrida*. New York: Syracuse University Press, 2018.

Ogden, Thomas. *The Primitive Edge of Experience*. Northvale, NJ: Aronson, 1989.

Oliver, Kelly. "Kristeva's Sadomasochistic Subject and the Sublimation of Violence." *J. Fren. Franc. Phil.* 21, no. 1 (2013): 13–26.

Osserman, Jordan. *Circumcision on the Couch: The Cultural, Psychological, and Gendered Dimensions of the World's Oldest Surgery.* London: Bloomsbury Publishing, 2022.

Paige, Karen Ericksen and Paige, Jeffrey M. *The Politics of Reproductive Ritual.* Berkeley: University of California. Press, 1981.

Palgi-Hecker, Anat. *From I-mahut to Imahut* (in Hebrew), Tel-Aviv: Am Oved, 2005.

Parker, Rozsika. *Torn in Two: The Experience of Maternal Ambivalence.* London: Virago Press, 2005.

Pilowsky Bankirer, Yael. "'I Really was the Mummy' the Double Act of Matricide." *Conversations* (in Hebrew) 3, no. 2 (2022): 155–162.

Pilowsky Bankirer, Yael. "The Mother's Name of the Father: On Names and Subjectivity." *MA'ARAG: The Israel Annual of Psychoanalysis* (in Hebrew), 11 (2023): 19–40.

Pilowsky Bankirer, Yael. *Between Our Tongues,* (in Hebrew) Tel-Aviv: Catharsis Publishing, 2023.

Rank, Otto. (1924). "The Trauma of Birth in Its Importance for Psychoanalytic Therapy." *Psychoanal. Rev.* 100 (2013): 669–674.

Reik, Theodor. *Ritual: Four Psychoanalytic Studies.* New York: Grove Press, 1946.

Róheim, Géza. "Transition Rites." *Psychoanal. Q.* 11 (1942): 336–374.

Róheim, Géza. *The Eternal Ones of the Dream: A Psychoanalytic Interpretation of Australian Myth and Ritual.* New York: International Universities Press, 1945.

Róheim, Géza. "The Symbolism of Subincision." *Am. Imago* 6 (1949): 321–328.

Raphael-Leff, Joan. "Psychoanalysis and Feminism." *Brit. J. Psychother.* 12 (1995): 84–88.

Raphael-Leff, Joan. "Pregnancy—Procreative Process, The 'Pacental Paradigm' and Perinatal Therapy." *J. Amer. Psychoanal. Assn.* 44S (1996): 373–399.

Raphael-Leff, Joan. *Psychological Processes of Childbearing.* London: Chapman & Hall, 1999.

Raphael-Leff, Joan. *The Dark Side of the Womb: Pregnancy, Parenting and Persecutory Anxieties.* London: Anna Freud Centre, 2015.

Ricoeur, Paul. *Freud and Philosophy: An Essay on Interpretation.* (D. Savage, Trans.). New Haven, CT: Yale University Press, 1970.

Said, Edward. *Freud and the Non-European.* London: Verso, 2003.

Silverman, Eric Kline. "The Cut of Wholeness: Psychoanalytic Interpretations of Biblical Circumcision." In: Elizabeth Wyner Mark (ed.) *The Covenant of Circumcision: New Perspectives on an Ancient Jewish Rite.* London: Brandies University Press, 2003. pp. 43–57.

Silverman, Eric Kline. "Anthropology and Circumcision." *Ann. Rev. Anthropol.* 33 (2004): 419–445.

Silverman, Eric Kline. "Circumcision and Masculinity: Motherly Men or Brutal Patriarchs?" In: Harry Brod and Shawn Israel Zevit (eds.) *Brother Keepers: New Perspectives on Jewish Masculinity.* Harriman, TN: Men's Studies Press, 2010. pp. 34–56.

Slavet, Eliza. *Racial Fever: Freud and the Jewish Question,* New York: Fordham University Press, 2009.

Smith, W. Robertson. *Lectures on the Religion of the Semites.* London: A. & C. Black, 1894.

Spencer, Herbert. "The Origin of Animal Worship". *The Fortnightly Review* 7, (1870): 535–550.

Sprengnether, Madelon. *The Spectral Mother: Freud, Feminism, and Psychoanalysis.* Ithaca: Cornell University Press, 1990.

Sprengnether, Madelon. "Reading Freud's Life." *Am. Imago* 52 (1995): 9–54.

Stone, Alison. "Against Matricide: Rethinking Subjectivity and the Maternal Body." *Hypatia* 27, no. 1 (2012): 118–138.

Thompson, Clara Mabel. "Towards a Psychology of Women." *Pastor. Psychol.* 4, no. 34 (1953): 29–38.

Terence, Turner. "Social Body and Embodied Subject: Bodiliness, Subjectivity, and Sociality Among the Kayapo." *Cult. Anthropol.* 10 (1995): 143–170.

Tzur Mahalel, Anat. "The Wolf Man's Glückshaube: Rereading Sergei Pankejeff's Memoir." *J. Am. Psychoanal. Ass.* 67, no. 5 (2019): 789–814.

Van Gennep, Arnold. *Rites of Passage*. Translated by M.B. Vizedom and G.L. Caffe. Chicago: University Press, 1960.

Wakefield, Jarome C. "Concept Representation in the Child: What Did Little Hans mean by 'Widdler'?" *Psychoanal. Psychol.* 34, no. 3 (2017): 352–360.

Whiting, John W.M. and Kluckhohn, Anthony R. "The Function of Male Initiation Ceremonies at Puberty." In: T.M. Newcomb, E.L. Hartley, and E.E. Maccoby (eds.) *Readings in Social Psychology*. New York: Henry Holt & Co., 1958. pp. 359–370.

Winnicott, Donald Woods. "Primary Maternal Preoccupation" [1956]. In: *Through Paediatrics to Psycho-Analysis*, London: Routledge, 1984. pp. 300–305.

Winnicott, Donald Woods. *The Child and the Family*. London: Tavistock Publications; New York: Basic Books, 1957.

Winnicott, Donald Woods. "The Use of an Object." *Int. J. Psycho-Anal.* 50 (1969): 711–716.

Wundt, W. Elemente der Völkerpsychologie, Leipzig. Trans.: *Elements of Folk Psychology*, New York and London, 1916, 1912.

Yerushalmi, Yosef Haim. *Freud's Moses: Judaism Terminable and Interminable*. New Haven: Yale University Press, 1991.

Yerushalmi, Yosef Haim. *Zakhor: Jewish History and Jewish Memory.* Seattle: University of Washington Press, 1996.

Young, Iris. *Throwing like a Girl and Other Essays in Feminist Philosophy and Social Theory.* Ann Arbor: University of Michigan, 2000.

Ziv, Efi. "Incest." *Mafte'akh A lexical Journal of Political Thought* (in Hebrew) (2020): 15, 13–34.

Index

Note: Page numbers followed by "n" denote endnotes.

For Product Safety Concerns and Information please contact our EU
representative GPSR@taylorandfrancis.com
Taylor & Francis Verlag GmbH, Kaufingerstraße 24, 80331 München, Germany

www.ingramcontent.com/pod-product-compliance
Lightning Source LLC
Chambersburg PA
CBHW050640280326
41932CB00015B/2726